BORDERS OF VIOLENCE & JUSTICE

BORDERS OF VIOLENCE & JUSTICE

Mexicans, Mexican Americans,
and Law Enforcement
in the Southwest,
1835–1935

Brian D. Behnken

THE UNIVERSITY OF NORTH CAROLINA PRESS
Chapel Hill

© 2022 The University of North Carolina Press

All rights reserved

Designed by Jamison Cockerham
Set in Arno, Sentinel, Cutright, and Scala
by Jamie McKee, MacKey Composition

Cover illustration: Harry Ransom Center, University of Texas at Austin.

Manufactured in the United States of America

LIBRARY OF CONGRESS CATALOGING-IN-PUBLICATION DATA
Names: Behnken, Brian D., author.
Title: Borders of violence and justice : Mexicans, Mexican Americans, and law enforcement in the Southwest, 1835–1935 / Brian D. Behnken.
Description: Chapel Hill : The University of North Carolina Press, [2022] | Includes bibliographical references and index.
Identifiers: LCCN 2022017134 | ISBN 9781469670119 (cloth ; alk. paper) | ISBN 9781469670126 (paperback) | ISBN 9781469670133 (ebook)
Subjects: LCSH: Law enforcement—Mexican-American Border Region—History—19th century. | Law enforcement—Mexican-American Border Region—History—20th century. | Vigilantism—Mexican-American Border Region—History—19th century. | Vigilantism—Mexican-American Border Region—History—20th century. | Discrimination in law enforcement—Mexican-American Border Region—History. | Mexican Americans—Mexican-American Border Region—History. | Mexican-American Border Region—Race relations. | Mexican-American Border Region—History.
Classification: LCC HV7936.R3 B464 2022 | DDC 363.2/308968720721—dc23/eng/20220711
LC record available at https://lccn.loc.gov/2022017134

FOR MY FAMILY

Monic, Brandis, Elleka, and Aven

Contents

List of Illustrations   viii

Acknowledgments   xi

Note on Terms   xix

INTRODUCTION   1

1 Reign of Blood: The Unending Mexican War and the Creation of the Criminal Justice System in the Southwest   15

2 Mob Law: Vigilantism as Law Enforcement in the Nineteenth Century   49

3 Stars and Shields: The World of Mexican American Law Enforcement Officers   81

4 Unknown Mex: Mexican and Mexican American Criminality and the Justice System   117

5 Bandits Everywhere: Anti-Mexican Violence, Mexican and Mexican American Resistance   147

6 The Pendulum of Change: Mexican Americans and Law Enforcement in a Time of Transition   183

CONCLUSION   215

Notes   227

Bibliography   275

Index   301

Illustrations

Early depiction of the Texas Rangers   14

Mexican jail in Texas   19

Kearny declares New Mexico annexation   23

"Hanging" windmill, Las Vegas, New Mexico   63

Notice from the Socorro Committee of Safety   64

Henry Garfias   83

Perfecto Armijo   85

Elfego Baca   97

Juan Murrieta and Martin Aguirre   111

Women's prison cell, Yuma Territorial Prison   134

Wanted postcard for Eugenio Ortegas   144

Front Cover of *Utah's Greatest Manhunt*   168

Chico Cano   171

"El Bandolero"   205

Acknowledgments

In 2005, I visited the Dallas Public Library to conduct research for my doctoral dissertation on the civil rights movement in Texas. Archivist Carol Roark brought out stacks of documents related to the city's civil rights history and in that stack were newspaper clippings and pictures of Santos Rodriguez, a twelve-year-old Mexican American boy executed by Dallas police officer Darrell Cain on July 24, 1973. The images, which still haunt my memory, showed a child seated in the front seat of a patrol car, a gaping hole in his head, blood everywhere. How in the world could a cop kill a twelve-year-old boy in this manner? Turns out Cain used a game of Russian roulette to try to get Rodriguez to confess to a crime he didn't commit and instead blew his brains out. This case was so egregious and yet at the time relatively unknown outside of the Mexican American community in Dallas. Clearly something was amiss, something was not right in our understanding of how law enforcement treated Mexican-origin people. And so I set out to learn. In 2010 I returned to Dallas to begin the research for this book. It turned out to be a much bigger story than I had anticipated. I travelled across the Southwest and the research kept taking me further back in time, from the seventies to the sixties, back to the forties, to the teens, and the next thing I knew I was researching in the 1830s. Such a lengthy chronology ultimately couldn't be contained in a single book, so *Borders of Violence and Justice* represents the first part of a two book story. Santos, who started everything off for me, appears in the second book, *Brown and Blue*, which I hope will be published in the next few years.

I could not complete such a lengthy process of research and writing and learning on my own. I owe a lot of debts. These acknowledgments won't really do justice to all the people who have helped me along the way, but they're a start. I will surely miss some people who have assisted me, and for that I apologize. Please know that I did value your assistance.

I mentioned Carol Roark above and for good reason, at the center of my work are the archivists, research librarians, and their staff who aided me in libraries across the Southwest. Many of those folks I also get to call friends. Carol is one of them. She was for years a dedicated public servant at the Dallas Public Library. I always enjoyed researching at the DPL, mainly because I knew I'd get great help and the chance to interact with Carol. After she retired, Rachel Howe became my go to person at the DPL, along with Adrianne Pierce, who helped me track down illustrations for this project. I deeply appreciate their help and the help of all of the staff at the DPL.

In San Antonio, Donna Guerra started me off on a solid footing when she worked at the San Antonio Municipal Archives. I'm blessed to say that Donna, like Carol, also became a friend. Over the many weeks I spent in San Antonio at the Municipal Archives, it was usually just me and Donna in a cramped little space, doing our work, getting to know each other. For years after she sent me material that she came across that related to Mexican Americans and policing. Now, that's dedication! I also received a great deal of assistance from the staff in the Texana/Genealogy Department at the San Antonio Public Library. In Austin, the staff at the Briscoe Center for American History at the University of Texas and at the Austin History Center were always super helpful. I also thank the staff at Special Collections at the University of Texas, Arlington.

In New Mexico, I benefited immensely from the experts at the Center for Southwest Research and Special Collections at the University of New Mexico. I especially appreciate the help of Suzanne Schadl, Nancy Brown-Martinez, and Terry Gugliotta. Additionally, Cindy Abel Morris did a lot to help me track down some important illustrations for this book. She has my thanks. Similarly, I had a wonderful experience at the Albuquerque and Bernalillo

County Special Collections Library. Many thanks go to Brandon Gonzalez for all the help he gave me when I visited there. Also in Albuquerque, I found a lot of useful information at the National Hispanic Cultural Center and thank senior librarian Greta Pullen. I also had a fabulous experience at the Fray Angélico Chávez History Library in Santa Fe hanging out with director Tomas Jaehn. Most of my time there, it was just me and Tomas, and he made my research experience extra fun. Special thanks also go to Kathleen Dull and Heather McClure, who helped me acquire several images from the Chávez Library. Also in Santa Fe, I found reams of material at the New Mexico State Records Center and Archives. Special thanks are due to Samantha M. Tubbs, Elena Perez-Lizano, and Rachel Adler for their help. And finally, Kathleen Gray at New Mexico Highlands University and Sonia Gomez at the Carnegie Library in Las Vegas both helped me get access to the (in)famous "hanging" windmill photo.

In Arizona, as in Texas, I not only got to do research but also got to make more new friends. I would like to especially acknowledge my friend Christine Marin for her help. For years, Christine helped researchers like me when she worked at Archives and Special Collections at Arizona State University. Now that she's retired, I simply message her over Facebook and get instant answers to my incessant questions. I also greatly benefited from the staff at the Arizona State Library Archives and wish to acknowledge Melanie Sturgeon and the rest of the archival staff there. I also received excellent help from Wendi Goen in tracking down some illustrations for this book. Similarly, at the Arizona Historical Society, Rachael Black was fabulous in helping me find illustrations, my friend Lora Key searched for images on my behalf as well, and James Burns was also a huge help.

In California, I received outstanding assistance from Lynda Claassen and the rest of the amazing staff at Special Collections and Archives at the University of California, San Diego. I had a wonderful experience at the Huntington Library and thank Clay Stalls, Claudia Funke, and the curatorial and front desk personnel there. After having lived in California for nearly a decade, researching in southern California was in many ways like coming home. The archivists there certainly made me feel very welcome.

I also received a great deal of assistance finding illustrations for this book from individuals at libraries and some businesses. At Granger, I thank Griff Thomas and Silka Quintero. At the Mary Evans Picture Library, I thank Lucinda Gosling and Jessica Talmage. Robert Demlong at the Phoenix Police Museum helped me get the image of Henry Garfias, one of the only known pictures of him. Nicki Ittner at the Marfa Public Library and Jake Mangum at the University of North Texas both helped me secure a scan of one of the few known photos of Chico Cano. Cristina Meisner and Jessica McDonald at the Harry Ransom Center at the University of Texas at Austin helped me obtain the permissions to use that scan. I thank all of you for your help.

For financial assistance I only received support for this project from Iowa State University in the form of Small Grants from the College of Liberal Arts and Sciences and a larger research grant from the Center for Excellence in the Arts and Humanities. Those grants gave me the ability to make multiple research trips to southwestern archival holdings. I also received a Faculty Professional Development Assignment (that's ISU speak for sabbatical) and a Humanities Scholarship Enhancement Initiative grant so that I could cobble together a year of leave to devote my time to writing. I also have a supportive group of colleagues in the Department of History, the U.S. Latino/a Studies Program, the African and African American Studies Program, and other departments and programs at Iowa State. While those folks know who they are, I would like to single out my various bosses who over the years supported my work, including Drs. Pam Riney-Kehrberg, Michael Bailey, Simon Cordery, Loreto Prieto, Lucía Suárez, and Tunde Adeleke. Your support has been truly appreciated.

Part of the fun of writing a new project is telling your friends and colleagues about it. Whether at a conference panel or over a meal, a beer, or a coffee, talking with colleagues and friends often produces a better-finished product. Simon Wendt, my best friend, brother from another mother, and doppelgänger is one of these special friends. He has opened more doors for me than I can count. While he has a keen intellect, always willing to comment or question or criticize my ideas and thinking and writing, he has on a number of occasions invited me to deliver talks at the University of Heidelberg and the University of Frankfurt. There, supportive and questioning crowds probed my work in ways that we academics find enormously beneficial. I also got to make new friends who helped me think through my own ideas, especially Fanja Razafimbelo, Fara Razafimbelo, Martin Lüthe, Peggy Preciado, and Pablo Dominguez Andersen. Thanks to you all. I owe Simon a huge debt of gratitude for his continued support and friendship.

In addition, friends and colleagues such as Greg Smithers, Chris Danielson, Gordon Mantler, Max Krochmal, Jorge Mariscal, David Montejano, Jimmy Patiño, Oliver Rosalas, Dan Berger, Cecilia Márquez, Brent Campney, Andrew Sandoval-Strausz, Cathleen Cahill, Clarence Walker, Ben Johnson, Monica Muñoz Martinez, Annette Rodríguez, Wes Phelps, Danielle Olden,

Michael Goebel, Brianna Burke, Max Viatori, Isaac Gottesman, Lora Key, Matthew Whitaker, Santos Nuñez Galicia, Jehan Nuñez al Faisal, Katherine Thatcher, Russell Contreras, and a number of others were always willing to share a drink or a meal and listen to me go on and on about policing. I also appreciated the folks who were willing to exchange an email or two with me to answer questions. My thanks go to John Bardes, Brent Campney, Monica Perales, Bill Carrigan, and a host of others. Brent Campney also graciously shared with me some of the research material he had located. Brent is a model of good colleagueship, which I greatly appreciate. Those conversations and emails and such are always important because friends and colleagues are quick to answer questions, they tend to ask you questions you wouldn't ask yourself, and those questions lead to new insights and answers as you progress in your research and writing.

I also have friends and colleagues who've helped in other ways. I wish to particularly single out my friend Dr. José Angel Hernández for his help. When I encountered Spanish phrases I did not understand, I relied on José's assistance for good translations. He's always been generous with his time but having a friend who is a native Spanish speaker and who didn't mind helping me figure out aspects of Spanish I had trouble fully understanding is a huge blessing. I wish to acknowledge and thank him for his help. I also received assistance with some last minute difficult translations from my friend Kristin MacDonald York and I similarly owe her my thanks.

I also benefited greatly from colleagues and friends when I presented my research findings at a variety of conferences and other events. My thanks are due to Alexander Byrd, Emily Straus, Monica Perales, Mario Garcia, David Montejano, Jose Moreno, Luis Moreno, Oliver Rosales, Marc Simon Rodriguez, Aaron Bae, Eric Larson, Ethan Blue, Greg Smithers, Scott Bowman, Roy Janisch, Abigail Rosas, Dwight Watson, Chris Haight, Guadalupe Quintanilla, and a host of conference audience members too numerous to name. I thank you all.

The fabulous staff at the University of North Carolina Press once again supported this project from idea to finished manuscript. My first editor, Chuck Grench, encouraged me to complete this project when I brought it up to him in about 2008. He assured me it would have a home at UNC Press. When Chuck retired, I began working with Debbie Gershenowitz, who made Chuck's assurances a reality. I've really enjoyed working with Debbie and can now say that I've had the privilege of working with two of the finest editors in the business. In addition, the staff at UNC Press is beyond topnotch and I wish to thank Andreina Fernandez, Andrew Winters, Valerie Burton, Lindsay Starr, Jamison Cockerham, and the rest of the staff at UNC Press. I also wish to thank the individuals who evaluated and wrote blurbs for this book, including Sonia Hernández, Miguel Levario, Bill Carrigan, and Brent Campney.

I would be remiss if I didn't mention the academic world that lives on Twitter. In particular, the host of twitterstorians who I've gotten to interact with over the years have been immensely helpful. These folks, and they are too numerous to list here but they know who they are, shared my ideas, critiqued my nerdy tweets, and asked insightful questions or for more information. Moreover, many of them are content area experts in fields that directly relate to my research. Those individuals, through their own tweets or comments on my tweets, seriously informed my research and writing because they actively worked to educate me via their own research and expertise. Twitter is ... interesting. The twitterstorians and academictwitter more broadly make it a community that is unlike any other.

My family has always been my most consistent group of supporters. Monic, my best friend, confidant, colleague, and wife, for years (years! bless her soul) listened to me talk about the things I discovered while researching or the moments I was writing about as this book came together. She of course had pertinent questions and critical commentary that helped strengthen the final product or, as was just as often the case, she offered many a commiserating "my god I don't know how you can write about this stuff" kind of statements. Even more importantly, her keen intellect and legal training allowed me great insight into how the criminal justice system works, what certain laws and statutes meant and how they worked, how criminal or civil trial courts operate, what state supreme court and U.S. Supreme Court decisions actually did, and a host of other topics. There were many times when I was writing this book that I felt like a law degree would have really helped me; I'm all too fortunate to have an attorney who lives with me! I truly appreciate Monic's friendship and love and dedication to helping me produce great work. My children, too, were always there. By the time this book is published my daughter, Elleka, will be fifteen years old. She's an amazing, bright young woman who also listened to my never-ending stories and commented on more than a few at the dinner table or on a long car ride. Similarly, my son, Aven, a wonderful, smart young man who will be thirteen by the time this book comes out, paid close attention to these same conversations and often weighed in with his own commentary. I love my children more than words can describe and am forever grateful to my family for their love, support, and encouragement. Finally, I acknowledge and remember my firstborn son, Brandis, who would have been sixteen by the time this book is published. Not a day goes by where I don't think of him, even though so many years have passed since he died. In some ways, he's always been there, even though he hasn't been. It's weird, grief is weird. My family gives me daily reassurance that our world is a good one and that my life is, as well. This book is dedicated to them.

Note on Terms

Properly designating Mexican-origin people can be challenging. Terms such as "Mexican" or "Mexican American" in part indicate an individual's citizenship status, but it is not always possible for scholars to accurately determine someone's citizenship. Moreover, additional terms that were commonly used during the period covered in this book and are occasionally used today—Tejano, Hispano, Californio, Latin American—can create confusion or misunderstanding for contemporary readers and as such I avoid using these terms. Historical records don't always make it clear if a person is of Mexican ancestry, and I occasionally rely on Spanish surnames to make that determination, an admittedly clunky and imprecise way of establishing heritage. Throughout this book I utilize "Mexican," "Mexican national," or "Mexican people" when it is clear the person or persons are citizens of Mexico. I use the term "Mexican American" to describe persons of Mexican ancestry who are American citizens. When speaking of Mexican and Mexican American people as a group, I mainly rely on "Mexican-origin people" or "people of Mexican ancestry." I also infrequently use "Latino/a/x" when referencing the entirety of the Latin American community in the United States.

This book also utilizes a number of Spanish language resources. In some of those sources spelling and usage of diacritical markings, especially the accent mark and tilde, are inconsistent. For example, in some sources "Pena" may have been "Peña" or "Garcia" may actually be "García." For names and phrases in Spanish, I follow the usage of diacritical markings as they appear in the sources or as they were preferred by the historical actors using such markings. Similarly, Mexican-origin people usually follow Spanish naming conventions wherein an individual's first last name (paternal surname) and second last name (maternal surname) are either equally important, or they mainly use their paternal surname. Thus, Joaquin Murrieta Carrillo is Joaquin Murrieta. In some cases, however, Mexican Americans for a variety of reasons utilized their maternal surname. Throughout this book I use the names Mexican-origin people preferred to use. Finally, I follow proper law citations and have omitted diacritical marks from titles of legal cases. All translations are my own unless otherwise noted.

The terms of ethnoracial identification for persons of European ancestry can also be problematic. While many Americans of European ancestry would be called "White" or "Caucasian" by the mid-nineteenth century, the governments of the Southwest also categorized Mexican-origin people as White. The terms "Anglo" and "Anglo American" also came to be common terms of identification for people of European heritage, even if many of those people did not originate in England. To avoid confusion, I use the term "White" throughout this book to describe individuals of European heritage only, making sure that it is clear when Mexican-origin people might also have been considered White.

For African-descent people I use the terms "Black" and "African American." For Indigenous people I utilize, when possible, their tribal affiliation or community attachment. When speaking of Indigenous people as a group I use the term "Indigenous people." I also occasionally use the term "Indian" when speaking of Indigenous people in historical context. Finally, throughout this book I capitalize all racial and ethnic terms of identification.

Many of the terms mentioned above are freighted with meaning and their usage is complex and even potentially controversial. The terms I use and how I use them are not intended to be in any way disrespectful toward the various ethnoracial communities mentioned in the pages that follow.

BORDERS OF VIOLENCE & JUSTICE

INTRODUCTION

The people of Yavapai County, Arizona, liked Manuel Mejía. He was a friendly, hardworking, thirty-two-year-old miner who knew the county like the back of his hand. Local people could always count on him for help planting a field, putting in a fence, or for advice related to mining in the Arizona Territory. His good reputation, however, did not stop the mob that attempted to lynch Mejía in September of 1886. The sheriff's office in neighboring Maricopa County had erroneously arrested him for the murder of a White family. Upon his release, a mob of ten men beat him, tied him up, beat him some more, dragged him by horse through the streets of Phoenix, and attempted to lynch him not once, not twice, but four times! Manuel Mejía thus has the strange distinction of having endured a quadruple hanging. Amazingly, he lived to tell about it.[1]

Manuel Mejía's attempted lynchings underscore how White people, and occasionally Mexican-origin people as well, conceived of vigilante justice as a legitimate form of justice in the Southwest.[2] They argued that law enforcement across the region was weak or nonexistent, which necessitated mob law. But all southwestern governments had made founding criminal justice institutions a priority in the 1830s and 1840s, so these perceptions were fictions, although they served as an effective excuse for vigilantism. Mejía had committed no crime; local authorities had arrested and then released him, which shows that the justice system did exist and work. But that outcome did not satisfy the mob. Instead, they assumed Mejía's guilt and sought to exercise their own version of justice even though he had done nothing wrong. His example only differs from hundreds of other cases of mob violence in the Southwest in that he lived.

Mejía's attempted lynchings tell us more about justice in the U.S. borderlands. He survived because he escaped the lynch mob. When he did, he fled to the home of a local Mexican family for protection, which shows how community networks could offer a measure of safety for those in need. That family called for assistance from Phoenix town marshal Enrique "Henry" Garfias, one of a handful of Mexican American law officers in the region. Garfias's position demonstrates that not only did Mexican Americans serve in law enforcement but they could also function as trusted sources of protection for the Mexican-origin community. He secured additional aid for Mejía from the Maricopa County Sheriff's Office, the same office that had originally arrested him. Additionally, the Mexican government, through its diplomatic corps, put pressure on the United States and the Arizona Territory to prosecute those in the lynch mob. The role of the Mexican government in the affairs of Mexican nationals such as Mejía—and Americans of Mexican descent as well—proved an important source of power for Mexican-origin people. The Maricopa County district attorney did bring charges against Mejía's attackers. Although a jury acquitted these men, the fact that the territory prosecuted them at all means that the system also worked for people of Mexican ancestry, even though the result of the trial hardly seems like justice.

Borders of Violence and Justice explores the Mexican-origin community's relationship with formal and informal law enforcement in the U.S. Southwest from 1835 to 1935. That period includes the formative development of the region and its criminal justice institutions in the early to mid-1800s and concludes with the modernization of law enforcement in the Southwest in the 1920s and 1930s. The book analyzes the ways in which legal and extralegal police agencies treated Mexicans and Mexican Americans in the border region. The book also reveals the ways Mexican-origin people challenged the often abusive nature of southwestern policing. They creatively adapted themselves to the local law enforcement landscape across the Southwest, resisted police abuse, and pioneered changes in policing that significantly reformed police procedure in ways still visible today.[3] To fully introduce the contents within this book, the following pages demarcate how White people regarded Mexican-origin people; how and why they implemented the criminal justice system they did; what went into that system; and how Mexicans and Mexican Americans responded to both.

Law enforcement efforts and manifestations of the broader criminal justice system pervade the foundational history of the border region. From the earliest days of American settlement, White people transported with them to the Southwest not only a sense of social, moral, and racial superiority—what would come to be called "Manifest Destiny"—but also a belief that they brought stable government and order to a region that had neither. Law enforcement became one of the first institutions crafted by White people in power to foster those beliefs. Developing a strong criminal justice system served to legitimize government in the region, gave it the necessary power to control people there, and allowed White leaders to use it to advance American colonialism in the borderlands.[4]

The American takeover of Mexico's territory was at base a process of settler colonialism.[5] Popular versions of American history don't really tell this story, preferring instead to see the spread of the United States from sea to shining sea as the logical outcome of the growth of the American population. But first in Texas, which wrested its independence from Mexico in 1836 and became a state in 1845, and later during the 1846–48 Mexican-American War, which saw the remainder of Mexico's northern territories fall to Americans, the United States used its military might to forcibly take possession of another country's lands. The Texas Army and the U.S. Army also became the first agencies of law enforcement in the region, initially controlling the Mexican population, Indigenous people, African Americans, and others, which simultaneously allowed for the settlement of White Americans.

The logic of colonization meant different things for these groups. Enslaved Black people, bound and controlled as they were via chattel slavery, factored into this colonial experiment in the borderlands as a group that assisted White settlers through forced work, since they did much of the labor of building the homes, farms, and other edifices of White society, especially in Texas. After the Civil War, White people reacted viscerally to Black freedom and curtailed the rights of African Americans until the civil rights movement.[6] Black people remained a small minority of the Southwest's population, except in East Texas, until well into the twentieth century.[7]

Indigenous people experienced colonization differently. Colonization largely meant ongoing warfare and genocide as White people actively attempted to eradicate or isolate them. This proved especially true for Indigenous people in the border region and in the West. The ongoing Indian Wars of the nineteenth century and the displacement of Indigenous peoples—for example, the Navajo Long Walk of 1864—decimated these communities. Those things also show the continued work of the American military in controlling nonwhite people to allow for White settlement. Additionally, the development of the reservation system further isolated and marginalized Indigenous people.[8]

Mexicans experienced colonization yet differently. Although protected by treaty and viewed by some Whites as potentially assimilable into the United States, they faced a kind of multifaceted colonialism that included marginalization, violence, and dispossession, but in some cases inclusion and even a measure of power sharing.[9] Once southwestern states and territories began to develop their justice systems, law enforcement became the military force that controlled Mexican-origin people and allowed for the in-migration of thousands of White Americans. Police agencies as well as extralegal mobs represented a broad, colonial regime that worked to maintain American power in the border region. The settlement process lasted more than a generation. The institutions created to make it happen remain with us today.

Law enforcement and White Americans often treated Mexican-origin people as a "foreign" population that they deemed undesirable and suspect. White people had a host of racist perceptions about Mexicans and Mexican Americans generally and their supposed criminality specifically. For example, popular sentiments construed Mexican-origin people as not just criminally prone but as having a proclivity to commit certain crimes such as murder. While incorrect, such viewpoints meant that law enforcement tended to treat Mexican-origin people with a heavy hand.[10]

The Mexican population thus encountered systems of government and people that deemed order and control as the necessary mechanisms for state building. It should be noted that while Americans saw themselves as bringing order and stable government to a barbaric and uncivilized region and people—even though the region did of course have institutions of government and the people weren't barbaric—those same Americans acted with a great deal of barbarity and violence when advancing this mission. Numerous instances of violence bear this point out, but the "Texas Cowboys" provide one notable example. Beginning in the 1850s, Texas ranching interests spread to New Mexico. They brought with them different groups of Texas

Cowboys, usually a conglomeration of skilled cowpokes, men searching for adventure, outright criminals, and otherwise desperate people seeking to escape problems, who acted as a law unto themselves and abused and murdered Mexican-origin people. Thus, state building via law enforcement and individual or collective action via groups such as the Texas Cowboys both cemented American control with violence, creating formal and informal systems of justice.[11]

What went into the criminal justice system? Like other locales, the Southwest had multiple and overlapping criminal justice institutions. Almost all southwestern governments authorized the establishment of sheriff's offices as the first stage of development of the justice system. Sheriffs are elected officials, their jurisdiction is at the county level, and they hire their officer corps of deputy sheriffs. The sheriff's office in most counties operates and supervises a jail; it staffs that facility with employees of the sheriff's department. A sheriff's office has historically presided over all matters of criminal justice: it investigates crimes, makes arrests, engages in traffic safety, and deals with civil matters such as evictions.[12]

Southwestern governments next mandated the formation of town and city police forces. Many towns first had an informal committee of public safety or other such extralegal police force (often akin to a lynch mob) before founding official, legally codified police departments. Houston, Los Angeles, and Santa Fe all serve as useful examples of this phenomenon. Once local governments established an official police force, they usually chose one of several options. Some founded police departments, some established a constable's office with an elected constable, and some had both (some locales had a marshal's office that acted like and in many cases eventually became a police department). Generally speaking, in the nineteenth and early twentieth centuries a police department and a constable's office operated similarly. They were responsible for local law enforcement, as well as handling civil matters such as traffic control, within the town or city limits where they were located. Most police forces also operated a city jail. Some constabulary's jurisdictional boundaries were the county, or segments or precincts of a county such as in Texas or Arizona. There was often overlap in the role and jurisdiction of police departments and constable's offices. For example, today Houston has a citywide police force, the Houston Police Department, which serves as the paramount law enforcement agency in the city, but also has a constabulary of eight precincts, the Harris County Constables, with jurisdiction over different county precincts. Constables usually, although not always, have less juridical authority than a police department or sheriff's office.[13]

Some southwestern states and territories also attempted to establish state or territory-wide law enforcement agencies. The most famous of these, the Texas Rangers, originated in the 1830s during the Texas Revolution (1835–36) and still exist today. Other states and territories attempted to establish similar police forces in the nineteenth century, with varying success. The New Mexico Territory established a short-lived Ranger force in the late nineteenth and again in the early twentieth century. The Arizona Territory also had several different Ranger forces, in 1860, 1882, and 1901, all of which disbanded. California launched a state Ranger force in the 1850s, the California Rangers, that eventually became the California State Police in the 1880s. For these state and territorial police forces, the entire state was their jurisdiction, and they handled all matters of law enforcement.[14]

Last, the federal government also operated several different branches of law enforcement in the border region. Most importantly, the U.S. Marshals Service employed a number of marshals in the Southwest. As federal officials, a marshal's jurisdiction pertained to federal laws, for example supervising federal prisoners or apprehending fugitives. In the Southwest, marshals also often provided local-level law enforcement when needed, meaning their job had local implications, not just federal ones. Border security was another aspect of federal law enforcement, one largely conducted by the U.S. Army and the U.S. Customs Service until 1924. That year the U.S. government created the Border Patrol to handle border security, further augmenting federal law enforcement.[15]

The broader criminal justice system also actively played a part in the lives of Mexican-origin people. While state and territorial governments established police agencies, they also developed other aspects of the system. If an interaction with a police officer represented the first step in the system, the formal charging of individuals after arrest, their trial, and depending on the outcome of that trial their punishment, from fines to jail time to execution, all represented subsequent steps in the system. In most locales, a county district attorney had responsibility for charging and trying arrested individuals. District attorneys could empanel a grand jury to charge individuals accused of a crime before a subsequent trial occurred. While district attorneys handled all manner of charges, including those for violent crimes, in some instances the state attorney general or federal prosecutors handled violent offenders. In addition to the local trial court system and the federal district court system, most states and territories operated other courts—including police courts wherein police tried minor cases such as drunk and disorderly conduct; a coroner's inquest (often with a jury) wherein the county coroner conducted a judicial inquiry, like a trial, to determine whether a homicide was accidental or intentional; a justice court wherein a judge or justice of the peace adjudicated minor, petty crimes during a bench or juryless trial; and state and federal appellate courts, with the state supreme court and U.S. Supreme Court serving as final arbiters in the outcome of a lower court's trial.[16]

Last, southwestern governments established a variety of corrections systems to incarcerate the individuals adjudicated in the courts. City police forces built jails, county sheriff's offices built jails, territorial and state governments built prisons or penitentiaries and other correctional facilities, the federal government built penitentiaries and other forms of human caging. Even individuals operated jails, such as plantation jails. Most incarcerated people served their time in county jails and usually had short sentences. The state imprisoned more serious and violent offenders in state or federal prisons, usually with lengthier sentences. Those prisons also carried out executions. This web of legally codified criminal justice agencies provided the foundation for a system that exercised a great deal of authority and power over all residents of the Southwest.[17]

But a legally codified criminal justice system wasn't the only one operating in the region. As the case of Manuel Mejía makes plain, extralegal justice worked in conjunction with the official criminal justice system. White people used a number of legalistic sounding terms to name their mobs—vigilance committee, vigilante society, committee of public safety, citizens patrol—further connecting their actions to criminal justice institutions. Such terminology offered an air of legality and legitimacy to an illegitimate body that committed unlawful acts. Extralegal justice also often included trials, convictions, and sentences, almost always death, which worked to terrorize Mexican-origin people and others to be sure. In other cases, people simply took the law into their own hands, exerting an individual-level version of a criminal justice system. Throughout the borderlands, White people actively argued that the justice system did not function adequately or effectively, necessitating the need for vigilante justice. As noted, White people clung to such falsehoods in order to exercise power over Mexicans and Mexican Americans.

The Mexican-origin population in the border region—which stood at about 100,000 people in the 1840s, contracted to about 75,000 people in the decade or so after the Mexican-American War, and then expanded rapidly in the late nineteenth and early twentieth centuries to several million people—found itself somewhat powerless when dealing with these newly created systems of governance.[18] For example, the criminal justice system insulated itself from criticism and change. The system and those that operated it found numerous ways to protect law officers accused of wrongdoing. Authorities frequently disparaged Mexican and Mexican American victims of police abuse (a practice that still occurs today). They labelled those victims as bad people, published their criminal record if they had one, made them seem like the aggressors, all with the goal of justifying their victimization and exonerating the officers accused of that victimization. One of the easy ways to visualize this process is through the concept of ley de fuga (law of flight) or more simply ley fuga. Ley fuga permitted law enforcement to shoot and kill suspects who fled. In many parts of the border region it was an actual law, but it also worked as a kind of informal rule where its legality was unclear. In numerous instances where law enforcement killed Mexican-origin people, police claimed the individual had attempted to escape, necessitating their killing. In fact, law enforcement simply executed those people and used the law of flight to justify the killing. Ley fuga legally excused police from their culpability in slaying people.[19]

Mexican-origin people found themselves at the mercy of the system in other ways. For example, White people frequently labelled them "bandits" whether or not they were outlaws. Whites applied the term "bandit" to just about anyone, and this labelling automatically categorized a person as a dangerous, violent lawbreaker. Once so named, mobs and law enforcement could then more easily eliminate such individuals from southwestern society. This labelling became especially problematic in the early twentieth century as more Mexicans arrived in the United States as refugees from the 1910–24 Mexican Revolution. For White Americans at this time, Mexican bandits seemed to materialize everywhere, and White people responded with increased violence, culminating in a number of murders and massacres of Mexican and Mexican American people, most notably the 1918 massacre of fifteen unarmed men and boys at Porvenir, Texas.[20]

Mexican-origin people did attempt to resist abuse from the criminal justice system and mob law. They fought against the United States military when it appropriated Mexican territories. Once warfare had ended, they continued to fight back against White encroachment and violence. Stipulations in the Treaty of Guadalupe Hidalgo, which ended the Mexican-American War, granted American citizenship to Mexicans, and they often attempted to rely on their rights as citizens for protection. They also utilized the newly created governmental systems to their advantage. They elected individuals to different positions in the criminal justice system, especially law enforcement officers. In fact, Mexican Americans served in law enforcement throughout the nineteenth and twentieth centuries. And some of those Mexican Americans became police officers because they wanted to protect the Mexican population, as the example of Henry Garfias shows. Their service, then, worked as a kind of early civil rights strategy for redressing wrongs. Mexican Americans correctly viewed law enforcement as the first level of justice in the Southwest and they pushed police to administer that justice fairly. They challenged heavy-handed policing, helped craft unique solutions to law enforcement problems, and resisted the harsh treatment they experienced in a variety of ways. Beyond that, Mexican Americans had roles in other aspects of the criminal justice system: they became attorneys, staff in prisons or jails, served as jurors, and were appointed to oversight committees within the justice system across the border region. Their efforts provide a rich history of service that demonstrates Mexican American willingness to ensure that the system worked and worked fairly.

Mexican-origin people resisted lynch mobs as well. They fought back, sought safety from the legitimate criminal justice system, fled their attackers, formed anti-lynching civic groups, and sought aid from Mexico. They also occasionally formed their own vigilante groups or joined the lynch mobs formed by others, an interesting aspect to this history that reveals that mob law wasn't solely the purview of White people. Focusing on resistance to vigilantes shifts agency away from an all-powerful White mob and onto the Mexican and Mexican American people who suffered from this violence and also found ways to combat it.

Mexican Americans found other ways to resist. In some cases, well-known groups such as Las Gorras Blancas, or White Caps, formed in New Mexico in 1889, actively fought against White dispossession of Mexican-owned lands and the unremitting greed of White land speculators, as well as against abuses in the justice system. The efforts of the White Caps represented a bold example of Mexican American agency, one that had much to say about law enforcement. In other cases, Mexican-origin people became the very bandits White people feared. They actively opposed injustice by becoming outlaws. A good number of so-called bandits only became outlaws because of a problematic encounter with White law enforcement. Francisco "Chico" Cano engaged in banditry after a former Texas Ranger illegally attempted to arrest him. He later became a militia leader in the Mexican Revolution; members of the U.S. military and police attempted and failed to have him murdered on several occasions. And then some bandits weren't bandits at all, such as Gregorio Cortéz of Texas, who killed two White law enforcement officers in self-defense and found himself railroaded by the criminal justice system. But they also received support from the Mexican American community. In Cortéz's case, Mexican

Americans developed a support network that advocated for him and collected funds for his legal defense. These efforts resulted in several acquittals during Cortéz's various trials and ultimately his pardon and release from prison.[21]

Mexican Americans also demanded reforms in the criminal justice system. When police agencies began to professionalize their officer corps and policies and procedures in the early twentieth century, Mexican Americans often initiated or took part in this process. Police departments, such as the Albuquerque Police Department, began to actively recruit Mexican American law officers at this time. Perhaps the most important reforms occurred in Texas with modifications to the Texas Ranger force in 1919. State representative José Tomás "J. T." Canales, the only Mexican American in the Texas Legislature, put the Rangers on trial for border murders they had committed in the 1910s. He also authored legislation that successfully altered the power of the Rangers.[22] Such examples demonstrate the creative adaptations of Mexican Americans to the law enforcement climate in the border region.

This book, then, merges Mexican and Mexican American agency with police action. It focuses on law enforcement by placing community activity and police authority, both broadly conceived, side by side. By adapting themselves to the local law enforcement environment, Mexican-origin people not only resisted police abuse but they also helped craft unique solutions to law enforcement problems. That history matters to both the Mexican American and the law enforcement communities.

Borders of Violence and Justice is set in the borderlands and focuses primarily on California, Arizona, New Mexico, and Texas, especially the southernmost parts of these states and territories where Mexicans and Mexican Americans predominated. While national boundaries are important, and many of the events described in this book occurred near the border itself, borderlands scholars see the frontier as less a line on a map and more a space defined by concepts such as power, race, ethnicity, gender, and national belonging. In this regard, borderlands serve as a meeting place for diverse peoples, each negotiating, making, and remaking a new or developing society. White people sought to control the border region by exercising power, especially the institutions of the criminal justice system; Mexican-origin people both resisted and joined that effort. And those interactions happened across the region, which seemed always in a state of flux. For example, New Mexico operated as a kind of super territory during much of its early history. It encompassed present-day New Mexico and Arizona, and parts of Texas, Oklahoma, Colorado, Utah, Nevada, and Kansas. The territory's borders shifted constantly—for instance, when the United States expanded its size after the 1853 Gadsden Purchase or when

Arizona broke away from New Mexico in 1863 to become a new territory. New territories with different boundaries meant new or revised criminal justice institutions with altered jurisdictions and powers, all of which people had to build and understand. Delineating the borders separating violence and justice, the boundary line between what is just and unjust, or the fact that violence and justice were quite often one and the same underscores the importance of the borderlands to American history. The Southwest, often overlooked and ignored by scholars, the media, and the public, has much to tell us about the policing of communities of color.[23]

This book also demonstrates how racism became institutionalized within the police profession in the border region, an important subject that has ramifications for policing today. Scholars and many in the public understand that law enforcement and the criminal justice system have roots in racism. The policies, practices, and procedures of police forces in the Southwest reveal a part of this institutionalization of racism, going back to their origins in colonial regimes and growing out of the military power that initially controlled the region. But other aspects of anti-Mexican racism—the discourse about their criminality or banditry, the White sense that Mexican and Mexican Americans were untrustworthy or barbaric or to be feared—also went into this system. The justice system as well as extralegal justice fed off those racist sentiments and reified them within the institution. The problem with systemic racism in law enforcement was that whether people committed a crime or not, police tended to treat them in wholly inappropriate ways because of their ethnoracial identity. It also meant that law officers who did good, fair-minded police work—and many of those officers existed—could make little impact on racism within law enforcement because it was an institutional part of the system and not correctable by individual action.[24]

I have structured this book topically to focus each chapter on distinct themes in this history. The first chapter explores the ways in which the United States took over the Southwest and how White Americans established the criminal justice system. That foundation is important because it demonstrates the colonial nature of the U.S. acquisition of Mexico's territories while simultaneously showing how the criminal justice system became an important first building block in American statecraft in the region. The second chapter examines mob violence by exploring extralegal justice that masqueraded as legal justice. Mob law acted in tandem with legitimate law enforcement and served to additionally cement American power and control in the region. In chapter 3, I uncover the history of Mexican American law enforcement officers. Many people might assume that Mexican Americans did not serve in law enforcement until police agencies began to actively recruit them in the mid-twentieth century. This chapter demonstrates otherwise, showcasing some important moments in the Southwest's policing history, especially the service of those Mexican American officers who saw their work as a type of early civil rights effort. The fourth chapter focuses on Mexican and Mexican American criminality. While White people often considered Mexican-origin people as predisposed to certain criminal activities, especially murder, the available historical record shows instead that police tended to arrest them for suspicion, vagrancy, or for property crimes. This chapter also demonstrates that while police officers often treated Mexicans and Mexican Americans with a heavy hand, the broader criminal justice system tended to treat them more fairly. In chapter 5, I address the issue of banditry in the Southwest. While social bandits have always existed in frontier societies, White Americans had an exaggerated fear of Mexican bandits, saw them everywhere, and actively attempted to rid the region of these so-called bandits. But one of the oddities of this fear of bandits is that law enforcement, tasked with apprehending outlaws, often created the very bandits it feared. Many of the Southwest's most notorious desperados only became bandits after an unfortunate encounter with White law enforcement. The final chapter shifts attention to the transformation of southwestern policing in the early twentieth century. From 1900 to the 1930s, law enforcement underwent important evolutions, especially police professionalization. Mexican Americans were often at the forefront of these professionalization efforts. And yet they continued to experience violence and abuse at the hands of law enforcement and lynch mobs. The oscillatory history of this period, shifting between progress and regress, represents the end of the Southwest's early policing history and the establishment of revised, professional police forces in the mid-twentieth century.

This is a hard history. The U.S. Southwest was an incredibly violent region. The pages that follow seem stained with blood. This history may be difficult for some; readers should be aware of the extent of the violence discussed in this book. For Mexican-origin people and others who have experienced racial violence from law enforcement, this book will no doubt be painful. The scars that result from police violence have created for many communities of color a kind of generational trauma that remains agonizing today. Those in law enforcement might also find this book hard to read. They may view it as an embarrassing indictment on policing or perhaps as an aspersion on their own police work. But many in law enforcement want police to do better, accept criticism, and work daily to avoid the mistakes of the past. Reckoning with this past is long overdue. Understanding the origins of how we got to where we are today may help us build a better future. I hope this book contributes to that process.

In sum, the level of violence detailed throughout *Borders of Violence and Justice* may be hard to fathom. Much of it derived from the ways in which legitimate law enforcement, the broader criminal justice system, and extralegal mobs conceived of and treated Mexican-origin people. The battles, massacres, lynchings, shootings, stabbings, beatings, maimings, and other forms of bloodshed that occurred from the 1830s to the 1930s ultimately demonstrate that the Southwest was a very violent borderland.

One of the earliest depictions of the Texas Rangers, this engraving appeared in an 1842 edition of the *London Illustrated News*. An article about the "Texas Mounted Militia" detailed the Rangers' attempts to halt incursions of Mexican forces and to maintain the border between the Republic of Texas and Mexico. This image also demonstrates that Mexican-origin people often served as or participated with the Rangers, as at least one and possibly two of the individuals appear to be of Mexican ancestry.
Mary Evans Picture Library.

1

REIGN OF BLOOD

The Unending Mexican War
and the Creation of the Criminal
Justice System in the Southwest

I
n the midst of the siege of Béxar in late 1835, an incredibly tense time in the Texas Revolution with Mexico, the provisional government of Texas met in session for the first time. The delegates had a lot to worry about: founding and funding an army to prosecute the war with Mexico, recruiting soldiers, feeding and arming them, along with the other mundane aspects of government such as mail service, the erection of government buildings, or the selection of a site for a capital. In addition to many of these things, the provisional government also took the time to pass "an ordinance and decree to establish and organize and establish a corps of rangers." In fact, the legislation establishing a Ranger force came before the legislation that decreed the raising of an army. The first incarnation of the

Texas Rangers would conduct law enforcement in the Republic of Texas and for generations after.[1]

White leaders were so preoccupied with law and order that the criminal justice system became the first government institution founded in many parts of the border region. The formation of the Texas Rangers serves as a case in point. The Republic of Texas began organizing other aspects of the criminal justice system while the Texas Revolution took place. Similarly, New Mexico and California began creating their criminal justice systems while the Mexican-American War transpired. Moreover, the U.S. Army conducted itself as a law enforcement body in the Southwest during the Mexican-American War and after. Several of the battles of the war were in essence police actions, and their aftermaths resulted in criminal trials for the Mexicans who participated in those battles. That history shows how law enforcement originated in the border region as well as how it came to regard Mexican people.

The American acquisition of Mexico's northern territories began in the 1830s and technically concluded in 1848 at the end of the Mexican-American War, with the signing of the Treaty of Guadalupe Hidalgo. But the violence of this period and the acquisition process did not end with the treaty. Instead, both the war and the manner by which Americans took possession of what became the U.S. Southwest continued well after 1848. Historian William Deverell has accurately referred to this time as the "unending Mexican war" era and as a "social hangover" wrought by the "recklessness of American occupation, warfare, and statehood [in California]."[2] While the war seemed unending, the process of establishing American forms of government and especially the criminal justice system was ongoing.

White Americans who ventured into Mexico's northern territories saw themselves as bringing law, order, and civilization to the region. They viewed their mission through the prism of Manifest Destiny and as such believed they embodied the nationalizing spirit and mission of the United States. Mexican people stood in the way of that vision. As a writer for the national *Democratic Review* made clear, "The Mexican race now see... their own inevitable destiny. They must amalgamate and be lost, in the superior vigor of the Anglo-Saxon race, or they must utterly perish. They may postpone the hour for a time, but it will come, when their nationality shall cease."[3] Or, to put it even more bluntly, as John L. O'Sullivan (who is generally credited with coining the term "Manifest Destiny") did in the *Democratic Review*, "Imbecile and distracted, Mexico can never exert any real governmental authority over such a country.... In the case of California this is now impossible. The Anglo-Saxon foot is already on its borders. Already the advance guard of the irresistible army of the Anglo-Saxon emigration has begun to pour down upon it, armed with the plough and the rifle."[4]

In the period immediately following the Mexican-American War, the United States gained control of the new American Southwest. They did this largely via military might and through the creation of agencies of government, especially law enforcement.[5] Americans established the criminal justice system as a first step in the state-building process. This process of settler colonialism utilized the U.S. Army, the criminal justice system, and vigilante justice as police powers to control a region White folks viewed as empty or devoid of people and government institutions.[6] When White Americans did consider the people who lived there, they tended to see Mexican, Indigenous, and Black people as inferior, barbaric, and dangerous. Interestingly, Americans often acted with a great deal of barbarism and violence themselves, projecting their own savagery upon Mexicans and then using the army or later police departments and lynch mobs (sometimes simultaneously) to halt the violence that they had created. Moreover, many of the individuals who came to serve as law officers in the Southwest had first served in the army. Once mustered out of service, they found similar jobs in law enforcement. This further connected the military to policing.

Mexicans responded to this situation in a variety of ways. Some joined with Americans to oppose Mexican rule. Many of these individuals later helped state and territorial governments create government institutions. Others actively fought against American encroachment into Mexico's territory during the Mexican-American War. They also continued to resist and fight in the postwar period. But between the 1830s and 1850s, Mexicans were rather defenseless against the onslaught of the United States.

The initial phase of Mexican and U.S. interactions began with the founding of American colonies in Texas in the 1820s. By the early 1830s, Texians outnumbered Mexicans in the state of Coahuila y Tejas. During the Texas Revolution, organized law enforcement was largely absent in Texas. Policing during the war and after fell to the Texas Army and the small force of Texas Rangers. Most Mexicans felt ambivalent toward the war. Some fought with the Texians, such as Juan Seguín, who participated in the Battle of San Jacinto.[7] Other Mexicans fought for Mexico. Vicente Córdova originally supported the Texians because of corruption within the Mexican government, but he switched sides when Texians coupled their call for independence with pro-slavery rhetoric. He later helped the Mexican Army recapture San Antonio in a failed bid to reconquer Texas.[8]

The Texas Legislature began establishing the criminal justice system throughout the revolution. While the legislature passed bills on how to form and fund the Texas military to prosecute the war early on, it simultaneously passed the first legislation governing criminal justice in what would become the Republic of Texas. Their focus on the criminal justice system, given the tense nature of the revolution period, demonstrates how important policing was to White Texians. As noted, during the First Session of the provisional government in 1835, legislators created the Texas Rangers.[9] Another law established a "justice court system," the local court system in the republic, and decreed the appointment of prosecuting attorneys, clerks, and other personnel.[10] Article 269 of the *Early Laws of Texas* provided for "the election of sheriffs, coroners and constables, and defining their several duties."[11] Article 275 established the powers of district courts. This article, one of the longest and most detailed of those passed in 1836, contained forty-seven sections explaining the role of the courts.[12]

After the Texas Revolution ended in 1836, the Texas government continued to modify the laws governing the criminal justice system. In the 1838 legislative session, Article 483 amended Article 275, revising the district court system by changing the power of district court judges, specifically their ability to alternate or recuse themselves in certain cases.[13] Article 509, "an act to better define the duties of sheriffs," decreed that in cases where the sheriff was a party to a suit, oversight of the case would fall to the town constable.[14] Article 580 augmented the Rangers, authorizing the "raising of a company of fifty-six men for the ranging service."[15] Article 768, passed in the 1840 Session, authorized the president of the Republic to "offer a reward of one thousand dollars for arrest of any person who shall flee from justice."[16]

The only things missing from the development of the criminal justice system during the years of the Texas Republic were jails and prisons. In fact, the initial legislation did not mention jails. It seems like the republic expected the various counties and sheriff's offices to provide their own jails, which they did. The republic only addressed incarceration in a concrete manner in the Sixth Session in 1841–42. During that session the legislature debated Article 1145, "an act to provide for the erection of a penitentiary."[17] The act failed to pass, however, and Texas did not erect its first penitentiary until 1849.[18] That prison, the Texas State Penitentiary at Huntsville, is still in operation today. After Texas became a state, the legislature authorized specific counties to construct jails. Article 1973, for example, called for Jasper County to collect taxes for "the building of a court-house and jail for use of said county."[19] That

This jail in Independence, Texas, was originally constructed in 1834–35 by the Mexican government and used for decades after by Washington County. While Texas, and later other southwestern states and territories, focused on building human caging facilities, often those facilities already existed. This jail was later transformed into a personal residence. The photo was taken circa 1935.
Historic American Buildings Survey, Creator. Mexican Jail, Farm Roads 390 & 50 Vicinity, Independence, Washington County, Texas, 1933.

type of legislation became the most common way southwestern governments established jail facilities.

Many of the laws passed by the government of the Republic of Texas and later the State of Texas seemingly had little to do with persons of Mexican ancestry. They could and would be used against Mexicans, though. For example, Article 374, "an act to provide for the punishment of crimes and misdemeanors committed by slaves and free persons of color," could be extrapolated to other ethnic communities.[20] Article 632 provided for "the raising of three companies of mounted volunteers for frontier service against hostile Indians," but such a group of Rangers would be deployed against Mexicans too.[21]

Like other governments, Texas continued to modify its laws as the nineteenth century progressed. One of the most important modifications came in the 1850s when the state established a penal code. While many other states

Reign of Blood

had lengthy criminal law or criminal code books, Texas was one of the first to create a penal code. The legislature initially passed the act for this code in 1856 and then revised and reapproved it in 1871. The revisions to the original act focused on the crimes of murder and attempted murder.[22] Since the legislature had established criminal statutes somewhat haphazardly, with new laws added to the books since the days of the Texas Republic, having a penal volume that compiled all laws into a single body was important. The Texas Penal Code was also massive, demonstrating yet again the importance of law and order at this time. Texas became the first state in the Southwest to create a penal code.

The relationship between Mexican people and local law enforcement is hard to discern in Texas's early history, but after the revolution it becomes clearer. Take the creation of the city of Houston in 1837. Founders Augustus and John Allen utilized enslaved Black people and Mexican prisoners of war to clear the grounds for the building of the town. The use of Mexican prisoners of war was a semilegal law enforcement solution to the messy conclusion of the Texas Revolution. The military imprisoned several hundred Mexicans on Galveston Island, doling out dozens of men to rebuild homes, restore property, and lay the foundation for Houston after the war had ended. The Constitution of Texas made no clear mention, nor established any law, governing prisoners of war.[23] The public version of the Treaty of Velasco, which ended the war with Mexico, asserted only that Texas would treat Mexican prisoners of war humanely (the private Treaty of Velasco made no mention of prisoners of war).[24] So the army decided the fate of prisoners of war and used them as a prison chain gang.[25]

In some Texas communities law enforcement began informally and extralegally. After Houston's founding in 1837, White residents developed an unofficial "citizens patrol." Extralegal and beholden to no one, these types of citizens patrols, often called "committees of public safety" or "vigilance committees" in other locales, closely monitored enslaved Black people and Mexicans.[26] Such citizens patrols appeared in numerous parts of the Southwest. The historical record of Houston's Citizens Patrol has been lost. The election of a sheriff in 1837, the development of a constabulary in 1837, and the official founding of the Houston Police Department in 1841 probably changed little in the day-to-day interactions of Mexican-origin people and police. The Mexican population in Houston remained numerically small throughout the nineteenth century—the 1850 census counted only six Mexicans and only eighteen in the 1860 census. Despite the small population, Mexicans still aroused the ire of Houstonians. In an 1839 letter to the editor of the *Houston Morning Star*, one

Houstonian complained about "idle, thieving Mexican vagabonds prowling about." "How long?" he asked, "before the proper authorities will take it into their hands to investigate the matter?" He also advocated for vigilante justice: "Unless the law will take hold of them, the citizens must take the matter in their own hands, and the transgressors must abide by the consequences."[27]

Other Texas cities followed a similar pattern. San Antonio first developed a town marshal system. Even though the town was officially incorporated in 1837, residents did not elect a marshal until 1846. The San Antonio Marshal's Office eventually morphed into a police force in 1873. It appears that between 1837 and 1846, the town utilized a vigilance committee and occasionally the Texas Rangers for its law enforcement needs.[28] Austin followed the same path and first had a vigilance committee before founding a marshal's office in 1840 and the Austin Police Department in 1862.[29] The police force in Dallas also began as a vigilance committee. White residents formed the Dallas Vigilance Committee in the summer of 1846 to police Dallas County, which had a small population of around fifty people. The Dallas Vigilance Committee primarily protected White folks from Indigenous people. It also seems likely that the committee, like other such entities, controlled the area's population of enslaved Black people. Few Mexicans lived in Dallas County at that time. The first record of a Mexican individual in Dallas, sixteen-year-old Lucio Bamarus, was counted in the 1850 census.[30] The Dallas Vigilance Committee eventually gave way to a town marshal, and in 1881 town leaders officially founded the Dallas Police Department.[31]

The Mexican-American War of 1846–48 exacerbated many of these policing issues. Much of the initial hostility began once again in Texas, which officially became a state shortly before the war started in 1845. The primary battlefronts of the war, though, occurred in the Mexican states of Nuevo México and Alta California. Many Americans have learned that the U.S. military heroically entered the region and won New Mexico and California for the United States without having to fire a shot. Moreover, popular accounts of the war in New Mexico especially, but California as well, often conveniently leave Mexicans out of the story. They were either invisible historical actors living in an unpopulated region, or they wholeheartedly welcomed the Americans into their lands. Neither was the case. The American military also did not triumph so easily. In fact, this military venture was like many others in the history of the United States: poorly planned and haphazard.[32]

As in Texas, some Mexicans did welcome Americans to New Mexico before the war. Charles Bent had lived in the region for a number of years. He had married into a prominent Mexican family and seemed to conform to Mexican people's expectations of American settlers.³³ But if American immigrants displeased Mexicans, they often had a hard time. For example, in about 1841 a White rancher known only as "old man Lane" lost forty head of cattle and found a note on his door demanding that he vacate his property, possibly for squatting on someone else's land. "Lane suspicioned a Mexican, by the name of Martinez," author Fred Lambert wrote. Lane went to Cimarron and swore out a warrant with the constable against Martinez. But Martinez didn't appreciate Lane's accusation and he went to Tiendetas (a town south of Cimarron that no longer exists) and filed charges against Lane before a Mexican magistrate. The judge authorized a group of men to form a posse and apprehend Lane, which they did. After delivering Lane to the judge, the "Justice acted quickly," Lambert wrote, "declaring Lane guilty and sentenced him to be hung." After handing down this harsh sentence, the judge reconsidered and allowed a group of sympathizers to bail Lane out of jail. He left New Mexico and never returned.³⁴

Old man Lane's experience demonstrates a couple of things. First, clearly Mexico had established institutions of government. Second, Mexican justice was swift, and Lane luckily escaped with his life. Third, Mexicans did not tolerate bad behavior on the part of Americans. When the American military arrived in New Mexico, many soldiers would treat Mexican people poorly. Such behavior did not go over well.

The U.S. government sent General Stephen Watts Kearny to secure Nuevo México for the United States in 1846. He took a force of about 2,500 men, the Army of the West, into New Mexico in August. Contrary to popular belief, Mexicans in New Mexico did oppose American forces. History has remembered New Mexico governor Manuel Armijo as a coward who gave in to the Americans and fled when the U.S. Army arrived. In fact, Armijo organized early on to resist the Americans. He mailed proclamations to various officials in New Mexico as well as to the government in Mexico City warning of coming hostilities with the United States and asking for measures to defend the region.³⁵ Shortly thereafter, Padre Mariano Lucero, a confidant of Governor Armijo, published a circular ordering the inhabitants of northern New Mexico to defend their homes and properties against the Americans.³⁶ Jose Pablo Gallegos, a military leader who later fought in the American Civil War, also strongly demanded that New Mexicans fight the Americans. He published several circulars in an attempt to raise a militia to halt the American military advance in New Mexico.³⁷

As American forces approached northern New Mexico, Governor Armijo again sent several desperate requests to Mexico City in an effort to raise

General Stephens Watts Kearny proclaims New Mexico a part of the United States to residents of Santa Fe, New Mexico, on August 18, 1846. This stylized engraving by an unknown artist from 1882 details how Americans viewed their acquisition of Mexico's territories as peaceful and ignored the military conflicts that occurred after these events. One month later Kearny would announce his Kearny Code of Law. *GRANGER – Historical Picture Archive.*

military forces. On August 8, 1846, and again on August 10, 1846, he wrote two highly patriotic letters calling on loyal Mexicans to defend their country: "I urge you countrymen and compatriots so that united to the military you will re-enforce those sentiments of union and true harmony, with your defenders, and at the void and always companions in arms, because only this sincere union can conduct us to a glorious triumph.... The Mexican Republic will know how to make her enemies respect her."[38] Armijo also commented specifically on the rapacious nature of the American invasion. Mexico, he asserted, "would soon be the prey of the greed and enterprising spirit of our neighbors to the north."[39] While he had hoped to outfit about 12,000 soldiers, Armijo raised a fraction of that number. He prepared for battle in a canyon pass, but ultimately abandoned these defenses when the weakness of his forces became evident. He had no choice but to flee to Mexico, allowing General Kearny to enter Santa Fe.[40]

Many writers have commented on Governor Armijo's escape and how the Americans took Santa Fe without firing a shot. These accounts described Armijo as a coward who shirked his duty.[41] Armijo's various letters reveal him to be a patriot who valued his country and feared what might happen if the Americans took over. His resolve and dedication should not be questioned. His actual ability to defend his territory, however, was in question and the governor seemingly saw the writing on the wall. He did not want to collaborate with the Americans, but he also wanted to avoid a bloodbath, and at the end of the day the only way he could achieve both was to flee.

Other Mexican officials also attempted to defend their country. Politician Antonio Maria Trujillo had instructed leaders throughout New Mexico to prepare to defend the territory, noting, "We have declared war with the Americans and it is now time that we all take our arms in our hands in defense of our abandoned country that we may try if possible to regain the liberty of our unhappy country."[42] General Jesus Tafolla called for a general revolt against the Americans to "shake off the yoke bound on us by a foreign government."[43] While the American military would come to view New Mexico as pacified and secured, Trujillo and Tafolla both understood that hostilities had not ended.

After Kearny captured Santa Fe in August of 1846, he declared himself military governor of the new Territory of New Mexico and issued the Kearny Code of Law. The code, which violated U.S. law because such powers are delegated to Congress, established American civil government in New Mexico and worked as a kind of pseudo constitution. If read carefully, the document becomes something more: a blueprint for American colonialism that made law enforcement the key mechanism for the control of the population.[44]

The Kearny Code had three parts, beginning with a bill of rights and a list of those he had appointed to the various political offices in New Mexico. The third part, "Laws for the Government of the Territory of New Mexico," was the longest and most important. It began with a detailed explanation of property rights, inheritance, and credit, which made this part of the code all about economics. The following sections of the code dealt primarily with criminal justice. They established an office of attorney general and a system of circuit attorneys. They also put forth a method for hiring constables (four for each county), sheriffs (one per county), a court system, a lengthy discussion of crimes and their appropriate punishments, the establishment of jails and the hiring of jailors, and the practice of civil and criminal law. Out of the twenty-five total sections of the third part of the Kearny Code, fifteen (or 60 percent) dealt exclusively with the establishment of the criminal justice system. Kearny devoted over 11,000 words to these parts in the code. The sections that dealt with economics, the collection of debts, tax revenues, and other economic items received about 8,000 words altogether. What emerged, then, was a document concerned with two things: money and criminal justice.[45]

Many people understood the Kearny Code this way. President James K. Polk made this point quite clearly: "The immediate establishment of territorial government and the extension of our laws over these valuable possessions are deemed to be not only important but indispensable to preserve order, and the due administration of justice within their limits, to afford the protection of the inhabitants and to facilitate the development of the vast resources and wealth which their acquisition has added to our country."[46] For Polk, like Kearny, the two important features of the American colonial enterprise in the Southwest, capital and law enforcement, were twins.

Another part of this history purports that the American appropriation of Mexican lands served as a kind of positive good for Mexico. Secretary of State James Buchanan's instructions to the minister to Mexico John Slidell, who attempted to negotiate to buy parts of Mexico's northern territories in 1845, made this argument clearly. "The province of New Mexico should be included within the limits of the United States, this would obviate the danger of future collisions. Mexico would part with a remote and detached province, the possession of which can never be advantageous to her, and she would be relieved from the trouble and expense of defending its inhabitants against the Indians.... It would seem to be equally the interest of both powers that New Mexico should belong to the United States."[47] This paternalistic type of thinking clearly benefited the stronger, more aggressive country—the United

States—while it simultaneously provided the United States with another positive justification for making war on a neighboring nation.

After he promulgated his code, General Kearny departed New Mexico in late September 1846 for California. He left Charles Bent in place as New Mexico's first civilian territorial governor and put General Sterling Price in command of the American military forces that remained in New Mexico. Kearny had no real power to do these things (nor to promulgate his code). The U.S. Congress had the responsibility for making these decisions, but Kearny made them anyway. Charles Bent had lived in the region for nearly two decades and knew New Mexico well. He seemed to apprehend developing tensions between the U.S. Army and Mexican people soon after the Americans arrived, mainly because Kearny and the soldiers acted badly toward Mexicans. For example, Kearny had mocked the New Mexican government and its governor, Manuel Armijo, as cowardly. He gloated about the superiority of the American forces and what he viewed as the timidity of the Mexicans. Bent saw otherwise, noting that the American soldiers had arrived "half-starved and sick, even their commander—Kearny . . . yet they plan[ned] to run ol' Armijo and his soldados all the way to Durango. Ha!"[48] As opposed to the formidable foe that proved so intimidating that the Mexicans simply gave up, the Americans arrived sick, poorly trained, and ill tempered.

Part of the trouble in New Mexico resulted from the individuals Kearny placed in positions of power before he left for California. Only Governor Bent seemed a logical choice, given his long-standing presence in New Mexico. But Kearny also appointed his friends and high ranking military personnel to government offices. For example, he made Donaciano Vigil, a cousin of Governor Bent's wife, territorial secretary. He appointed Charles Beaubien as chief justice of the New Mexico Supreme Court. Many New Mexicans hated Beaubien; he had unscrupulously acquired thousands of acres of land in the region. Kearny named Beaubien's son in law, Stephen L. Lee, sheriff of Taos. Kearny appointed Francis Blair, who had joined the Army of the West as it marched into New Mexico, attorney general. Blair had already aroused the ire of local people for insulting and offensive behavior. To put this another way, almost all the positions Kearny filled with his cronies were offices in the criminal justice system.[49]

The fact that Kearny appointed individuals whom Mexicans already strongly disliked was, of course, problematic. For instance, Francis Blair and George Bent, the brother of Charles Bent, had angered Santa Fe's Mexican population shortly before the arrival of the American military. In May of 1846, about thirty men attacked Blair and George Bent, allegedly because of crooked business deals and the general bigotry of the two men toward Mexican people. They beat the two and did considerable damage to Blair's business office. Charles Bent defended his brother and expressed anger that "justice would take no steps in the affair." "If this mob," he warned, "is not punished I would not answer for the peace of this place."[50] Bent seemed to forget that at that time Mexicans controlled "the peace of this place."[51] He also complained to Manuel Álvarez, the American consul in Santa Fe, and openly questioned whether Governor Armijo actually cared about protecting Americans who resided in New Mexico.[52]

After his appointment as governor, Bent understood the growing tension a little better. General Sterling Price did not. Price's soldiers formed the bulk of the local law enforcement, were a visible sign of American dominance and control in the region, and according to Governor Bent, abused the Mexican population. Bent complained about General Price, noting that there was "a great want of discipline and subordination of the troops here." He argued that Price should impress upon soldiers the need for "rigid care with regard to the treatment of the inhabitants," adding that the Americans "must conciliate, not exasperate."[53] Bent further commented on the conduct of the American soldiers, noting that they "undertook to act like conquerors." He begged military officials to intervene and use their "authority to compel the soldiers to respect the rights of the inhabitants." Bent remarked, "These outrages are becoming so frequent that I apprehend serious consequences must result sooner or later if measures are not taken to prevent them."[54]

Governor Bent's warnings about the behavior of American soldiers went unheeded. An English observer named George Ruxton wrote that the Americans "have not been very anxious to conciliate the people, but by their bullying and overbearing demeanor toward them, have in great measure been the cause of this hatred."[55] General Price and his men treated the New Mexican population with disdain, insulting, beating, and harassing local people. Many Mexicans came to fear that the Americans would dispossess them of their property. Americans later confirmed those fears. Moreover, the American soldiers regarded the Mexicans as enemies, even though the U.S. government considered New Mexico "pacified," and many Americans believed hostilities had ended. Some Mexicans responded viscerally to this treatment.

A group of Mexican leaders began planning to expel the Americans in late 1846. Various members or close associates of the Ortiz family, which had a long history in New Mexico, instigated these plans. Tomas Ortiz, a captain in the Mexican military, and Diego Archuleta, a colonel, led this group. They met in Santa Fe on December 1, 1846, to plan the reconquest of New Mexico.

They had a good plan. On Christmas Eve, Ortiz would gather a contingent of soldiers in Santa Fe Plaza's parish church while Archuleta went to communities surrounding Santa Fe to rally Mexicans to fight against the Americans. When the church bell sounded at midnight, these two groups of soldiers would merge and then attack the Palace of the Governors and the nearby quarters of the American Army, capturing Governor Bent and General Price. They had also planned to seize several cannons and aim them at American strongholds around Santa Fe to halt any American resistance. If successful, Ortiz would become the new governor and Archuleta the commanding general of Mexican forces in New Mexico.[56]

In order to secure as many soldiers as possible, Ortiz and Archuleta sent word of the planned revolt to a number of nearby communities. It seems they publicized the plan a little too much because the Americans discovered this plot. Colonel Price sent troops to arrest Ortiz, Archuleta, and five others. Interestingly, the American authorities generally viewed these insurrectionaries as unintelligent individuals of low status, but most of those captured and later tried as leaders of the planned revolt came from the upper crust of New Mexican society. Tomas Ortiz, for example, was a wealthy, well-educated individual who came from a long line of New Mexicans. He was also a patriot who not only loved his country but also saw through the pretenses of the American invasion. Diego Archuleta was similarly well established.[57] Perhaps because of their standing, Ortiz and Archuleta escaped prosecution. American authorities released two other men, but they tried three others for treason. Their attorney, Captain William Angney, argued that the men were "patriots acting in defense of their country," an argument that defined these individuals as Mexican nationals whom the United States could not prosecute for treason because they were not American citizens. That understanding would be lost in subsequent trials, but in this case it worked. All were acquitted and released.[58]

An actual insurrection followed the December 1846 planned revolt. In January of 1847, Pablo Montoya, a longtime Mexican politician, and a group of New Mexicans began planning to overthrow the Americans in Taos. This Taos "revolt" was really a major battle of the Mexican-American War. The revolt was organized by, among others, Montoya and Tomás Romero, an Indigenous leader of the Taos Pueblo. They gathered a small contingent of soldiers and on January 19 attacked Governor Bent's home. They killed him, Sheriff Stephen Lee, and half a dozen others, many of whom held positions in the criminal justice system. The group also besieged a local distillery and killed several other Americans. They then marched on Santa Fe. The attacks shocked the Americans in New Mexico. As one reported, "We cannot believe that the Mexicans have been able to make [so] much head[way] against our troops in Santa Fe."[59]

Additional insurrectionary battles occurred in Santa Cruz de la Cañada and Embudo. General Price engaged a large group of New Mexicans numbering as many as 1,500 at la Cañada on January 24, 1847. The Americans killed thirty-six of these Mexican soldiers. This contingent of insurrectionary forces regrouped at Embudo. They fought another short battle against the Americans, losing about twenty more men before retreating to Taos. American forces engaged in another battle on January 24 at Mora, a town adjacent to Las Vegas. Here the Americans met a stiffer defense, and the Mexican forces killed the leader of the expedition, Captain Israel Hendley. Another twenty-five Mexicans died, and the Americans captured seventeen prisoners of war who later stood trial for treason. U.S. forces ultimately withdrew from Mora, but they returned on February 1, 1847, and killed an unknown number of Mexicans and burned the town to the ground.[60] In all these battles, the Americans killed at least several hundred Mexicans, destroyed villages, and displaced families. One report noted that the Americans attacked and killed women who had gone to collect water.[61]

Many insurrectionists fled to Taos. General Price besieged Taos beginning on the night of February 3, 1847. Residents of the Taos Pueblo and its surrounding communities had gathered at the San Geronimo de Taos church as the American Army approached. The church bells rang as a warning for Mexicans to flee to the sanctuary for protection. About 550 Mexicans escaped to the church where they mounted a weak defense to 600 American soldiers. The adobe walls of the church offered some protection; cannon balls and bullets simply embedded themselves in the adobe. Eventually the continual shelling opened a large hole in the adobe walls. Some Mexicans attempted to flee; American soldiers shot them down as they ran. On February 4 the Americans set fire to the church. The conflagration consumed the roof of the building and caused the people inside to surrender. Of the 550 who sought shelter there, at least 150 died in the fire and from the battle. The church bells never sounded again.[62]

After Governor Bent's death, Donaciano Vigil became governor. He reported that the U.S. military had suppressed the rebellion.[63] He was wrong. Instead, the Taos Revolt continued. Mexicans killed three American soldiers whose bodies were discovered outside of Los Valles, south of Las Vegas, in July of 1847. Although American officials never determined the circumstances of their deaths, the army dispatched a group of soldiers who killed six Los Valles residents, arrested forty others, and burned the town to the ground. As historian Robert Tórrez has written, the "American troops descended on Los Valles and literally erased the community from the face of the earth."[64] A final battle at Cienega Creek, south of Taos, occurred on July 19, 1847. A group of Mexicans and Indigenous allies attacked a small encampment of Americans. While this group killed five Americans, a larger contingent of U.S. soldiers arrived and decimated the group. Twenty-five Mexicans and Indigenous people died in the fighting.[65] That battle brought the Taos Revolt to an end.

The aftermath of the revolt reveals a great deal about the nature of law and order in the American frontier. For example, U.S. forces captured and imprisoned Tomás Romero, but an angry American soldier murdered Romero in his jail cell, which made his death more like a lynching. A military drumhead court quickly tried and convicted Pablo Montoya of treason. Unlike the trials of the December 1846 planned revolt, this charge, which assumed that the conspirators were citizens of the United States (they were not), stuck. The military hanged Montoya.[66] American forces arrested about forty other individuals for the revolt. Sterling Price conducted another series of drumhead courts-martial and seven men stood trial for murder. They convicted and summarily executed six of these men.[67] Given the charges and that a military tribunal adjudicated nonmilitary cases—which shows how the military was a criminal justice institution—the trials were highly unusual. But the irregularities did not end there. The government conducted some of the trials utilizing relatives of the Americans who had died in the fighting, an obvious conflict of interest. The primary judge was Charles Beaubien, whose son had died during the Taos Revolt. George Bent, the brother of Governor Bent, served as the foreman of the grand jury. Elliot Lee, one of the jurors, was a relative of Sheriff Stephen Lee. Francis Blair, who had treated Mexicans poorly since his arrival, worked as the prosecuting attorney.[68]

Several of these kangaroo courts charged Mexican nationals with treason or "high treason." For instance, the court charged Trinidad Barcelo on March 10 and Pantaleon Archuleta on March 11 with treason.[69] Barcelo and Archuleta both pleaded not guilty.[70] Both cases had juries that deadlocked. The district attorney then made a "nolle prosequi" declaration before the court, which translates to "unwilling to pursue/prosecute" and meant that he would halt the cases.[71] On March 17, 1847, the kangaroo court indicted Pedro Vigil for "high treason." It is unclear why the court changed the language from "treason" to "high treason" considering no such crime existed in U.S. law. Perhaps it felt the more stringent wording of "high treason" might resonate better with jurors. In this case, it did not. Vigil pleaded not guilty on March 22 and on May 3 his case resulted in another hung jury and another nolle prosequi declaration.[72] The kangaroo court also tried Polio Salazar for "high treason," found him guilty, and hanged him. The court convicted and executed five more men for the same crime. A month later the court processed ten more cases of treason. All resulted in convictions and executions.[73] While some questioned the validity of charging Mexican nationals as traitors to the United States, Secretary of War William L. Marcy gave General Price wide latitude to allow the court to make charges as it saw fit.[74] As one individual put it, "It certainly did appear to be a great assumption on the part of the Americans to conquer a country and then arraign the revolting inhabitants for treason."[75]

The treason case against Antonio Maria Trujillo serves as a typical example of the lengths court officers would go to in order to ensure the law worked the way they wanted it to. On March 9, 1847, the kangaroo court charged Trujillo with treason. He pleaded not guilty.[76] The indictment declared that Trujillo was "a citizen of the United States of America" who had "with force and arms" joined "with diverse other false traitors" to "wickedly and traitorously" make "war against the said Government of the United States." The indictment repeated the words "traitorously," "maliciously," and "wickedly" a number of times to hammer home Trujillo's traitorhood. Despite the fact that Trujillo, like the others, was not a citizen of the United States, the jury found him guilty.[77]

The language used in Trujillo's sentencing was equally bombastic: "A jury of twelve citizens [not all of whom were citizens] have found you guilty of the high crime of treason against your government." Again, the United States was not his government, but the court sentenced him to die by hanging. "You have nourished bitterness and hatred in your soul," the sentencing paperwork reads, "you have been found seconding the acts of a band of the most traitorous murderers that ever blackened with the recital of their deeds the annals of history."[78] Trujillo appealed. His attorneys listed seven reasons why the court should overturn the conviction, including the fact that he was not a U.S. citizen and that the court had presented improper and illegal evidence to the jury.[79] It is not altogether clear what happened to Trujillo. According to historian Robert Tórrez, Trujillo asked President Polk for a pardon. Tórrez speculated that General Price may have released him.[80]

For those Mexicans who revolted, whom they attacked mattered. This was not an unplanned or spontaneous revolt. They were not a "roaring mob . . . some of them drunk on whisky," as one contemporary writer put it badly.[81] Instead, they organized the revolt carefully and purposefully killed those individuals in authority, including the governor, a judge, a district attorney, several army officers in Governor Bent's cabinet, and Sheriff Lee. One of the first to die, Sheriff Lee, represented the hollowness of American criminal justice to Mexicans. They also killed Narciso Beaubien, the chief justice's son; J. W. Leal, the district attorney in Taos; and Prefect Cornelio Vigil, the cousin of Donaciano Vigil, who served as the administrative head of Taos as well as the acting justice of the peace.[82] Having felt the sting of racist American justice, the Mexicans who revolted purposefully targeted not just the agents of American authority, but the agents of the justice system. That targeting demonstrates that Mexicans were not simply displeased with the Americans in general but more specifically with the actions of those involved in the nascent criminal justice system.

During this period, more than 300 Mexicans died in battles with American soldiers. This fact alone should discourage our understanding of the bloodless manner by which the United States acquired New Mexico. Additionally, American leaders executed nearly thirty men after kangaroo courts-martial for treason or murder and one for "rebellious conduct" (whatever that means), in what have come to be called the "1847 Treason Trials." In hanging the rebels, one bystander observed that the Americans had acted with "a strange mixture of violence and justice."[83] The motives of those who fought back seem easy to apprehend. For the Americans, as General Price himself noted on the first anniversary of these events, they succeeded in the "complete extinction of the band of murderers who under the pretense of patriotism killed and robbed so many defenseless innocents." The U.S. Army was the law of the land until 1851.[84]

The American takeover of Alta California mirrored what happened in New Mexico. General Kearny had hoped to also get credit for securing California, but he underestimated the length and difficulty of the voyage from Santa Fe to Los Angeles. Instead of Kearny, Commodore Robert F. Stockton gets most of the credit for acquiring California for the United States. The situation in California differed from Nuevo México because of the Bear Flag Revolt, which began in Sonoma in June 1846. The revolt exacerbated tensions between Mexicans and Americans before the American military arrived in California. Captain John C. Frémont took charge of the rebellion, which for many Mexicans signaled that the Bear Flag Revolt was an American military coup.[85]

Like the Mexican authorities in New Mexico, those in California hoped to resist American encroachment. Governor Pío de Jesus Pico had corresponded with California's military officials, particularly General José Antonio Castro, as well as with Mexico City in an attempt to gather forces. Governor Pico's correspondence, like the letters and proclamations written by New Mexican governor Manuel Armijo, proved that both men were highly patriotic and critical of the United States. He called the American invasion "the depraved plans of that piratical Nation."[86] Pío Pico and General Castro made hasty plans to head north to oppose the Americans, explaining to the central government that he and Castro had "both agreed to defend at all costs the integrity of the national territory."[87]

The U.S. Navy soon confirmed Pío Pico's apropos reference to piracy. Commodore John D. Sloat, the commander of the U.S. Pacific Squadron, landed at Monterey in July of 1846, shortly after the Bear Flag Revolt. He issued a rather bombastic proclamation declaring that a state of war existed between the United States and Mexico and that the United States intended to annex California. This "proclamation" lacked the military force of both the Kearny Code of Law and a proclamation issued by Commodore Robert Stockton the following month in August 1846. Sloat's proclamation also made few references to law and order such as those in the Kearny Code. One of the wise things that Sloat did was to "invite the judges, alcaldes, and other civil officers, to retain their offices and to execute their functions as before." That left existing government structures in place, a decision that could have ameliorated tensions between Mexicans and Americans, but instead made Sloat appear cowardly to other American military officers. His unwillingness to leave his ship also contributed to this perception. In fact, Sloat was sick, and the U.S. military soon replaced him with Commodore Stockton.[88]

Stockton arrived in Monterey and began plans to lay siege to Los Angeles in August 1846. Frémont had left Sonoma a few weeks earlier and planned to also attack Los Angeles. General Castro stood ready to oppose Stockton and Frémont. He had written to Governor Pico as well as to Mexico City requesting more soldiers. Pío Pico had, of course, done the same. The Mexican government ultimately rebuffed both men. Like Governors Pico and Armijo, Castro was a patriot who despised what he viewed as the greedy nature of the United States. He called Americans "a horde of bandits" (an interesting choice of words considering that Americans would castigate Mexicans as "bandits" in the decades that followed). Alas Castro had only a small contingent of soldiers, about one hundred men, and little hope of acquiring more. Moreover, the Los Angeles area had a small population of around 1,500 people, and Castro knew he could not gather enough soldiers from this population to effectively oppose the Americans.[89]

Commodore Stockton landed at the Port of San Pedro (present-day Port of Los Angeles) in August of 1846. General Castro did the only thing that seemed acceptable to him: he proposed an informal truce and requested a meeting with Stockton. Stockton agreed to a meeting if California declared independence from Mexico. For Castro, Stockton's request should have come at the end of the negotiations, not at the beginning. Since Stockton had basically asked the general to commit treason, he responded angrily, calling Stockton's demands "degrading propositions." "Never shall I consent to commit the baseness of doing such a thing," he wrote. As for raising the American flag over Los Angeles, which Stockton had also demanded, Castro responded simply by saying, "Never, Never, Never!"[90] Castro had no real ability to oppose Stockton. He called a war council with other Mexican leaders that made this quite clear.[91] He would get little additional support from Mexicans in the area or from Mexico City. Governor Pico had already explained it to the Mexican population: "Your Governor being placed in the hard alternative of ignominy or migration, has chosen the latter and from today he separates himself from you, taking with him the acute sorrow that he leaves you in the power of the unjust conqueror."[92] Castro fired off a final angry letter to Stockton and then, like Governor Pico, withdrew to Sonora, Mexico.[93]

Commodore Stockton, joined by Frémont and his soldiers, entered Los Angeles and quickly declared the town part of the United States on August 13, 1846. Again, the lore surrounding these events suggested that the Mexicans refused to put up a fight and that they welcomed the Americans with open arms. As Otis Singletary, an early chronicler of the war, explained, "The occupation of California was accomplished without firing a gun."[94] Such statements magnified both American courage and Mexican cowardice, while of course wholly downplaying the resistance that Mexicans like Pío Pico and José Castro hoped, but were unable, to mount. This version of the story also neglects the later resistance that surfaced in Los Angeles.

Like Kearny, Stockton issued his own proclamation. The Stockton proclamation, much like the Kearny Code, violated American law. It also focused heavily on criminal justice and law enforcement. For example, Stockton declared, "The Territory of California now belongs to the United States, and will be governed, as soon as circumstances permit, by officers and laws similar to those by which other Territories of the United States are regulated and protected." Because Americans had yet to establish those "officers and laws," the "proclamation" established the military as the law of the land: "Military law will prevail, and the commander-in-chief will be the governor and protector of the Territory." In another section, he noted a second time that the military would serve as law enforcement in the region. Stockton also commented on specific crimes: "All thieves will be put to hard labor on the public works, and there kept until compensation is made for the property stolen." He also established a curfew "from 10 o'clock at night until sunrise in the morning."

Moreover, the American military jailed any Mexican who resisted or who seemed anti-American.[95]

Commodore Stockton, and the Americans in California more broadly, quickly declared California pacified and secured. As in Nuevo México, they were wrong. Shortly after arriving in Los Angeles, Stockton began plans to leave to invade Acapulco, Mexico. Frémont had already departed to attempt to apprehend José Castro. That left Captain Archibald Gillespie in charge of Los Angeles. Gillespie, like Sterling Price in New Mexico, exacerbated tensions and caused an uprising of the Mexican population. Gillespie was a racist who loathed Mexicans. He commanded fifty soldiers who seemed to enjoy Los Angeles about as much as their commanding officer did. Stockton had warned Gillespie to balance the "rigors of indispensable military law with appliances of peace."[96] Gillespie ignored this warning and instead, according to author Neal Harlow, "laid down needlessly oppressive regulations."[97]

The spark that lit a rebellion in Los Angeles came on Mexican Independence Day, September 16, 1846. Many Mexicans in the Los Angeles area of course hoped to celebrate the holiday. Gillespie unwisely and unnecessarily forbid it. At a secret independence celebration, Cérbulo Varela announced that he would expel the Americans. He gathered a force of several dozen men and a week later attacked the American stronghold at the government house, where Gillespie and others had bivouacked. After a brief skirmish, the Americans repulsed the Mexican insurgents. Captain Gillespie then decided to ransack a series of randomly chosen homes, looking for Varela and the other conspirators. One of the individuals tasked with these raids was James Barton, who would become the Los Angeles County sheriff a few years later. The Americans found none of the conspirators and instead only succeeded in angering more Mexicans.[98]

Captain Gillespie had, like Sterling Price in New Mexico, caused a popular uprising against American rule. More than 300 Mexicans joined the Cérbulo Varela insurrection. On September 24, Varela and his compatriots released their own proclamation. They listed a number of grievances against the Americans, many of which focused on the despotic nature of Gillespie's rule and, more importantly, the abusive form of military law enforcement that Mexicans now encountered. "They dictate despotic and arbitrary laws and burden us with onerous levies," the proclamation read. "Shall we wait to see our wives violated, our innocent children beaten by American whips, our property sacked, our temples profaned, to drag out a life full of shame and disgrace?" they asked. The answer: "No, a thousand times no!"[99] To organize their resistance, Varela and others chose Captain José María Flores as commander in chief of the insurrection's armed forces, now called "las fuerzas nacionales" (the national forces). Flores organized the national forces into three squadrons, in total 400 men, and even acquired a cannon.[100]

Captain Gillespie dispatched a rider to contact Commodore Stockton and have him send reinforcements. Captain Flores wrote to Gillespie to say that he would permit American forces to leave Los Angeles. Interestingly, the American who translated Flores's note from Spanish to English added a note of his own begging Gillespie to surrender, which he did. It was the only good decision he made during his ignoble career in California. On September 30, 1846, the Americans marched out of Los Angeles with a great deal less fanfare than when they had marched in.[101]

By the time the retreating American forces reached the port in early October, another ship had docked. That ship carried 350 American soldiers dispatched by Commodore Stockton, who had received word from Gillespie's courier about the situation in Los Angeles. This contingent assumed it could easily defeat las fuerzas nacionales and began marching to retake Los Angeles. The Mexican forces engaged the Americans in a running fight in retreat, slowing the Americans' march, wounding and killing numerous American soldiers, and sustaining few losses themselves. After a day of this kind of fighting, the Americans retreated to their ships.[102] Stockton finally arrived to find his acquisition of Los Angeles totally undone. His plans to retake the town were fairly simple: Frémont would travel from Santa Barbara, Stockton from San Diego, and their forces would simultaneously attack Los Angeles. While Stockton began preparing his forces, Captain Flores began harassing Frémont's soldiers near Santa Barbara. The audacity of this action threw the Americans into a bit of a panic. They expected the Mexicans to simply defend Los Angeles or to surrender, not to engage in offensive strikes against American forces.[103]

Captain Flores soon received word that he would have to deal with another American adversary. In December 1846, General Stephen Watts Kearny finally arrived in California. Since leaving New Mexico, his luck seemed to have dissipated. The grueling trek across the Southwest had exhausted his men. Kearny's first engagement in California ended in defeat when he attacked a group of Mexican soldiers led by Pío Pico's brother, Andrés. The Mexican forces killed seventeen Americans and forced Kearny to order a hasty retreat to Los Angeles. But now las fuerzas nacionales would more than likely have to fight a three-pronged attack against Kearny, Stockton, and Frémont.[104] That attack came on January 8, 1847. The forces of the United States and those of las fuerzas nacionales met in battle at the Río San Gabriel on the outskirts of Los Angeles. The choice was a good one for Mexican forces because of the river's sandy bottom, which would slow the Americans. But American forces outnumbered the Mexicans and drove them back. The battle lasted an hour. The following day the Americans marched into Los Angeles. After another pitched battle, most of Flores's soldiers abandoned the field.[105]

The hostilities officially ended on January 12, 1847, with the signing of the Treaty of Cahuenga, often called the Capitulation of Cahuenga because it was in fact not a treaty but rather a ceasefire or a truce. Unlike the Stockton proclamation and the Kearny Code, the capitulation said little about law and order and instead focused mostly on the rights that Mexicans would have in California, basically granting them equal rights. One of the interesting aspects of the treaty focused on the citizenship status of Mexicans. "No Californian or other Mexican citizen shall be bound to take the oath of allegiance," Article III read. This suggested that the Americans would not assume Mexicans were citizens of the United States and, as such, would not subject them to the same treason trials as they had in New Mexico.[106]

The Mexican-American War officially ended with the signing of the Treaty of Guadalupe Hidalgo in February of 1848. The treaty did a number of important things. For instance, it firmly established the boundary line between Mexico and the United States, something that earlier treaties such as the Treaty of Velasco failed to do. For Mexican-origin people, the treaty had two important components. Article VIII guaranteed Mexican property rights in the new American territory and granted them rights as citizens. Article IX offered further guarantees of citizenship. Most Americans respected neither of these two articles.[107]

After the war had ended, state and territorial governments focused sustained attention on completing their criminal justice system, especially police forces and jails. As noted, Texas had formulated much of the state's justice system during the period of the Texas Republic. Numerous towns such as Houston and San Antonio also founded police departments. Even though most counties and towns established some form of police agency in the 1830s, 1840s, and 1850s, White Americans also formed vigilante groups in the 1850s. Along with the continuing violence that occurred after the conclusion of the Mexican-American War, Mexican-origin people also experienced violence and social marginalization for their perceived opposition to slavery in Texas.[108] Texans became obsessed with the presence of so-called Mexican "peons," whom they believed enticed enslaved Black people to run away to Mexico. They responded to this obsession by forming lynch mobs and challenging law enforcement to arrest, remove, and eradicate Mexicans who seemed threatening or subversive.

Texan anger over the supposed threat Mexicans represented to the slave system reached a critical mass in the mid-1850s.[109] After ongoing economic crises in the late 1840s and early 1850s, and after continuing border disputes with Mexico, many White people believed Mexicans —many of whom were now Mexican Americans—threatened Texas from within and without. In many western and southwestern counties, Mexican-origin folks predominated. As a result, a number of counties and cities banned the in-migration and settlement of Mexicans. For instance, in 1854 citizens in Seguin, a small town east of San Antonio, organized an anti-Mexican convention and succeeded in passing a resolution banning Mexican people from entering and living in Guadalupe County. The members of the Seguin convention referred to Mexicans as a group as "a vagrant class," "robbers," "thieves," and "idle vagabonds." The tone of this convention, like others that came after it, had a law and order quality even though a legitimate criminal justice system existed in Seguin.[110] Colorado and Matagorda Counties, among others, also drove out their Mexican and Mexican American populations in the 1850s.[111]

These anti-Mexican efforts flourished in south Central Texas. In Gonzales, White leaders called a "convention" on October 21, 1854. At least twenty "delegates from the different western counties of the State will be holden [holding] in Gonzales [a convention] for the purpose of devising means to remedy the evil resulting from the transient Mexican peon population in our midst." "By placing themselves on an equality with the slave, they stir up among [White people's] servants a spirit of insubordination . . . and are always ready to assist the runaway slave in effecting his escape to the Mexican frontier," wrote the *Texas State Gazette*. In flowery language, these delegates blamed the state government for neglecting to provide law enforcement to address this "evil." This was a lie. Gonzales County had established a sheriff's office in 1836 and the town of Gonzales had founded a police department in the late 1840s. But the convention delegates needed the lie to justify their desire to implement an extralegal form of law enforcement.[112] They ultimately adopted a list of resolutions, titled "Peons," that resolved that citizens would form a "Vigilance Committee."[113] A follow-up list of resolutions went further and declared, "All transient Mexicans . . . be warned to leave within ten days from the passage of this resolution . . . all remaining after that time [will] be forcefully expelled." It also clarified that "ten energetic gentlemen" would constitute the vigilance committee.[114] The committee would "expel those Mexicans whose guilt is apparent, 'peaceably if they can, forcibly if they must.'"[115]

The Gonzales convention reveals a great deal about the nature of extralegal justice, legitimate law enforcement, and their treatment of Mexican-origin people in the early to mid-nineteenth-century borderlands. For the convention delegates, the fact that Gonzales County had existing law enforcement agencies meant very little. The delegates disliked the fact that Mexican people had allegedly allied themselves with enslaved Black people. So the delegates decided to take the law into their own hands and form a vigilance committee to monitor them, intimidate them, and ultimately drive them from the county. At least five of the twenty convention delegates identified themselves as major or captain and one as a judge, which demonstrates how military service could transform into mob justice.[116]

Travis County quickly followed the example of Gonzales County, although it one-upped its neighboring county by forming a vigilance committee composed of twenty men. The leaders also listed those individuals appointed to the committee. They included two U.S. Army majors, one army captain, and one judge, which again shows how the military morphed into vigilante justice.[117] Newspaper editorials of the time described the vigilance committee in patriotic terms and Mexicans as a "serious evil," "pernicious," and "peons."[118] "Peon" was a dehumanizing and emasculating term at the time. The *Texas State News* reported on October 28, 1854, two weeks after the vigilance committee had formed, that through warnings and violence, "the vigilance committee have discharged their duties."[119] The *Annals of Travis County* also reported that "no further trouble was apprehended."[120]

Gonzales County revised its vigilance committee the following month. Another "convention" called specifically for "an efficient police organization" to control "the interference of evil disposed persons and Mexicans." The reference to "an efficient police organization" denigrated the work of the Gonzales County Sheriff's Office and the Gonzales Police Department. This convention included two generals, a colonel, and at least two judges.[121] The delegates again founded a vigilance committee and encouraged "each county" in the state to form its own "committee of vigilance."[122] A writer in San Antonio went further, calling Mexicans a "troublesome class" and "a bad element" and suggested "that every strange Peon Mexican coming to San Antonio be compelled to register his name at the Mayor's office" and, if unable to explain the reason for visiting, "be required under a penalty to leave the city forthwith."[123]

Scholars have examined the antislavery views of Mexican-origin people and why they would assist runaway enslaved Black people. Mexico had outlawed slavery decades before the United States did.[124] Beyond their fear that Mexicans assisted runaway slaves, these vigilance committees acted as law enforcement. White people closely monitored Mexican people's lives because they saw them as a threat not only to slave owners but also to law and order. In addition to demeaning these individuals by calling them "robbers," "peons," or "a troublesome class," Texans violently drove them from their communities. And they proposed a law and order solution, the founding of multiple vigilance committees, to eradicate what they saw as a problem. This type of reaction did not end in the mid-1800s. In Austin in 1918 the press reported, "Sheriff Matthews is doing some 'still hunting' . . . running down those who will neither work nor fight [in the Great War]." The sheriff had come across "three idle Mexicans" and taken "them to jail to await the coming of some farmer in need of help." The example shows how ridding areas of Mexican-origin people, as well as peonage (discussed further in chapter 6), became legitimate parts of law enforcement.[125]

The New Mexico Territory organized its criminal justice system initially via the Kearny Code of Law, but after 1851 the territory revised almost all institutions of government. Territorial leaders focused heavily on the justice system. Many of those in power were veterans of the Mexican-American War who had become important government officials. They had a distinct sense of law and order, especially after the treason trials. For example, in 1852 then acting governor Edwin V. Sumner, a career U.S. Army officer, Mexican-American War veteran, and a colonel at the time, issued a proclamation in English and Spanish that noted that there was "no probate judge, no sheriff, and no justice of the peace, (Alcalde), in the county of Doña Ana." Because of the growing importance of Las Cruces, Doña Ana's county seat, Sumner authorized the immediate election of these officers. This occurred before authorities organized other aspects of the county, making the establishment of the justice system the first step in bringing government to Doña Ana County.[126]

In late 1852, Governor William Carr Lane had also hoped to modify the criminal justice system. He described the territory as "over-run with Red and White thieves and robbers." He added, "Your prisons are insecure, and no appropriation has yet been made by Congress, for a Territorial Penitentiary." He elaborated further, "A well-organized Volunteer Militia force will protect your stock from *Red* thieves; and a penitentiary will rid you of *White* thieves." Governor Lane also suggested revising the territory's laws, especially criminal law. He further planned to ask the United States for, among other things, arms and ammunition for the defense of the territory and the enforcement of law and order and for funds that would establish a territorial prison at Yuma. By the time construction began on the Yuma Territorial Prison, Yuma was in the Arizona Territory, which had formed in 1863.[127] Congress did eventually set aside funds for a penitentiary in New Mexico, which would become the

Penitentiary of New Mexico in Santa Fe. Since that complex did not open until 1885 (it is still in operation today), in 1866 acting governor William Arny in his message to the territorial legislature recommended "the passage of a law requiring each county in the Territory to build and keep in repair a county jail for the safe detention of persons charged with a crime."[128]

The New Mexico government also focused on establishing police forces throughout the territory. Although the New Mexico Territorial Mounted Police did not begin operation until the early twentieth century, a discussion about creating such a group of rangers began in the 1850s. One of the first ideas came in 1856 and proposed the formation of a one-hundred-man body of rangers who would protect citizens and defend against Indigenous attacks. This measure failed.[129] The territorial legislature did pass a "police law" authorizing the development of police forces in 1856, especially in towns located far from a justice of the peace. The law also required townspeople to aid the police in the execution of their duties. This, in essence, allowed police officers to easily gather a posse to assist them, a measure akin to the legalization of a lynch mob.[130]

Various cities and towns acted on these messages to found police agencies. Like Houston or Los Angeles, the Santa Fe Police Department began as a lynch mob, or, as writer Benjamin Read called it, "a vigilante organization," in 1866. After the Civil War, a large number of soldiers mustered out of both the Union and Confederate militaries had found their way to New Mexico. After someone murdered a Californian named Foster (first name unknown), city leaders called for a general meeting and issued a resolution that authorized a group of ten men to organize police rules. No one had appointed or elected these individuals. They drafted a report that called on residents to "aid and assist each other and all good citizens in all lawful ways to end the reign of crime," which sounds a lot like a vigilance committee. They also formed an executive committee that would officially form a police department and hire officers.[131] In 1868 Santa Fe leaders submitted to acting governor Herman H. Heath a draft of police regulations for the city. This draft would become the blueprint for the Santa Fe Police Department. The individuals who drafted these regulations did so "for the better government of [their] city," showing how founding government institutions meant police.[132] Moreover, the proposed police regulations also dealt with crimes, meaning they laid the groundwork for local criminal ordinances in Santa Fe.[133]

The legislative initiatives in New Mexico continued into the 1870s. The Twenty-First Session (1873–74) of the New Mexico Territorial Legislature was particularly concerned with the justice system. A new act authorized counties to erect jailhouses and to issue warrants for bonds to raise the necessary capital to build jails.[134] The legislature also modified the existing 1856 "police law," which it revised in 1871–72 and again in 1873–74. During the Twenty-First Session, the legislature modified it further by extending it to San Miguel and Mora Counties. Those counties had been too sparsely populated to warrant inclusion in the original legislation, but by the 1870s the legislature decided they should form police forces.[135]

Other acts of the Twenty-First Session also modified existing laws or established new ones. The legislature approved a law authorizing the governor to issue rewards for the apprehension of individuals accused of a crime. The law specifically mentioned "murder or other felony" as necessitating rewards.[136] Another act granted additional powers to justices of the peace. It specifically gave them the power to imprison individuals for crimes against property if the value of the property was less than fifty dollars, the sentence was not to exceed thirty days.[137]

New Mexico continued to modify its laws and expand police forces into the 1880s. In 1881, Governor Lionel Sheldon proposed beefing up law enforcement in certain counties to mollify the generalized perception of lawlessness in the territory and to try to dissuade local people from founding vigilante groups. He settled on San Juan County and authorized the formation of the San Juan Guards. They operated as a police force in San Juan County, but in the end, Sheldon could not escape the collision of legal and extralegal justice: the San Juan Guards were really just a lynch mob that acted like a police force.[138]

Like New Mexico, California developed its criminal justice system shortly after the conclusion of the Mexican-American War. Many of the initial officeholders in Southern California had served in the U.S. Army. Los Angeles's first American mayor, Stephen C. Foster, had worked as an interpreter for the army. Foster had some serious problems, though. He resigned as mayor to preside over the lynching of a man and then promptly won reelection. He also aroused the ire of the Mexican community when the public execution of a Mexican man went badly.[139] James Barton, who had served with Stockton and Gillespie, went into law enforcement after the war. He was elected as sheriff in 1851 and killed in a shoot-out with members of Flores Daniel Gang in 1856.[140]

The Los Angeles Police Department, like police in Houston or Santa Fe, began as a lynch mob. Local people formed a vigilance committee, variously called the Committee of Safety or the City Guard, to police Los Angeles. According to historian Richard Griswold del Castillo, the City Guard was Los Angeles's first police force.[141] Writer Horace Bell put it succinctly: "Los Angeles was ruled by a lawless mob. The law, as administered by the Courts, was not much better than that administered by lynch law, for the reason that the mob elected the judges, and the sheriffs, and the other officers of the county. . . . And hence it was that the mob ruled as it chose to rule."[142] Bell's observations reveal how legal and extralegal justice barely differed. This led to violence, not justice. William Wallace turned the American civilizing mission on its head when he described it as "the dangers, the vices, the self-sacrifices, the cold-blooded crimes through which the pioneers have guided this unformed and malformed community."[143] Violence pushed leaders to lynch law, actual law enforcement, and incarceration. As historian Kelly Lytle Hernández has noted, "imprisonment was the first act of governance in Anglo-American Los Angeles."[144]

The California Legislature also began forming the state's criminal justice system shortly after the war had ended. Beginning in December of 1849 and ending in April of 1850, the First Session of the legislature produced a massive amount of law. At nearly 500 pages in length, the statutes the legislature authorized ranged from the adoption of United States laws, which anticipated California's admission to the United States in September of 1850, to the creation of important state agencies like the offices of the treasury and the secretary of state. The legislature also paid close attention to the creation of the justice system.[145]

The first aspect of the developing system of criminal justice related to the organization of counties in California. County development meant establishing the "seats of justice," the first step in designating the location of courts in the counties. Chapter 24, one of the many statutes creating the justice system at the First Session, detailed the manner by which the people of each county would elect almost all county positions, including district attorney, county judge, county clerk, coroner, and sheriff.[146] Chapter 39 established the office of county attorney and specifically spelled out its duties, while Chapter 40 did the same for the office of district attorney.[147] The legislators also passed Chapter 44, "An Act Concerning Jails and Jailors." It made the county courts responsible for erecting a jail or "some suitable place for the safe keeping of prisoners." The sheriff had charge of the jail and appointed a jailer who would oversee the day-to-day operation of the jail.[148]

The various legislation passed during the First Session periodically mentioned the office of sheriff and constable, but legislators did not specify the duties of those offices until chapters 106 and 112. For Chapter 106, "An Act to Prescribe the Duties of Sheriff's," the legislature gave sheriffs broad latitude in the execution of their duties; they could appoint as many deputies as they saw fit, hire a jailer, and play a role in all court facilities a county might create. As in most states, the legislators made the sheriff's office the first law enforcement body formed in each county, stating specifically that "Sheriffs shall be Conservators of the Peace in their respective Counties."[149] Chapter 112 detailed the formation of constabularies. In California most towns and cities established police departments, not constabularies, and the legislature left it to the cities to write the ordinances that would govern their police forces.[150]

California differed from other states in that legislators at the First Session passed Chapter 119, entitled "An Act to regulate proceedings in Criminal Cases." This chapter, the longest of any at fifty-seven pages, worked as a penal code that dealt with a host of crimes, their investigation, prosecution, and punishment. Other states and territories had piecemeal and haphazard criminal laws, or they established a collated penal code like Texas. California basically followed both paths by creating a patchwork of criminal laws and within those criminal laws was Chapter 119, which acted like a penal code. The California Legislature did write a penal code in 1872, one that cut and pasted from Chapter 119 significantly.[151]

In many ways the writing of penal codes in Texas and California represented the final step in the establishment of their criminal justice systems. The other parts of the Southwest, especially the territories of New Mexico and Arizona, continued to revise their criminal codes throughout the nineteenth century, although they did not condense those statutes into a penal code at that time. Arizona differed from the other parts of the border region in that it did not become an independent territory until 1863. The New Mexico Territory had already established much of the framework for local criminal justice institutions in what became the Arizona Territory before 1863, but the First Session of the Arizona Territorial Legislative Assembly in 1864 demonstrated that Arizona would develop its own justice institutions.

The First Session of the legislature in Arizona revealed the fluid nature of the borderlands and the development of its criminal justice institutions. The writing of a new code of laws fell to Judge William T. Howell, who authored *The Howell Code*, a 400-page tome that left no aspect of the criminal justice system untouched. The second chapter, for example, dealt with the formation of counties and their courthouses, jails, and other facilities for Arizona's four original counties of Yuma, Yavapai, Pima, and Mohave. Section 4, the first section to discuss criminal justice, mandated that each county build "a suitable and sufficient jail." Chapter III focused on the establishment of sheriff's offices. The next chapter dealt with coroner's offices, another important part of the system. Chapter VII dealt with justices of the peace, while Chapter VIII discussed the development of constabularies that would perform local law enforcement and operate as an arm of the justices of the peace. These chapters firmly established law enforcement bodies in Arizona.[152]

The next three chapters, nearly one hundred pages of text, dealt with criminal law in the territory. Much of this part of the code unsurprisingly concentrated on violent and property crimes. These pages borrowed heavily from *The Statutes of California*. As in California, *The Howell Code* operated as a general code for the development of the criminal justice system in Arizona, but the chapters focusing on criminal law in essence worked as a kind of penal code within the broader code.[153] *The Howell Code* also devoted a good deal of attention to the development of the court system, the appointment of judges, and their jurisdictions.[154]

The Howell Code had little to say about police officers or the formation of police departments. In fact, the only mention of police came in one of the sections on criminal law and stated that "the organization and regulation of the police in cities and villages in this Territory, are governed by special laws." The following section declared that the mayor had authority over police.[155] That language, while vague, left it to city officials to develop their own police forces via city ordinances. The legislature revised these brief statutes in 1889, detailing further the role of police chiefs and police judges.[156] They revised those statutes again in 1901, but the new statute entitled "Police in Cities and Towns" barely clarified the role of police, leaving the specifics to city governments.[157]

The development of the Arizona Territory's criminal justice institutions demonstrates how the border region remained in a state of flux. With the refinement of existing criminal justice statutes, as well as the addition of new territories and states, the administration of justice seemed stuck in a state of perpetual modification. And the same thing occurred in still other parts of the Southwest, especially as Nevada, Utah, and Colorado became new territories. What that process showed, again and again, was just how preoccupied Americans were with the establishment of these bodies of laws. Once the U.S. Army, the first type of law enforcement in the region, ceded its authority to the Southwest's states and territories, it fell to them to create institutions for the administration of justice. And these institutions were often the first forms of government developed in the Southwest. While the states and territories had many things to worry about—infrastructure such as good roads and bridges; monitoring trade; decent mail service; attracting new residents; establishing facilities like libraries, hospitals, and parks—the thing they concentrated on, the thing that they built, was the criminal justice system. That system, like the military, became the mechanism by which the United States colonized the border region.

State and territorial legislatures decreed what local communities were required to do. Those local governments quickly complied. If, as in Houston, Santa Fe, or Los Angeles, the police force began as an informal body, that group gave way to official police departments or constabularies. In other communities the county jail, sheriff's office, or police force originally developed as a codified legal body. Many White people also called for the establishment of lynch mobs or vigilance committees because they argued that no official law enforcement existed. This lie justified mob law. Legal justice and extralegal justice existed simultaneously, and quite often the two worked together. These institutions acted as the army had before them, as a military power to control the people in the region, and of course to exercise that control over people deemed a threat by White society: Mexican-origin people, African Americans, Indigenous people, and White people who did not conform to the dictates of White society.

Keep in mind that the U.S. military augmented state and territorial criminal justice offices as well as conducted border security for decades following the Mexican-American War. For example, in 1879 an American soldier on the U.S. side shot and killed José Maria del Valle. The fourteen-year-old del Valle had gone with some friends to let their horses drink from the Río Bravo River on the Mexican side. An unnamed American soldier saw these children and for unknown reasons opened fire. One shot hit del Valle in the chest. He died next to the river. The Mexican government pleaded with the U.S. government to investigate the case. It is unclear, and unlikely, that any investigation took place. The soldier guarded the U.S.-Mexico border as an agent of national law enforcement akin to the U.S. Border Patrol. Why he chose to murder a fourteen-year-old child remains a mystery.[158]

Mexican-origin people did not simply accept the American immigrants. Contrary to popular belief, Mexico's northern territories were not an empty space, and the U.S. government did not acquire them without having to fire a shot. While some Mexicans sided with the Americans, many more resisted. In New Mexico and California especially, that resistance, begun by leaders like Manuel Armijo and Pío Pico, among others, became full-scale resistance movements once local people felt the sting of American racism. The popular revolts in Taos and Los Angeles were major battles in the Mexican-American War. The way Americans policed Mexicans spurred these revolts and the people Mexicans targeted, especially in New Mexico, were members of the criminal justice system.

Mexican American resistance did not end as the nineteenth century progressed. There were of course examples of outright confrontational violence.

Mexican Americans also attempted to resist White racism from within the criminal justice system by becoming law officers, attorneys, or jailers. Americans have almost entirely forgotten this legacy. Despite the formation of the criminal justice system, White people still formed lynch mobs and murdered Mexican-origin people. Those of Mexican ancestry resisted this abusive extralegal justice and even, on occasion, resorted to lynching themselves. Lynchings, other types of violence, and the massacres of Mexicans and Mexican Americans that occurred in the late nineteenth and early twentieth centuries were all a part of the American takeover of the Southwest, a reign of blood instigated by the military and one continued by legal and extralegal law enforcement.

2

MOB LAW

Vigilantism as Law Enforcement in the Nineteenth Century

Santa Fe, New Mexico, had a long history of law enforcement and extralegal justice that seemed to blend seamlessly. The city's unofficial police force, established in 1866, began as what writer Benjamin Read called "a vigilante organization."[1] That informal group transformed into the official police force in 1868.[2] Yet in 1876 lynch justice could still rear its ugly head. That year a group of men had robbed and murdered Dr. John P. Courtier, a well-known elderly White physician.[3] In the days following, Santa Fe police arrested six individuals for the crime, a Black man named Ramon Winters and five Mexican men, Juan Benavides, Crespin Gallegos, Gavino Gallegos, Jose Pais, and Eugenio Gabaldan.[4] Authorities later released Gavino Gallegos for lack of evidence, but indicted the other five on charges of first-degree murder.[5] Then in early 1877 authorities released Pais and Gabaldan also due to lack of evidence. That left Winters, who decided to testify against his accomplices, which meant Juan Benavides and Crespin Gallegos would stand trial for the murder of Courtier.[6] The jury convicted both men and sentenced them to one year in prison.[7]

Juan Benavides and Crespin Gallegos never served their time. Anger in Santa Fe over the length of the sentences turned to talk of lynching. One writer castigated the justice system, calling it an "utter failure or rather farce trial by jury."[8] It seems part of the frustration White people experienced had to do with the jury itself, which was mainly composed of Mexican Americans. A group of White men soon formed a ten-person vigilance committee. They asserted that such a light sentence "may prove a very bad example for other young bandits." "To protect ourselves," the vigilance committee explained, "we have decided to surprise the jailor, take these murderers outside the city and hang them to a tree." And "the two murderers were hung." As such, mob law superseded the actual justice system.[9] According to writer Flora Spiegelberg, who recounted this incident, "It was the first lynishing [sic] party in old Santa Fe."[10]

The lynching of Benavides and Gallegos underscores how White people conceived of extralegal justice as a legitimate form of justice in the borderlands.[11] They argued that mob law was necessary because law enforcement across the region remained weak or even nonexistent in the nineteenth century. Since all southwestern state and territorial governments had made founding criminal justice institutions one of their first orders of business, these viewpoints were falsehoods that served as effective justifications for vigilantism. The criminal justice system had, after all, acted effectively: authorities made arrests, weeded out the individuals not involved in the crime, and tried, convicted, and sentenced Benavides and Gallegos. But that outcome did not satisfy the mob, which decided to substitute itself for the legitimate justice system. Although mobs asserted that extralegal justice was justice, their real goal was to exert vengeance or to punish. Mobs killed hundreds of innocent Mexican-origin people who had committed no crime, they simply fit a description or satisfied the mobs' bloodlust. Vigilantes murdered hundreds of others who had allegedly committed crimes. Of course, even people who had broken the law deserved their day in court—extralegal justice usurped the criminal justice system in ways that violated the law as well as the rights of the accused. And mobs also murdered those, like Juan Benavides and Crespin Gallegos, who had actually experienced the legal administration of justice.

Mob violence was so multifaceted in the Southwest that it is difficult to accurately categorize.[12] Lynching, the extralegal execution of an individual or individuals accused of a criminal offense or of a violation of social norms, itself took many forms. Lynching could include hanging, shooting, stabbing, burning, and torture, among other types of violence, or some combination of all those things. Mobs often, although not always, carried out these executions. One type of mob, vigilance committees or citizens patrols, were often well organized. They engaged in policing, trials, and killings, usually executions by shooting or hanging. In other cases, mobs formed spontaneously to murder people. In some instances, these spontaneous mobs did not simply kill individuals, they massacred large numbers of Mexican-origin people. In other examples, a group of two or three men would join to execute an individual. Extralegal violence also took the form of individual action: a person felt wronged, sought out the person that was supposedly guilty, and in vengeance killed that person. In some cases, individual vigilantes murdered several people, or killed them to cover up a crime, or for a host of different reasons. While they acted like a mob, individual action is of course not mob action. Because of this variety, I mainly explore extralegal violence that acted as law enforcement in the pages that follow. So many instances of lynching occurred in the borderlands from the 1850s to the 1920s that one chapter cannot capture them all—readers will find multiple examples in the other chapters in this book.[13]

Extralegal justice in the Southwest grew out of several similar circumstances. Unlike the lynchings of African Americans in the South—whom White people executed to enforce White supremacy when Black people exercised their rights, for fictitious violations of sexual taboos, or because White people believed they could function as the law better than the law could—the lynchings in the Southwest were practiced almost exclusively because White folks erroneously believed that the law didn't work. Many White people held the idea that lawlessness and major crimes like murder ran rampant. Petty thieves or horse rustlers committed crimes because law enforcement could not stop them; murderers got away with killing people because police did not arrest them or because a judge let them off. And many White people wrongly believed that Mexican-origin people were prone to such criminality. Therefore, it fell to individuals or groups of people to exercise justice. Crime and violence did of course happen, but White people often committed this violence and then used it as a justification for more lynch mobs and increased law enforcement to control and kill Mexicans and Mexican Americans.

White people also used vigilantism when a trial did not result in the conviction or punishment they sought, as the example from Santa Fe makes clear. These individuals too argued that the law was lax, but they probably did not realistically believe their own rhetoric and instead simply used it to engage in extralegal justice. Thus, they lied about the need for vigilante justice to be able to successfully carry out a lynching. It is also the case that Mexican Americans used extralegal justice and for similar reasons, usually in show trials and lynchings of other Mexican-origin people. They also occasionally joined with White people to perform lynchings. Communities of color utilizing extralegal justice is not widely known or understood.[14]

The variety of extralegal violence and the various methods of killing have caused a great deal of misunderstanding about what was justice and what was injustice. White folks created a number of legal sounding names for their mobs—posse, vigilance committee, vigilante society, committee of public safety, citizens patrol—all in an effort to make an illegal act appear legitimate. This terminology demonstrates how White people either saw or argued that their actions served as a stand-in for legitimate law enforcement. The terminology gets more confusing considering that on occasion writers misuse the term "lynching." For example, some have labelled the 1836 execution of Josefa "Chipita" Rodriguez in Texas a lynching, but the San Patricio County sheriff arrested her for allegedly robbing and killing a man and properly jailed her, and the district court tried, found her guilty, and legally executed Rodriguez. Her trial had some abnormalities (the sheriff had served on the grand jury, for instance), but that means that she had an unfair or irregular trial. In fact, law enforcement prevented a lynch mob from killing her twice, so to call her execution a "lynching" is wrong and contributes to the misunderstandings that exist about extralegal violence.[15]

Other writers applied a host of different labels to lynchings, which adds to the confusion about this terminology. Take, for instance, the 1855 Rancheria Massacre, so named because five White people and one Indigenous person died in an attack allegedly committed by Mexicans. But the vigilante violence that followed resulted in the deaths of, at a minimum, twelve Mexicans whom a vengeful mob murdered. Why are their deaths called lynchings and not the Rancheria Massacre? Author Peter Hertzog tabulated a list—literally a directory of New Mexico desperados, to borrow the title of his book—that detailed the exploits of 568 outlaws in the territory. He commented on a number of mob killings but used similarly imprecise language. For instance, he noted the lynchings of some desperados, such as Narciso Montoya, whom a mob "lynched at Taos, June 10, 1881, for the murder of Luis Gallegos," by using the term "lynched" appropriately. But in other cases he used different language. Hertzog described Juan Alvarid's murder in the following manner: he was "mob-hung for raping an eight year old girl" (law enforcement determined

Alvarid's innocence the following day, a fact that Hertzog chose not to report).[16] Or, in the case of Manuel Cardenas, Hertzog wrote he was "shot by a mob as a murder suspect in the death of Reveren [sic] F. J. Tolby." Cardenas's murder was a clear-cut case of lynching. Marino Leyba's listing is also worth mentioning. He led "a gang of horse thieves and robbers who killed Colonel Charles Potter. Murdered by [a] deputy sheriff at Golden." Given that a law officer killed him, it is hard to discern from Hertzog's account whether the deputy "murdered" Leyba or killed him in the discharge of his duties. But we know that two deputy sheriffs, Joaquin Montoya and Carlos Jacomo, tracked Leyba and killed him in a shoot-out, which is not murder. Such inconsistent use of terminology has led to a great deal of confusion as to what a lynching actually entailed.[17]

Mexican-origin people resisted mob violence. They were not helpless victims and fought back in any number of ways. Like other people in the region, they carried guns and they engaged in self-defense. They also looked to legitimate law enforcement to protect them. While law officers did occasionally join with lynch mobs, they also did their duty and protected Mexican-origin people from mobs. Mexican Americans also pushed criminal justice authorities to punish vigilantes. Additionally, they elected officials, including sheriffs and others in law enforcement, who assisted those targeted by vigilantism. They also fled mobs, a type of resistance that suggests that they understood the slim odds they had of living through such an ordeal. Mexicans and Mexican Americans could also call upon Mexican consular officials for aid. That tactic gave them a strategy of resistance that other communities of color did not have.

As noted in the previous chapter, White leaders founded government institutions such as the criminal justice system to bring government to a place they believed had none. Mob law contradicted White people's assertions about civilization and government. Some sympathetic White folks saw through the pretense and noted that Americans in fact brought violence and barbarity, which they somehow viewed as civilization, to the region. "Blood flows in the streets, justice weeps. All is anarchy," William Wallace noted about this violence.[18] In the post–Mexican-American War period, such violence continued. In this period, newly formed agencies of law enforcement and, simultaneously, lynch mobs replaced the military. Thus, legal and extralegal justice, law and mob law, became rather indistinguishable.

California was exceedingly violent in the nineteenth century. Writer Horace Bell commented on the period of early American involvement in Southern California with clarity and honesty. Bell wrote about the United States' acquisition of California. He explained,

Had our Government, at one fell swoop, confiscated every league of land owned by the transferred inhabitants and all the cattle and horses, constituting the wealth of the Country, it would have been an act of mercy as compared with that that followed, to-wit: Turning loose upon the hapless inhabitants, a hungry horde of licensed sharpers [swindlers] and Shylocks that came from all lands under the dome of heaven, to prey upon an unsuspecting and confiding people [Mexicans].... Our Government ought to have protected them.... Our Government did not protect them, but it did protect the Shylocks and sharpers, and thus wrought ruin and desolation to a theretofore happy and prosperous people.[19]

Bell's words could be applied to other parts of the Southwest.

One of the first and most well-known lynchings to take place in California was that of Josefa Segovia, also often referred to as Josefa or Juana Loaiza, which occurred on July 5, 1851. Segovia's case merits attention because she was a woman, allegedly the only woman lynched in California, and because her murder followed the pattern of mob violence acting as criminal justice.[20] She lived in Downieville, a normally sleepy small town in the gold region of northeast California, but then overflowing with people because of a July 4 visit from a popular state senator. That night as the town celebrated, miner Frederick Cannon decided to extend his revelry to Segovia. He and a group of men went to her home and kicked in the door. When Cannon attempted to rape Segovia, she fought back and drove him and the others from her home. Cannon left but returned early the next morning. Another confrontation ensued, possibly a second attempted sexual assault, and Segovia plunged a knife into his chest. Cannon died quickly.[21]

The Downieville area had an extralegal vigilance committee, which tried and quickly convicted Segovia for killing Cannon. Had her case reached a legitimate court, a jury may well have exculpated her of her crime because she had acted in self-defense. That did not happen. So, on July 5, 1851, she ascended the gallows, allegedly placed the noose around her own neck, and was hanged. According to most sources, a crowd of some 2,000 people had gathered to watch Josefa Segovia die.[22] Her case serves as a typical example of how an illegally organized vigilance committee could act much like the criminal justice system, with an arrest, a trial, a conviction, and an execution.

The violence in Northern California did not end with Josefa Segovia. One of the worst mass lynchings took place in 1855 near the town of Rancheria, which no longer exists. While many papers reported on Mexican outlaws as the cause of the violence, the policing of those people may have actually spawned the incident. In early August 1855, a group of "outlaws" had appeared in nearby Drytown. These "Spaniards... looked rather suspicious," and some townspeople decided "to watch them for a short time and see that they committed no crime in town." This group of people then violently drove the "Spaniards" out of Drytown. These "outlaws" allegedly proceeded to Rancheria and robbed a store and in the process killed five White Americans and one Indigenous person.[23]

A massive mob of over 1,000 men gathered to track down the killers. White townspeople who assisted local law enforcement as "special police" rounded up just about every Mexican person in the area, thirty-six in total, and placed them in a makeshift prison.[24] The mob tried all of them and found three Mexican-origin people guilty of the attack on Rancheria. They hanged all three. They ordered the remaining Mexicans to leave town and then burned their homes to the ground. The mob lynched several others as they fled. One writer commented, "How many Mexicans have been caught and hung it is hard to say." This writer estimated that the mob had hanged seven Mexicans and shot several others in the first few days after the incident at Rancheria.[25]

The following evening, "one of the supposed robbers was taken from the jail, where he had been placed by the citizens until they could collect evidence sufficient to hang him." As a point of clarity, law enforcement does not search for evidence in order to justify a sentence. Evidently they tired of waiting and took him from the jail. They "run him up on the famous old tree; he was then let down for five minutes to confess, but he would not. He was run up again, and now (10½ P.M.) is hanging over the road on Main street." The legitimate criminal justice system had operated effectively since this individual was already in jail, but the mob chose to usurp its efforts.[26]

Meanwhile the sheriff, William Phoenix, had gone in search of the outlaws that attacked Rancheria. He apprehended several suspects whom he transported to jail in Drytown, but the mob later took them from the jail and hanged them. Sheriff Phoenix died when he encountered two of the alleged Rancheria attackers. Although they fled, one managed to get off several shots, killing Sheriff Phoenix. Two deputy sheriffs then shot Phoenix's killer. The other Mexican man fled to a nearby home. After another shoot-out, the officers simply set the home on fire and burned the individual alive.[27] In total, the mob lynched an estimated dozen, and quite probably more, Mexican-origin people for the killings at Rancheria.[28]

Many of the news reports of the time offered telling testimony as to the motivations for these lynchings. The *Daily Alta California* offered a critical (and rare) stance and called the murders the work of "irresponsible mobs and vigilance committees, that defy and set aside the law... and are governed by nothing but their own cruel passions and prejudices."[29] Other papers went in the opposite direction and encouraged their readers to police the Mexican community, again tying extralegal efforts back to law enforcement. "We trust that our citizens will watch strictly the conduct of the Mexicans who may be living about the various camps," the *Sacramento Daily Union* intoned, "and arrest any of them who are not known to be industrious and well-behaved, and bring them before the proper authority for examination." Such a request, while patently illegal, remained a common way White people controlled Mexicans and Mexican Americans. In fact, as noted, such treatment may have spawned the violence at Rancheria, since White people had driven alleged "outlaws" from Drytown.[30] The *Daily Union* also wrote, "Some public measures will be adopted forthwith for the protection of our population against the fiendish cruelty of these semi-barbarous persons who infest our country."[31] In another article, the paper called for the "annihilation and expulsion of every Mexican from the mines, if not from the state," which showed the excessiveness of violence in the White mind.[32]

Writers of the period called the incident at Rancheria the "Rancheria Massacre" because White people died. But it was in fact a massacre of Mexicans that came in the form of hangings, burnings, and shootings. Some people fought back, as the example of Sheriff Phoenix's shooting makes clear. The Rancheria incident also shows how lynch mobs saw themselves as, and acted like, a form of criminal justice. That they had arrests, trials, and executions all signal a desire on the part of the mob to make their actions appear legal, even though in reality they acted wholly against the law.

Like the Gold Country, Southern California was extremely violent. Author Horace Bell described the first lynching in Los Angeles, that of a man he called Zavalete, really Doroteo Zabaleta, in 1852. Law enforcement had arrested Zabaleta for murder, but he escaped from jail. Sheriff James Barton—who had come to Los Angeles as a soldier during the Mexican-American War and when mustered out had gone into law enforcement (he served as sheriff from 1851 to 1857)—had left town to find Zabaleta, leaving the city in the hands of the City Guard, Los Angeles's vigilance committee. A mob of men found Zabaleta and brought him and two other Mexicans into town. The mob conducted what historian John Mack Faragher has appropriately called a "vigilante trial," found the three guilty of murder and sentenced them to hang.[33] A group of White and Mexican-origin people came out to watch the execution, which Sheriff Barton performed. After Zabaleta, Horace Bell wrote, "mob rule and lynchings followed year after year."[34]

J. Ross Browne, a writer for *Harper's Weekly*, visited LA and described what he called "the question," which was : "'Well, who did they catch today?' 'Who was killed?' 'Did they hang anybody?'" Horace Bell seemed embarrassed by Browne's commentary on the nature of law and order in Los Angeles. "And such was the plane of civilization to which our people had attained at that early period of our American Los Angeles history," Bell observed, "Fourteen years of American rule had certainly demonstrated to the benighted Sons of Mexico the superiority of our civilization.... A man was either a man hunter or he was hunted. If neither, he was a nonentity. Honest people wondered where it would all end." "Lynch law as administered in Los Angeles in the early times was not a marked success," according to Bell, "and after a half century of thought and careful observation it has been noticed that most of the people who indulged in the pastime usually came to untimely or miserable ends." And yet it continued.[35]

"To shoot these greasers ain't the best way," another American declared, instead "give 'em a fair trial, and rope them up with all the majesty of the law. That's the cure."[36] John Franklin Burns remembered two other important moments in the early history of Los Angeles and Southern California relating to lynching and law enforcement. The first was the killing of Sheriff Barton, and the second was the subsequent lynchings of Juan Flores and Pancho Daniel in 1857. Sheriff Barton had pursued Juan Flores and Pancho Daniel, who with a number of other men made up the Flores Daniel Gang. This group had engaged in livestock stealing and stood accused of killing a man named George Pflugardt. Sheriff Barton and four deputies died in a shootout allegedly with Flores and Daniel while tracking them. A posse of over one hundred men formed to hunt down Flores, Daniel, and the rest of their gang. This posse lynched about a dozen suspected gang members during the search. They finally captured Daniel and Flores and after a brief show trial found them guilty and hanged both.[37]

More violence followed. In 1856, for instance, Los Angeles deputy marshal William Jenkins killed Antonio Ruiz after he resisted having his guitar repossessed. In an interesting twist, the Mexican-origin community organized a posse of about 300 men to find and arrest Jenkins, a good example of resistance. This role reversal did not sit well with White authorities, though. The City Guard mounted its own posse and eventually captured the Mexican posse's leader, Fernando Carriaga, which seemed to defuse the tension in Los Angeles. Still, many of the racist stereotypes of this period appeared in this incident. Mexican-origin people, in forming their own vigilance committee, had fomented "revolution," unlike when White Americans did the same. In a final twist of fate, Officer Jenkins stood trial for killing Ruiz. An all-White, all-male jury acquitted him.[38]

Even well after the unending Mexican War period had ended, Whites continued to lynch Mexican-origin people in the Los Angeles area. In 1874, for example, an officer arrested Jesus Romo for an alleged robbery and attempted murder. A mob took Romo from this officer and hanged him. Repeating the refrain of civilized American "justice" over Mexican criminality, the *Los Angeles Star* called Romo "a hardened and blood-stained desperado, who deserved richly the fate which overtook him."[39] Jesus Romo represented White distaste for banditry, the fear of which had serious repercussions throughout the Southwest.

On December 22, 1877, in Bakersfield a mob of at least one hundred White men lynched five Mexican men. The Kern County sheriff had apprehended Antonio Maron, Francisco Encinas, Miguel Elias, Fermin Eldeo, and Bessena Ruiz for allegedly stealing horses in the Tehachapi Mountains. While awaiting trial, a mob gathered at the jail, overpowered the jailor, and broke into the jail cell holding the five men. The mob actually took the men upstairs to the courtroom, impaneled a jury, and had a short trial. The jury found all five guilty and sentenced them to death. This kangaroo court then marched Maron, Encinas, Elias, Eldeo, and Ruiz outside and lynched them as a group. A subsequent coroner's inquest found that "the cause of their death was being hung by some person or persons, to the jury unknown," although none in the lynch mob had disguised their identity.[40]

This Bakersfield lynching is yet another example of how White people conceived of extralegal justice as justice. Clearly the criminal justice system worked effectively. But the mob decided their authority, of which they had none, outweighed the legally codified authority of Kern County and Bakersfield. To give the lynching an air of legality, the mob conducted a trial—in the actual courtroom—and found the men guilty and executed them. So, they acted like legal authorities to conduct an extralegal trial and execution. The newspapers that reported on this event characterized the five Mexican men as "robbers" and "bandits" to further validate their alleged guilt. Those papers also noted that the Mexican and Mexican American population in the area was incensed but could do nothing to change the situation.[41]

The record in Texas is about as violent as in California.[42] According to available data, vigilance committees such as the one in Gonzales County did not lynch any Mexican-origin people, although they did drive the Mexican populations out of Colorado, Gonzales, Matagorda, and possibly Travis Counties. Mob violence also resulted from White fears that Mexicans assisted enslaved Black people in escaping to Mexico. But as in other locales, many of the lynchings in Texas derived from the need of some White people to exercise their own version of criminal justice.

Mid-nineteenth-century lynchings of Mexican-origin people occurred sporadically in Texas. But when they did take place, they tended to be dramatic and exceedingly gruesome. The lynching of an unnamed Mexican man near Eagle Pass in about 1865 or 1866 offers a good example. This murder mirrored the lynchings of African Americans for fictitious violations of sexual proscriptions. In this case, the mother and father of the Wood family had travelled from their ranch to Eagle Pass for supplies, leaving behind their twelve-year-old son, fourteen-year-old daughter, a Black farmhand, and a Mexican farmhand. The Mexican man bludgeoned the son to death and tried to do the same to the Black man. He then kidnapped the daughter and fled to Mexico. The African American farmhand alerted authorities. Soon a massive manhunt commenced, but another Mexican-origin individual spotted and then apprehended the Mexican man and kidnapped girl. He delivered them to officers at Fort Duncan, a U.S. Army base. When the Woods went to retrieve their daughter, the commander at Fort Duncan, Captain Hiram Mitchell, turned her and the Mexican man over to the parents.

What happened next was grisly. On the outskirts of Eagle Pass, a mob consisting of the Woods, a family friend named Robert Owens, a number of soldiers, and White townsfolk gathered and built a large fire. "While the fire was getting well lighted they commenced to torture the Mexican with their knives," wrote Jesse Sumpter, who recorded this event in a short autobiography. "They cut off his nose, cut off his ears, stuck their knives through his hands, and split them out. They likewise split out his feet[,] cut off various members of his body, gouged out his eyes with their knives, and finally picked him up and threw him into the fire." The Mexican man crawled out of the fire. "They then picked him up and threw him back into the fire," Sumpter reported, "they kept him on the fire till he was dead."[43]

This horrific lynching offers some compelling information about extralegal justice. For one thing, like the spectacle lynchings of African Americans in the late nineteenth and early twentieth centuries, the unnamed Mexican man experienced brutal torture that may have included castration: "they ... cut off various members of his body." Additionally, the U.S. Army turned over the Mexican suspect to the mob, which indicates that military officials continued to serve as an arm of law enforcement in the Southwest. That wing of law enforcement could also give way to extralegal justice, as several of the soldiers participated in the lynching of the unnamed Mexican. While Mexican-origin people had gathered to observe the lynching from a distance, it does not appear that they participated in the carnage. Yet, their presence tells us something about resistance because it seems likely that they had gathered to make sure only the unnamed Mexican would die, a killing that did not seem to sit well with them. Mexicans showed their displeasure a week later when Robert Owens visited Piedras Negras and bragged about killing the Mexican man. A group of Mexicans beat him and shot at him as he attempted to flee across the Río Bravo. Owens tried to swim to a ferry skiff, but Mexicans yelled to the skiff operator "mátalo," or "kill him." The Mexican ferry skipper took his oar and brought it down on Owens's head with a loud crack. Owens sank under the water; his body finally floated to the surface a week later. Some Mexicans dragged him to the banks of the river on the Mexican side. When his family asked to reclaim the body, they were told to "come and take the dog away."[44]

Another gruesome killing similar to the one in Eagle Pass occurred near San Antonio in 1896. This murder also was about a perceived violation of sexual taboos. Aureliano Castellón had allegedly attempted to court Emma Standfield (most accounts refer to her only as a "weak-minded" fifteen-year-old girl).[45] Her brothers Hugh and Watson confronted Castellón, shot him eight times, and then doused his body in coal oil and burned his corpse. Authorities found Castellón's body the next day and arrested the brothers. It is unclear, and doubtful, that authorities prosecuted the brothers for lynching Castellón.[46]

Most examples of mob violence in Texas appear more mundane and less detailed than the Eagle Pass and Aureliano Castellón lynchings. The following five serve as good examples. First, a mob lynched two Mexican men near San Marcos in March of 1870. The *Dallas Daily Herald* waxed dramatic when it reported, "The live oaks about San Marcos, Texas, are said to be bearing a new kind of fruit namely, Mexican horse thieves."[47] Second, a mob killed several Mexicans in Nueces Country: "Several Mexicans were seen hanging last week near the pasture fence of Capt. R. King. They have expiated their crime in a summary manner, the supposition existing that they were hung for stealing cattle."[48] Third, the *Galveston Daily News* reported on an 1875 lynching in Cameron County: "The Mexican who murdered one of the Morel brothers, on the Rio Grande a few months ago, was found hanging by the neck to a mesquite tree a few days ago."[49] Fourth, in 1880 a group of White and Mexican men shot Francisco Villareal to death near Uvalde for allegedly stealing livestock. As the *Dallas Daily Herald* noted, "The man it is concluded had an insatiable habit of sequestering loose stock, and his violent taking off is generally regarded as retribution and a warning to others in this vicinity."[50] Finally, in 1881 a group of Texas Rangers crossed the Mexican border to apprehend Onofrio Baca on a charge of murder. They captured him but then delivered Baca to a mob that "strung [him] up to the cross beams of the gate in the court house yard until he was dead."[51] This is one of numerous similar incidents wherein the Rangers violated international law by crossing into Mexico to arrest people and then turning them over to mobs for execution.

All these examples demonstrate how mobs used extralegal justice as a form of legitimate justice. From kidnapping to livestock theft to murder, White folks employed mob law to punish Mexican-origin people in Texas for their alleged crimes. In all these cases, legally codified bodies of law enforcement existed that could have altered the situation but did not. And even when they did, as the last example makes clear, vigilante justice still occurred.

Not only did White Texans lynch Mexican and Black people but the fear of lynching also became so pervasive that White people could use the threat of a lynch mob to control Mexicans. Whites could even use this form of terrorism to make the criminal justice system work the way they wanted it to. For example, when authorities found "an old Mexican tenant" dead at the O'Connor Ranch in San Patricio County, suspicion fell on "two Mexicans." A White posse soon captured two Mexicans (it's not clear whether they were *the* "two Mexicans" in question), both youths in their teens. Although they professed their innocence, the posse believed they had committed the murder. So, to elicit a confession they tortured the younger child. "They denied their guilt," the *Houston Daily Post* reported, "but after the younger of the two had been strung to a limb he acknowledged the whole affair." It seems a faux lynching could coerce a confession. Beyond that, the newspaper recounted, "There was strong talk of lynching the murderers, but coolness and judgement finally prevailed and the law will be allowed to take its course." While the mob debated and rejected lynching the "two Mexicans," it was only because they "allowed" justice to occur that legitimate justice prevailed. It is unclear what happened to the two youths.[52]

The record of White extralegal violence against Mexicans and Mexican Americans in Texas is fragmentary at best. We know, for example, that vigilante groups, such as the one in Gonzales County, formed for particularly racist reasons, but it does not appear those mobs killed anyone. Examples of lynching often appear as routine vignettes in newspapers with few details other than someone found a Mexican person hanging. Many of the examples of extralegal violence, though, underscore the fact that for some White people mob justice was justice. In the early twentieth century, this type of "justice" would give way to outright massacres of Mexican-origin people.

Of the different regions in the Southwest, Arizona's and New Mexico's records of extralegal violence were basically unparalleled. New Mexico has a particularly nasty lynching history.[53] Further complicating this picture, Mexican Americans occasionally joined White New Mexicans to form vigilance committees, often working side by side with legitimate law enforcement. Both legal and extralegal justice worked to stop the perceived lawlessness in New Mexico, especially outlaws or desperados. But, of course, you didn't have to be a desperado to face mob justice.

In 1877, as noted at the beginning of this chapter, a group of White men formed a vigilance committee in Santa Fe after Juan Benavides and Crespin Gallegos murdered Dr. John Courtier. Las Vegas also saw the formation of a vigilance committee in the 1880s. The group placarded the town with flyers warning "thieves, thugs, fakirs and bunko-steerers [swindlers]" to leave town or "be invited to attend a GRAND NECK TIE PARTY." "100 SUBSTANTIAL CITIZENS" signed the flyer. According to John Murphy, whose grandfather witnessed these events, residents awoke daily to find men hanging from a windmill in the center of town. The windmill became known as the "hanging windmill" because of the number of people lynched there. "The Vigilante activity for a time bore daily fruit," Murphy recalled, "and the inhabitants woke in the morning to find men hanging on the old windmill." These hangings grew so frequent that the owner of the windmill, who erected it to provide water for horses, had it torn down.[54]

Another group, whose location and formation have been lost, developed in New Mexico at about the same time as the Las Vegas vigilance committee. This group, known only as the S. C. of S. (possibly the Socorro Committee of Safety), posted broadsides that stated, "Notice is hereby given that all violations of peace and good order by any person or persons irrespective of nationality and condition will be inevitably followed by speedy and sure punishment."[55] Again, notions of "peace and good order" had a distinctive law enforcement sound, and the "speedy and sure punishment" more than likely meant extralegal lynching. Like other locales, Socorro had established policing agencies.

Other New Mexican locales also had violent reputations, especially Cimarron, and more specifically the St. James Hotel. The Lambert family, including Fred Lambert, a prominent law officer, owned the St. James Hotel. The hotel became known for the host of colorful characters who patronized the establishment and died there.[56] In a list of the deaths that occurred at the St. James, someone (possibly Henry Lambert, Fred's father) tabulated the killings in great detail, including a narrative about each death and a sketch

The infamous "hanging" windmill on the plaza of Las Vegas, New Mexico. A local farmer built the windmill to supply water to livestock in 1876. Its height and size made it unfortunately ideal for lynchings. According to Elfego Baca, the owner had it torn down in 1880 when the hangings became too numerous. Alas, local residents simply moved to lynching people from a nearby bridge. *Father Burke Collection, Carnegie Library, Las Vegas, New Mexico.*

of the individuals involved. In one instance, Lambert listed four "Mexicans" among the dead (in a list of thirteen incidents wherein a total of twenty-two people died). Those deaths included Juan Borrego, killed by David Crockett (a relative of Davy Crockett); Francisco "Pancho" Griego, shot down by infamous gunfighter Clay Allison; Feliciano Butarus, murdered by Sam Tipton; and Tomas Rodriguez whom hotel proprietor Henry Lambert killed. Each of these deaths are compelling, but the nature of the killing of Pancho Griego and Feliciano Butarus merit greater scrutiny because of how they relate to extralegal violence.[57]

The killing of Francisco "Pancho" Griego tells us a great deal about life, death, and mob violence. It was also a very big story. Griego owned a ranch, served as a deputy sheriff in Colfax County, and dealt monte at the St. James Hotel in the early 1870s. As a Cimarron County deputy sheriff, he was an example of a Mexican American who worked in law enforcement, but he lost his badge after he allegedly killed three Fort Union soldiers at the St. James,

NOTICE.

To all whom it may Concern: Notice is hereby given that all violations

OF PEACE

and good order by any person or persons irrespective of nationality and condition will be ~~inevitably~~ *inevitably* followed by speedy and sure punishment.

By order of the

S. C. OF S.

Notices from vigilance committees often placarded communities in the Southwest as a warning to lawbreakers or those who violated "peace and good order." This one, circa 1880, was probably from the Socorro Committee of Safety. These extralegal vigilante groups often existed in locales that had established law enforcement bodies or, if they originated in towns with no police force, they eventually morphed into legitimate law enforcement. *Mauro Montoya Collection (AC152), Fray Angélico Chávez History Library, New Mexico History Museum, Sante Fe.*

an incident for which a grand jury no-billed his charge. Griego had a great deal of political acumen and opposed the activities of the Santa Fe Ring, a corrupt group of politicians who used their influence to acquire large tracts of land, often at the expense of Mexican American and Indigenous landholders.[58] These issues culminated in a murder, at least two lynchings, and the execution of Pancho Griego.

The lynchings and Griego's death all commenced with the murder of a minister named Franklin James "F. J." Tolby. Reverend Tolby had publicly advocated for the farmers and ranchers mistreated by the Santa Fe Ring. The ring probably wanted to silence Tolby, and they certainly managed to kill other detractors, but when authorities found Tolby dead, suspicion fell instead on Cruz Vega, a mail carrier and Pancho Griego's nephew.[59] Vega probably had nothing to do with the murder of Tolby; local authorities had questioned him, Vega had a sound alibi, so they released him. Nevertheless, a colleague of Tolby's, Reverend Oscar P. McMains, convinced of Cruz Vega's guilt, led a lynch mob to apprehend Vega. McMains, gunfighter Clay Allison, and a mob of about five other men seized Vega in late October of 1875. They tortured him for some time in an attempt to elicit a confession for the role he played in the killing of Reverend Tolby. Vega refused to confess although he did allegedly implicate another Mexican American man, Manuel Cardenas. The mob lynched Vega anyway. According to the *Santa Fe Daily New Mexican*, Vega was "hung to a telegraph pole by a vigilance committee for being an accomplice in the death of Rev. J. F. [sic] Tolby." We can again see how the press legitimized extralegal justice by referring to the lynch mob as a "vigilance committee." Vega also went from murderer to "accomplice," although his fictitious complicity evidently warranted lynching too.[60]

These events infuriated Pancho Griego, who vowed to kill Clay Allison in 1875. Not one to ignore a challenge, Allison soon showed up at the Lambert Saloon at the St. James Hotel where Griego dealt monte. The details of their encounter are sketchy, but according to most accounts Allison and Griego met at the hotel bar, moved to a corner, engaged in quiet conversation, and then Allison simply shot Griego three times, once in the forehead and twice in the body after he had fallen to the floor. He died instantly.[61] The *Pueblo Chieftain* explained away the murder and commented, Griego "'has killed many Americans and was considered a dangerous man. His death occasions little regret.'" A local court deemed the killing a justifiable homicide.[62]

The extralegal killing of Manuel Cardenas came next. Colfax County law enforcement arrested Cardenas on suspicion that he had participated in the Tolby killing after Cruz Vega had allegedly implicated him. They released

Cardenas a short time later due to a lack of evidence. That caused enough anger for another mob to form. The *Santa Fe Weekly New Mexican* reported, "An armed band of men ... bent on violence, lawlessness and ruling to suit themselves; they declare they are assisting civil authorities, but from all we can learn compel them to do as they see fit."[63] Here we see again how extralegal justice worked as a stand-in for law enforcement that in this instance purported to assist local authorities. The Colfax County sheriff rearrested Cardenas. As the sheriff transported him to the courthouse, someone shot Cardenas in the head, a final lynching victim in the Tolby case.[64]

It seemed as though the drama stimulated by Reverend Tolby's murder might have ended the day Cardenas died, but almost two years later authorities arrested Oscar McMains for the lynching of Cruz Vega. Reverend McMains appeared before a grand jury in neighboring Mora County in 1877. His testimony demonstrated yet again how extralegal justice often stood in for legitimate justice. At his trial, he acknowledged his role in the murder and stated bluntly, "We are not a mob of lawless men, as has been reported abroad, bent upon violence and defiance of law, but on the contrary, have assembled legally and quietly for the purpose of securing the doings of justice and the punishment of crime."[65] McMains statement was, of course, a fantastic explanation of the role of lynch justice in the Southwest, but also factually inaccurate. McMains, Clay Allison, and the others involved *were* in fact a mob of lawless men that did act violently in defiance of the law. Moreover, since authorities had questioned and released Vega, the legitimate criminal justice system worked, it simple had not worked the way McMains had wanted it to. They had certainly not assembled legally, and murder was not justice. The Mora County grand jury found McMains guilty of fifth-degree murder and fined him $300. However, they set that sentence aside. Later, a judge granted the prosecution a new trial, but it never happened. As such, McMains went free.[66]

This whole bloody affair encapsulated a great deal about extralegal violence at the time. It began with a lynching of one man, Cruz Vega, a lynching in which Clay Allison participated, led Allison to commit yet another murder against Griego, and only ended with the lynching of Manuel Cardenas. Now, Pancho Griego sought to commit extralegal violence against Allison to avenge Vega. If Griego had actually attacked Allison in some way, Allison could have killed him and later claimed self-defense. Instead, Allison preemptively killed Griego, more than likely because he knew he could get away with it, and he did. It is doubtful that either Vega or Cardenas killed Reverend Tolby, whose murderer was never captured.

Griego was not the only Mexican-origin person killed under questionable circumstances at the St. James Hotel. Feliciano Butarus's murder serves as a reminder of the passion that horse stealing aroused in the Southwest. As a point of legal clarification, horse stealing was a form of larceny and courts tended to punish it with fines and time in jail or prison. But western lore suggests that the punishment for stealing horses and other livestock was death. The extralegal justice that occurred because of horse stealing, as in the case of Feliciano Butarus, certainly demonstrates the seriousness with which people took it.

Butarus, a Mexican national, had lived for twenty years with the Comanche in New Mexico. He rode into Cimarron one day in about 1880 with three horses, two of which he promptly sold at the corral adjacent to the St. James. As he negotiated the sale of the third horse, Sam Tipton passed by. Someone had recently stolen several of Tipton's horses and when he and Butarus locked eyes, Butarus fled. As he ran, Tipton fired two shots. The first missed, the second hit Butarus in the back. He died on a billiard table at the St. James Hotel. Now, if Butarus did steal Tipton's horses then he had certainly committed a crime. But Tipton decided to take the law into his own hands and kill Butarus. No arrest nor trial of Sam Tipton took place after the killing of Butarus, even though shooting a person in the back would not seem permissible.[67]

Popular writers have covered many of these stories, especially the Tolby killing. In their coverage, however, they have tended to extol the courage and shooting prowess of the White individuals involved while simultaneously excusing their culpability for the murders they committed. They have also portrayed the Mexican-origin people involved in these events negatively. For instance, an account of Clay Allison's exploits written in the 1960s described him in glowing terms. After the murder of Tolby, Allison, "properly indignant ... arrived at a just and honorable decision" to lynch Cruz Vega. According to this writer, Pancho Griego, "a person of doubtful habits and ancestry," was also a coward. The murder of Griego reads like a punch line, Allison simply "decided he would be happier with Pancho dead."[68] Some newspapers at the time, however, painted a different picture. The *Santa Fe Daily New Mexican* published an anonymous letter in 1875 from a citizen "who feared that more bloodshed is likely to occur between bad Mexicans and equally bad Americans." He wrote, "Such affairs are a disgrace to our people and all good citizens will hope that the end of lawless violence is reached." This writer at least acknowledged the lynchings and murders honestly as lawless vigilantism.[69]

Like in New Mexico, White men in the Arizona Territory founded vigilance committees and lynched individuals of Mexican ancestry. A group of men proposed forming a vigilance committee in 1871 to combat lawlessness and "the alarming frequency of deeds of violence in our community." Calling vigilance committees "the self-constituted arbiters of justice," and noting that "society has been outraged," these men blamed "lawless and desperate men," a veiled reference to Mexicans, Indigenous people, and suspect Whites. In 1877, some Whites proposed a new vigilance committee to combat a rash of stagecoach robberies. While asserting that they hoped to prevent lawlessness, this group made sure to note that they did not advocate disrespect of the law or lawlessness themselves by forming such a committee. Beyond the vigilance committee, this group also asserted quite openly that the string of robberies would cease if a few of the robbers were "strung up to limbs, or shot down like sheep-killing dogs." In Phoenix, an 1881 newspaper editorial advised the formation of a vigilance committee. "We never counsel violent or hasty action," the paper argued, but suggested nonetheless that "a little wholesale hanging of bad characters" would help alleviate problems.[70] In 1881, individuals near the Arizona–New Mexico border region formed a vigilance committee to halt horse stealing between the United States and Mexico. "Hanging," the *Arizona Weekly Journal-Miner* noted, "is the antidote employed."[71] White people clearly suggested forming lynch mobs as a substitute for legitimate law enforcement. They also coded their language in a manner clearly intended to separate White people, whom they saw as decent and law abiding, from their lawbreaking Mexican counterparts.

The vigilance committees in Arizona did not simply threaten to lynch people of Mexican ancestry. For example, shortly after the organization of the 1871 vigilance committee, a mob murdered an unnamed Mexican man in the mining district near Prescott in Yavapai County. A White man named Robert Williams was dealing faro in a saloon when a "'half-breed,' of Mexican nativity" attempted to place a bet. This individual put down twenty-five cents in scrip, a common practice at the time, but the bet was under the table limit. This upset the Mexican man who became demonstrative and so the bartender ordered him to leave. As he walked outside, he withdrew a pistol and shot at Williams. The bullet grazed Williams's cheek and hit another man in the leg. A group of men in the saloon gave chase but lost its quarry. The next morning, they located this unnamed Mexican and shot him dead. "We regret to have to chronicle a case the proceedings in which are so closely allied to Lynch law," the *Weekly Arizona Miner* stated, "yet it would be wrong to censure those men for the act." The paper repeated the oft told fiction about the inaction of law enforcement: "The law in Arizona is too imbecile, too weak, too cowardly, to punish dangerous characters, which fact suggests to men the propriety of defending themselves." While refusing to censure the lynch mob, the paper simultaneously insulted law enforcement and argued that individuals had the right to take the law into their own hands. The Yavapai County Sheriff's Office and the Prescott Constable's Office would surely have disagreed.[72]

White Americans of course resorted to lynch justice even when legitimate law enforcement had done its job. In 1872, for instance, Maricopa County sheriff Tom C. Warden arrested Ramon Cordova for a string of alleged stagecoach robberies. A few days later, a group of men broke into Cordova's cell in the county courthouse and hanged him. In an odd twist, a coroner's jury found Cordova, in absentia, guilty the following day. As the *Weekly Arizona Miner* put it, "this is harsh medicine, but a sure cure."[73] In 1878, an unnamed Mexican allegedly shot and killed a Mr. Kimble near the small town of Planet. Although he fled to Mexico, a local law officer named Hank Williams retrieved this individual. The townspeople, convinced of his guilt, lynched the unknown Mexican. The *Weekly Arizona Miner*, which had come to serve as the voice of vigilante justice, jokingly reported that the people at Planet "let him go, and he was turned loose." The newspaper continued, "Whether there might have been a rope around his neck, and it tied to the limb of a cottonwood tree, when he was let loose, is a horse of another color. Served him right."[74]

Even when law enforcement acted quickly, the perception that guilty parties would, or did, escape punishment drove lynch mobs. A vigilance committee in Tucson formed in 1872 for this reason. Several murderers had escaped the local jail. "The only comment we need make on these cases," the vigilance committee noted, "is to state that pretty good men are again talking of the necessity of a vigilance committee to administer that punishment which the law says shall be (but is not) for the terrible crime of murder. Murder upon murder is committed in Arizona, and yet not one murderer has ever been punished as the law dictates."[75]

In Tucson a similar situation provoked violence and lynching. In August 1873, Leocardo Cordova, Clemente Lopez, and Jesus Saguaripa allegedly murdered Vicente Hernandez and his spouse, Labrada Chaves, during a botched robbery attempt. The murder was gruesome: the killers bashed their skulls with a club and slashed their throats. The crime scene was horribly bloody, and investigators learned a short time later that Chaves was pregnant. Barely a day after the murders, Tucson constable Frank Esperanza arrested Cordova and Lopez. A group of local people created a vigilance committee called the Committee of Safety led by a man named William Zeckendorf. They descended on the jail and managed to elicit confessions from both men (the press did not disclose how they got those confessions). The confessions led the vigilance committee to Saguaripa.[76]

Word spread quickly that law enforcement had the murderers in custody. Soon townsfolk began to talk of "an expressed purpose to hung [sic] the three (and also John Willis [who was in jail for killing a man named Robert Swope in an unrelated incident]) immediately after the funeral of the murdered man and wife." The funeral took place, shops closed, and hundreds of people gathered at the jail. "Very soon thereafter," the *Arizona Weekly Citizen* reported, "the four men above named, were brought out of jail, with small black bandages over their eyes, put in wagons, ropes adjusted to their necks, and the wagons drawn out and all four hung side by side."[77]

In a fascinating postscript to this story, the Pima County coroner, Solomon Warner, conducted an in absentia inquest into the guilt of the four lynched men, much like the case of Ramon Cordova. The jury found them guilty and exonerated the townspeople who participated in the lynching. "We further find," the coroner's jury stated, "that the said hanging was committee [sic, committed] by the people of Tucson, en masse; and we do further say that in view of the terrible and bloody murders that had been committed by the three Mexicans above named and the tardiness with which justice was being meted out to John Willis, a murderers [sic], that the extreme measures taken by our fellow citizens this morning in vindication of their lives, their property, and the peace and good order of society, while it is to be regretted and deplored that such extreme measures were necessary, seems to the jury to have been the inevitable results of allowing criminals to escape the penalties of their crimes."[78]

As for John Willis, a Pima County jury had previously found him guilty of murder and sentenced him to death, but he had escaped jail, hence the language about criminals escaping their penalties. The lynch mob strung him up with Leocardo Cordova, Clemente Lopez, and Jesus Saguaripa. Their hangings were a classic example of lynch justice, replete with all the justifications used to excuse the behavior of the mob. The postlynching inquest also saw the legitimate criminal justice excuse an illegal act. Moreover, Mexican-origin people participated in the lynching. Constable Esperanza had assisted in the arrests and more than likely in the lynchings. Tucson had a large Mexican-origin population, probably around 50 percent of the total population, and surely some attended the executions. Moreover, they may well have favored lynching considering the murdered individuals were well-liked Mexican Americans. According to one account, Zeckendorf, who helped organize the lynching, asked the crowd what punishment the men should receive. The response was "¡que mueran!," or "let them die," which certainly suggests the participation of Mexican-origin people.[79] They joined with White townspeople to lynch three Mexican men who had killed a Mexican American family and Willis, a convicted murderer thrown into the mix for good measure. Mexican-origin people were not solely the victims of lynchings; sometimes they helped perpetrate them.

In another example of lynch law taking over for legitimate law, the *Weekly Arizona Miner* reported on a lynching in January of 1875. Ventura Nunnas (possibly Nuñes) allegedly murdered G. R. Whistler, for whom Nunnas worked. The sheriff dispatched a posse and they captured him. They also turned "him over to the proper authorities." And yet, even though law enforcement clearly existed and surely the "proper authorities" would do their duty, Nunnas "was taken out [of jail] by a party of men and hung to a tree nearby."[80]

In other cases, both government officials and individual Arizonans complained about what they saw as lawlessness and what they viewed as the poor workings of the criminal justice system, even after arrests and trials had occurred. Take the case of David Estes. He and an accomplice had allegedly robbed a card game at a Galeyville saloon. To make his escape, Estes also allegedly stole a horse. His total haul including the horse was about $500. Deputy Sheriff Jim Goodman quickly arrested Estes, and Justice of the Peace G. W. Ellingwood, the sole court official in Galeyville, initiated trial proceedings. The witnesses, however, could not conclusively identify whose money Estes had stolen. So Ellingwood released Estes. This caused some frustration in Galeyville since the trial did not go as some thought it should. One man, who identified himself only as "Clipper," noted sarcastically after the trial, "Thus you see a single pair in Galeyville wins five hundred dollars." That the processes of the criminal justice system went forward—even in a recently formed town like Galeyville, which never amounted to much and no longer exists—did not seem to mean much to "Clipper." But it demonstrates that legitimate forms of justice existed, a direct refutation to the common argument put forward by lynch mobs.[81]

Mexican-origin people did not simply suffer at the hands of lynch mobs. They resisted in a variety of ways, including by appealing to state and territorial governments and especially to the Mexican government and its ambassadorial staff. Mexico took a keen interest in policing issues in the Southwest because many of the cases of brutality and lynching involved Mexican citizens and because Mexico well understood that Mexican Americans might not always receive the impartiality they deserved from the criminal justice system. Mexican-origin people understood this as well, and they frequently called on Mexican authorities to investigate, protest, and push for the prosecution of the murderers of Mexicans and Mexican Americans. This proved true for Mexican-origin people killed by lynch mobs and police.

Envoy Manuel de Zamacona y Murphy represents a good example of this work. Zamacona served as ambassador from 1878 to 1882. He frequently vocalized concerns he had with the U.S. criminal justice system, often criticizing the outlandish excuses used when legal and extralegal forms of justice conspired to rob Mexicans of their rights and lives. His correspondence tells us a great deal: he exposed lynchings that we have little information about otherwise, he demonstrated a legalistic and conscientious approach to law enforcement that differs considerably from what often occurred at the local level, and he represented another avenue for understanding the ways in which Mexicans attempted to protect and creatively adapt themselves to the law enforcement landscape in the Southwest.

Zamacona wrote to Secretary of State James G. Blaine in August of 1881 to express his concerns about "the hanging of certain Mexicans near Wilcox." Those hangings came after a series of robberies allegedly committed by Texas Cowboys, who abused and murdered Mexican-origin people with relative impunity. Unfortunately, Mexican people bore the penalty that came from robberies committed by Texas Cowboys, such as when a mob hanged José Ordoña and Rafael Salcido for allegedly stealing horses.[82] Wilcox authorities seemed little inclined to investigate the case. Sheriff Robert H. "Bob" Paul, who may have participated in the lynchings, explained to consular officials "that a number of persons, usurping the functions of the proper authorities, declared the Mexicans in question to be thieves, and thereupon hung one and retained the other in custody."[83]

Envoy Zamacona complained not only about the lynchings but also about the sheriff's response. "The most remarkable feature [of the sheriff's reply] is that the officer ... justifies the outrage referred to, considering it beneficial and necessary," he stated. Zamacona called this viewpoint "absurd and alarming." While he referenced treaty stipulations and the exercise of good government, Zamacona was mainly concerned with what he correctly viewed as murder under the color of law. He hoped that Secretary of State Blaine would push the Arizona territorial government to investigate and bring the guilty parties to justice. Blaine lamented that such events stemmed from "mob violence in disregard of the laws and constituted authorities." While he noted that such outrages occurred on both sides of the border, he demanded that the "public authorities of Arizona ... use of every legal means within their power to put a stop to such outrages and to bring to justice all persons who shall be found to have been engaged in their perpetration."[84] Arizona territorial governor John C. Frémont had of course never shown himself to be an advocate for Mexican American rights; he wasn't even in the territory at the time. Instead, acting governor John Gosper responded by siding with the sheriff and basically dismissed the lynchings as justified because Ordoña and Salcido "were probably outlaws."[85]

Zamacona protested other abuses committed by the Texas Cowboys against Mexicans. For example, he complained about the ways they abused Mexican merchants. On two separate occasions they had assaulted Mexican traders, in one instance attacking a caravan of herders travelling from Mexico to the Arizona Territory and in another instance robbing a train of Mexican goods while leaving the goods of American entrepreneurs untouched. Zamacona rightly saw the robbery of the herders as an international incident since it had occurred in Mexico.[86] In addition to writing to Governor Frémont about the Wilcox murders, Blaine also asked the governor to investigate these robberies.[87] Frémont, again, did nothing.[88] Acting governor Gosper did, however, criticize this situation. He lamented what he saw as law enforcement's failures, commenting that "the very best law abiding and peace loving citizens has no confidence in the willingness of the civil officers to pursue and bring to justice that element of outlawry."[89]

One of the more notorious cases that brought together Mexican consular officials and American authorities was the lynching of Francisco Quiñones Jr., a well-liked youth whose murder preceded a host of killings.[90] Officers found him hanging from a cottonwood tree in July of 1884 for possibly witnessing the theft of a rifle.[91] Pima County sheriff Bob Paul initially investigated the lynching but discovered that it had actually occurred in Cochise County. He therefore alerted Cochise County sheriff Jerome Ward. These jurisdictional issues slowed the legal proceedings, which frustrated local people who considered Quiñones a good youth, as well as law enforcement and consular officials who wanted the case solved.[92]

Several more murders followed the Quiñones lynching. One man named James Rafferty had allegedly witnessed Quiñones's murder. Rafferty approached the sheriff and the local offices of the Mexican legation to offer his testimony. Alas, before he could make a statement, Rafferty and three companions, Joseph Raymond and husband and wife Winfield and Mary Fritz, turned up dead. The Fritzes and Raymond died horribly at their home; unknown parties shot Joseph Raymond and Winfield Fritz multiple times. They shot Mary Fritz "through the head . . . the weapon having been held so close to the body as to singe the hair." Authorities found Rafferty's body a short distance away from the house, down a path that led to where he grazed livestock. The killers had shot him once in the head from a distance.[93] Arizona territorial governor Frederick Tritle soon posted a $500 reward.[94] The *Arizona Daily Star* reported that "Rafferty and the Fritzes were murdered because they had all declared their intention to testify against the parties" that had lynched Quinoñes.[95]

Francisco Quiñones's lynching angered Mexican-origin people in the region. "The Mexicans," the *Arizona Daily Star* reported, "were much excited over the affair, and threatened vengeance on Americans living in that vicinity." While understandably angry, the way the press reported Mexican frustrations veered into dangerous territory. The paper warned, "Settlers are armed and ready for any attack, and the state of affairs is anything but pleasing."[96] Then someone began to circulate a rumor that Mexicans had killed Quiñones, Rafferty, the Fritzes, and Raymond. Cochise County authorities received spurious information, possibly from the real killers, that a man named Eduardo Romero had committed the murders. They arrested him but released him because he had nothing to do with the killings.[97] Mexican consul Antonio V. Lomeli dismissed accusations of Mexican involvement, noting that they wouldn't have killed Quiñones and that if they wanted to avenge Quiñones by killing Rafferty, Raymond, and the Fritzes they would have done so quickly, not months later. Lomeli speculated that the real killers had simply attempted to cast blame on Mexicans. "A careful examination of all the facts confirms the first suspicion of the [*Arizona Weekly*] *Citizen*," the paper reported, "that the murder was not the work of Mexicans, but was the desperate act of men who found it necessary to kill everybody on Rafferty's ranch for their own protection."[98]

By November of 1884, law enforcement had finally begun to focus on brothers David and Thomas Duncan (and possibly a third brother named Daniel), as well as a man named "Stormy" Jim McFarland, as the murderers of Quiñones, Raymond, Rafferty, and the Fritzes. The story seemed clear by this point: Quiñones had seen the men stealing a rifle (quite possibly the rifle used to kill Rafferty) and they lynched him to cover their crime. Considering the violence in the region, they probably thought another lynched Mexican wouldn't receive much attention.[99] But witnesses had seen David Duncan in the area and Rafferty had witnessed the lynching of Quiñones. So the Duncan brothers had killed him, Raymond, and the Fritzes to cover their tracks. They had also fled Arizona after Consul Lomeli and others had shifted suspicion away from Mexican culprits. Authorities collared the Duncan brothers and Jim McFarland in San Francisco and returned the men to Arizona.[100]

The Cochise County grand jury indicted the Duncan brothers, McFarland, and a man named Hawkensmith for the murders of the Fritzes, Rafferty, and Raymond (the role Hawkensmith played in the murders is unclear). They did not indict the men for murdering Quiñones since they had killed James Rafferty, the only person who could testify that they had lynched Quiñones.[101] As the trial got underway, Mexican consul Joaquín Díaz Prieto convinced Francisco Quiñones Sr. to come to the United States to testify about his son and retrieve the youth's body for burial in Mexico. But after testifying, Quiñones Sr. vanished, leaving many to believe the same fate that befell his son had befallen the father! Several reports speculated that he had been kidnapped, lynched, or both. But Quiñones Sr. turned up a few days later. Someone had evidently drugged him and left him to die in the nearby Huachuca Mountains.[102] In May the case went to trial. Alas, while it seemed likely that they had murdered Mary and Winfield Fritz, James Rafferty, and Joseph Raymond, little evidence existed to support a guilty verdict. The jury acquitted the Duncan brothers, McFarland, and Hawkensmith in May 1885.[103]

As strange and as violent as this story was, it had not yet ended. The Duncan brothers, McFarland, and Hawkensmith went their separate ways. The Duncan brothers stayed in Cochise County and kept to themselves on their ranch. But in March of 1887, newspapers across the Southwest reported that someone had murdered the Duncan brothers. This sensational news turned out to be a fiction, or "a canard," as one paper put it. "The Duncan brothers are full of life."[104] The Mexican government continued pushing for the prosecution of Francisco Quiñones's murderers in 1888. U.S. secretary of state Thomas F. Bayard wrote to Arizona territorial governor C. Meyer Zulick in March of that year to ask for an update. Bayard explained that he had received another demand for action from Envoy Matías Romero. Nothing came of these inquiries.[105]

Finally, in 1890, Thomas and Daniel found their brother David dead in a pool of blood. He had been ill and bedridden. In February of 1890, an unknown assailant entered the Duncan's ranch house after Thomas and Daniel had left to plow a field. The individual stabbed David "through the heart with a long knife, the blade passing entirely through his body." The killer or killers then ransacked and robbed the home. One newspaper speculated that this deed "was supposed to have been committed by Mexicans." That may have been the case, but no proof existed to support this speculation, and as noted people frequently blamed "Mexicans" for borderlands crimes. Interestingly, no one connected the murder of David Duncan to the five murders he allegedly committed. In fact, acting territorial governor Nathan Murphy called Duncan a "reputable citizen of this territory" and issued a $500 reward for the apprehension of his killers.[106] No one ever came forward with information; authorities charged no one with the murder. And with that, the violence that had begun with the lynching of Francisco Quiñones Jr. finally came to an end.[107]

The Mexican government intervened in other lynchings and near lynchings, such as the multiple attempted lynchings of Manuel Mejía, discussed in the introduction. Mejía might have become another victim of lynch justice but for a curious set of circumstances, the stupidity of his attackers, and his own will to live. Mejía was a well-liked miner who had lived in Yavapai County for about fifteen years. Because of his knowledge of the county and its terrain, the Maricopa County Sheriff's Office asked Mejía to assist them with an investigation into the murder of Yavapai County store owner Barney Martin, his wife, and two children in August of 1886. Authorities located their bodies near the southeastern border of Yavapai and Maricopa Counties. For unknown reasons, Deputy Sheriff J. W. Blankenship, whom the Maricopa County sheriff had tasked to meet with Mejía, instead took him into custody for the murders. Blankenship had no suspicion that Mejía had played any part in the murders, nor had he gotten an arrest warrant for him, yet Mejía spent seventeen days in jail before Blankenship finally released him.

Upon his release a group of around ten men led by Charles Genung and Thomas Bryan captured Mejía and attempted to lynch him. As Mejía walked out of jail, the mob pounced upon him. Although he fought back, the mob beat him nearly unconscious. They then gagged him, beat him some more, bound his hands and feet, and dragged him by horse through the streets of Phoenix. After beating him some more, the mob placed a rope around Mejía's neck and hanged him from a cottonwood tree. They left him hanging while they discussed getting a drink at a nearby saloon. After letting him hang for a while, the mob lowered Mejía to the ground, demanded he confess, and beat him yet again. They then hanged him a second time. They let him down again, beat him some more, and lynched him a third time. They repeated this pattern again, but on the fourth lynching attempt the mob wandered off to the saloon and left Mejía to die.[108]

But he did not die. Instead, Mejía had managed to bite down on the rope and contort his body in such a way that he could still breathe. He had also retrieved a knife from his boot. And then he miraculously cut himself free. Unfortunately, when he cut the noose, he fell painfully onto a barbed wire fence and rolled down an embankment into a creek below. The mob heard this commotion and ran from the saloon to try to apprehend Mejía again. He managed to cut the rope from his feet and cross the river. The lynchers proceeded to rush to the embankment and shoot at Mejía as he fled. All their shots missed. Mejía made it to the nearby home of a Mexican family and begged for help. They tended to his wounds and called Phoenix town marshal Henry Garfias for aid.[109]

Though he lived, Mejía received lifelong injuries from his ordeal. The lengthy beating left him blind in one eye. The fall onto the barbed wire fence so badly lacerated his left arm that he lost the use of that appendage.[110] Justice also came slowly for Mejía. He had received some initial assistance from Marshal Henry Garfias, who had already helped Mejía by securing his release from the Maricopa County Jail after Blankenship had falsely imprisoned him. At that time Garfias had contacted Maricopa County district attorney Frank Cox who, upon looking into the case, authorized Mejía's release. Cox also revealed in a deposition following the attempted lynchings some of the ways in which the deputy sheriff had manipulated the justice system. Blankenship did not charge Mejía with the murders but held him for "complicity in the murder of Barney Martin and family." The deputy sheriff also later stated he held Mejía for stealing Barney Martin's horse. That never happened and if it did it would have happened in Yavapai County, so Blankenship had exceeded his jurisdictional authority. He had no evidence to support any formal charges in the murders, thus the sheriff's office had evidently switched tactics and made up the claim about the stolen horse in order to continue holding Mejía. In an attempt to further delay releasing him, Blankenship requested that eyewitnesses travel from Yavapai County to Phoenix to testify. Instead of the eyewitnesses, Yavapai County sheriff William J. Mulvenon arrived to speak on Mejía's behalf. He told Cox that "he did not think there was anything in it [Mejía's involvement in the murders]." These legal maneuvers meant that Mejía spent an unnecessary seventeen days in jail.[111]

Envoy Matías Romero came to Manuel Mejía's defense and wrote to Secretary of State Thomas F. Bayard in September of 1886, asking him to pressure the territorial government to find the would-be lynchers.[112] Romero wrote again the following month and included a letter from Henry Garfias detailing the nature of the case.[113] Garfias explained in his letter that the lynch mob had hanged and beaten Mejía multiple times in order to elicit a confession for the Martin killings. They wanted him to confess to the crime or to name the actual killer or killers. When Mejía could do neither, the mob decided to leave him hanging until he died.[114] Garfias also noted that he had secured the aid of District Attorney Cox, who had "directed the Sheriff four or five times to discharge Mejias [sic]," but the sheriff had refused. Garfias, of course, also aided Mejía after his ordeal.[115] Acting U.S. secretary of state Alvey A.

Adee responded by writing to Governor Zulick, asking him to investigate the matter.[116] Secretary of State Bayard followed Adee's letter with one of his own, again imploring Zulick to investigate the case.[117] The sheriff of Yavapai County issued a reward for information in the murder of the Martin family, which would have also assisted the Mejía case. The territorial government offered a reward of $1,000 (about $31,000 in 2022 dollars).[118]

District Attorney Cox also did his duty in the case. Cox and Garfias convinced a frightened Mejía to swear out a complaint against his attackers. Cox then issued a warrant for the arrest of Charles Genung, Thomas Bryan, Antonio Soto, and "John Doe (a Mexican whose true name is unknown)" for assault with intent to murder. Other parties had identified Genung and Bryan as the ringleaders. Antonio Soto and "John Doe" were of Mexican origin, which again shows that Mexican people sometimes participated in lynchings. Cox's investigation did not result in a trial of these men. They successfully produced alibi witnesses and the only evidence against them came from Mejía.[119]

Manuel Mejía's own testimony was incredibly compelling. While recounting the astonishing story told above, he also added some additional details. He estimated, for instance, that the mob had dragged him to the hanging tree over a distance of more than a half mile. He also explained how he survived the hangings. Upon the third attempted lynching he managed to free his hands without his captors noticing. He also managed to retrieve his knife, palming it until the mob hanged him a fourth time. In addition to freeing his hands and secreting his knife to cut the ropes, he "managed to take a hold of the rope with [his] teeth and thus prevent . . . being strangled to death" the final time the mob strung him up. He also noted that after escaping he had wandered aimlessly "suffering intense agony" until he passed the home of a "Mexican" who first gave him "some relief" and who contacted Henry Garfias on Mejía's behalf. And yet, "After an examination lasting several days," Mejía noted, "the Judge discharged my aggressors."[120]

In early 1887, the Mexican government also issued a formal complaint demanding that the U.S. government punish the would-be lynchers as well as the authorities who failed to protect the rights of Manuel Mejía. While the various correspondence from Mexican consular officials certainly implied that the Mexican government regarded the treatment of Mejía as an international incident, until Envoy Matías Romero issued a formal petition (a reclamación in Spanish, or claim) the government's efforts carried little weight. Romero, writing at the direction of Mexico's secretary of foreign affairs Ignacio Mariscal, sternly rebuked the U.S. government as well as the Arizona territorial government while relaying the details of what happened to Mejía. Mariscal had, moreover, directed Romero "to present a formal complaint to the United States Government on account of the failure of the Arizona authorities to punish the parties who were guilty of those outrages [against Mejía], to present a reclamation based upon the evident lack of the proper administration of justice which, in the opinion of [his] government, there has been in this case, and to ask for the punishment of the delinquents and of the authorities what have been derelict in the performance of their duties."[121] The presentation of this claim represented a major diplomatic step that amounted to an official declaration by the Federal Republic of Mexico that an international incident had occurred. The U.S. government should have taken the claim seriously. Although Secretary of State Bayard forwarded the Mexican government's claim to Arizona territorial governor Zulick, it seems he did nothing.[122]

It took until 1889 for law enforcement to identify a suspect in the murder of the Martin family. Martin had recently sold his store to a man named Charles Stanton, who then hired a man named Francisco Vega and others to rob Martin of the money Stanton had just paid out for the store. Yuma County deputy sheriff Will Smith located Vega in Sonora, Mexico, and attempted to extradite him to Arizona. But the Mexican government refused. Whether he actually participated in the killing of the Martins is unclear. Clearly Manuel Mejía had nothing to do with the crime: he was simply a Mexican that Deputy Sheriff Blankenship singled out as a murderer and who endured a quadruple hanging.[123]

The brutality that Mexican-origin people endured at the hands of vigilantes is hard to fathom. While the majority of these cases of extralegal violence occurred in the Southwest, mob justice against Mexican-origin people happened in states as far away as Oregon and Nebraska.[124] The number of lynching victims remains a mystery. Historians William Carrigan and Clive Webb have estimated that thousands of Mexican-origin people died at the hands of mobs, and they provided detailed data on 547 victims. They caution against strictly looking at numbers, however, noting that focusing on numbers reduces victims to a data point and a seemingly hard total when in fact a true number "will never be known because it is impossible to recover the names and dates and places of all those killed by mobs."[125] Numbers create another problem in that they cause readers to reductively fixate on victimhood. Those who died at the hands of vigilantes were more than victims. Victimhood silences those attacked by mobs and relegates them to nothing more than a dead body.

Mexicans and Mexican Americans did resist. They fought back with guns and fists, they fled extralegal justice, they joined lynch mobs, and they appealed to law enforcement, elected officials, and Mexican consular officials, as numerous cases make clear. To put this simply, Mexican-origin people did not simply die passively at the hands of mobs.

Some White people believed that vigilante justice served as an effective form of criminal justice. While we can see today that many of these beliefs were fictions and lies, numerous newspapers, vigilance committees, White mob leaders such as Oscar McMains, "Clipper," and law officers such as Sheriff Robert H. "Bob" Paul all argued in favor of extralegal justice. That White people claimed so vociferously that vigilantism was law enforcement and that mob law was legal justice is revealing. And such assertions did not end in the 1800s. Instead, another wave of anti-Mexican violence and murder also occurred in the early twentieth century. White people asserted once again that extralegal violence could solve the problems of perceived Mexican criminality, unleashing a torrent of racial violence that left hundreds, and some speculate thousands, of Mexican-origin people dead.

3

STARS & SHIELDS

The World of Mexican American Law Enforcement Officers

Surely Elfego Baca wondered whether he would live through the night. He had hidden himself inside a small home in Frisco, New Mexico, on a cool night in October of 1884 to avoid eighty angry Texas Cowboys who wanted him dead and had vowed to "get this dirty little Mexican."[1] To fulfil that promise, those Cowboys surrounded the home and then sent hundreds of bullets crashing through the walls, windows, and front door of the house. To hear Baca tell it, nothing scared him. Perhaps that explains how in the middle of the fusillade, with dust and bits of wood and debris raining down on him as the bullets flew, he decided to do something seemingly unusual: cook himself breakfast. A pot of coffee, some sizzling beef, even handmade tortillas! One has to wonder what those eighty Texas Cowboys thought when they caught the smell of fresh brewed coffee and tacos. Elfego Baca survived the night.

While the Texas Cowboys thought of Baca as just a "dirty little Mexican," what really angered them was that he acted as a law officer who stood up to the Cowboys and the racist violence they had unleashed on the Mexican-origin community in New Mexico. Indeed, White Texas Cowboys had plagued Mexicans and Mexican Americans from Texas to California, and they had killed untold hundreds of people. Elfego Baca not only refused to let the Cowboys kill him but he also refused to let them abuse and murder other Mexican-origin people, and he did so by pinning a badge to his chest and becoming an officer of the law. He was not alone. Mexican Americans served in law enforcement across the Southwest from roughly the mid-nineteenth century to the present day. All they needed was a star or a shield. Their examples merit attention.

Despite what Old West lore has told us, the peace officer of the nineteenth and early twentieth century was not always a White man. Mexican Americans also served in law enforcement. These officers tended to predominate in heavily Mexican areas of the Southwest, especially New Mexico. They were elected or appointed and often, although not always, served with distinction. Examining these officers illuminates a number of interesting and salient facts. First, Mexican American police sometimes began their careers as social bandits. Having worked on one side of the criminal justice system—the criminal side—they became police officers or sheriffs later in life. Second, they usually had no qualms about exercising their authority on anyone. They understood their role and power and any person who failed to respect it soon learned the error of their ways. These officers also worked alongside, and in some cases over, White counterparts. That suggests a more equalitarian and cooperative working relationship than we might otherwise expect. Third, the role of the nineteenth and early twentieth-century law officer provided a concrete example for the individuals who came later, especially in the mid-twentieth century as police departments attempted to diversify their officer corps by hiring more Mexican Americans. And fourth, while Mexican American law officers expressed a variety of reasons for choosing their profession, from simply needing a job to being the only one who would take it, a good number, such as Elfego Baca, chose law enforcement because they viewed policing as a kind of civil rights strategy to help the Mexican American community.

We know a good deal about some Mexican American police and very little about others. As noted in the previous chapter, Francisco "Pancho" Griego had served as a deputy sheriff before Clay Allison murdered him. We know next to nothing about his time in law enforcement. Spanish surnamed law officers

Phoenix town marshal Henry Garfias (*far left*) in front of the Justice Office with two other men, circa 1881. Garfias was a well-respected law enforcement officer for many years in Arizona. *Phoenix Police Museum.*

appear quite regularly in the historical record, but oftentimes a name is all we have. The frequent mention of Mexican American officers in newspaper accounts or letters indicates that they had some measure of prevalence in the Southwest, especially in Arizona and New Mexico. But those thumbnails tell us little about them beyond their name.

One of the earliest and most important borderlands law officers was Arizona's Enrique "Henry" Garfias, who helped protect Manuel Mejía, as noted in the introduction and previous chapter. He initially came to policing in the early 1870s, after he arrived in Phoenix. The city appointed him constable when no one else wanted the job. This occurred with some regularity across the Southwest: only people who did not mind dying, as an old saying goes, served in these capacities. Garfias wanted the job. He held several other positions in the local government, including court translator and city gravedigger. He ran for office for the first time in 1878, one of six candidates to file for two constable positions. He won easily.[2]

Soon after his election, however, Garfias became embroiled in a controversy. A man named Jesus Romero had for unknown reasons attacked a crowd of people with a sword. Garfias and Maricopa County deputy sheriff Jesus Vasquez (whom we know little about), captured Romero, who became known as the "saber slasher." Garfias then learned that a lynch mob planned to murder

Stars & Shields

Romero. He attempted to seek protection for him by gathering an armed posse to guard the jailhouse. But while Garfias worked to gather this posse, a mob broke into the jail and shot and killed Romero. This early encounter served as both an example of lynch justice—even when the established criminal justice system was clearly at work—as well as a failure for Garfias, who took it as a negative mark on his record.[3]

After Phoenix was incorporated as a city in 1881, Garfias ran for the newly created city marshal position. He won again. Interestingly enough, because of how and when the city was incorporated, Garfias served as town constable and city marshal simultaneously. Shortly after this election, Garfias became involved in another controversy. This time a group of Texas Cowboys had come into town and in a drunken state began shooting up Phoenix. Garfias refused to tolerate this lawlessness. He formed a posse, rode out to meet these Texas Cowboys, and engaged in a shoot-out with the men. Garfias wounded one man, while two others fled. He soon captured those men, but as Garfias and the posse transported them to jail, a group of angry Phoenicians, White and Mexican-origin people, gathered to lynch the prisoners. This time Garfias did his duty more effectively than he had with Romero. "The officers," the *Arizona Daily Star* reported, "came to their rescue and removed them to jail."[4]

Marshal Garfias also served as a Maricopa County deputy sheriff in the 1880s and 1890s. He had another encounter with an individual who attacked people with unusual weapons as a deputy sheriff in 1895. Like Jesus Romero, the so-called saber slasher, Antonio Cuarento was apprehended by Garfias for "a deadly assault committed with an axe upon a man," south of Phoenix. Cuarento had allegedly committed "a half dozen cutting and stabbing affrays." Garfias tracked him for nearly a year before capturing him.[5] He retired shortly after this event. Alas Garfias suffered major injuries after a fall from his horse in 1896. While recuperating, he probably contracted pneumonia and died that same year. The press at the time lamented his death and highlighted his fair-minded attitude toward the law. Like other frontier officers, Garfias had an interesting and exciting career.[6]

Perfecto Armijo's legacy roughly mirrors Henry Garfias's. Armijo was one of the finest law officers the New Mexico Territory produced in the nineteenth century. He served for years as Bernalillo County deputy sheriff and then sheriff. He also inspired numerous other law officers, especially Elfego Baca. Armijo first ran for sheriff in 1871.[7] The available record is unclear, but it seems that he lost because the following year he served as a justice of the peace in Tularosa.[8] In 1878 Armijo ran for Bernalillo County sheriff again.

Sheriff Perfecto Armijo (*far right, wearing a hat*) with others in front of the Spanish Shack Cafe and Old Town Chili Parlor, Albuquerque, circa 1880s.
This photo would seem to confirm that Armijo did not carry a gun.
Emma Moya Collection, Center for Southwest Research and Special Collections, University of New Mexico Libraries, Albuquerque, #B1F44.

This time he won.[9] According to popular lore, Armijo never wore a gun, a fact the image above would seem to confirm. That is perhaps surprising given the danger he faced daily.

One of the first major events of Sheriff Armijo's career involved the eradication of the Marino Leyba Gang that operated in the Sandia Mountains. The gang engaged in horse stealing and killed a lot of people. In 1880, the gang had participated in the robbery and murder of Colonel Charles Potter, a surveyor for the U.S. Geological Survey, which aroused considerable attention in the region. Armijo first attempted to apprehend gang members Pantaleon Miera and Santos Benavides in connection with the murder of Potter. The initial search for Miera and Benavides took place with all the required legal procedures. Bernalillo County justice of the peace Jose Candelaria Estrada (whom we know little about) issued a warrant for their arrest. Armijo arrested the men and jailed them temporarily at the home of Constable Pedro Valdez (whom we also know little about). But here all pretenses to legality ended. A group of vigilantes overpowered Miera and Benavides's jailors and hanged the two men from a cottonwood tree. Local residents found their bodies the next morning, "dead and frozen" and still hanging from the tree. A writer for the *Santa Fe New Mexican* reported on this "neck-tie social," noting that Miera especially deserved his fate: "Judge Lynch tried, sentenced and executed him." Given the locale and those involved, White and Mexican-origin people may well have joined in these lynchings.[10]

Sheriff Armijo later learned that Miera had directly participated in the Potter robbery and murder; Miera had also pawned Potter's watch in Albuquerque. Since Miera was dead, Armijo used this evidence to implicate the entire Marino Leyba Gang. He soon arrested three other gang members, Escolástico Perea, Miguel Barrera, and man named California Joe. Under interrogation, Perea gave the names of the others in the gang. He also led Armijo to the location where they had murdered Potter.[11] As with Miera and Benavides, the legal soon gave way to the extralegal. A vigilance committee of 200 men, White and Mexican, broke into the jail, removed the prisoners, and "lynched them into eternity." The *Santa Fe New Mexican* again came to the defense of lynch justice, writing the following:

> Though lynching in general is to be condemned, yet to every case there is an exception. In the instance of the dastardly murder of Charles Potter, it is very doubtful whether justice can be too swiftly meted out. There is a band of outlaws in the neighborhood of Albuquerque which to a man, full deserves the fate which has overtaken their three companions, and while having every respect for law and order, the NEW MEXICAN refrains from saying that the sooner such a fate does overtake them the better will it be for that section of country and New Mexico at large.

In defending lynching, the paper certainly did not have respect for law enforcement, although as noted the news media often aired such sentiments. The examples of Perea, Barrera, and California Joe show again how the legitimate justice system could fall prey to extralegal justice. Moreover, this serves as another example of how Mexican-origin and White people could join forces to engage in mob justice.[12]

A short time later Sheriff Armijo succeeded in capturing Faustino Gutiérrez in connection with the Potter murder. He too made it to jail, but a mob lynched him soon after. A note fixed to Gutiérrez's body identified him as "assassin of Col. Potter" and read "hanged by the 601." According to lynching lore, "601" stood for "six feet under, zero trials, one rope."[13] Armijo dispatched five deputies who finally collared Leyba in March 1881.[14] The territory put him on trial, not for the Potter killing, but for several cases of stock stealing and for the attempted murder of Pat Garrett, whom Leyba had shot at several months before. A Las Vegas jury convicted Leyba and sentenced him to seven years at Leavenworth Penitentiary. He served two years, was transferred to the Penitentiary of New Mexico in Santa Fe, and in 1886 Governor Edmund Ross pardoned him. Leyba had evidently saved the life of the warden, meriting his pardon.[15]

Marino Leyba returned to his criminal activity. He next participated in the murders of Joseph Lackey, a well-regarded sheep rancher, his partner Julian Tessiere, and farmhand Juan Trujillo in early 1887. Leyba and at least two others had evidently confronted Lackey and Trujillo at Lackey's ranch house, robbed and killed them, and then burned their bodies in the house. They shot Tessiere in the back as he fled for his life. Authorities quickly rounded up, tried, and convicted Ricardo Valdez and Porfirio Trujillo, two men in Leyba's group.[16] Local people again proposed founding a vigilance committee in Valencia County. "The organization of a vigilance committee," an anonymous writer to the *Santa Fe New Mexican* opined, "it is thought by many, would afford the desired protection to life and property and cause all bad characters to give this region a wide berth."[17] It is unclear whether they founded this vigilance committee, but the public discussion of such a group demonstrates again how easily talk could turn to mob law even when the legal system worked effectively.

Marino Leyba eluded capture and allegedly vowed that no man would take him alive. Santa Fe County sheriff Frank Chavez dispatched Deputy Sheriffs Joaquin Montoya and Carlos Jacomo (yet more law officers we know little about) who fulfilled this vow.[18] They encountered Leyba at a mountain pass near Golden, New Mexico. Leyba resisted arrest and drew his gun. The sheriffs drew theirs as well and all three men fired. Leyba's bullet skimmed Montoya's head. At least one of the officers' shots hit Leyba in the head, killing him instantly. They brought his body to Santa Fe where Sheriff Chavez allowed a public viewing of Leyba's corpse to demonstrate he was dead. Over 2,000 people chose to see his body.[19]

With Leyba's death the work begun by Perfecto Armijo in eradicating the Marino Leyba Gang came to an end. Armijo no longer held the position of sheriff when Leyba died, and the Santa Fe County Sheriff's Office finished the job. But Armijo had engaged in dogged police work to bring the gang to justice. This case also demonstrates how legal justice could overlap with extralegal justice since so many of the gang died by lynching. Armijo disliked lynching and prevented more than one. It's hard to discern how so many lynchings could have occurred on his watch. Only one thing excuses him: he was in and out of town looking for other members of the gang when the mob hanged Pantaleon Miera, Santos Benavides, Escolástico Perea, Faustino Gutiérrez, Miguel Barrera, and California Joe.

Perfecto Armijo became involved in another major case when a constable named Milton Yarberry murdered two men. Armijo had actually recruited Yarberry to serve as Albuquerque's first town marshal in 1880. In March of 1881, Yarberry killed Harry Brown, the son of John C. Brown, former governor of Tennessee, after the two men exchanged words. He shot Brown four times.[20] The constable stood trial for murder, but the jury acquitted him, and he got his job back.[21] In June of 1881, Yarberry killed again. He shot Charles Campbell for unknown reasons. According to one account, Yarberry and another man had heard a gunshot, had run to a nearby restaurant, and found Campbell walking down the street. Suspecting him of the shooting, Yarberry called out to Campbell who turned as if to shoot. Yarberry opened fire, killing Campbell.[22] Elfego Baca tells a different version of what happened. According to Baca, Yarberry and his colleague had encountered Campbell as described above. Yarberry called for him to halt and Campbell complied. But then Yarberry just shot him dead. As a crowd emerged from the nearby Martinez Saloon, Yarberry exclaimed, "He tried to get me, [but] I got the draw on him."[23]

This police killing would have gone undisputed and forgotten but for the actions of Sheriff Armijo. According to Baca, who was enraged by this murder and followed Yarberry into the saloon to confront him, Armijo entered the saloon and demanded to know "who had killed that man out there." Yarberry responded, "I did, what about it?" Armijo quickly disarmed Yarberry and, according to Baca, picked him up by his collar "just like a cat will a mouse." Armijo placed Yarberry in jail. When a crowd gathered to lynch him, Armijo stepped out, confronted the mob, and convinced them to disperse. A jury found Milton Yarberry guilty of murder. He actually escaped from prison, only to have Santa Fe sheriff Frank Chavez recapture him. Sheriff Armijo expressed some concern about the death sentence Yarberry received—namely, because he would have to carry out the hanging. "There is no one that feels more than I do that Yarberry should not hang," Armijo admitted, "but I have a warrant to hang him and I will execute it."[24] Armijo hanged Yarberry in 1883.[25]

Sheriff Armijo was a well-respected and fair-minded law officer who executed his duties with impartiality and a great sense of responsibility. He won election as sheriff of Bernalillo County from 1879 to 1884.[26] In 1884, however, Armijo got in some trouble when his accounting books didn't add up correctly. Part of his responsibilities as sheriff entailed collecting taxes and fees for licenses. It seems that Armijo failed to properly collect these taxes and fees resulting in a deficit of nearly $5,000. The Bernalillo County Board of Commissioners removed him from office because of these irregularities.[27] Although Armijo ran for sheriff again in 1884, he lost to Santiago Baca.[28] He continued to try to get his accounts in order even after his shrievalty had ended.[29] According to one report, he also accepted a position as a deputy sheriff in Arizona.[30] Oddly enough, despite his collection problems as sheriff, Armijo served as the Bernalillo County assessor beginning in about 1890. According to several newspaper reports, he did a good job.[31]

In 1905 Perfecto Armijo got his job as sheriff back. That year District Attorney Frank Clancy removed Bernalillo County sheriff Thomas Hubbell and two others from their offices for malfeasance. Sheriff Hubbell evidently charged the county for individuals incarcerated in the county jail who had served their sentence and had already been released. He then pocketed that money. Governor Miguel Otero appointed Armijo as sheriff to replace Hubbell.[32] In an interesting bit of political intrigue, Hubbell refused to step down and turn his office over to Armijo, so Sheriff Armijo established a separate sheriff's office and even a second jail. The county eventually had to have Hubbell arrested for refusing to vacate his office; Armijo had to break down the door to the jail with an axe and sledgehammer to take possession of the facility![33] Hubbell appealed his termination up to the New Mexico Territorial Supreme Court and won. In late 1906 the court declared that Governor Otero had exceeded his authority in removing Hubbell and replacing him with Armijo. Hubbell's original term expired two days after the supreme court ruling and a new election was already underway.[34]

Armijo had already announced his candidacy for sheriff for the 1906 election.[35] He won, beating Hubbell by a wide margin.[36] He served his term and retired in 1909. Sheriff Jesus Romero replaced Armijo.[37] Perfecto Armijo died at the age of 68 in September of 1913.[38] His passing was deeply felt in the territory. *La Revista Popular de Nuevo Mexico* noted that his "muerte ha sido lamentado en todo el estado." (death has been regretted across the state.)[39]

Perfecto Armijo had a long, eventful, and distinguished career. He had a relatively simple philosophy: work hard with fairness and equanimity. The fact that he could serve for so many years, handle so many hardened criminals, and do so without a sidearm remains a testament to his legacy. He preferred to use his words, soothing dangerous situations, such as the lynch mob that gathered to kill Milton Yarberry, with diplomacy. It is no wonder that so many Mexican American law officers, especially Elfego Baca, found Armijo's example valuable.

Elfego Baca's career was as extensive and distinguished as Perfecto Armijo's. Similar to Jose Chavez y Chavez, discussed below, Baca went from outlaw to law officer. Unlike Chavez y Chavez, Baca served with distinction. He was born in Socorro, New Mexico, in February 1865. He had an interesting childhood. When he was an infant, Navajo people captured and held him for several days. After they returned him to his parents, Francisco and Juanita, the family moved to Topeka, Kansas. Juanita died in 1872 and Elfego returned to New Mexico in 1880. He worked for a number of years on his grandfather's ranch. Francisco returned to the territory in about 1881 and settled in Belen. A short time later, he became the town marshal of Belen. As such, Baca's father became the first example of a conscientious law enforcement official the young Elfego would come to know.[40]

Like other parts of the New Mexico Territory, Belen was a rowdy town. Marshal Baca soon got down to the difficult business of bringing law and order to the region. The Mexican-origin community welcomed his efforts. They had come to detest the violence and racism they experienced at the hands of yet another group of Texas Cowboys. Baca ran afoul of some of those Cowboys and their employers, who took umbrage at his efforts. Several Cowboys from the nearby village of Los Lunas confronted Marshal Baca in October 1881. That confrontation led to gunfire. Baca walked away unscathed; two White Cowboys died at the scene. While it appears he acted in self-defense, Marshal Baca was arrested for murder. As author Frank Ross observed, "Francisco had not started the fight; he was the local peace officer; he was being shot at with intent to kill—nevertheless, he was a 'Mexican' who had killed two 'White' men."[41]

Elfego was outraged. He quickly left for Los Lunas with a friend named "Chavez." They arrived at the beginning of the feast of Saint Teresa celebration, which meant that security at the courthouse would probably be lax. The jail that held his father was located on the ground floor of the court building. On the night of October 15, Baca and Chavez snuck into the jury deliberation room located on the second floor above the jail. They speedily cut a hole in the floor and helped Francisco escape. They secreted him to Mexico and Elfego returned to Socorro.[42]

Elfego Baca at this point could easily be dismissed as simply another outlaw who committed a jailbreak. But he knew the work his father had done as town marshal mattered and that his arrest was a farce. He believed his father deserved better. Moreover, he assumed his father would probably not get a fair trial. Many people suspected Elfego had broken Francisco out of jail, but no one could prove it.[43] At about the same time, Baca started riding with

Billy the Kid. This and the jailbreak contributed to the perception that Baca was a bandit. Elfego and Billy became friends and rode together for several months.[44] Baca learned some important lessons about frontier justice with Billy. On a bright moonlit night in 1881, Billy and Elfego were lounging against a telegraph pole near the Martinez Saloon in Albuquerque when they witnessed Constable Milton Yarberry murder Charles Campbell. Baca actually thought about intervening and had drawn his gun, but then he saw Sheriff Perfecto Armijo walk into the saloon and quickly arrest Yarberry.[45]

This event began Baca's transition from bandit to law enforcement officer. Now he had two examples of conscientious law enforcement officers, his father and Perfecto Armijo. Like other Mexican Americans, Baca valued and respected Armijo's service as sheriff. Moreover, as someone who witnessed the senseless murder of Campbell, Baca appreciated that Armijo not only did his duty and did it quickly but also that he continued to do his duty in a surely uncomfortable situation when he executed Milton Yarberry. It seems clear that Perfecto Armijo's example inspired Baca in much the same way that he found inspiration from his father.

After the incident in Albuquerque, Billy the Kid and Baca parted ways. Baca drifted around before he eventually returned to Socorro in about 1884. After working for a local merchant, he took his first job in law enforcement, electioneering for Socorro sheriff Pete Simpson as he ran for reelection. At the same time, Baca also met another Mexican American law enforcement official, Deputy Sheriff Pedro Saracino. He hailed from Lower San Francisco Plaza (Frisco for short and today called Reserve) in western New Mexico. This village had three distinct plazas—Lower, Middle, and Upper Frisco—all along the San Francisco River.[46] Deputy Sheriff Saracino confided in Baca about some of the difficulties he had as a law officer. Much like Marshal Francisco Baca, Deputy Sheriff Saracino encountered a violent and unwelcoming White population and an abused Mexican-origin population. John Slaughter, a wealthy Texas cattleman who had bought large tracts of land in western New Mexico, employed a large group of Texas Cowboys in the Frisco area. As elsewhere, these Cowboys drank heavily, frequently shot up the town, and made it a sport to abuse the Mexican population. To borrow the words of Baca biographer Kyle Crichton, "the Slaughter outfit, in short, was a law unto itself."[47]

These abuses stood in stark contrast to everything Baca had come to understand about law enforcement. He called the Cowboys in Frisco "a notorious lynching gang." "This gang was hanging all the mexicans they could," he noted.[48] Even worse, Deputy Sheriff Saracino told Baca about an instance of brutality against an intellectually disabled Mexican youth. According to Saracino, a group of Texas Cowboys had accosted the youth, known only as "El Burro," in a bar. They roped this young man, tied him down to the bar, and, in Baca's words, "one of the boys sat on his chest and arms and the other on his lap and that right there and then poor Burro was alterated in the presence of everybody."[49] Baca went on to explain what he meant by "alterated": "they castrated him."[50] Another Mexican American man, Epitacio Martinez, attempted to aid El Burro. "The result," Baca explained, "was that after they finished with Burro, the same Cowboys got hold of Epitacio Martinez and measured about twenty or thirty steps from where they were and tied him [up]. They then used Epitacio as a target and they betted the drinks on who was a better shooter. Martinez was shot four different times." Despite being severely wounded, Martinez lived through this encounter, as did El Burro.[51]

Baca was outraged at these injustices and questioned Deputy Sheriff Saracino's commitment to law enforcement. "You should be over in Frisco," Baca told Saracino. "No, no. Not me," Saracino replied, "I want to live." "So do the people on the Frisco!" retorted Baca, "they want to live in peace. And you're the peace officer!" Then Saracino allegedly made what might seem a strange offer: "You are welcome to my badge—if you think you can do better," he said. Baca's response was simple: "Hand it here. Now I am the deputy."[52] While it remains unclear how Baca became a lawman (some accounts agree with this one, some suggest Sheriff Simpson made him a deputy, others note that Saracino returned to Frisco with Baca and that upon arriving made him a deputy, while another account suggests Baca got his badge out of a mail order catalog),[53] Baca left for Frisco on a mission to bring justice to this small town. "I went up there and pacified them," he explained, "I made them understand that I was afraid of no one."[54]

His visit to Frisco would leave an indelible mark on Baca's life and southwestern history more broadly. Upon arriving in Frisco, he immediately set out to apprehend who had castrated El Burro and shot Epitacio Martinez. A day or so later, Baca met another Mexican American official, Justice of the Peace Lopez (first name unknown).[55] While Baca was conversing with Lopez, some of the Texas Cowboys road into town. One individual, Charles McCarty (sometimes McCarthy), road his horse up and down the street shooting wildly.[56] He also clubbed a man "on the head two or three times."[57] Baca demanded that Lopez intervene, but he refused, saying that Slaughter employed 150 men and that he could not stop them. A disgusted Deputy Sheriff Baca decided to arrest McCarty himself. When he approached McCarty, he shot Baca's hat off, but Baca quickly subdued McCarty and took him into custody.[58]

McCarty's arrest sent the Texas Cowboys into a rage. They decided they would teach Baca something about "justice." That night eight Cowboys rode into town and descended upon the home of Pedro Saracino, where Baca was staying. Perry Perham, the foreman of the Slaughter Ranch, led the group. He demanded that Baca release McCarty. Baca refused. Perham then launched into an expletive-filled tirade against Mexican-origin people in general and Elfego Baca in particular. Baca stood his ground and told Perham, "I'm a peace officer. I'll give you and your pack up to the count of three to get out of here."[59] The Cowboys seemed perplexed, but Baca was serious. He had at some point in his life adopted this credo: "Never say you are to do something unless you intend to do it."[60] And so he began counting.

When Baca got to "three" he drew his revolver and opened fire. He shot one Cowboy named Tabe Allen in the knee. The gunfire also startled Perry Perham's horse, which reared back and fell on its rider, killing Perham. The Cowboys made a hasty retreat. Word of this incident spread quickly. For the Mexican-origin community, Baca's actions prompted both fear and respect. The Texas Cowboys had weapons that could easily outmatch the arms that local people possessed. Moreover, the Cowboys had shown little compunction about using violence. But Mexican-origin people also had a good understanding of what law and order should look like, and Elfego Baca represented a more genuine version of law enforcement to them. Baca knew his actions would probably cause him no small amount of trouble and could easily end up harming other people in Frisco. When several townsfolk came to him, Baca instructed them to gather villagers into the church for safety, which they did.[61]

For the Texas Cowboys, Baca's actions prompted both anger and a sense of caution. A large cohort of Cowboys talked about taking action and putting Baca in his place. Some could not fathom that he had acted alone. One of the Cowboys, James Cook, later wrote about these events. He and other Cowboys had received word that "the Mexicans had gone on the warpath" and that *they* "had killed one of Mr. Slaughter's cowboys and were going to try to wipe out all the Americans living near their settlement." Cook also noted that the Cowboys formed what he called a "committee" to defend "the Americans living near the Mexican settlement."[62] Cook's words serve as a reminder that White people continued to view vigilance committees as a legitimate form of justice, one that superseded the authority of Deputy Sheriff Baca or any other law enforcement official. Cook's account was also wholly fictional, the type of fiction that led to countless deaths in communities of color across the United

States. Thankfully cooler heads prevailed. Several of the Cowboys decided to seek the aid of Justice of the Peace Ted White. Despite the fact that White had no jurisdiction in Frisco (he was from neighboring Grant County), the Cowboys convinced him to order Baca to present Charles McCarty for trial.[63]

Baca and a friend named Francisco Naranjo delivered McCarty to the justice of the peace's office in Upper Frisco as ordered. Upon his arrival Baca encountered a group of nearly one hundred angry Cowboys. One took a pot-shot at Baca, but the bullet missed. Baca boldly marched McCarty through this group of men and into the justice of the peace's office. Ted White quickly began the trial, charging McCarty with assault, assault with a deadly weapon, and resisting arrest. After a few minutes of testimony, mainly from Baca himself, White found McCarty guilty of all charges. He assessed McCarty's penalty at a ridiculously light five-dollar fine. McCarty paid his fine and walked out of the building a free man. Baca was incensed. He had not secured his prisoner, nor had he gone through the trouble of confronting the eight Cowboys who came to Saracino's home the night before, nor had he marched his prisoner over dangerous territory to trial to see it all end in a manner that seemed unjust. "But justice," as writer Clee Woods put it, "still blindly tipped the scales in favor of the *Americanos*."[64]

While the Texas Cowboys celebrated in a local bar, Baca walked to the nearby jacal (a common dwelling composed of upright poles daubed together with adobe) of an acquaintance named Geronimo Armijo. While he conversed with Armijo a mob of around eighty Texas Cowboys gathered outside of the jacal. Baca quickly ushered Armijo's family out the back door and to safety. A Cowboy named Bert Hearne had taken charge of the group and shouted for Baca to come out. Baca refused. "I'll get this dirty little Mexican out of there," Hearne stated as he approached the front door, which he kicked twice.[65] Baca retorted with two shots. Hearne, mortally wounded, staggered back saying, "Boys, I'm killed."[66] The Cowboys opened fire on the jacal.

According to Elfego Baca this first fusillade lasted thirty minutes. When it stopped, several Cowboys approached the jacal again in an attempt to see whether they had killed Baca. He fired several shots to let them know he still lived. This process continued throughout the remainder of the day and into the night. At one point, Baca lit a fire and cooked a breakfast of beef, homemade tortillas, and coffee, which he somehow prepared while the shooting continued. Sometime after midnight, the Texas Cowboys tossed a bundle of dynamite at the house, which shattered one side of the jacal and started a fire. Baca once again retorted with shots of his own. The back and forth shooting continued throughout the night and until early the next morning.[67]

News of the shoot-out spread quickly, and Deputy Sheriff Frank Ross from Socorro arrived in Frisco to try to end the violence. Francisco Naranjo accompanied Ross. They approached the jacal with their hands up. Baca knew Ross through the election work he had done for Socorro sheriff Pete Simpson, and he knew Naranjo since his arrival in Frisco. The three spoke for some time before coming to an agreement. Ross promised that the Cowboys would disperse and that he would protect Baca, but he said that he would also have to arrest Baca for the deaths of Perham and Hearne and take him to the jail in Socorro. Baca reluctantly agreed to these terms but added several of his own: First, he would not disarm. Second, he would not be bound or handcuffed. Third, Baca would travel behind, following Ross and any others who went to Socorro. Ross agreed to Baca's terms. As it turned out, six of the Texas Cowboys chose to travel with Ross and Baca. These men acted as "guards," although they rode, per Baca's terms, about thirty paces ahead of Baca and Ross. This way, Baca could guard those who guarded him.[68]

According to one of the Cowboys, Baca's trepidation had merit. Alfred Hardcastle reported that after Baca had shot Hearne, the Cowboys had removed his body to a bar. There, a group of White men initiated a makeshift inquest. They elected a court clerk, judge, formed a jury, elected Hardcastle as jury foreman, and elected the bartender as coroner. This kangaroo court found Baca guilty of first-degree murder and sentenced him to death. Here we see yet again the way extralegal justice frequently operated in the Southwest: improvised, unofficial, and designed to punish Mexican Americans. Baca surely worried that his captors might kill him, in effect carrying out the death sentence of this phony court.[69]

The Frisco shoot-out went on for over thirty hours. The Cowboys fired an estimated 4,000 rounds into the jacal; the front door alone had 400 bullet holes in it. Baca killed one man that night and wounded nearly a dozen Texas Cowboys. He emerged from the jacal unharmed. Baca survived because the house had a sunken floor, allowing him safe cover as the bullets flew harmlessly overhead (which explains how he was able to cook breakfast). The event cemented his legacy as a no-nonsense lawman and badass. Of course, El Burro, Epitacio Martinez, and the other Mexican-origin people terrorized by the Texas Cowboys got lost in the sensationalism of these events; they probably never got their justice. But Baca did. Ross successfully delivered him to the newly constructed Socorro County Jail. The district attorney charged Baca with first-degree murder for the killing of Perry Perham. His attorney requested and received a change of venue to Albuquerque. They transferred Baca to the Old Town Jail (Baca would later serve as jailor of this same calaboose). At

Stars & Shields

trial the jury found him not guilty. The trial for the killing of Bert Hearne took place in Socorro a few weeks later. The jury once again found Baca not guilty.[70]

The Frisco shoot-out reveals a great deal about the nature of justice in the Southwest. First, the presence of Mexican American law enforcement officials demonstrates one of the ways Mexican-origin people fought for law and order. The Mexican-origin community and more specifically individuals such as Elfego Baca and Pedro Saracino demanded equal rights for all and a fair criminal justice system. Saracino returned to Frisco vowing never to let White people intimidate him again, and as one author asserted after these events, "There are no further reports of atrocities against Hispanics in western Socorro County."[71] Second, numerous authors have described a cowed and cowardly Mexican community in Frisco, a perspective that magnifies Elfego Baca's bravery.[72] Certainly they were scared, but they did not leave the fight solely to Baca. Writer Clee Woods noted that "some defiant men got out old guns [and] worked over their mechanisms" to assist Baca.[73] When the Frisco shoot-out took place, historian Marshall Trimble observed, "Citizens [Mexican Americans] gathered to cheer him [Baca] on."[74] James Cook acknowledged that a large group of armed Mexican-origin people had gathered in the Frisco foothills to aid Baca if necessary.[75] A group of Mexican Americans also travelled to Socorro to secure aid for Baca. This party convinced Deputy Sheriff Frank Ross to come to Frisco to end the conflict.[76] As such, the Mexican-origin community, hardly cowardly, actively participated in these events. Third, the ever-present vigilance committee, such as the one described by James Cook, or the kangaroo inquest detailed by Alfred Hardcastle show again how Whites manipulated the concept of criminal justice. In these instances, their version of law and order failed, but in numerous other instances this type of "law enforcement" often prevailed, with deadly results. Last, Elfego Baca prevailed in court, twice.

Elfego Baca continued to work in criminal justice and held multiple jobs in the justice system. In 1886 he relocated to Albuquerque and became the city jailor at the Old Town Jail, the same facility that held him during the Hearne trial. Even as jailor, Baca continued to defend the Mexican-origin community. For example, he had noticed an interesting pattern in arrests at night; law officers would arrest Mexican people for drunkenness and the judge, William Heacock, would fine the arrestees the exact amount of money they had in their possession. To put it differently, while a standard fine for drunkenness existed, Heacock based his fines on the amount of cash the person had, for the profit of the city. When Baca witnessed Albuquerque town marshal Eugene Henry arrest Jesus Romero, an acquaintance of his, for drunk and disorderly conduct,

Elfego Baca (*right*) with another man identified only as John, in the Manzano National Forest outside of Albuquerque in 1907.
At this time, Baca worked as an attorney in New Mexico.
Goddard Collection of Elfego Baca Papers, Center for Southwest Research and Special Collections, University of New Mexico Libraries, Albuquerque, 2 #1F31.

he intervened. He approached Henry and asked him to release Romero. Henry refused and the two men got in a scuffle. Baca knocked Henry unconscious and a large crowd assisted another officer in arresting Baca. And then Baca appeared before Judge Heacock, who charged him with drunk and disorderly conduct and gave him the choice of a thirty-day jail sentence or a fine that, unsurprisingly, totaled the exact dollar amount Baca had in his possession when arrested. He chose to spend the thirty days in jail, at the Old Town Jail, where he of course served as jailor. It would seem that only Elfego Baca could jail Elfego Baca.[77]

Baca's arrest exposed Heacock's actions, which ceased afterward. He served his time and continued to work in the jail. After his service as jailor, Baca returned to Socorro and began a short stint as a U.S. deputy marshal beginning in 1891. He won election as county clerk in 1893, a position he held for four years. Baca also served as mayor of Socorro from 1896 to 1898. He began a different phase of his work in the criminal justice field when he became an attorney. In 1894 he passed the bar exam and practiced law as a criminal defense attorney for decades. He parlayed these various jobs into other political ventures, from district attorney and mayor to superintendent of the Socorro school district in 1900. He was also appointed district attorney of Socorro and Sierra Counties in 1900 and again in 1905. He also founded the Baca Detective Agency in the 1920s, a business he ran for over a decade.[78]

Baca also continued to support those Mexicans and Mexican Americans who came to him in need. For instance, a cousin named Conrado Baca approached Elfego shortly after the affair in Frisco regarding trouble he had with White miners in the mining town of Kelly. These miners and cowboys had forced Conrado out of his store. Elfego agreed to help and travelled to Kelly. He went to the store and told the White men who had seized the business to leave. They left.[79]

Residents of Socorro County elected Baca as sheriff in 1919. His understanding of policing remained as unorthodox as always. For example, he famously used people incarcerated in the county jail to do some of his police work. In one instance, he tasked a prisoner with apprehending a fugitive. The man left the jail and returned with the fugitive. Baca also wrote infamous arrest warrants, which went out as a form letter: "Dear Sir, I have a warrant here for your arrest. Please come by and give yourself up. If you don't, I'll know that you intend to resist arrest, and I will feel justified in shooting you on sight when I come after you. Yours truly, Elfego Baca, sheriff." According to most accounts, everyone who received such a letter turned themselves in.[80]

Despite his unorthodox approach to law enforcement, Sheriff Baca not only understood the law but he also enforced it with equability. For example, he arrested a murder suspect named Jose Garcia in 1919. Garcia had allegedly killed a man and kidnapped his wife, whom he had also later murdered. Sheriff Baca arrested Garcia near the Kewa Pueblo, but as he prepared to transport the prisoner to Socorro, a large crowd appeared yelling "we want Garcia," "asesino" (murderer), and "lynch him!" As someone who had witnessed lynching done by White Americans, Baca refused to turn Garcia over to the mob, although this example again demonstrates that Mexican Americans could advocate lynch justice. He delivered Garcia to the Socorro County Jail.[81]

Sheriff Baca also broke up the Manzano Gang in 1919–20. This group had engaged in a variety of crimes, from petty theft to horse stealing in Socorro and Torrance Counties. They also murdered Abran Contreras. He owned a store in a town called Scholle (today Contreras). In November of 1919, two masked men broke into Contreras's home in an attempt to rob him, and when he resisted they shot him. Contreras died a short time later from his injuries.[82]

Baca set out to apprehend the killers. Suspicion fell on the Manzano Gang and Baca quickly arrested the first of six gang members: a youth named Pancrasio Saiz. Sheriff Baca probed Saiz for information about the other gang members. He divulged that almost all the gang hailed from either the Saiz family or the Padilla family. So Baca rode to the home of Saiz's father-in-law, Lazaro Cordova, and intimidated him to get information about the location of the other gang members. While Cordova evidently gave up little information about the gang, Baca learned that some of the men may have holed up near La Joya. He set out for La Joya and along the way encountered and arrested the other gang members, including Jose de Jesus Padilla, Luciano Padilla, Pedro Saiz, Antonio Saiz, and Emilio Peña.[83] After interviewing the gang, Baca determined that Pedro Saiz and Jose de Jesus Padilla had murdered Contreras. At trial their jury found them guilty of second-degree murder and the judge sentenced them to life in prison. The Torrance County court convicted the other four men of second-degree murder, and they received thirty-year jail sentences.[84]

Breaking up the Manzano Gang was one of Baca's triumphs as sheriff. It serves as a great example of Baca's dogged police work. He went out, gathered information, and found the gang members. While intimidating Lazaro Cordova for information would not be condoned today, as Baca noted, "To make a good sheriff you have to be a little bad, then you understand the people you have to arrest." He made a similar statement about being a jailor: "If you want a good jailor, you have to get someone who has been in jail once. He knows the ins and outs then."[85]

Baca considered running for governor in 1928. A number of newspaper editorial boards endorsed him before he even announced his candidacy. *La Opinion Publica* called Baca a "hardworking, altruistic, and diplomatic" individual with "deep wisdom" who would make a "splendid figure in the executive's chair in Santa Fe."[86] Baca's potential candidacy got a boost when he got into a fight with Alfredo "Fred" Otero, an acquaintance of Baca's and a rising political figure, in the lobby of an Albuquerque hotel. Otero had stated that "there wasn't a Spanish-American with the bones and brains to be governor of the state," to which Baca took offense. According to numerous accounts, Baca walked into the hotel and demanded that Otero rise from his chair because Baca was "going to lick" him. When Otero complied, Baca punched or slapped him, knocking off his hat. Hotel staff quickly intervened and ordered the two men outside where the fight continued. Baca landed two or three good blows to Otero's jaw before Police Detective Romulo Salazar (whom we know little about) intervened. He was fined fifteen dollars for the assault. Baca ultimately declined to run for governor.[87]

Shortly after his attempt to run for governor, Baca did run for district attorney in Socorro County. He put together a detailed platform that emphasized his work in law enforcement (and that downplayed or ignored the instances where he broke the law).[88] He lost this election, but it seems to have reignited his popularity. He toured the Southwest and spoke to numerous audiences about his exploits.[89] This popularity ultimately attracted a number of media outlets that wanted to tell Baca's story on film or on television. The Walt Disney Company won the story, and several years after his death it produced a miniseries called *The Nine Lives of Elfego Baca*.[90]

Baca also frequently spoke to police groups after his retirement. He often gave sage and meaningful advice. At the 1932 annual banquet of the New Mexico Sheriffs and Peace Officers Association, for instance, he counseled against heavy-handed law enforcement. Baca noted that he had never killed anyone as a lawman, a ludicrous statement but according to him, "all my killings were before I was an officer" (he seems to mean that he didn't kill anyone as sheriff). He also more accurately claimed that he rarely drew his weapon as an elected sheriff. He called the "use of a gun in making arrests . . . the mark of an amateur." Somewhat contradictorily, Baca stated that officers should "shoot first if the other party shows signs of resorting to 'Judge Colt' for a decision." He also mentioned his creativity as a sheriff and a jailor, recalling how he sent the prisoner to apprehend the fugitive. "I was criticized once for sending one prisoner to catch another, but the idea worked, all the same." Baca also remembered the existence of vigilance committees. "People had to go around in a committee," he noted, "until they found some fellow who didn't care when he died, and make him sheriff."[91]

The archival record contains many interesting documents about Elfego Baca. One of the more curious items was a paniological (a now defunct "science" analyzing patterns in the hand) study conducted by Guy Franklin Kelsey in 1939. In grandiose terms, Kelsey detailed the meaning of a handprint of Baca's right hand. This print, according to Kelsey, showed that Baca "had more courage than should be allotted to one man." Kelsey also pondered over the "Line of Mentality, or Head Line" and the "Life Line" on Baca's hand. These lines demonstrated Baca's "dramatic ability . . . whether he was exercising this dramatic ability when he was being tried for murder as a young man or later when he became a dramatic, compelling figure before a jury," Kelsey wrote.[92] In a follow up correspondence, Baca asked a question about what his hand showed about his enemies. "You asked about your enemies; your hand shows that you had plenty but now they don't register enough to show on the hand," Kelsey replied. Thus, despite his numerous encounters with death and danger, these events barely impacted him.[93]

Elfego Baca had a long career in the field of criminal justice. His no-nonsense police work worked. Baca did not shy away from violence, much of which would be unacceptable today, but as he noted, "I never wanted to kill anybody, but if a man had it in his mind to kill me, I made it my business to get him first."[94] He continued to make history after his death in 1945. When construction workers building a new federal building in Albuquerque unearthed a rusty .45 Colt in 1958, suspicion quickly mounted that the gun belonged to Baca. After cleaning the weapon, local historians discovered the initials "E. B." scratched into the barrel of the weapon. It "undoubtedly belonged to Elfego Baca, fabulous character of New Mexico's early days."[95] Fabulous character indeed, but he was not the only one.

New Mexico's Jose Chavez y Chavez, another fabulous character like Baca, also came to law enforcement in an unorthodox manner. Chavez y Chavez serves as one of the curious cases of a law officer who was also a bandit. He also provides a good example of a Mexican American law officer who did not distinguish himself in his police work. Chavez y Chavez, a compatriot of Billy the Kid, participated in two conflicts in Lincoln County, New Mexico, the Horrell War (often considered the first Lincoln County War) and the Lincoln County War (actor Lou Diamond Phillips portrayed him in the two *Young Guns* films). This contributed to his image as a bandit. But he also had several early forays into law enforcement: in 1873 when New Mexico governor Marsh Giddings appointed him to the Mexican Posse led by Juan B. Patrón, in 1878 when he joined the Lincoln County Regulators, and in 1879 as a part of Governor Lew Wallace's Lincoln County Mounted Rifles militia. The Mexican Posse came in response to the Horrell War, while the Regulators and the Mounted Rifles came in response to the Lincoln County War.[96]

Governor Giddings formed the Mexican Posse in 1873 in an attempt to halt violence in Lincoln County. The governor and many Mexican-origin people in the area had grown weary of a group of Texas Cowboys, especially brothers Tom, Ben, Merritt, Martin, and Samuel Horrell, who stole the property of Mexican Americans and killed several people, including at least two law officers.[97] The most egregious example of this came when Ben Horrell murdered Lincoln constable Juan Martínez (whom we know little about), a well-regarded Mexican American officer.[98] The resulting battles between the Mexican Posse and the Texas Cowboys were incredibly violent. The posse typically operated by riding into town, heavily armed, and parading as a display of power. They would then disarm the Cowboys. In late 1873 in Lincoln the Cowboys resisted. A firefight ensued and the Mexican Posse killed three Texas Cowboys. According to historian Donald Cline, the posse shot one man "nine times, his body dragged to a nearby stream and tossed in." One member of the Mexican Posse died in this battle.[99] The following day the Texas Cowboys murdered two Mexican-origin people not affiliated with the posse. These back and forth killings occurred regularly over the next year. In another example of this violence, a group of Cowboys raided the home of a Mexican family having a party. They killed four men and wounded two women. The Mexican Posse retaliated by burning the Horrell ranch to the ground and killing hundreds of their cattle. The Horrells fled New Mexico, ending the violence.[100]

Chavez y Chavez held several positions after the Horrell War had ended. In September of 1874 Lincoln County residents elected him constable.[101] In 1875 he won election as a justice of the peace in Lincoln County. He lost this position a year later when county officials revised the number of precincts in the county, which eliminated Chavez y Chavez's precinct. As a possible recompense for his loss of position, the county appointed him constable in San Patricio for two years. He also served as a deputy sheriff in San Patricio.[102]

When Lincoln County erupted in violence again after the murder of John Tunstall in 1878, Chavez y Chavez joined the Lincoln County Regulators. James Dolan, a business rival of Tunstall, allegedly had him killed. Justice of the Peace John Wilson deputized the Regulators, making them a legitimate law enforcement group in the territory. But in truth they executed their authority by, well, executing the individuals they deemed responsible for Tunstall's murder.[103] In 1879, Governor Lew Wallace formed the Lincoln County Mounted Rifles to halt this violence. Chavez y Chavez enlisted as a private. As such, Chavez y Chavez served on two law enforcement groups trying to end the Lincoln County War. But the Mounted Rifles evidently accomplished little, and the governor disbanded the group early the next year.[104]

Jose Chavez y Chavez's specific role in the Mexican Posse and the Mounted Rifles remains hard to discern, as is much of his law enforcement work that preceded the violence in Lincoln County. After the Lincoln County War in about 1881 or 1882, he moved to Las Vegas and became a San Miguel County deputy sheriff. It is unclear how Chavez y Chavez achieved this position; in one story he bested Bob Ford (who killed Jesse James) in a duel and won his badge in the process. But he likely got his star the way others did; he went into town and asked for it. It would also seem likely that his reputation with a pistol and previous law enforcement work had earned him a modicum of respect among local people.[105]

His police work in Las Vegas seemed uneventful, until he crossed paths with Las Gorras Blancas (the White Caps). Las Gorras Blancas actively opposed unlawful land acquisition and speculation in New Mexico (discussed more fully in chapter 5). Seeing the way the White Caps defended the Mexican-origin community, Chavez y Chavez joined the group. As such, he served as a law officer while simultaneously working with a group that operated as a type of extralegal law enforcement. To further muddy the waters, he also joined La Sociedad de Bandidos (Society of Bandits). So Chavez y Chavez was a lawman, a "lawman," and a bandit all at the same time.[106]

Vicente Silva, a notable political figure and criminal boss in San Miguel County, had formed La Sociedad de Bandidos and possibly Las Gorras Blancas.[107] He headed La Sociedad, a group of about forty men who ranged from outlaws to landowners to politicians. Silva also owned a saloon and rustled cattle and sheep. He relied on Chavez y Chavez and the other Las Vegas deputy sheriffs, Julian Trujillo and Eugenio Alarid, to supply him with information. Events came to a head in 1892 with a shake-up in the local political structure in Las Vegas and in La Sociedad de Bandidos. The society had broken into two factions, and some members of the original group became angry when a rancher named Patricio Maes left the organization. Fearing he might give away society secrets, the Las Vegas deputy sheriffs arrested Maes. They soon discovered that he would, if called to do so, testify against Silva and expose the inner workings of La Sociedad. The deputies relayed this information to Silva.[108]

Vicente Silva and a group of his confederates decided to put Patricio Maes on trial. The Las Vegas officers delivered Maes to Silva's tavern, where he convened a kangaroo court. That "court" found Maes guilty of treason against the Society of Bandits. They sentenced him to death. Because the famous "hanging" windmill had already been removed, they hanged Maes from a nearby bridge. The hanging went badly, though: the rope broke or came untied and Maes fell to the icy river below. The mob had to hang him a second time. Here we can see again how Mexican Americans occasionally engaged in lynching. However, this lynching did not end well for the deputy sheriffs, who according to most accounts had supplied information to Silva that led to Maes's death and possibly participated in his murder. The next morning, Chavez y Chavez and the other sheriffs investigated the lynching. They recorded "that the person of Patricio Maes had come to his death by strangulation at hands of person or persons unknown."[109]

Here the situation began to spin out of control. Silva became desperate to uncover other defectors like Patricio Maes. Strangely, his suspicions soon turned to his own wife, Telesfora, and her brother, Gabriel Sandoval. With the help of Deputy Sheriffs Jose Chavez y Chavez and Julian Trujillo, Silva lured Sandoval to a meeting in February of 1893. Shortly after this meeting began, Silva stabbed Sandoval to death. Silva and the deputy sheriffs dumped his body in a cesspool. Silva then began making plans to murder his wife. Chavez y Chavez, Trujillo, and Alarid, however, had begun to seriously question Silva's sanity. In May of 1893, Silva tricked his wife into coming to a meeting with the now deceased Sandoval. Instead of Sandoval, Telesfora found herself ambushed by her own husband. Silva stabbed her to death too. He and the group of deputies dumped her body in a ravine. The Mexican American law officers had already decided to act against Silva, and they tasked another man named Jose Valdez to kill him. Valdez shot Silva in the head after they had disposed of Telesfora in the ravine. They then dumped his body in the ravine next to his wife.[110]

The role of the deputy sheriffs in these crimes soon came to light and they all fled. Authorities quickly arrested Trujillo and Alarid. Chavez y Chavez managed to stay on the loose for several months.[111] Police found him tending sheep in south Socorro County in 1895.[112] The territory put Chavez y Chavez on trial for the murder of Gabriel Sandoval in 1896. The jury convicted him and sentenced him to death, but Chavez y Chavez successfully appealed and had the judgement overturned. The territory tried him once more, again found him guilty, and sentenced him to death in 1897. Governor Miguel Otero commuted that sentence to life in prison a short time later, more than likely because Chavez y Chavez had not actually murdered Sandoval but rather was an accessory to this murder. Interestingly, Governor George Curry paroled him in 1909 because he had assisted prison guards during a riot. He lived the rest of his life quietly and died in 1923.[113]

Jose Chavez y Chavez had a rather mixed record as a law officer. The fact that he basically lived most of his life as both an outlaw and an officer might seem unusual, but in the borderlands at this time such things were not uncommon. Chavez y Chavez blurred the line between the two fairly effectively given that much of the time when he ran with Billy the Kid he also served as a deputized member of two law enforcement bodies. And it would seem he did both jobs well until he moved to Las Vegas. There he used his position and power improperly, not only running afoul of the law but also of the people he had sworn to protect.

Other Mexican Americans worked in different aspects of the criminal justice system in New Mexico. A case involving Joseph Ancheta offers a good example. Ancheta, a rising political star in Doña Ana County in the late 1880s, had won election as district attorney in 1886 and to the territorial legislature in 1889. In 1891, Ancheta attended a meeting with two wealthy territorial politicians, Thomas B. Catron and Elias Stover. An unknown assailant, or assailants, fired into Catron's office where the meeting took place. Ancheta was hit in the back with buckshot, the only one wounded in the attack. The shooting exposed an unusual web of conspiracy and political intrigue that, in part, revealed the workings of the Santa Fe Ring.[114]

The territory launched a major investigation into the shooting and offered reward money of up to $10,000 (a massive sum equivalent to over $321,000 in 2022). The legislature also authorized a $10,000 budget for the apprehension of the guilty party.[115] Governor L. Bradford Prince engaged state law enforcement and also hired investigators from the Pinkerton National Detective Agency. The agency dispatched Charles Leon, "one of our oldest Opts." James McParland from the Pinkerton Denver office wrote, "He is conversant with Mexican habits and, while he does not speak the language very fluently, he understands it enough to carry on conversation with any Mexican." It seems that despite the limited amount of evidence, then, suspicion fell on the Mexican-origin community.[116]

The New Mexico government seemed interested primarily in using the shooting as a pretext to undo Las Gorras Blancas, which perhaps explains why they focused on a Mexican or Mexican American suspect. Operative Leon quickly connected Ancheta's shooting to "the White Cap crowd," signaling this supposed link between Las Gorras Blancas and the Ancheta shooters.[117] Law enforcement began to focus on two rather convenient suspects: two "heavily armed" Mexican men who had passed through Gallup at around the time of the shooting.[118] Another detective, the famous Charles Siringo, floated an alternative theory that the target of the shooting had actually been Catron, not Ancheta, by Democrats "with a view of getting Catron out of the way." Catron, a Republican and a prominent member of the Santa Fe Ring, had angered a number of rivals, so having him "out of the way" made sense.[119] Of all the theories, Siringo's was the most credible. Thus, the shooting had nothing to do with the White Caps. Siringo also concluded that Santa Fe sheriff Frank Chavez had organized the shooting.[120] A year later someone assassinated Chavez. The territorial government then sought the apprehension of Chavez's killer.[121] Authorities surmised that the Borrego Gang killed Sheriff

Chavez. The sheriff had allegedly arrested and beaten Francisco Gonzalez y Borrego. Interestingly, Gonzalez y Borrego served as Santa Fe chief of police at the time, which suggests that all these events may have been connected to internecine police warfare.[122]

Authorities arrested Francisco Gonzalez y Borrego, Antonio Gonzalez y Borrego, Laureano Alarid, and Patricio Valencia and charged them with killing Sheriff Chavez. Police killed another suspect, Hipólito Vigil, when he resisted arrest. Oddly enough, Thomas B. Catron represented the four men at trial. A jury convicted them of Chavez's murder. The territory hanged them all in April 1897. Sheriff Chavez had distinguished himself on several occasions, such as when his deputies found and killed Marino Leyba or when Chavez himself captured Milton Yarberry after he had escaped from jail. But his career evidently took an ugly turn.[123]

As for the Ancheta investigation, it eventually grew cold, and law enforcement never identified Ancheta's shooter. But the event itself and the specifics of the investigation are quite revealing. First, the fact that the territory authorized such a massive manhunt for the wounding of a person of Mexican ancestry is significant. Many other people got shot and died and did not warrant this kind of attention. Second, while suspicion immediately fell on a Mexican-origin perpetrator, little evidence specifically linked the shooting to anyone. While Ancheta had surely made enemies, the focus on a Mexican or Mexican American assailant seemed nothing more than a weak attempt to link the shooter to the White Caps in order to discredit that group. The two heavily armed Mexicans who passed through Gallup served as another rouse. Siringo's speculation seems most likely: the shooters meant to kill Catron. The investigation, itself a sign of egalitarianism since it paid such close attention to a Mexican American victim, ultimately fell prey to the racist presumptions of the time that a Mexican person must have done the shooting.

Mexican Americans served in other aspects of the criminal justice system in New Mexico. Take Zacarias Padilla, justice of the peace in Valencia County. In 1907, a former Mounted Police officer, or "ranger," named George Murray had come to feel it his duty to intervene in the private affairs of Mexican-origin people, particularly as those affairs related to drinking and sex. Padilla personified Murray's disdain. Padilla had two children with his wife, two with a lover, and according to Murray drank heavily. That was a pretext. Murray really disliked the fact that Padilla had power and played a part in the county's law enforcement establishment. "His father is one of the wealthy Mexicans there," Murray wrote, "they cannot do anything with him as he is the J.P. there and he does what he likes." Thus, Murray used Padilla's personal matters as an excuse to remove him as justice of the peace.[124]

Although he was not a law officer and no agency sanctioned Murray to apprehend Justice of the Peace Padilla, who had committed no crime, in October 1907 Murray arrested Padilla for the "abduction" of his mistress and put him under a $1,000 bond.[125] The arrest caused quite the local controversy. R. L. Baca wrote to Governor George Curry to protest the "illegal arrest" of Padilla.[126] T. J. Sawyer, the superintendent of the American Lumber Company wrote to the Chief of the Mounted Police, Fred Fornoff, to find out whether Murray actually served in the Mounted Police.[127] In responding to this letter, an unnamed lieutenant in the Mounted Police reported to Sawyer that Murray "in no way [was] connected with the New Mexico Mounted Police."[128]

Impersonating an officer was a serious offense and Captain Fornoff decided to launch a full investigation into George Murray's actions. Much of the investigation focused on the character of Zacarias Padilla and George Murray. M. J. Haverkamp, a resident of San Rafael in Valencia County, praised Murray and claimed, "Padilla has always been connected with the bad element [and] is the worst drunkard in this community and the most lawless man that we have, and it is stated that he has seduced many girls. I do not consider Zacarias a proper person for a peace officer." Manuel Padilla y Chavez, a large landowner in the area and Zacarias Padilla's father, testified that he had asked Murray "what the charges were against Zacarias." He continued, "He told me he did not have any. . . . I asked him what order he had to arrest him." Murray had none. For his part, Zacarias Padilla flipped the script on Murray and said that Murray had "put handcuffs on me, because he had been drunk the night before, and was nervous and did not know what he was doing." "Nearly all the time Mr. Murray comes here," Padilla added, "he behaves badly towards the people." Most of the testimony in the investigation oscillated between those who considered Murray an alcoholic and a bad person and those who considered Padilla an alcoholic and a bad person. The investigation exonerated Murray of wrongdoing, even though he had clearly impersonated an officer and illegally arrested Zacarias Padilla.[129]

In the end, justice came for George Murray. A short time after arresting Padilla, he killed a man in a shoot-out in the town of Ketner. A jury convicted him of manslaughter and sentenced him to three years in the penitentiary.[130] The territory also charged him with "selling liquor to Indians," a serious crime.[131] He pleaded guilty and was fined.[132] Murray failed to harm Zacarias Padilla, who went on to win election to the first state legislature in New Mexico in 1911.[133]

In addition to county level positions, city police forces in New Mexico hired Mexican American officers. In 1904, for instance, the city of Santa Fe employed fifteen Spanish-surnamed officers (out of a force of seventeen).[134] In 1914, the city appointed Nicolas Serna as city marshal and four Spanish-surnamed individuals as police officers.[135] In 1922, the city appointed James Baca to the position of marshal. Baca had previously served as a town alderman. He promised to enforce the ordinances in the city, but also "that he would court suggestions and fair criticisms of his work as marshal."[136] In 1923, Tomas P. Delgado served as sheriff in Santa Fe County.[137]

Like other localities, Santa Fe utilized a police magistrate for most of the minor cases the city had to handle. This position serves as another important example of the roles Mexican Americans played in the criminal justice system. For many years Santos Ortiz held the position of police magistrate. Judge Ortiz's record offers compelling evidence. For one, while he began most of his reports to the Santa Fe City Council in English, he wrote up all the cases he oversaw in Spanish, which denotes how both languages were official languages in many parts of the Southwest. Second, while New Mexico employed a number of Mexican American law enforcement officers, Mexican Americans rarely held the job of police magistrate. This makes Ortiz unique, given the importance of the job, the fact that most cities had only one police judge, and because of his ethnicity. Lastly, Judge Ortiz presided over a court that saw a good number of Mexican and Mexican American defendants, and he treated those defendants the same as he did non-Mexican defendants, demonstrating his impartiality as a judge.

Take, for instance, the March 8, 1909, case of Nicolas Maes. Police had arrested him for "embriaguez," or intoxication. Judge Ortiz wrote, "en esto causa Del Defindiente, Fue' Precentado a La corte Y la corte le inpuso, $5.00 De multa Y los costos, de corte, Y endefecto de dicha Multa Y costos, 10 Dias en la carcel del condado, O Apricion de la cuidad bajo la diricion Del marisc al Atrabajos publicos. El Commitemet Fue Depocitado en las manos del mariscal de la cuidad." While his typing seems hasty and his spelling imperfect, Ortiz's findings in the case proved typical. The translation: "In this cause of the defendant, was presented to the court and the court imposed a $5.00 fine and court costs, and failing to pay the fine and costs, 10 days in the county jail or city prison under the direction of the town marshal to [complete] public works. The principal was deposited into the hands of the town marshal."[138]

Judge Ortiz tried thirty-two cases like Nicolas Maes's and reported these in his March-June 1909 report to the city council. Of these cases, twenty-eight ended exactly as had Maes's. Ortiz suspended four cases that quarter for good behavior. All the individuals tried in his court during that period had Spanish surnames. In 1912, City Marshal Rafael Gomez issued a similar report. He reported twenty-two cases for the month of June, mostly drunkenness again, but also four cases of breech of the peace and one speeding case. Of these cases, five individuals had English surnames and seventeen had Spanish surnames. All the intoxication cases resulted in a similar outcome as the cases Ortiz presided over: a five-dollar fine and court costs, a jail sentence of around 10 days, or public works for the city.[139] In 1915 a new police judge, Alberto Garcia, presided over eighteen cases for the month of July, all cases of intoxication. Sixteen men had Spanish surnames, two had English surnames. Almost all the cases went the same as before, with a five-dollar fine or jail time and public labor. Nicolas Maes appeared again in the record; this time he paid his five-dollar fine and was released.[140]

In some cases, Mexican-origin people fought back against what they saw as aggressive policing, even if the officer was of Mexican ancestry. The case of Santa Fe officer Amado Sena represents a good example of this. Local people disliked Sena; those familiar with him found him abusive and mean spirited. On the morning of November 7, 1906, he came off duty and encountered a group of Mexican men leaning against a wall in front of a downtown store. According to Sena the men had blocked the sidewalk, so he ordered them to move. They complied, but Juan Antonio Ortega did not move enough for Sena. "He didn't want to move," Officer Sena reported, "but he did move a little." Sena removed his nightstick and demanded the men move again. Cleofas Jimenez, who had moved already, retorted, "What else do you want when we have all moved?" Sena ordered the men to move once more. They turned on him. Jimenez and Ortega grabbed Sena's arms while Emilio Gutierrez wrestled the billy club from Officer Sena and began beating him about the face with it. One of the men ripped Sena's badge from his chest, a sure sign of the disrespect they felt for the officer. Other officers arrested Ortega, Gutierrez, and Jimenez for beating Sena. It is not clear what happened to these men.[141]

The New Mexico example of Mexican American service to the law enforcement profession remains impressive. Because of the large Mexican-origin population in New Mexico, Mexican American involvement in policing occurred with great regularity. Not all law officers did a good job; Jose Chavez y Chavez's motley policing record or the possible rivalry between the Santa Fe Police Department and the Santa Fe sheriff revealed by the shooting of Joseph Ancheta suggest a mixed legacy. Perfecto Armijo and Elfego Baca had more admirable records. Compared to other southwestern states and territories, the number of Mexican Americans who served in law enforcement in New Mexico is basically unparalleled.

Of all the southwestern states, California had the weakest record of Mexican Americans in law enforcement. There were some early examples, though. Tomás Avila Sanchez won election as Los Angeles County sheriff in 1860 and served for seven consecutive terms.[142] Martin Aguirre followed Sanchez and had a lengthy career in law enforcement in Southern California. He was elected as constable in 1885, became a deputy sheriff the following year, and a sheriff in 1888. Aguirre, like Perfecto Armijo, disliked carrying a gun and instead preferred to carry a knife. He also disliked having to perform executions, again like Armijo, and successfully petitioned the state to move the site of executions from LA to the penitentiary at San Quentin. Ironically, the state later appointed Aguirre warden of San Quentin. His duties included overseeing executions during a time when the prison hanged more incarcerated individuals than during any previous period. He served a single four-year term as warden and then left the United States for several years to work in Central America. When Aguirre returned to LA, he became a deputy sheriff in 1907 for the second time in his life. "It might have been beneath some former sheriffs to accept a lesser position," a short history of the Los Angeles Sheriff's Office noted, "but Aguirre was a professional lawman. He was apparently unimpressed by the number one position, and wished only to serve the people of Los Angeles County as a law enforcement officer."[143]

The state had other Spanish-surnamed officers at the turn of the century, such as Juan Murrieta. While mainly known for bringing the avocado to California and for having the town of Murrieta named after him, Murrieta had a long career in law enforcement. He originally immigrated to Mexico from Spain and then came to California. He was appointed a Los Angeles deputy sheriff in 1887 and served for forty years in that role. Murrieta also trained other officers, such as Eugene Biscailuz. The Biscailuz family had a long-standing presence in Los Angeles and traced its origins to the American settlement of the city. Eugene Biscailuz would go on to serve as Los Angeles sheriff from 1932 to 1958 and organize the California Highway Patrol in 1929. Since Juan Murrieta had trained him and so many others, Murrieta earned the nickname "Father of Sheriffs." As a report on the Los Angeles Sheriff's Office noted, "Although Murrieta was never elected sheriff, he was the trainer and mentor of several. No public official ever gave more satisfactory service. He devoted practically his entire life to the public interest, and grew old and gray in the service of Los Angeles County."[144]

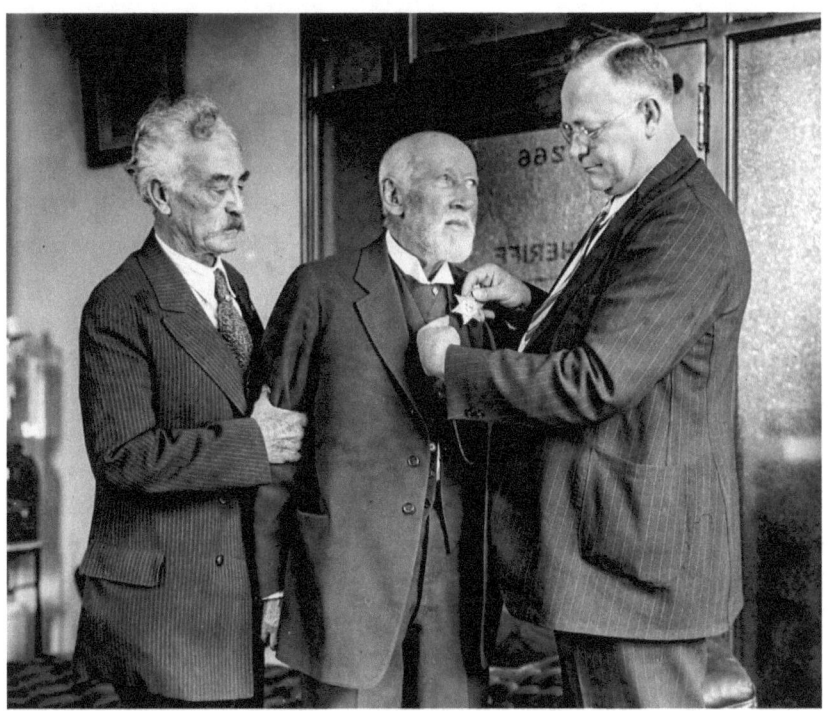

Los Angeles County sheriff William Traeger pins an honorary badge on the chest of former deputy sheriff Juan Murrieta. The man holding Murrieta's arm is former sheriff Martin Aguirre. This photograph was taken circa 1925 at a gathering celebrating Murrieta's retirement and acknowledging his long service to law enforcement.
Murrieta Family Materials, HM 73230–73256, Huntington Library, San Marino, California.

Texas has perhaps the most hidden histories of Mexican American police officers. They existed, but the archival record of their activities remains thin. Santiago Alvarado, for example, one of the earliest Mexican American officers in the El Paso Police Department, served as a "special police officer" beginning in 1889 (one out of twelve officers). Departments often reserved this designation for Mexican American officers who patrolled Mexican sections of town. Alvarado had a rocky career and first made it into the news when he shot a Mexican man who had beaten another man.[145] He also experienced several examples of frustrating racism. In 1889, Alvarado served on a security detail for mayoral candidate Adolph Krakauer. At a campaign speech, Krakauer "assailed Officer Alvarado in language too indecent for publication."[146]

Alvarado allegedly tried to convince El Pasoans not to vote for Krakauer. The El Paso Police Department suspended him for politicking as an officer, but the city council later reinstated him.[147] In 1890, Officer Alvarado discovered that he received less pay than his White counterparts, a common form of discrimination for Mexican Americans in numerous areas of employment. Alvarado earned sixty dollars a month compared to the seventy-five dollars a month White officers received. While Alvarado did not get a pay increase, by 1894 the city equalized the remuneration all officers received.[148]

Officer Alvarado did his duty well. In a good example of his policing, in November of 1890 he tracked down an alleged horse thief named Francisco Baca. He had made off with a horse from nearby Ysleta and travelled to Ciudad Juárez, Mexico, to sell the animal. Alvarado received a detailed description of Baca, went to Juárez, and discovered that Baca had already sold the horse and headed back to the United States. He located Baca near the El Paso ASARCO smelter and placed him under arrest. Baca had in his possession two revolvers, a fine watch, and a suit of clothing "such as are worn by Mexican gentlemen." Baca offered Alvarado these items if he would let him go, but "the officer was not to be bribed and accordingly brought him to jail." An El Paso jury convicted Baca of horse stealing and sentenced him to six and a half years in the penitentiary.[149]

Officer Alvarado's career did not last long. He left the El Paso Police Department over the pay dispute and went to work for the El Paso Constable's Office in 1891. But he was wounded when he and Deputy Sheriff Juan Franco (discussed below) responded to a disturbing the peace call. Someone shot the officer in the arm, destroying the appendage and ruining Alvarado's police career.[150]

The number of Mexican American officers on the El Paso police force increased throughout the late nineteenth century and into the twentieth. Officer Santiago Alvarado had been the only Mexican American out of twelve officers in 1891. By 1896 there were five Mexican Americans out of sixteen officers. In around 1901, Ramon Gonzalez joined the force as a patrol officer.[151] The numbers continued to rise until the 1910s, at which point they declined. By 1918 only three officers of Mexican ancestry served on a force that had grown to ninety. Historian Mario García speculates that this situation resulted from heightened anxiety due to the Mexican Revolution.[152]

El Paso also saw Mexican Americans serve in the county sheriff's office. Several sheriffs had Spanish surnames, including Juan Armendariz (1870) and Benito Gonzalez (1880).[153] The name "Sheriff Garcia" shows up quite often in the nineteenth and early twentieth centuries records. One of these Garcias was

Deputy Sheriff Tomas Garcia. He originally became a deputy in the El Paso County Sheriff's Office in 1895, stationed in San Elizario, and later transferred to the El Paso office in 1900.[154] Garcia had some interesting moments in his career. One involved San Elizario police officer Dionicio de Soto, whom a group of "tough characters" had beaten unconscious. Garcia initiated a search and quickly discovered a number of suspects whom he arrested for beating Officer de Soto.[155] Unfortunately, de Soto later died from his injuries. Two of the men Garcia had arrested, Jose Sierra and Severo Cordero, stood trial for the murder. A jury convicted them and sentenced Sierra to five years in prison and Cordero to a ten-year prison term.[156]

In another case in April 1899, brothers Blas, Celso, Epitacio, and Anastacio Aguirre, Adolfo Chacon, and "an Italian, known as John" left San Elizario for a saloon in San Ignacio on the Mexican side of the border. After drinking for some time, they beat and shot the tavern keeper, Juan Jose Escajeda, who died. The ruckus alerted townsfolk who surrounded the saloon. The six men shot their way through the crowd, killing two men in the process, but the townspeople regrouped and, with the help of the Mexican Guardia Rural (Rural Police), caught the six at the Río Bravo before they could cross. In a hail of bullets, they wounded all six men. Anastacio Aguirre and the Italian named John died. Adolfo Chacon, while also wounded, escaped to the American side. The Mexicans captured the other men.[157]

Deputy Sheriff Garcia learned of the case that same night, tracked Chacon, who bled profusely from a bullet that had entered his shoulder and then lodged in his jaw, and found him holed up at a nearby ranch. Garcia originally intended to turn Chacon over to Mexican authorities, but when Blas, Celso, and Epitacio Aguirre escaped from a Mexican jail to the United States, Chacon held Garcia instead. Law enforcement in New Mexico eventually captured the three Aguirre brothers. A grand jury indicted them all for conspiracy to commit murder.[158]

Here things got complicated because most of the evidence remained in Mexico and no one could conclusively say who killed Juan Jose Escajeda. So starting with Blas Aguirre, juries began acquitting the men. The Mexican government intervened and demanded that the United States extradite Blas Aguirre to Mexico for trial. The United States complied with this request. A Mexican jury convicted him of murder and sentenced him to execution by firing squad.[159] It seems both Celso and Epitacio Aguirre testified against their brother, so the state did not try them.[160] Blas Aguirre died by firing squad in February of 1901.[161] It is unclear what happened to Adolfo Chacon; he likely shared the fate of Blas Aguirre.[162]

There were other Mexican American officers in Texas whom we know little about. For instance, while newspapers reported on the beating and murder of Officer Dionicio de Soto, that's all we know about him. Similarly, El Paso constable Leon Chavez served but a few years in the 1890s before he too was cut down in the line of duty.[163] El Paso deputy sheriff Juan Franco had worked with Chavez in 1893 before he died.[164] Deputy Sheriff Franco's name appears frequently in local papers, but most of the reporting is mundane. For instance, Franco arrested a man who stabbed another man in 1906.[165] He arrested several men for selling liquor unlawfully in 1908.[166] In 1909 he arrested a fugitive.[167] Franco's record demonstrates many of the routine aspects of early twentieth century policing.

Contrary to popular discernment, Mexican Americans did serve in the Texas Rangers.[168] One of the important early Rangers, Jesse Perez, held a host of law enforcement positions. His first foray into policing came in 1887 when Bexar County sheriff T. P. McCall recruited him as a deputy sheriff. Perez found himself called to assist in a good deal of policing outside of San Antonio because of his facility with the Spanish language and because he was of Mexican origin. This service caught the attention of the Rangers; they recruited Perez for the first time in 1889. Perez seems to have enjoyed ranging, but he left the service to begin a family. He joined the San Antonio Police Department in about 1895 when his first child was born. He returned to the Rangers for two years in 1898, but left to become "pound master," or the head of animal control, which was also a position in the San Antonio Police Department.[169]

By 1906, Jesse Perez became a Ranger yet again. But times, it seems, had changed. He began noticing an uptick in the number of Mexicans, supposed bandits, killed by the Rangers. That year he wrote the Rangers had "killed half a dozen poor Mexicans for nothing." It seems the Rangers killed these men in retaliation for the murder of Judge Stanley Welch (discussed in chapter 5).[170] Perez also noted that the Rangers killed at least two other Mexican men during the investigation into Welch's killing. Perez left the Ranger service yet again and became chief deputy sheriff of Starr County in 1907. In 1908 he left that position to join the U.S. Secret Service, but he quit that job and returned to the Rangers once more in late 1908 and stayed with the Rangers for nearly two decades. He spent most of his time trying to halt bootlegging after the passage of the 18th Amendment. He continued doing the same thing when he left the Rangers in 1924 and joined the Customs Service.[171]

In his writings and in the available historical record, Jesse Perez operated as an effective law officer. He also commented on the general racial climate in Texas at the time, especially regarding the treatment of Mexican-origin people as well as the so-called bandit trouble of the early twentieth century. For example, Perez noted that most White people thought of Mexicans as "shiftless," but he countered that instead Mexicans and Mexican Americans were so resourceful that others "would starve to death while [they] fattened."[172] In commenting on border banditry, Perez mainly discussed border fighting done by Mexican revolutionaries. He did not ridicule all Mexican-origin people as bandits, as many White Americans did. Instead, he simply listed a number of possible bandits captured or killed by the Rangers, without any value judgment on their alleged banditry. His descriptions stand in marked contrast to those who seemed to think all Mexican-origin people engaged in banditry.[173]

Other Mexican American Texas Rangers existed who did not distinguish themselves in their duty. Such was the case of Texas Ranger Daniel Hinojosa. Ventura R. Sanchez, the constable in the town of San Diego, had unpleasant dealings with Hinojosa. He testified about Hinojosa in 1919 at a major Texas legislative hearing into Ranger violence. Sanchez recounted an incident in which Rangers George Hurst and Daniel Hinojosa came into town, got drunk, and shot up a saloon. When Sanchez intervened, they threatened his life. This short account is really all we know about Constable Sanchez.[174]

We know more about Daniel Hinojosa, who had a long career in law enforcement. Alas, like Jose Chavez y Chavez and others, Hinojosa's record was not the best. For example, during the so-called Bandit Wars (discussed in chapter 5), then deputy sheriff Hinojosa and a town marshal named Frank Carr were transporting a prisoner named Adolfo Muñoz to jail in Brownsville when they encountered a group of masked men. This mob took Muñoz and hanged him. Hinojosa may have participated in the lynching, given the propensity of law enforcement to murder Mexican-origin people.[175] Hinojosa served in Ranger Company A until the state disbanded it in 1919. Later, in 1931, San Benito constable Dave Ferguson appointed him to the constabulary there. Ferguson touted Hinojosa's record on the Rangers and claimed, "He is one of the stalwarts among the Mexican-Americans." Hinojosa had a stroke and died the following year.[176]

Henry Garfias, Perfecto Armijo, Elfego Baca, Jose Chavez y Chavez, Martin Aguirre, Santiago Alvarado, Juan Franco, Tomas Garcia, these are just a few of the many names of law enforcement officials of Mexican ancestry who worked in the Southwest long before "minority recruitment programs" of the mid-twentieth century came on the scene. Those programs, a product of the civil rights era, seemed new and novel, as new and novel as the Mexican American officers who joined police forces then. But Mexican American service in the justice system was neither new nor novel. Mexican Americans served in law enforcement for generations before the civil rights period.

Like any other group of people in law enforcement, some Mexican Americans performed their duties well, while others did not. Henry Garfias, Perfecto Armijo, Martin Aguirre, Tomas Garcia, and Juan Franco, among others, did good police work. They were decent, effective law officers who carried out their jobs with a commitment to professionalism. They had good ethics and moral character. Other Mexican Americans skirted the line. Elfego Baca is a good example of an officer who operated effectively but sometimes went outside of accepted practices to get results. And then we have officers who simply did not do their jobs well, such as Amado Sena, Jose Chavez y Chavez, and Daniel Hinojosa. Again, Chavez y Chavez seemingly started off as a decent law officer but then later did a truly terrible job.

Most importantly, some Mexican Americans became law officers to protect the Mexican-origin community. They saw their service as a kind of civil rights strategy. Elfego Baca is perhaps the best example of this, but others had a similar motivation. For Baca, White outlaws such as the Texas Cowboys abused and hurt the Mexican population. Law enforcement should have done something about this situation but did not. So Baca took it upon himself to become a law officer and seek justice. His legacy remains important because it represented the kind of law enforcement as public service or social work that would come into existence during the civil rights era. His legacy also inspired many of the law officers who came after him.

The historical record of Mexican American law officers is unfortunately spotty. While some parts of the Southwest, especially New Mexico and Arizona, had large numbers of officers, other parts did not. Scholars in New Mexico and Arizona have made it a point to memorialize and valorize the efforts of these officers; other states have not made those efforts. They should, because the work of these officers stands in stark contrast to what many contemporary Americans think about Mexican Americans and policing. They did not simply come on the scene when departments attempted to diversify in the mid-twentieth century. Rather, they were there one hundred years before that.

4

UNKNOWN MEX

Mexican and Mexican American Criminality and the Justice System

In December of 1885 in the Arizona Territory, Valerio Garcia allegedly stole 500 sheep from James Houck!¹ Apache County district attorney Charles L. Gutterson charged Garcia with grand larceny. Gutterson learned that Garcia had fled to Albuquerque, so he dispatched Deputy Sheriff Frank Hubbell to apprehend him. Garcia eluded the deputy sheriff.² In 1890, the county issued a new warrant for his arrest; an official order from the governor also authorized his arrest.³ Apache County sheriff St. George Greaghe barely missed Garcia when he attempted to apprehend him in Albuquerque in May 1890. Sheriff Greaghe submitted a bill for his attempted apprehension in the amount of $175.60, a significant sum (about $5,600 in 2022).⁴ Another sheriff also failed to apprehend Garcia in February of 1891.⁵ These attempts to secure Garcia show that these officials took their jobs seriously. Despite this flurry of law enforcement activity, they never collared Valerio Garcia, who more than likely fled to Mexico.

Valerio Garcia's case proved fairly typical in the criminal justice systems in the border region. The law enforcement response also was typical. Law enforcement worked hard to apprehend him, although it failed in its efforts. Garcia's crime, except for the large number of sheep, was also typical. Most cases recorded in criminal dockets and arrest records across the Southwest were for larceny, or theft. The same remains true today. To put this another way, if a standard type of crime or criminal existed in the Southwest, Valerio Garcia was it, except for the 500 sheep part (that's a lot of sheep).

Americans in general, and White Americans specifically, stereotypically believed that Mexican-origin people were criminally prone. According to popular White conceptions of the era, Mexicans and Mexican Americans could not resist drink or gambling, were so lazy that they would rather steal than work, always had a knife at the ready, had no compunctions about violence or killing, and possessed a corrupt culture lacking in morality.[6] These viewpoints were racist and erroneous. White people also tended to view Mexican-origin people in the nineteenth and early twentieth centuries as having a proclivity to commit certain crimes such as murder or sex work. While murder certainly shows up in the record books, prostitution in many locales wasn't a crime or was tolerated.[7] Instead of these crimes, police mainly arrested Mexican-origin people for common nonviolent crimes such as theft or vagrancy or the nondescript charge of "suspicion."

The problem with prejudices in law enforcement lay in their power to drive a highly punitive criminal justice system. Those in the justice system responded to their beliefs about crime by augmenting the power and number of law enforcement agents and by constructing jails, prisons, prison farms, youth camps, detention centers, and other forms of human caging. The criminal justice system, and the penal system specifically, rarely had reform as a goal. Instead, the goal was to punish. As noted in the first chapter, White leaders in the Texas Republic, the states of Texas and California, the Territories of New Mexico and Arizona, and in many other parts of the Southwest founded criminal justice institutions early on partly in response to these perceptions about the criminality of Mexican-origin people.[8]

Other misconceptions also existed. Given the general propensity for racism during this period, we might expect juries to easily convict Mexicans or Mexican Americans and to punish them more harshly than other segments of the population. Certainly the criminal justice system continued to exist as a racist institution founded to control Mexican-origin people and others.

But while lynch mobs and vigilance committees and law enforcement often brutalized Mexicans and Mexican Americans, other aspects of the criminal justice system, from attorneys to judges and from prison wardens to state boards of corrections, tended to treat them more justly.[9] Juries, for example, convicted Mexican-origin people at about the same rate as other groups in southwestern society and handed down the same punishments for them as they doled out to members of other ethnoracial communities. Mexican-origin people also received pardons and compassionate releases from prisons. This lasted until the eve of the Mexican Revolution. Alas, during the revolution the number of arrests and prosecutions of Mexicans especially, as well as modifications to the punishments for a variety of crimes, increased significantly, a racist response to the large number of Mexican refugees fleeing the revolution to the United States.

Additional curiosities pervaded the criminal justice system in this period. For instance, law enforcement cataloged Mexican-origin people in unusual ways by frequently omitting their names from civil and criminal records. Of all the various ethnic and national communities described in these records, police regularly recorded only Mexican-origin men by their first name, with no name, or with an ethnoracial designation. Instead of a name, law enforcement wrote things like "mex" or "John Doe Mex" or "Unknown Mex." to describe the people they arrested or imprisoned. The erasure of an individual from the criminal record simultaneously erased that person from the historical record, a double whammy that in a few cases followed a person from arrest, to trial, to imprisonment, to release.

The available arrest and court records demonstrate the inaccuracy of many of the misconceptions described above. Criminal records, fragmented and dispersed in archival holdings across the Southwest, come primarily from the period between 1860 and 1930. This period encapsulates the initial phase of American establishment of the criminal justice system while the Mexican-origin population remained relatively small, as well as the use of that system in the period of the Mexican Revolution, when the Mexican and Mexican American population in the Southwest increased rapidly. After the 1930s, the court and prison records became standardized and massive, creating a ubiquitous type of quantitative data that provides less narrative detail. Most local and state governments shifted to an aggregate type of data in that period that listed total numbers of arrests and convictions, which tells no clear story and provides less helpful information for this book. The narratives revealed by the data from the 1860–1930 period are, however, instructive. Contrary to popular stereotypes, Mexican-origin people had no proclivity to criminality. They were not wanton murderers. In fact, homicide was statistically the least common crime that anyone committed during this period. Theft, assault, drunk and disorderly conduct, or disturbing the peace were far more common criminal offenses. And the criminal justice system took all these offenses seriously, disputing the arguments of lynch mobs and vigilance committees about the ineffectiveness of the justice system.

The first arrest record I located in California, that of Antonio Garcia, is an example of compassionate jurisprudence. While generally seen as a modern concept, compassion in justice is very old. The basic principle involves district attorneys, judges, prison administrators, and other individuals in the criminal justice system taking into consideration a defendant's health, physical well-being, psychological condition, age, and other factors before subjecting that individual to trial or incarceration. If a judge or prosecuting attorney felt a defendant was, say, too ill or infirm to stand trial, the individual might be released. Similarly, a warden might request clemency or a pardon from the governor if an incarcerated person had a terminal illness, a process called compassionate release. Now, this kind of compassionate jurisprudence had many critics, from those who believed people should answer for their actions no matter their physical or emotional condition to those who felt courts simply tried to save money by releasing someone who might die, thus this type of release had little to do with compassion and more to do with cutting costs.[10]

Antonio Garcia's case is an instructive example of how compassionate jurisprudence worked. In November of 1860, the Los Angeles authorities issued an arrest warrant for Garcia. He had allegedly robbed Pedro Pison of twenty dollars the previous September. Police apprehended Garcia and placed him in the county jail to await trial. But, in late November, as the trial moved forward, the court received word that Garcia was "dangerously ill." The sheriff worried that a trial would only hasten his demise. Officials decided not to try Garcia, who died a short time later. Interestingly, his case file noted, "Case stricken from Docket. Deft [defendant] dead and buried."[11] Authorities spared Garcia from trial because of his illness, which not only humanizes him but also demonstrates how the criminal justice system in Los Angeles treated individuals of Mexican ancestry with compassion when it seemed warranted.

The case of Juan N. Padilla also revealed an important aspect of how the criminal justice system operated at his time. The Los Angeles district attorney charged Padilla in February of 1861 with assault and battery on Marta Abila de Padilla (the exact nature of their relationship is unclear). He had allegedly beaten and injured her for reasons not disclosed in court documents. The Los Angeles County grand jury indicted him, but Padilla appealed the indictment claiming that the grand jury was prejudiced against him. In particular, two grand jurors, Ygnacio del Valle and Francis Mellus, had aired "an unqualified opinion that Defendant was guilty of the charge for which the indictment was found" before the grand jury met.[12] In other words, they had already decided Padilla's guilt. That is contrary to the law and the district attorney set the indictment aside and did not prosecute the case. No record exists to show the state ever revisited the case, which prevented an injustice from happening to Juan Padilla (he deserved a fair trial) while simultaneously allowing an injustice to happen to Marta Abila de Padilla (she deserved her day in court).[13]

A final revelatory aspect of the Los Angeles court system involved cases that never went to trial. In the vast majority of cases handled in the 1860s and involving Mexican-origin people, the district attorney discontinued the cases using the legal term "nolle prosequi," or "unwilling to pursue/prosecute." This meant that for a variety of reasons, usually a lack of evidence or the inability to locate witnesses, the prosecution had decided not to move forward with the case. The declaration of nolle prosequi gave district attorneys the ability to collect data and potentially try these cases at a later date, but courts rarely revisited nolle prosequi cases. Such a dismissal shows that the court system did not railroad Mexican-origin defendants but instead attended to their cases as seriously as others.[14]

The cases that went to trial provide the most detail. About half of these ended in convictions and half ended in acquittals. For example, the Los Angeles grand jury indicted Jose Machado for grand larceny after he allegedly stole a saddle, two bridles, and other equipment valued in total at one hundred dollars from J. S. Griffin and J. C. Welch. Machado's attorney offered no testimony whatsoever, which either indicates Machado's guilt or that he had ineffective counsel. The jury convicted Machado and sentenced him to a five-year term at San Quentin State Prison.[15]

Criminal trials also frequently ended in acquittals for Mexican and Mexican American defendants. In 1863 Ramon Carrillo allegedly murdered John Rains. His trial ended thusly: "The said District Attorney declares and says that the people of the State of California have no complaint against said Carrillo, and that he knows of no testimony against said Carrillo upon said charge.... It appearing to me that there is no reasonable cause to believe said Carrillo guilty of the charge in said warrant mention, he is hereby discharged."[16] A jury found Gabriel Rodriguez not guilty of stealing two horses from Jose Gonzales for similar reasons.[17]

Women, whether victims or perpetrators, infrequently encountered the criminal justice system at this time. Statistically speaking, today fewer women in the United States commit crimes than men, a fact true even more so in the past. A purposeful exploration of criminal records reveals some unfortunate realities about women: rape was the most common crime committed against women, and most criminal offenses committed by women had connections to sex work.[18]

Sexual assault cases in the historical record unfortunately represent female victimization. Rape laws across the United States at this time were extremely lax and, frankly, sexist by contemporary standards. The justice system considered rape a property crime, specifically a crime against a male protector, usually the father or husband of the woman, and not a crime against the woman herself. The state often measured the consequences for rape based on the victim's chastity. If courts deemed a woman chaste or a virgin, the penalty for her attacker increased in severity; if she had engaged in previous sexual activity then courts viewed her chastity as questionable and punished the perpetrator less severely.[19] Prosecutors also found rape hard to prove if no witnesses beyond the victim came forward. Victim testimony usually proved insufficient as the system viewed such cases through a "he said, she said" lens. Finally, the punishment for rape was often a fine.

In one of the few cases of rape brought to trial at this time, the State of California charged Epifano Valdez with assaulting Francisca Rodriguez in January of 1864. In this case, Rodriguez testified against Valdez, and her friend Francisca Alvisa, who witnessed the attack, corroborated her testimony. That testimony showed one of the ways women supported one another in rape cases. The jury found Valdez guilty and, because of Alvisa's testimony especially, the judge sentenced him to a five-year prison term at San Quentin.[20]

In California and other states, women seldom appeared in criminal court cases as defendants. But they did commit crimes. In one of the few cases in which the state accused women of a crime, they tried Josefa Ybarra and Polonia Acosta for accessory to grand larceny. Evidently two men, Tomas Rodriguez and Perfecto Escalante, had stolen goods from Joseph Kasllet. Acosta and Ybarra helped hide Rodriguez and Escalante while authorities searched for them. The jury convicted Acosta and sentenced her to two years in the Los Angeles County Jail. Ybarra received a lighter sentence of six months in the county jail. The records do not explain the difference in sentences.[21] In a case of theft in 1862, the state accused Isabella Esquerer of stealing a silver watch valued at twenty dollars. They charged her with petit larceny, found her guilty, and assessed a twenty-five-dollar fine or, if unable to pay that fine, she would go to jail, the term not to exceed twelve days. She served the twelve days.[22]

Arrest and court records for the Territory of Arizona mirror those of California. In 1873 Manuel Pacheco and several others allegedly killed a man named Griffin near Phoenix. Police arrested Pacheco and jailed him for trial. A jury initially found him guilty of murder in the first degree.[23] But Pacheco's attorney appealed and asked for a new trial. The judge in the case agreed. The district attorney decided not to retry Pacheco and declared the case nolle prosequi. The court then discharged Pacheco.[24] This decision angered a number of Phoenicians. F. L. Hayes, for example, complained to Governor Anson Safford about the trial. "Manuel Pacheco had been tried by a jury of twelve men and found guilty of murder in the first degree," Hayes began, "but the sentence had not been pronounced. Since then, much to the surprise and I may say indignation of every white citizen in the valley, the judge set aside the verdict of the jury ... and the parties were set at liberty. [I] will simply say that there is not a doubt existing in the minds of the citizens of the Co[unty] as to the guilt of the parties."[25]

Hayes's letter demonstrates many of the common conceptions that White people had about the criminal justice system. According to him, "every white citizen" believed Pacheco guilty. And yet a judge and a district attorney, both of whom were White, had agreed to dismiss the case. This occurred fairly regularly in the justice system, even today, and the fact that White men had made such a decision would indicate that not "every white citizen" believed Pacheco guilty. Likely something improper occurred during Pacheco's arrest or trial necessitating the dismissal, the available record does not make this clear. While Hayes makes no mention of a vigilance committee, the "surprise" and "indignation" he described frequently led to the formation of lynch mobs so that Whites could acquire the type of justice they felt a suspect deserved. Hayes's letter also reminds us that White people often believed the criminal justice system lax or weak-kneed, even though it worked properly in the Pacheco case.

Despite what the leaders of lynch mobs and individuals like Hayes attempted to argue, the record suggests that the criminal justice system in the Arizona Territory acted with a serious commitment to law and order. For example, in 1886 Apache County district attorney Charles L. Gutterson sought four Mexican American men for grand larceny. The evidence against one of these men, Jesus Valenzuela, proved so compelling that when Gutterson learned that authorities in Hillsboro, New Mexico, had jailed Valenzuela, he immediately dispatched Deputy Sheriff Frank Hubbell to retrieve Valenzuela so that "the accused may be brought to justice" and "be dealt with according to law."[26] Hubbell returned Valenzuela to the town of St. Johns, the county seat in Apache County. After a short stay in the county jail, however, Valenzuela escaped. He was killed in June 1896 in undisclosed circumstances.[27] As noted in the beginning of this chapter, the Arizona Territory expended similar efforts to bring Valerio Garcia to justice. In a final, comparable example, Gutterson and Hubbell pursued Juan Moreno for months, but they failed to apprehend him.[28]

As in any state or territory, the treatment of Mexican-origin people by the justice system varied by locale. In Maricopa County, for example, District Attorney Frank Cox acted with impartiality no matter the ethnic origin of the individual on trial (recall how he assisted Manuel Mejía). The August 1885 trial of Francisco Yanez and the July 1886 trial of "John Doe," whom the court later identified as Tiburcio Ruiz, both represent textbook examples of the working of the court in Phoenix. Both were grand larceny cases, in Ruiz's case horse theft (Yanez's case does not specify). Justice of the Peace W. T. Woods found Yanez guilty, assessed him a $1,000 bail (a massive amount, $32,000 in 2022), and ordered him confined to the county jail until he could produce this bail money. In the Ruiz case, however, District Attorney Cox made a motion to dismiss charges because "from the best information the horse was not stolen therefore he did not to make any costs to the County." "There is nothing in the charge," Woods wrote, and he ordered Ruiz discharged.[29]

The Maricopa County District Attorney's Office handled several cases that involved Mexican-origin women, which reveal similar details as seen in California. In one case the county tried Manuela Cruz for "using vulgar and offensive language in the presence of women and children" in January of 1893. Phoenix marshal Henry Garfias arrested Cruz and Justice of the Peace Henry Wharton tried the case. After hearing testimony from several witnesses, the jury found Cruz guilty and ordered her to pay a one-dollar fine and court costs.[30] Guadalupe Corrales faced the same charge in May 1894. The court also found her guilty, but she could not pay the fine and was instead incarcerated.[31]

White people commonly regarded Mexican-origin women as sex workers. While they sometimes engaged in sex work, they were of course not alone in this profession, and local communities often tolerated prostitution or it was legal. In fact, law enforcement seldom arrested women for sex work, but rather they listed their occupation as "prostitute." The cases of Luz Miranda and Manuela Pesquiera serve as useful examples. Officials arrested the two women for "residing in a room apartment and house of ill-fame resorted to for the purposes of prostitution situated within four hundred yards of a school building." Thus, the crime was actually the location of the "house of ill-fame." Justice of the Peace Henry Wharton dismissed charges against Miranda but ordered her to pay court costs. Pesquiera's attorney successfully quashed some of the testimony against his client. Wharton dismissed the charges against her. While he gave the prosecution additional time to press new charges against Pesquiera, it seems that the district attorney declined.[32]

Of the crimes tried in courts across the Southwest, murder was the most serious, as well as the most infrequent. The case of Manuel Baca is a good example. In 1891 in Apache County, Arizona, Baca shot Matias Anaya in the neck, killing him.[33] Baca fled and a short time later the governor authorized a reward of $300 for his capture. Apache County sheriff O. B. Little offered an additional award of $250.[34] Newspapers across Arizona reprinted the governor's reward and arrest proclamation.[35] Despite the large award ($17,666 in 2022 dollars) and a massive manhunt, Baca disappeared from the record. That the government would authorize such a large sum for Baca's capture is again proof the territory took murder very seriously.

Other counties operated as Apache County did, with similar degrees of success and failure. For instance, authorities in Cochise County went to great lengths to track down Domingo Laguna for the murder of Cayatano Ferazon in 1891. Laguna had allegedly escaped to Mexico, a common occurrence at the time that may also explain what happened to Manuel Baca, Valerio Garcia, and others.[36] An additional urgency pushed officials to apprehend Laguna; the state had already arrested and convicted another man named Esteban Dorame for killing Ferazon. Law enforcement did capture Laguna, and Governor Louis C. Hughes pardoned Dorame. A jury convicted Laguna and sentenced him to ten years at the Yuma Territorial Prison.[37] Similarly, in Pima County, Manuel Gonzales murdered a well-regarded Mexican American man named Felipe Robles in March of 1887. Sheriff E. O. Shaw engaged in a large-scale manhunt for Gonzales, but the killer eluded him. Shaw suspected that Gonzales had fled to Mexico. Although the governor offered $500 in reward money, authorities never apprehended Gonzales.[38]

Perhaps no example better demonstrates the fastidious working of the law in Arizona in the late 1800s than the case of Reyes Baca and Martin Duran. The case excited the passions of Arizonans and was a major news item for well over a year. Duran murdered Baca in Flagstaff on September 18, 1887.[39] A large group witnessed the murder, so the circumstances of the case were pretty clear. Baca and Duran had a romantic relationship that soured, and she left him in the summer of 1887. Baca began residing with her friend Martina Gonzales, who witnessed the murder, which occurred in her home. On the night of September 18, Martin Duran and a group of his friends had gotten drunk at the San Juan Saloon. Duran convinced these men, all musicians, to accompany him to Gonzales's home to serenade Reyes Baca in the hopes of wooing her back. Baca then invited the men into Gonzales's home. At some point Duran and Baca went outside to converse and then returned to her bedroom to talk some more. Both sat on the edge of the bed. Baca lit a cigarette. "As she [Baca] turned I saw the defendant [Duran] slip out a revolver and shoot her with it," explained Martina Gonzales. Duran shot at her four times; two shots entered her head near her right ear.[40] According to another witness Baca "quivered . . . for about four minutes" before dying. Several of the people present held Duran until Constable Sandy Donahue arrived and arrested him.[41]

The Arizona Territory tried Martin Duran for first-degree murder in November of 1887 in nearby Prescott. Since the eyewitness testimony proved so overwhelming, the defense attempted two strategies to spare Duran from the noose. The first involved maligning Reyes Baca. The defense asked almost every witness whether Gonzales's home was "a house of ill-fame," implying that Baca engaged in sex work.[42] The defense, it seems, hoped this would justify Duran's actions. Such an implication may seem revolting today, but this common strategy often worked at the time because the defense could demonstrate that the victim's supposed infidelities had excited the defendant's passions. The witnesses all responded that Gonzales's home was not "a house of ill-fame." The second defense tactic involved showing that Duran was drunk, which served as a kind of capacity defense. The defense asked the witnesses about the quantity and type of alcohol consumed that night, going so far as to ask one whether Duran was "so much under the influence of liquor as to be unconscious?" The response of one witness did not help the defense: "I don't think that he was so drunk as not to know what he was doing."[43] The prosecution countered this second strategy by asking the eyewitnesses whether they believed Duran had the "capacity to distinguish right from wrong." Every witness stated that he had such a capacity.[44] The prosecution even asked Constable Donahue whether he thought Duran was "sane or insane." "I should say that he was sane," Donahue replied.[45]

Martin Duran decided to testify on his own behalf. He told the jury that shortly after he and Baca had begun their relationship, he found a love note from another man to Baca. He also claimed to have caught Baca in bed with another man. According to Duran, Baca and the man fled, with Baca taking refuge in the home of Martina Gonzales. This fictitious account probably didn't happen. When Duran went to Gonzales's home the night of September 18, he stated that he believed Baca and some of the men from the saloon were talking behind his back. "I seeing this couldn't hold my temper," Duran told the jury, "so I shot four shots at her, and then the men got hold of me although I didn't want to run away, for I wanted them to leave me alone as I intended to die to[o], because I was so sad and I knew that they would punish me for it anyway." Upon cross-examination Duran stated, "She forced me to kill her." When the prosecution asked, "How did she force you?" Duran responded by saying, "By treating me so bad when I didn't give her any occasion for it." "Is that the only reason you had for shooting her?" the prosecutor asked. His response, "yes, sir," basically nullified the defense's contentions that he was aroused to kill her because she had engaged in sex work and that he had been drunk and therefore not in control of himself. The defense attempted to refocus the court's attention by asking once again about Duran's consumption of alcohol and his "state of mind," but the prosecution objected, and the defense withdrew the question.[46]

The *Mohave County Miner* succinctly noted the cause of the killing shortly after it had occurred: "Martin Duran shot and killed a woman named Reyes Baca at Flagstaff last Sunday morning.... Cause, jealousy."[47] Indeed, despite the attempts to claim that Duran was not in his right mind because of alcohol or that Baca had provoked him by engaging in sex work (a fiction that no one seemed to believe and that even Duran refuted in his own testimony), Duran was simply a jealous and angry person who committed a violent act, either simply a murder or, if Duran is to be believed, a failed murder-suicide. The jury found him guilty of first-degree murder and sentenced him to death.[48]

But the case would not go away. Shortly after the court handed down the sentence and set the execution date for March 2, 1888, Arizonans inundated Governor C. Meyer Zulick with petitions and letters asking him to commute Duran's sentence to a prison term. For example, fourteen residents of Yavapai County, where Duran had worked and where both Flagstaff and Prescott were at the time located, signed a petition asking for commutation.[49] They claimed that he deserved a different sentence "because of his youth" and because "the act was committed while in a fit of passion, and jealousy, and under the influence of liquor, amounting, in our opinion, to temporary Insanity."[50] L. F. Eggers, an attorney in Globe, wrote a five-page letter to Governor Zulick explaining how the relevant criminal law at the time did not fit a sentence of death. "I do most sincerely and honestly believe," Eggers concluded, "that he should be tendered a commutation of said sentence."[51] Eggers was not much of an attorney because all the evidence, eyewitness accounts, and even Duran's testimony indicated first-degree murder. Zulick, therefore, refused to commute Duran's sentence. The territory hanged him in Prescott on March 2, 1888.[52] The *Arizona Silver Belt* waxed poetic in its description of the execution:

"Hempen cordage, in Prescott, March 2d, noosed in a coiling fold the felon neck of Martin Duran, who murdered his mistress in Flagstaff, and when cut down he was food for worms."[53]

The prolonged attention to the case tells us a great deal about criminal justice during this time period. First, as opposed to the vigilance committees and lynch mobs that claimed they had to take the law into their own hands because legitimate law enforcement didn't work, here we see the criminal justice system operating effectively. Second, the case tells us something of the gender climate at the time. Many of the appeals on Duran's behalf contained outright sexist language and stereotypes. According to those appeals, Baca was an older, sexually promiscuous women who had manipulated a much younger, naïve man. In reality, Duran was eighteen and Baca was twenty-three. In labelling her a sex worker, the defense and the writers who later asked for a commutation of Duran's sentence effectively blamed Baca for her own murder. The fact that she did not engage in sex work seemed lost on these writers. American society did not treat Mexican-origin women particularly well and labelling Reyes Baca a prostitute fit many of the misperceptions White people had about them. Their value was evidently so degraded that in a trial wherein a Mexican American woman was the victim, Reyes Baca became the cause of her own murder, while Martin Duran, the murderer, was an innocent dupe who, as he had said during trial, was "forced to kill her." The jury and, later, the governor thought otherwise.

Incarceration also tells us a great deal about criminal justice and the most important prison in the Arizona Territory at this time was the famous Yuma Territorial Prison. The incarceration of Mexican-origin people at the prison fluctuated depending on the year. Most of those incarcerated, almost always men, typically served time at the prison for grand larceny. The number of individuals sentenced to the prison for manslaughter or murder was low because these crimes occurred less frequently. The length of prison terms for any crime often, but not always, differed by the county where the trial took place. In most cases, the punishments meted out for Spanish-surnamed people did not differ markedly from the punishments given to English-surnamed people.[54]

In April 1884, Pima County sentenced Bernadino Martin to a term of ten years in the Yuma Territorial Prison for grand larceny.[55] A Mohave County jury handed down the same punishment in September of 1884 to Crecentio Barrila.[56] The following year a Maricopa County jury sentenced Francisco Yanez, as noted above, to a five-year term for grand larceny.[57] Santiago Pedia received a three-year term for grand larceny committed in Yavapai County in 1887.[58] In 1888 the court in Cochise County sentenced Miguel Chicon to five years for grand larceny.[59] These sentences show that while no standard or mandatory sentence existed, Mexican-origin people usually received a sentence under ten years for larceny, the norm at the time.

The territory of course took murder and manslaughter very seriously and individuals convicted of murder received much lengthier sentences. Pima County sentenced Juan Marquez to thirty years' imprisonment in March of 1889 for murder.[60] The punishment for manslaughter was similar to that handed down for property crimes. Mohave County sentenced Albino Villa to a term of six years for manslaughter in 1886.[61] In 1888, A. Lopez received a six-year sentence for manslaughter by a Graham County jury, while Isadore Lopez got a two-year sentence from a Pinal County jury.[62] The last entry in the 1884–89 logbook was for H. Salazar Martin, who received a three-year term for manslaughter in Cochise County in 1889.[63] We might expect that Mexican-origin people received long sentences for killing people, that the criminal justice system preferred to simply lock them up and throw away the key, but that was not the case.

Individuals with English, Scottish, and other European surnames received similar terms in prison. Rich Downing received a three-year term for grand larceny in Yavapai County in July of 1888.[64] While James Henrickson only received a one-and-a-half-year term in prison for grand larceny committed in Yavapai County in 1888, William Hall got a three-year sentence from a Maricopa County jury for grand larceny.[65] For murder, a Yavapai County jury sentenced Fred Glover to life in prison in 1885.[66] Cochise County also sentenced Wilson Douglass to life in 1886.[67] Both L. W. Davis in Apache County and W. D. Harper in Yavapai County got twenty-five-year sentences for murder in 1888.[68] James Williams received a sentence of ten years for manslaughter in Maricopa County in 1885.[69] Gila County sentenced B. F. Thornton to four years for manslaughter in 1887.[70] What these records show is that the system did not significantly treat White and Mexican people differently and that while many Americans viewed Mexicans and Mexican Americans as violent criminals, the vast majority of violent offenders were White. Yuma prison records from 1883 to 1890 show no obvious change to the sentencing patterns noted above.[71] In 1892 and 1893, the overall number of prisoners increased slightly, but the lengths of sentences remained the same.[72]

Like all prisons, the Yuma Territorial Prison regularly released prisoners when they received pardons or once their terms of sentence had ended. A series of reports by prison superintendent Frank Ingalls to the territorial legislature in 1890 detailed the individuals released each quarter. For example, in the third quarter of 1890, Ingalls released seven men, four of whom had

Spanish surnames.[73] In the fourth quarter of 1890, the prison released ten men. Of these, four had Spanish surnames and six had English surnames.[74] In 1891 the prison released eleven individuals, three with Spanish surnames, two with Indigenous names, and six with English surnames.[75] In July of 1891, the prison logbook shows that Ramon Flores, who had received a two-year prison term in November of 1891 for grand larceny in Maricopa County, was "pardoned to restore citizenship."[76] Individuals with Spanish surnames predominated in the record book in the second quarter of 1892. The prison released eleven people, of which ten had Spanish surnames.[77] While 1892 saw an increase in the total number of those incarcerated at the prison, it also saw an increase in the number of releases. The third quarter of that year shows that the prison released twenty-five incarcerated people, of which twelve had Spanish surnames. Four of these individuals were also listed using only their first names: Miguel, Nicholas, Antonio, and Ramon. It seems odd that even after each had served nine-month sentences for burglary, the prison staff still could not deduce their full names.[78]

In 1893 prison superintendent Thomas Gates received a more detailed pardon application from an incarcerated individual named Lauterio Aguilar. He had received a seven-year sentence from the district court in Yavapai County for a charge of assault with intent to murder in 1891. The circumstances that led to this sentence reveal some of the ways in which Mexican-origin people experienced an unfair criminal justice system. Aguilar was employed as a cook's assistant at a hotel in Prescott. He decided to visit the Palace Saloon (which is still in operation today) to try his luck at the faro table. He placed a half-dollar bet, but another patron named William McRae pocketed the coin. Even after Aguilar protested and "hot words passed" between the two men, McRae refused to return Aguilar's money. McRae also hit Aguilar several times and then picked up a stool and bashed him with that as well. As several of McRae's friends approached Aguilar with pool cues positioned as clubs, Aguilar drew a knife and stabbed McRae three times. This not only stopped McRae's assault but it also sent his friends scurrying. Law enforcement quickly arrested Aguilar and charged him with assault with intent to murder.[79]

Lauterio Aguilar's trial occurred in June 1891 in the district court of Judge Edmund W. Wells. An all-White, all-male jury could not reach a verdict and Wells declared a mistrial.[80] Now, all-White juries did not tend to operate in this fashion at this time; the records do not show why they could not reach a unanimous verdict, but it probably had something to do with the fact that the incident was clearly a case of self-defense. The state tried Aguilar again a week later. This time an all-White, all-male jury found him guilty. Judge Wells sentenced Aguilar to seven years at the Yuma Territorial Prison.[81]

By all accounts, Aguilar was a model prisoner. Superintendent Gates described him as "in all respects good and satisfactory." Gates had even authorized Aguilar to become a prisoner trustee, which meant that he allowed Aguilar to work outside of prison grounds and with little supervision. In his case, Aguilar had served as a cook in the superintendent's and assistant superintendent's prison residences. As trustee Aguilar had "given entire satisfaction in the performance of his duties," Gates noted.[82] Aguilar applied to Governor L. C. Hughes for clemency, asking that he commute his sentence from seven to four years. In addition to support from the prison administration, he also secured the support of Charles McGarr who had witnessed the dispute between Aguilar and McRae and testified for the defense at Aguilar's trials. McGarr, as Aguilar himself had explained, saw the encounter between the men as a robbery during which McRae had assaulted Aguilar, who then defended himself.[83] Aguilar explained in his application that his conviction resulted from racism on the part of McRae, the other gamblers, and the prosecution: "A prejudice was raised in the minds of the public against me and my conviction and the sentence as above stated were the result."[84]

McGarr played an additional role in Aguilar's quest for clemency; he secured letters supporting Aguilar from several of the jurors who had convicted him, which is pretty unusual. Aguilar also wrote to several jurors himself, claiming to be in ill-health and asking for their help in securing his release.[85] At least three jurors wrote letters to the governor on his behalf.[86] Governor Hughes ultimately agreed to commute Aguilar's sentence to four years. In his Proclamation of Commutation of Sentence, Hughes went into detail about his motivations in Aguilar's case. "The offense for which he is now serving sentence," the governor wrote, "was committed in a measure if not wholly in self-defense, upon one McRae, who it appears assaulted the defendant striking him several times, and the defendant being driven to the wall, by his assailant, drew a knife and defending himself, cut his assailant McRae, whom it appears from the evidence was a quarrelsome, dangerous, and vicious man." Aguilar was released a few months later.[87] This case demonstrates that racism could motivate the justice system to convict an innocent person, but also that the government could intervene to correct that injustice.

In the early twentieth century, the quarterly reports from the prison superintendent became more complex biennial reports. This resulted from an increase in the prison population. Also, as the Mexican Revolution commenced, more Mexican-origin people found themselves incarcerated at the prison. In June of 1900, Superintendent Herbert Brown reported to Governor Nathan O. Murphy that the prison housed a total of 266 prisoners. All were men: "148 Caucasian, 101 (Mexican), 23 Indian, 15 Negro, 5 Mongolian" (that actually totals to 292, but the report says 266).[88] Interestingly, the report listed the term "Mexican" in parenthesis and indented beneath "Caucasian," which denoted that the territory and prison staff considered Mexican-origin people part of the White population, which was common across the Southwest. At this time the vast majority of people were incarcerated for property crimes: thirty-seven for burglary and thirty-nine for grand larceny. The number of individuals imprisoned for violent crime paled by comparison: fifteen for murder, six for murder in the second degree, and eight for manslaughter.[89] The prison listed one individual, Francisco, only by first name.[90] The territory spent about $43,000 on the prison, which was no small sum at the time (just over $1,496,000 in 2022 dollars).[91]

In the biennial report for June of 1902, Superintendent Herbert Brown reported to Governor Alexander O. Brodie that the prison housed 281 individuals, 3 of whom were women. Of the total, Brodie listed 132 as "Mexicans" and 123 as White.[92] Incarcerating these people cost the territory $49,502 for fiscal year 1900–1901 and $54,020 for fiscal year 1901–2, an increase of nearly $5,000, or 10 percent.[93] The report also noted that twenty-five individuals were paroled, and the territory pardoned twenty-six. Of those paroled, five had Spanish surnames; two of those pardoned had Spanish surnames.[94]

Few women, or at least female names, are to be found in the Yuma prison logbooks. As noted, women appeared infrequently in city arrest logs and court records. But prison records do help our understanding of how the criminal justice system treated women. One of the women incarcerated at the territorial prison was Manuela Fimbrez. A Pima County jury convicted her of murder and sentenced Fimbrez to fifteen years' imprisonment in March of 1889.[95] Prison staff listed her in a "Report on Prisoners" compiled from 1883 to 1890 as "female prisoner."[96] Her case was an interesting one. She had assisted her boyfriend, Juan Enriquez, in the murder of Ah Foy, better known as "'Sullivan' the Chinaman," in Tucson in 1889.[97] The case drew a great deal of attention because Enriquez claimed Ah Foy had attempted to sexually assault a friend named Carmen Molina. Enriquez and Fimbrez asserted that they had accidentally killed him while defending Molina. However, authorities learned that Enriquez, and most likely Fimbrez, had previously attempted to kill Ah Foy. A jury convicted Enriquez and Fimbrez of murder.[98]

The case became even more interesting when in November of 1889, about eight months after her conviction, Fimbrez gave birth to a healthy baby boy at the Yuma prison.[99] Births in prison, which have recently garnered a great deal of attention in the United States, clearly have occurred in the past.[100] She cared for the baby in her cell for the remainder of her incarceration. Shortly after the birth of her son, authorities began discussing pardoning Fimbrez. Some of their reasons were sexist. One newspaper article, for example, explained, "An effort has been made to secure her pardon, but without success. That she richly merits the full penalty given her is undoubted.... It must be confessed, however, that there is no place here for a woman." The paper made no mention of the child. The prison had no female ward, but prison staff had sequestered Fimbrez in her own cell in an area away from male prisoners.[101] A short time later a newspaper reported that she was near death due to an erysipelas infection. Erysipelas, an acute bacterial infection of the skin, was often fatal.[102] She recovered from the illness but being a sick prisoner with a baby may have also influenced authorities to release her. Governor John Irwin pardoned Manuela Fimbrez in October of 1891; the state deported her immediately thereafter.[103] Her pardon can be viewed as an example of a compassionate release, and the available information suggests that territorial authorities did care about the child. But the prison may simply have not wanted to expend resources and care for a sickly woman and her baby. The faqt that they deported her would indicate state officials didn't really care about her or her child.

It is difficult to gauge with any real accuracy the number of women imprisoned at the Yuma Territorial Prison. In some instances, prison staff listed the incarcerated by only a first initial, and thus some of these may have been women, although a newspaper article noted in 1891 that Fimbrez was "the only female convict in the Territorial Prison" at that time.[104] But women did enter the prison before and after Fimbrez. An 1890 prison logbook listed at least one other female prisoner, Matilda Garcia, whom a Pinal County jury convicted of grand larceny and sentenced her to a year in prison in October 1890. She would have served her time with Fimbrez. Like criminal records in other states and territories, the Arizona justice system also listed prisoners only by their first names. The same logbook listed two individuals this way: Antonia and Guadalupe. It is therefore possible that the prison incarcerated four women at the same time.[105] The 1902 biennial report listed three Spanish-surnamed women. Susana Chabio had received a two-and-a-half-year sentence for assault with a deadly weapon in Yavapai County; Rosa Duran served a three-year sentence for grand larceny in Yavapai County; and Elena Estrada received a seven-year sentence for manslaughter in Pima County, all in 1900.[106]

The Yuma Territorial Prison was one of the few penitentiaries in the nineteenth and early twentieth centuries that could be classified as a maximum

Women in one of the women's cells at the Yuma Territorial Prison.
(*From left to right, standing*) Elena Estrada, Pearl Hart, and Rosa Duran seated. Estrada killed her boyfriend, whom she allegedly caught in flagrante delicto with another woman in 1900. The state committed Hart for robbery in 1899 and Duran for larceny in 1900, many people considered them female bandits. This photo was probably taken in 1901.
Arizona Historical Society, PC 1000, Portraits-Hart, Pearl, #69152.

security facility. It lives in the lore and popular imagination of many Americans, primarily due to films such as *3:10 to Yuma*. Some of the ways in which racism was visible at the prison include the deletion of individuals' full name. Some incarcerated people may well have ended up at the prison because the system railroaded them, as the case of Lauterio Aguilar demonstrated. But just as surely, prison staff treated Mexican-origin people in the same way they did individuals from other ethnic groups, including releasing them after they had served their sentences, pardoning incarcerated folks of Mexican ancestry, allowing them to serve as trustees, and, most importantly, showing compassion to people such as Lauterio Aguilar and Manuela Fimbrez.

The prison records also demonstrate the over policing of Mexicans as the Mexican Revolution began and more refugees came to the United States. This Great Mexican Migration really began in the 1880s as economic problems in Mexico worsened and continued into the 1920s because of the violence of the revolution.[107] During this period, Americans in general and White people in the borderlands more specifically became alarmed at the presence of increasing numbers of Mexicans. This "re-Mexicanization" of the Southwest led to any number of odd conspiracy theories among White folks, most notably fears of a reconquest of former Mexican lands—a fear that seemed more real after the discovery of the famous Zimmermann Telegram of 1917—as well as the general racist angst that White Americans had about Mexicans, especially perceptions about Mexican criminality. The number of incarcerated people of Mexican ancestry at the Yuma prison did not increase at this time because there were more criminals, but because Mexicans were victims of an overbearing law enforcement situation that they could not effectively challenge.

Arizona law enforcement agencies also categorized Mexican-origin people with "John Doe" type designations. For example, officials in Tombstone issued a warrant for the arrest of "John Doe (a Mexican)" in 1892 for an undisclosed crime.[108] In a similar case, Tombstone officials issued warrants for "John Doe unknown Mexican" in February of 1893 and "John Doe Mex." in April of 1893. Interestingly, authorities later amended both "John Doe Mex." listings to record their actual names as Refugio Bernal and Ferdinand Rivera.[109] In a more honest example, an arrest warrant for a "Joe Doe—Mexican" noted "true name unknown." The record concluded with these words: "Said defendant could not be found, had cross the Mexican line into Old Mexico."[110] It would seem to be rather impossible for law enforcement to locate such an individual. Records in other Arizona locales utilized similar designations. In 1885, Maricopa County issued an arrest warrant and noted the subsequent arrest of "John Doe" for grand larceny. Only in the text of the justice court's logbook was the name of "John Doe" revealed as Serano Rodriguez. The judge dismissed the charges against Rodriguez due to insufficient evidence.[111] In 1886 the docket recorded the arrest of "John Doe, a Mexican" for allegedly wielding a deadly weapon. Even after a trial that lasted multiple days and resulted in the defendant receiving a fine of $4.25, the court still failed to determine his name.[112]

The arrest records in New Mexico correspond to the examples from other southwestern territories and states.[113] The common crimes that New

Mexican authorities collared Mexican-origin people for included drunkenness, fighting, and livestock theft. For example, law enforcement in Doña Ana County arrested Juan Villegas in October of 1893 for drunk and disorderly conduct. He pleaded guilty and the court fined him five dollars and court costs. Villegas paid his fine.[114] But he was back a few days later, charged again with drunk and disorderly conduct. The court again assessed him a fine of five dollars and court costs, which he paid.[115] In perhaps a more serious case, Doña Ana County charged Albino Gomez and Juan Benavides with resisting an officer. Resisting arrest, both then and now, could lead to serious bodily harm and death, usually for those under arrest. But the court found Gomez and Benavides not guilty.[116] On September 8, 1907, police arrested Placido Trujillo for "fighting and disturbing the peace." The court found him guilty and fined Trujillo five dollars.[117] In February of 1911, officers arrested Juan Barquello for assault and fined him ten dollars and one month in jail.[118] Both Trujillo's and Barquello's arrests occurred during the period of increased migration from Mexico and while Trujillo received the same penalty as others, Barquello's punishment was harsher than normal.[119]

The Santa Fe jail also saw an increase in Spanish-surnamed individuals as a result of the coming of the Mexican Revolution. In the fourth quarter of 1908, the jail had housed fifty-one prisoners, of whom forty-two had Spanish-surnames. For that quarter, 82 percent of the prisoners were Spanish-surnamed men.[120] With the onset of the Mexican Revolution and increased migration of Mexican refugees into the Southwest, these numbers continued to rise. For the fourth quarter of 1912, the Santa Fe jail housed ninety-two prisoners, of whom eighty-five had Spanish surnames, or 92 percent.[121] The number of incarcerated Mexican-origin people rose throughout the period of the Mexican Revolution.

While authorities arrested and imprisoned Mexicans and Mexican Americans with increasing regularity in the early twentieth century, New Mexican authorities also tended to parole or release them with the same frequency as people from other ethnic groups. Pardons for Mexican-origin folks appear just about as regularly as pardons for others. For example, Governor Bradford Prince pardoned Jesus Acosta from the Penitentiary of New Mexico upon certification from the superintendent of the penitentiary in 1889.[122] In March of 1919, the penitentiary board reviewed eleven cases for parole or release, five involved people with Spanish surnames, and of those the penitentiary board recommended four for full restoration of citizenship rights. The other six individuals had English surnames, of which the institution released four and denied release to two.[123] In January 1920 the penitentiary board reviewed seventeen applications for parole. Of these, twelve had Spanish surnames. They paroled all seventeen applicants.[124]

In most parole or pardon cases, the individuals granted or denied clemency were just a line item in a report, but in other cases the penitentiary staff went into greater detail about the applicants. The February 1919 pardon of Eliseo Valles serves as a good example. Socorro County convicted Valles of murder in 1906 and sentenced him to ninety-nine years in prison. The Board of Penitentiary Commissioners noted that he "was only 17 years of age when crime was committed and sentence imposed." Because of "his youth at the time he was sentenced, and also because of extraordinary good record as a prisoner," the board recommended a pardon, which the governor granted.[125] Similarly, Eddy County sentenced Agapito Nunez in February 1919 to five to six years in prison for involuntary manslaughter. The territory granted him a pardon that same month because "prisoner was suffering from complication of diseases, apparently incurable," and was expected to die. As such, Nunez serves as another example of compassionate release.[126]

Of all the southwestern states or territories, the criminal justice system in Texas tended to treat Mexicans and Mexican Americans the worst. Austin, like other locales, frequently resorted to the "unknown mex" type of cataloging of Mexican-origin arrestees. For instance, a Mexican man arrested by Austin city marshals on January 30, 1876, had no name written in the box for "name." The desk officer recorded the person's "nativity" as "Mexican," which means the officer reduced the man's identity to a national label.[127] On February 12, 1876, Austin marshals arrested a Mexican man for "intoxication." They listed his name as "unknown."[128] On November 26, 1876, Austin marshal Joe Smith arrested a Mexican man for disturbing the peace. Smith listed the individual's name as "Mexican."[129] On April 28, 1877, marshals arrested a "Mexican" for "intoxication" and listed his name as "unknown Mexican."[130] Similarly, on November 30, 1878, Austin marshals arrested a male Mexican laborer for "intoxication" and recorded his name as "Mex."[131] Most offensively, on March 1, 1876, and February 4, 1878, Austin police arrested a Mexican peddler and recorded his name as "Monkey."[132] In 1885, they arrested a Mexican man for disturbing the peace and recorded his name as "Rabbit."[133] Then in early 1886, police arrested "John Monkey" for disturbing the peace.[134] It is not clear whether "Monkey" and "John Monkey" were the same person. Assigning Mexican-origin people animal names was racist in a manner similar to describing Black people as simian.[135] Police also recorded Mexicans as "Mescican" or "Mescin."[136]

Unknown Mex

Austin was also one of the cities that regularly arrested Mexican-origin women. In 1885 Austin police arrested "Anastasia" for disturbing the peace. By 1885 the police force logbook had changed, so we also know that Anastasia was Mexican, engaged in sex work, and that the judge dismissed her case.[137] In similar cases, police arrested "Amelia" and "Maggie" for vagrancy in February 1877.[138] In these cases, like others across the Southwest, police arrested these women only to release them or see their cases dismissed, a common form of harassment.

In the Fort Worth area and Tarrant County more broadly, court records also illustrate the racism of nineteenth-century Texas. The earliest records show some of the same biases and issues seen elsewhere in the Southwest, especially the namelessness of Mexican-origin people. For example, the state tried a "Mexican Antone" in April of 1886 for aggravated assault. The Tarrant County court found him guilty and fined him a hefty thirty dollars, but "Mexican Antone" could not pay the fine, so he remained in jail. The state never bothered to learn his name.[139] "Mexican Antone" may well have been the first Mexican tried for a crime in Tarrant County. The criminal docket books from 1876 to 1879 and the sheriff's account book from 1876 to 1885 appear to have no Spanish-surnamed people listed.[140]

As in other locales, Tarrant County had a common crime: illegal gambling, usually recorded as "betting at gaming dice." Officers arrested L. Reno and charged him with this type of gambling in September of 1893. He received a ten-dollar fine.[141] A few months later in January of 1894, police arrested Reno again and this time tried him for five counts of "betting at gaming dice." He paid fines in the amount of sixty dollars and was released.[142] Mexican-origin people also had experiences similar to others involved in the justice system. For example, officers arrested Raul Orozco for carrying a pistol. Such a charge proved commonplace, but perhaps because of the prevalence of guns, the district attorney tended to dismiss these cases. Between 1902 and 1909, the district attorney dismissed about 300 carrying pistol cases. Orozco's was no different.[143]

In the early 1900s, Tarrant County saw an uptick in the arrest of Mexican-origin people, again a result of police targeting the increase in Mexican immigration. The most common crime at this time was theft, followed by aggravated assault. In almost every case of theft, the arrested individual paid a one-dollar fine. For example, police collared Luis Hernandez for theft on October 14, 1905. The court assessed him a fine of a dollar and released him.[144] For aggravated assault, we have the case of Santiago Mendoza, whom police arrested in May of 1907. The court released Mendoza on bond, the most common way all people got out of jail for this crime at this time.[145] About half the cases in the 1905–7 logbook were for theft and aggravated assault. Between 1910 and 1913, the court adjudicated another twenty cases of theft for individuals with Spanish-surnames, but only four cases of assault. The court tried thirty-four total cases involving Mexican-origin people, with theft coming in at just under 60 percent of the total and aggravated assault at 10 percent. Tarrant County saw a smaller increase in Mexican involvement in the justice system during the Mexican Revolution, probably because of the county's distance from the border.[146]

Dallas and Dallas County treated Mexican-origin people in a fashion similar to that of Fort Worth. Dallas authorities did, however, use the "Mexican," "Unknown Mexican," "John Doe, Mexican," or "Mex" designations with greater frequency. Dallas had no Mexican population when it incorporated in 1856 and only a small population at the turn of the century. When officers arrested and jailed Mexican-origin people, they tended to use their names or basic descriptors such as "Mexican" or "unknown Mexican" with equal frequency. For example, in March of 1891, P. P. Martinez spent a night in jail for violating the city sidewalk ordinance (in other words, he spit).[147] In September 1891, though, police booked a "Mexican" into the City of Dallas Calaboose for intoxication.[148] Police logged a "Mexican" into the jail in September 1901 for drunk and disorderly conduct. Jail staff listed his age as fifty-five and his occupation as "laborer," but could not discern his name.[149] Later that month police booked Frank Mercado into the calaboose for suspicion.[150] Similarly, in early 1902 the calaboose accepted two "Mexican" individuals, Frank Lopez and Joe Gonzales, both for "D&D," or drunk and disorderly conduct.[151]

It took until the 1920s for city criminal justice officials to arrest Mexican-origin people in larger numbers as their percentage of the population grew due to the Mexican Revolution. Officials continued to frequently catalog Mexicans with names like "Mexican." On July 12, 1920, the Dallas city jail recorded someone named "Mexican," whose nationality was listed as "Mex," for "SPP," or sleeping in a public place.[152] A few weeks later the jail took in a "Mexican" for "unlawfully riding a train."[153] And in 1922, police booked an "Unknown Mexica" for drunk and disorderly conduct.[154] The booking officer got a little more specific in 1923 when the arrest was cataloged as "Unknown—Mex. man" for "D & D." Police could somehow determine that this person lived in Dallas, was fifty-one, and a laborer, but could not figure out his name.[155]

The "unknown Mexican" description also found its way into other police documents. Police reports and complaints mirror other documents that used this terminology. In 1913, a Dallasite named Frank Wright reported to the police that he had been mugged of $2.60, "by two men, thinks they were mexicans." Wright's vague description of the muggers—"one low heavy set, other medium slender"—probably helped police very little in tracking down these two men.[156]

When authorities could identify a person's name, the crimes still remained fairly standard: arrests for vagrancy, gambling, and drunk and disorderly conduct predominated. Dallas police arrested C. Gomez, Jose Galindo, and Severo Romediaz for "gaming with cards" in March of 1921. They probably spent a night in jail and were released.[157] Carlos Tellez serves as an example of a vagrancy case; he spent two nights in jail for vagrancy in May of 1922.[158] Police booked L. Vasquez into jail for using abusive language, but then released him a few hours later.[159] M. Martinez spent a night in jail for drunk and disorderly conduct.[160]

Dallas police also occasionally booked Mexican-origin women. They arrested Belen Perales in 1926 for vagrancy. She pleaded guilty and was fined twenty-five dollars, a considerable sum for vagrancy and one that demonstrated how local authorities augmented such penalties as a result of the Mexican Revolution. As in other locales, police listed Perales's profession as "prostitute."[161] In 1931 police arrested Mary Garcia for vagrancy. She was one of the few women picked up by police in the 1930s. Like Belen Perales, the court found her guilty and fined her twenty-five dollars.[162]

Dallas law enforcement also did periodic sweeps to roundup "vagrants," one of the other ways we can see how police punished refugees. On March 10, 1921, for example, the Dallas jail took in sixteen Mexican men for vagrancy. Usually the jail records show one Mexican individual incarcerated per day, and the logbooks frequently have some days with no Mexicans listed, so it's unusual to see sixteen on one page and all for vagrancy. The jail staff listed their occupations as "laborer" and their residence as "Dallas," so it is unclear why police considered them vagrants.[163] In another sweep in 1922, Dallas law enforcement collared seven individuals for vagrancy, five of whom were Mexican. Those five included four women listed as "prostitute." The court later found all these individuals guilty of vagrancy and assessed each a ten-dollar fine.[164]

San Antonio differed from Fort Worth and Dallas in its treatment of Mexican-origin people, probably because of the city's long history of having a large Mexican population. For instance, the court charged Rafael Garza and Andreas Coy Jr. with "assault and battery on an officer in the discharge of his duty," a serious offense, on August 29, 1899. The judge dismissed the charges against both men.[165] Joe Martinez threatened Judge G. Lawther in

1914. Lawther had just pronounced Martinez guilty of disturbing the peace and the judge entered a hefty fine of one hundred dollars against Martinez. As Martinez left the courtroom, he told the judge "I'll get you yet." Judge Lawther found him guilty of contempt of court and sent him to jail for three days. And yet, the same judge later lowered Martinez's fine to thirty dollars for good behavior in jail.[166] As such, even with an offense like "assault and battery on an officer" or when an individual threatened a judge, the criminal justice system in San Antonio seemed to treat Mexican-origin people fairly.

In San Antonio during the period of the Mexican Revolution, police mainly arrested Mexican-origin people, almost always men, for drunk and disorderly conduct. While alcohol abuse remains a major social problem, in the list of criminal offenses at the time it was a fairly minor one.[167] Police also frequently charged Spanish-surnamed people, primarily men, with vagrancy only to later dismiss those charges. For example, on May 7, 1924, the docket shows four Spanish-surnamed men booked into the jail for "vag idle person," or vagrancy. All four had their cases dismissed.[168] That was good, given that authorities, like police in other places, cracked down on vagrancy in the 1910s and 1920s by significantly raising fines (in some cases as high as $200), again a common form of harassment.

Women appear infrequently in criminal court records in San Antonio. For a few examples, a judge fined Louisa Garcia and Julia Martinez two dollars for fighting on September 11, 1899.[169] Police booked Stella Ramirez and Josephine Gomez into the city jail for disorderly conduct on November 28, 1899. Both had those charges dismissed in court two days later.[170] In 1902, police arrested Valentina Puente for using "abusive language." The judge dismissed the charges.[171] Similarly, police collared Maria Ruiz for vagrancy in December 1915. She pleaded not guilty, and the judge dismissed her case.[172] Police arrested Isabela Rodriguez for disturbing the peace on New Year's Eve in 1915. She also pleaded not guilty, and the judge also dismissed her case.[173] Often more serious charges warranted a different result than the dismissals mentioned above. But not usually for women. In July of 1920, Maria D. Trevino was charged with assault. Though she pleaded guilty, the judge dismissed her case.[174]

The criminal justice system in San Antonio also tended to treat Mexican-origin defendants accused of property crimes fairly. When Guillermo Rodriguez allegedly stole the mule of Jose Maria Gonzalez, the state subpoenaed six people for the trial, a significant number for a livestock case. Rodriguez pleaded guilty to this charge and the court sentenced him to two to ten years in the penitentiary.[175] Like Guillermo Rodriguez, authorities charged Antonio

Jesus Lopez with stealing a horse. He pleaded not guilty, but a jury convicted Lopez and sentenced him to a two-year term in prison.[176] Juries found Mexican-origin defendants not guilty of the charges against them as frequently as they found them guilty. In November of 1909, the Bexar County District Court charged Andres Pena with burglary. Pena had allegedly broken into the home of Albert Ogden and made off with valuables not disclosed in the case file. The evidence against Pena was circumstantial and the jury found him not guilty.[177]

As elsewhere, San Antonio and Bexar County took violent crime very seriously. Police, for instance, arrested Louis Ramos for assault with intent to murder in June of 1908 for allegedly attempting to kill Charley Chong. The state subpoenaed five individuals and conducted a three-day trial. The jury found Ramos guilty and sentenced him to a two-to-fifteen-year term at the state penitentiary. The length of the trial and its outcome demonstrate the serious commitment of the criminal justice system to such cases. One might expect that a Mexican person who attempted to kill an Asian person might not warrant such proceedings—in other words, those in power might not care if two people from marginalized communities tried to kill one or the other—but the state did care. Moreover, this trial and many others like it show that the justice system worked effectively.[178]

The state also engaged in some measure of compassion in several cases. For example, the state charged Juan Gutierrez with forgery. But Gutierrez had advanced tuberculosis and "confinement would only hasten his death." The judge dismissed the case.[179] Several cases demonstrate compassion to young people or those who had no previous record. Take the case of Antonio Torres, whom the court found guilty of theft under twenty dollars. If he had received the standard sentence, Torres would have spent two years in the penitentiary. But the jury also stated, "The defendant has never before been convicted of a felony in this or any other state and we recommend that his sentence be suspended by the court." The judge granted that request.[180] Two months later the court similarly suspended a defendant's sentence because he had "a good moral character."[181]

A number of cases demonstrate the court's similar commitment to good jurisprudence. In December 1912, the State of Texas attempted to try Jesus Garcia for robbery, but the state's chief witness, a man named Flores, had evidently assisted Garcia in the alleged robbery. Since the state cannot solely rely on the testimony of a conspirator to convict a coconspirator and Flores's testimony was the only evidence the state had against Garcia, the judge dismissed the case due to a lack of evidence.[182] In the trial of P. G. Garza, who allegedly attempted to assault Guadalupe Rodarte, the judge similarly dismissed the case due to lack of evidence. "The evidence in this case is insufficient in that it fails to connect the defendant with the commission of the offense, but points to the act having been committed by another party," a court officer wrote.[183]

These cases demonstrate the overall fair working of the court system in San Antonio. Since American society did not treat Mexican-origin people particularly well, and law enforcement did treat Mexicans and Mexican Americans harshly, we might expect for prosecutors or judges or juries to follow suit by, say, considering prejudicial or problematic evidence. But these cases show the inaccuracy of that thinking. San Antonio also had fewer of the "Mex," "Unknown Mex," or "John Doe Mex" type of names in arrest and court logbooks. Relatively few instances of these designations appear in the record in the mid-1910s. For example, police arrested "mex" in December of 1915 for "drunk," or drunk and disorderly conduct. The individual pleaded guilty and was assessed and paid a five-dollar fine.[184]

Across the Southwest the various ways police agencies communicated with one another shows another way law enforcement operated, especially as they attempted to track down wanted suspects. Law enforcement agents communicated fairly effectively throughout the late nineteenth century, and communication only improved in the twentieth century. Before widespread use of photography or if they did not have a photo of a suspect, for instance, police often provided detailed descriptions of suspects in writing. Jake Giles, the sheriff of Jefferson County, Texas, wrote to the chief of police of Dallas in 1911 about a suspect named Bonifacia (probably Bonifacio) Garcia. Giles had a warrant for Garcia's arrest for assault with intent to murder. Giles described him as such, "Height about 5 feet 11 inches, blue eyes, smooth shaven, brown hair, light complected for a Mexican, about 35 years old, has scar on left arm from shoulder down towards elbow about 6 inches long, small scar under same arm about 2 inches long."[185] It is unclear whether Giles's thorough description aided his apprehension of Garcia. Other law enforcement officials tried to provide a similar level of detail while also looking for the mythical "Unknown Mexican." Sheriff Tom Whitson of Johnson County, Texas, wrote Dallas police searching for "one Mexican" wanted for murder. Whitson's poor wording, typing, and grammar probably did not help the search: "Description -5 ft 10 in high-165, lbs .long musstach very heavy,big scar on neck /big blue mole on left side of nice big scar on right wrist drinks considberbly White hat light gray coat Striped pants."[186]

Law enforcement officials also wrote letters to other authorities when they came across people they believed another agency might want. Such was the

$35.00 REWARD!

For Eugenio Ortegas. Age, 37 years; weight, 155 pounds; nationality, Mexican; complexion, light; and black hair. Wears black coarse, bristly mustache, which he keeps waxed and curled. Is stoop-shouldered; walks slowly and with a swing. Carries chin high, and raises it very high when spoken to. Not talkative, but of a very quiet disposition. Is a good musician and plays trombone. Speaks but very little English, and is a coal miner by occupation.

Will pay $35 for this man's arrest and return to me at Decatur, Texas.

JNO. M. BRANCH,
Sheriff Wise County.

Sheriff John M. Branch sent this wanted postcard for Eugenio Ortegas to various law enforcement officials in the Dallas–Fort Worth area in 1908. These types of postcards provided law enforcement with a great deal of information about the wanted individual. This one has some interesting details about Ortegas's physical features—for example, he seemed to meticulously coif his mustache. But Sheriff Branch also added additional details about some of Ortegas's personality traits or demeanor that don't often appear in these postcards, for instance that he had a "quiet disposition" and was "a good musician." It's unclear why Branch wanted Ortegas, but given the amount of the reward money, it is likely that he had committed a nonviolent crime or had escaped from jail. *Texas/Dallas History and Archives Division, Dallas Public Library.*

case with John Peno. William Young, the chief of police in St. Louis, Missouri, wrote to the Dallas police chief John Ryan that he had located Peno. Young believed Dallas might have wanted Peno for an 1898 murder. To remind Ryan about Peno, Young offered this description: "Peno is a half-breed Mexican, 40 years old; 5 feet, 9 inches tall; 145 pounds; slim build; black hair that is almost straight."[187] In a similarly racist letter, the superintendent of the Tarrant County Convict Camp, which utilized prison labor to complete road projects in Dallas, advised law enforcement to "look out for [a] yellow Mexican" who had escaped from a work crew.[188]

Understanding criminality in the Southwest can be challenging. The popular myths of the period have produced an unfortunate and distorted picture of what crime and the criminal justice system actually looked like. This proves especially true for Mexicans and Mexican Americans. In short, they were not the criminals that many White folks took them for. As today, sometimes police did the wrong thing, abused people, or killed suspects under questionable circumstances. Judges sometimes had racist prejudices against Mexican-origin defendants, juries did too. But the workings of many southwestern courts show that the entire courtroom work group in many locales operated effectively and fairly, demonstrating not only the impartiality of the system but also disrupting the lynch mob narrative about the laxness of the criminal justice system.

The Southwest's early history also skews our interpretations of Mexican and Mexican American women. The single, most damaging misconception White people had about Mexican-origin women was that they all engaged in sex work. That belief has entered the popular imagination as both a social and societal issue, but also as a criminal justice issue. Neither was true. The criminal record rarely mentions sex work connected with Mexican-origin women and crime, because it wasn't something exclusive to them and because it usually wasn't a crime.

Incarceration also tells us a great deal. In the Southwest, as in other parts of the United States, what developed in the nineteenth century was the seed that became today's prison industrial complex. The erection of jails and prisons began once Americans took over the Southwest. Many states and territories also began constructing penitentiaries such as the Yuma Territorial Penitentiary and the Penitentiary of New Mexico, which housed increasing numbers of Mexican-origin people at the turn of the century. The expansion of existing jails and prisons across the region also serves as a model example. Many jails and prisons, for instance, began adding women's quarters in the 1930s, the timing of which would seemingly have nixed the idea, but there were always funds for prisons. Authorities proved willing to build new prisons, expand old ones, and hire more guards and staff, all common facets of the carceral state today.

The odd designations for Mexican-origin people in the criminal record—the listing of someone as "Unknown Mex" or "John Doe Mexican"—demonstrates one type of racism in the criminal justice system. The elimination of an individual's name erased them from American society. For law enforcement in the Southwest, this meant that Mexicans listed as "Mex," "Mexican," "John Doe, Mexican," "Unknown Mex," "Monkey," or nothing at all became nonexistent. The expunging of a Mexican-origin person's name from the criminal and historical record indicated that they had no identity in southwestern society, were interchangeable one from the other, and were treated as a group with disdain and opprobrium. Law agencies treated no other ethnoracial community in this way. Records of arrests of Chinese nationals, Syrians, Ethiopians, Indians, Germans, Czechs, Japanese, Indigenous people, and African Americans, just to name a few, were all accompanied by a first and last name. Deleting the names of Mexicans and Mexican Americans further marginalized them as people in American society.

Finally, the early twentieth century witnessed an ugly revolution in the operation of the criminal justice system. The refugees fleeing the Mexican Revolution caused a great deal of fear and consternation among White folks in general, and law enforcement specifically. Some communities responded with periodic police sweeps to rid towns and cities of "vagrants." Other communities significantly increased the fines doled out for these crimes, either to profit from Mexican migrants, or encourage them to go elsewhere, or both. And some parts of the Southwest went further by forming new "border patrol" units to monitor the border for "bandit" activity or, in the case of Texas, by using existing law enforcement like the Texas Rangers to massacre Mexican-origin people. In many ways the criminal justice system oscillated between a general fairness in the late nineteenth century to a general abusiveness in the early twentieth century as more Mexicans fled the revolution to the United States. For many White people, the revolution represented a threat, and Mexican refugees were somehow all "bandits." Indeed, for White folks in the early twentieth-century Southwest, it seemed there were Mexican bandits everywhere.

5

BANDITS EVERYWHERE

Anti-Mexican Violence, Mexican
and Mexican American Resistance

In the 1910s, Chico Cano's name was everywhere. The press seemed to love his story: he led a "desperate band of Mexicans... engaged wholly in outlawry"[1]; was an "outlaw" and a "bandit" in a "Mexican gang"[2]; and he had, depending on the news account, "100 outlaws,"[3] "150 bandoleros (outlaws),"[4] or "bandits, 200 in number" under his command in the Texas border region.[5] But Chico Cano only became a bandit when White law enforcement turned him into one. U.S. customs inspector Joe Sitter, a former Texas Ranger, had simply decided in 1912 that Cano was an outlaw and in 1913, without proof or authorization, attempted to apprehend him. Chico Cano and his brothers fought back. They knew that Mexicans taken into custody by the Rangers often ended up dead. Cano avoided arrest, but he spent the rest of his life on the lam because Joe Sitter thought him a criminal. He turned Cano into a bandit, one law enforcement never caught.

Chico Cano's name lived on. Law enforcement used it to murder and massacre Mexican-origin people in Texas throughout the early twentieth century. While Americans in general, and law enforcement specifically, saw him and other Mexican people as bandits, they only became bandits after an unfortunate encounter with a police officer. Interestingly, many of the most famous Mexican bandits became outlaws in this manner. Many other people died during the late nineteenth and early twentieth centuries because of the "bandit" label. For White people in the border region and beyond, "bandit" became something of a racial code word: bandits were Mexicans and Mexican Americans, they were bad people, they were everywhere. Actual bandits did operate in the Southwest.[6] In fact, social bandits have always been a part of frontier societies.[7] The problem was that many bandits weren't bandits, they were simply Mexican-origin people who seemed threatening to White folks. So White people used extralegal and legal means to control and kill these people. The Texas Rangers did the most damage. Texas legally authorized the Rangers to kill. When they did, it was hardly ever considered a criminal act. Instead, it was a state-sanctioned police practice. White mobs also lynched a lot of so-called bandits. Now, bandit or not, Mexicans and Mexican Americans deserved the legal administration of justice, which they did not receive. Instead, police and mobs simply executed them or they died via legally excused killings such as ley de fuga (law of flight) cases.

The bandit label encapsulated many of the major events of the nineteenth and early twentieth centuries, from the Cart War and Salt War in Texas, themselves versions of the various land wars in the New Mexico Territory, to Las Gorras Blancas and the *Plan de San Diego*'s "Liberating Army of Races & Peoples." For White people bandits were bad; for Mexican-origin people bandits were heroes. Mexican-origin people understood that many of the major issues of the period related to policing, and bandits stood up to abusive law enforcement. Unfortunately, that seemed to confirm the worst fears White people had about people of Mexican ancestry, resulting in more bloodshed, death, and outright massacres.[8] Mexicans, like Chico Cano, and Mexican Americans did resist. They did so by fighting back, by fleeing, by forming their own protection leagues, and by becoming the very bandits White people feared.

One of the earliest and most important bandits in southwestern history, Joaquin Murrieta, appeared in California in 1849. Like others he sought to strike it rich in the gold rush. While his exact origins remain in dispute, it seems most probable that he came from Sonora, Mexico. He evidently did well at mining and soon brought his brothers from Mexico to California. But Murrieta also ran into some problems. In particular, White migrants, whom promoters and newspaper reporters had convinced would easily find gold in the mountains, found instead that mining was hard work and many of the most valuable claims already staked out by Mexican miners like Murrieta. White people resented this fact and blamed Mexicans like Murrieta for their misfortune.[9]

Despite the development of the criminal justice system in California and the presence of law officers in the gold region, vigilante committees populated the area. They not only acted as police but also in many instances as the broader justice system by having hearings and trials, even though the outcome for the "defendant" was always guilt and a sentence of death. Recall, for instance, the lynching of Josefa Segovia and the so-called Rancheria Massacre discussed in chapter 2. What happened to Murrieta remains a mystery; most scholars agree that White miners acting as a vigilance committee attempted to force him off his claim. Some accounts suggested that the vigilantes gang-raped and murdered Murrieta's wife, but this is doubtful.[10] In fact we don't fully know what happened to him, but we know he fought back and became an outlaw.[11]

Murrieta's exploits, then, resulted from an injustice, and an injustice that a White mob carried out under the color of the law. His response: seek revenge on anyone and especially those who acted as law enforcement. One of Murrieta's first victims was General Joshua Bean near Los Angeles in 1852. That would make his first killing a military official who possessed law enforcement power.[12] Murrieta scared White Californians of the time so much that almost any theft, assault, murder, or other crime got attributed to him, so it is difficult to accurately detail his exploits. But the fear he caused spawned a massive manhunt. A group of California Rangers allegedly hunted down and killed Murrieta in 1853 and from 1853 to 1854 took his embalmed head on a tour across California to assure White folks he was dead.[13]

Tiburcio Vásquez became a bandit after a regrettable encounter with law enforcement. Vásquez was born in Monterey and watched Americans take over California. In fact, when Commodore Sloat arrived, Vásquez could see his vessel from his home. His and other Monterey families also lost family members in the ensuing battles in California. That experience generated some hard feelings for Vásquez, so for young Tiburcio anyone who opposed the Americans garnered his respect. And no one piqued his interest as did California outlaws.[14]

One of the bandits operating near Monterey, Anastacio García, fascinated Vásquez. García and Vásquez were also related (García had married one of

Vásquez's cousins). Anastacio García allegedly became a bandit after White migrants forced him off his sixty-acre ranch, which occurred regularly across the Southwest.[15] García set out on his own path of revenge and began robbing and killing people. In 1852, Monterey County issued a warrant for his arrest and Constable William Hardmount eventually caught up with García. When the constable attempted to take him into custody, García shot Hardmount. While Vásquez may have witnessed the shooting, the county accused him of being an accomplice to the murder of Hardmount. He fled in fear of his life and went into hiding. Vásquez became a bandit to survive. A posse captured him in 1857, and a jury convicted him of horse theft. He spent five years in San Quentin.[16] Once he got out, he began robbing people again. In 1867 Vásquez was back in prison. This time when he got out, he organized a gang of outlaws who robbed frontier settlements, stealing horses and cattle. Authorities captured Vásquez when one of his men betrayed him. He stood trial for murder, the jury convicted him, and the state executed him in 1875.[17]

Both Joaquin Murrieta and Tiburcio Vásquez became bandits in part because that is what society made them. Their outlawry only began because of unpleasant encounters with White law enforcement or, in Murrieta's case, a White mob acting as law enforcement. In Vásquez's case, the accusation that he killed a law officer would surely have resulted in his death, so to flee from the law wasn't that surprising. There were others like them.

Juan Cortina also became a bandit after an ugly experience with a law officer. He viewed his resistance to White racism as supporting the rights of Mexican-origin people in Texas. As prominent attorney and state Representative J. T. Canales correctly noted, Cortina "sympathized with the 'underdog' among his fellow citizens and opposed human slavery, and that is the reason why he became popular with the common people."[18] Cortina was a well-respected individual in Brownsville. He came from a wealthy landowning family and became a political boss after the Mexican-American War. Cortina's family lost a lot in the conclusion of the war, however, and he nursed considerable anger over what he saw as the rapacious greed of White migrants. "Flocks of vampires, in the guise of men," he called them. They "came and scattered themselves in the settlements, without any capital except the corrupt heart and the most perverse intentions."[19]

In July of 1859, Cortina witnessed Brownsville town marshal Robert Shears brutally beating a Mexican man, Tomás Cabrera, whom Cortina had employed at his ranch. He intervened on Cabrera's behalf. "Why do you ill-treat this man?" he asked Shears, who responded impudently, "What is it to you, you damned Mexican?" Cortina did not appreciate seeing an officer beating a defenseless man who offered no resistance, and he did not appreciate Shears's flippant response. Cortina replied by withdrawing his pistol and shooting Shears in the shoulder. In Cortina's words, "I punished his insolence and avenged my countrymen by shooting him with a pistol and stretching him at my feet." Cortina gave Cabrera a ride out of town and then left for Matamoros, Mexico.[20]

Marshal Shears spent several months recovering, but he survived the shooting. Meanwhile, Sheriff James Browne organized a twenty-five-man posse and set out to capture Cortina. Just past the outskirts of Brownsville, the posse evaporated: twenty of the men quit in fear and returned to town. With no posse, Sheriff Browne also turned back. Interestingly, Cortina evidently tried to smooth the situation by writing Shears to see whether they could settle the affair. Not only did Shears refuse to settle but a Cameron County grand jury also indicted Cortina for attempted murder. Cortina responded by forming his own seventy-person militia and in September he invaded Brownsville. He broke his men up into small units each tasked with attacking specific targets in town, including Marshal Shears, who fled. Town Constable George Morris, who had allegedly murdered a number of Mexicans, also attempted to flee and the raiders cut him down. Robert Johnson, the town jailer, tried to escape but several of Cortina's men found him hiding in a store and killed him. The jail itself came under attack and one of Cortina's units freed a number of Mexican men in the jail. Cortina's forces also targeted William Peter Neale, who had murdered at least two Mexicans in Brownsville. Neale died after a short shoot-out. To analyze this succinctly, Cortina's raid specifically targeted nearly every aspect of the criminal justice system in Brownsville. Cortina and his men then occupied the town for two days before departing.[21]

A group of officers and angry White residents amassed a thirty-person posse, which they called the Committee of Public Safety, to capture or kill Juan Cortina. In November 1859 they attacked Cortina and his militia. Cortina repulsed their attack easily. But in late December a group of Texas Rangers reinforced this posse. They decisively beat Cortina in two battles, bringing to an end the First Cortina War. A few years later, in 1861 after Texas had joined the Confederacy, Cortina again invaded Texas in what became known as the Second Cortina War. This time Confederate captain Santos Benavides decisively beat him, which ended the Cortina insurrections for a time.[22] But in 1875 Cortina was allegedly responsible for the Nuecestown Raid. That raid supposedly involved a group of Mexicans who robbed ranches from the Rio Grande Valley to the Corpus Christi area.[23] Whether Cortina participated in the planning of the raid or the raid itself remains a mystery. He denied it, but the press dismissed his denial. Interestingly, some speculated at the time that White Texas outlaws, not Mexicans, committed the raid. The press also dismissed that speculation.[24] Whites in the region organized themselves into vigilance committees and killed dozens of Mexican-origin people in retaliation for the Nuecestown Raid. We know relatively little about these vigilante groups or their victims.[25] The Texas Rangers broke the vigilante groups up.[26] The Rangers also killed a number of Mexican-origin people. In one instance they ambushed a "party of raiders," killed thirteen, and then took their bodies to Brownsville as a public display of Ranger strength.[27]

Juan Cortina's resistance to Texas authority demonstrated Mexican displeasure over White racism. Cortina had several regretful encounters with White men, some who seemed nothing more than the greedy "vampires" he had described and others like Marshal Shears who only treated Mexican-origin people with violence. When Cortina resisted, he did not simply attack Brownsville in an indiscriminate manner. Instead, he attacked almost every vestige of the criminal justice system, which gave his attack a clear purpose. His initial success perhaps should have shown White leaders that they might reconsider the use of legitimate law enforcement such as Marshal Shears or Town Constable Morris and illegitimate law enforcement such as the Committee of Public Safety. Instead, White authority doubled down on law enforcement, brought in the Texas Rangers who killed a number of Mexicans and Mexican Americans, and later spawned the massacres associated with the Nuecestown Raid. Juan Cortina succeeded in raising the fears White people had about Mexican "bandits," while the violence of the Texas Rangers succeeded in raising fears among Mexican-origin people. Neither of those fears would soon dissipate, but the sides were hopelessly unbalanced with White law enforcement having the bulk of the power. In the ensuing decades, the Mexican-origin community would suffer horribly.

After the Civil War, "wars" between Mexican folks and law enforcement continued in Texas. Some represented the merging of capital interests and vigilantism. The Cart War of 1857, wherein White Americans who desired to control the lucrative Mexican cart trade that ferried goods from the coast to inland cities such as San Antonio, fits this pattern of violence (Whites hanged an estimated seventy Mexicans during the Cart War), but it also lacks the law enforcement angle important to this book.[28] The Salt War, however, provides a clear law enforcement perspective.

In the El Paso area in the 1870s, salt meant money. The town of San Elizario was the seat of El Paso County and a lucrative site for salt mining. This largely Mexican community had enjoyed free access to the nearby Guadalupe salt lakes, which were public property, for generations. The salineros, or salt gatherers, from the region worked in cooperation. But salt was a big business and various White migrants sought ownership of the salt lakes. When they tried to acquire these lakes, Mexicans resisted. That resistance spawned the Salt War.[29]

Tensions came to a head in San Elizario in 1877 with the arrival of Charles Howard, a well-established businessperson with ties to Texas and New Mexico. Howard claimed the salt lakes for himself. This obviously did not sit well with Mexican-origin people. They sought someone to represent them and found a friendly benefactor in Louis Cardis, a fierce rival of Howard and an elected member of the Texas House of Representatives. Mexican residents also formed a number of public committees, "juntas" in Spanish (administrative bodies akin to town councils). These juntas came to represent so many people that they became the power structure in the region and effectively displaced the county government. The White population as well as the local and state governments viewed these juntas negatively and, though they had committed no violence, as riotous mobs. As author Paul Cool has cogently observed, the juntas were "the product of a deliberate, community-based decision squarely in the tradition of the American nation's original fight for self-government," they "were not eliminating 'law and order,' merely redefining it through their own government 'of the people, by the people, for the people.'"[30] The juntas, determined to protect open access to the salt lakes, acted in many ways like an inchoate criminal justice system.[31]

Howard persisted in his efforts to take possession of the salt lakes and threatened to charge anyone who gathered salt with theft and trespassing. In September of 1877, two salineros, José María Juárez and Macedonia Gandara, made public their intentions to collect salt. Howard used his connections with El Paso County sheriff Charles Kerber to have them jailed. The Mexican-origin population was incensed. The leaders of the juntas, with Louis Cardis, made plans to capture Howard and if possible, Kerber. Howard countered by seeking out Cardis. When Howard found Cardis, he emptied two shotgun barrels into his enemy, killing him.[32]

The juntas again made plans to capture Charles Howard after he murdered Louis Cardis. Since the juntas had largely replaced local authorities, a vigilance committee formed to protect Howard. When the vigilance committee asked Governor Richard Hubbard to send in the Texas Rangers, he complied. The governor tasked Lieutenant John B. Tays with bringing the situation under control by forming a Frontier Force, a kind of pre–Border Patrol border patrol. Tays helped cobble together a contingent of twenty men to oust the juntas and reestablish White government. This Frontier Force exacerbated problems, as did Howard. When a group of salineros again made plans to harvest salt in December of 1877, Howard swore out arrest warrants against them, claiming that they were stealing his salt. He probably should have left well enough alone.[33]

The salineros were determined to protect their access to the salt lakes and the juntas were determined to captured Charles Howard and rid the region of the Rangers. The juntas had a good number of well-armed soldiers. Citizens of San Elizario joined their cause. A number of Mexican-origin people from El Paso also came to San Elizario to assist the juntas. And finally, a group of Mexican nationals crossed the border to assist the salt warriors. The juntas had at least 500 individuals, men and women, in their ranks. On the morning of Thursday, December 13, 1877, the war began. One of the juntas' leaders, Sisto Salcido, gave the Rangers an ultimatum to turn over Howard. When the Rangers refused, shots rang out. A raging battle began that lasted the day, resumed on Friday, and continued on Saturday and Sunday. The junta forces killed several Rangers during the fighting. Ranger John Tays surrendered that Monday, allegedly the only time the Rangers ever surrendered. He turned Howard over to the juntas, as well as John G. Atkinson, a former state police officer, and John McBride, who had defended Howard and whom Tays had made a sergeant in the Rangers. The juntas executed Charles Howard: they shot him, hacked his body to pieces with machetes, and dumped his remains in an abandoned well. They also shot and killed Atkinson and McBride. With their deaths, the siege came to an end.[34]

The juntas' victory did not last long. The U.S. Army ultimately unseated the juntas and restored Sheriff Kerber to his office. Many people remembered the Salt War long after it happened, but the various groups involved remembered it differently. Whites viewed the war simplistically as a "riot" committed by a Mexican "mob" that resisted modern business practices. It was, for many White people, a battle of modernity against what they stereotypically viewed as a backward and unchanging people. Mexican-origin people interpreted the Salt War quite differently. For them the Salt War represented resistance. It was about defending ancestral rights against greedy aggressors, as well as an attempt to create a more just society. Howard had used law enforcement to his economic advantage, so it is no wonder, then, that the juntas acted as a criminal justice system, that the institutions that they confronted were part of the criminal justice system, and that the individuals killed by the juntas were, except for Howard, members of law enforcement, which perhaps explains why White people remembered the Salt War so negatively.[35]

Both the Salt War and the Cart War represented economic competition that spilled over into law enforcement. The same factors were at work when Mexicans and Mexican Americans formed Los Gorras Blancas, or the White Caps, in New Mexico. Most scholars have emphasized the role Las Gorras Blancas had in resisting White dispossession of Mexican and Mexican American lands. As such, the group protected Mexican land rights. It achieved this by cutting fences, burning property, and destroying railroad trestles. David Correia and Mary Romero have examined the White Caps via a class struggle and social movement lens.[36] But the White Caps can also be analyzed through a law enforcement lens.

The White Caps worked to protect Mexican-origin people from land speculators *and* abusive law enforcement.[37] Many of the people they attacked, and the institutions they threatened, were part of the criminal justice system. Their "platform," which came in the form of several major declarations, focused on land issues in Las Vegas and, later, beyond San Miguel County. But much of their "platform" also focused on criminal justice:

> Our purpose is to protect the rights and interests of the people in general, and especially those of the helpless classes.... We are not down on lawyers as a class, but their usual knavery and unfair treatment of the people must be stopped.... Our judiciary hereafter must understand that we will sustain it only when "Justice" is the watchword. The practice of "double dealing" must cease. There is a wide difference between New Mexico's "law" and "justice." And justice is God's law, and that we must have at all hazards.... Intimidation and the "indictment" plan have no further fears from us.... Be fair and just and we are with you, do otherwise and take the consequences. The White Caps—1,500 Strong and Gaining Daily.[38]

These statements indicted the criminal justice system.

In the minds of many White New Mexicans, Las Gorras Blancas probably seemed like bandits, nothing more and nothing less. Given the presence of bandits such as Jose Chavez y Chavez in the group, as well as similar groups like La Sociedad de Bandidos, this perception perhaps made some sense. In reality, like other "bandits," White people only viewed Las Gorras Blancas as bandits because they opposed local and territorial authority in New Mexico.

The first iteration of Las Gorras Blancas developed in Las Vegas in 1889. The first ranch they attacked belonged to Lorenzo Lopez, sheriff of San Miguel County. Lopez serves as another example of a Mexican American law enforcement official, but one that seemed to side with American interests and whom

Mexican-origin people disliked. He owned large tracts of land and nearly 2,000 head of cattle. The White Caps cut his fences on several occasions and as one colleague noted in late 1889, "Lorenzo Lopez suffered severely."[39]

Sheriff Lopez eventually arrested three men for these crimes, but this only inflamed the situation and word began to spread that Las Gorras Blancas might attempt to break these individuals out of jail. Edward W. Wynkoop, the warden at the Penitentiary of New Mexico, wrote to Governor L. Bradford Prince in December 1889 explaining that "trouble is expected this pm."[40] A few days later Sheriff Lopez sent his own desperate request to Governor Prince asking for fifty rifles and ammunition, "I fear jail will be attacked by a mob over one hundred strong and I cannot get weapons here." Elisha V. Long, chief justice of the New Mexico Territorial Supreme Court and a Las Vegas resident, forwarded a supporting telegram to Governor Prince and advised "an instant compliance with the sheriff's request."[41] The indictments against the men ultimately fell apart when the court failed to locate witnesses, which probably contributed to even more fear from local leaders.

The single most common response by law enforcement to Las Gorras Blancas were calls for self-defense and weapons. We need "rifles with ammunition... for the purpose of self-protection," Deputy Sheriff Joseph Trumbly begged in early 1890.[42] The governor sent the weapons. Probate Judge Manuel C. de Baca asserted that the governor "must at once organize a militia."[43] To my knowledge not a single document in the extant record mentioned investigating or trying to understand the cause of the White Caps' activism. In fact, some like District Attorney Miguel Salazar believed that "in all this flagrant and wicked destruction of property, no apparent reason or excuse exist, or is given by these people for their felonious acts."[44] And yet he could also explain to the governor that he feared Las Gorras Blancas would entice various members of the territorial assembly to "oppose [his] re-nomination as District Attorney." "My re-appointment," Salazar continued, "will be a vindication of *law* and *order*."[45] Clearly Salazar understood the situation from both a criminal justice and a political perspective, his own.

Sheriff Lopez, District Attorney Salazar, and Judge C. de Baca all viewed Las Gorras Blancas as not just an affront to property but to the law. Judge de Baca called for organizing a militia that should remain until "the time of the next term of the District Court." He said, "We entertain some fears that the so called White Caps will make all efforts for an outbreak during the court, as many threats have already been made by them."[46] His concern was well founded. A list of the White Caps' activities in the following months noted, "Twice at night the 'White Caps' have ridden through Las Vegas in a compact body of two or three hundred, masked and armed with rifles. The second time they surrounded the Court jail, the Court House, and then Assistant Prosecuting Attorney Salazar's house, also the Sheriff's house,—this during the time District Court was in session." Following the session of the court, several hundred Mexican-origin people assembled, "some shooting pistols in the air, and all in the most excited way, denouncing the public officers and the laws."[47] Clearly the White Caps had concerns beyond property rights.

When a simple solution to Las Gorras Blancas failed to materialize, some leaders proposed forming vigilance committees to protect themselves from the White Caps. Thus, local leaders, many of whom held positions in the criminal justice system, proposed outlaw justice as a solution to outlaw justice. The chair of the San Miguel County Commission, Stephen E. Booth, wrote to the governor explaining, "There will be a meeting of the citizens of San Miguel County ... for the purpose of deciding some means whereby the depreditions [sic] now being committed in the county may be suppressed and the guilty parties brought to justice." While he was not explicit about it, Booth certainly seemed to suggest extralegal means. Moreover, people did gather for their own defense at this time, suggesting Booth's meeting may have borne fruit.[48]

Instead of dissipating, Las Gorras Blancas spread. A group developed in Taos County in the 1890s. The Taos example once again shows the connection between the White Caps and law enforcement. Sheriff Cesario Garcia used the group to cement his hold on power by working with Las Gorras Blancas to resist White land speculators. The White Caps, situated primarily in the village of Arroyo Seco, also engaged in their own law enforcement practices by removing two outlaw groups, the Vigils and the Maeres. While the sheriff assisted the White Caps, and vice versa, other groups such as La Sociedad de Proteccion y Justicia (Protection and Justice Society) also conducted informal law enforcement. La Sociedad was akin to a mutual aid society but one that punished lawbreakers with torture, such as the cepo de campana, or bell trap (whipping people on their knees with their hands bound under their shins).[49]

The community of Anton Chico, just south of Las Vegas, New Mexico, also had a group that operated like the White Caps in the early twentieth century. C. M. O'Donel, manager of the Bell Ranch, for example, had in 1906 hired Jose Sosteno Baca to investigate an outbreak of fence cutting that began in 1904. O'Donel employed Baca specifically because he was a Mexican American individual who could infiltrate the local community. Interestingly, Baca made his entry by pretending he worked for the New Mexico Mounted Police, or rangers. This aroused the suspicions of local people since no one knew him. They captured Baca, who revealed his identity, and they banished him from Anton Chico.[50]

The fact that someone had impersonated a ranger alarmed the territorial government, so they sent out an actual ranger to investigate. This time Ranger Cipriano Baca, a respected law officer and known member of the Mounted Police, went to Anton Chico. Baca discerned that a number of individuals had, like Jose Sosteno Baca, taken it upon themselves to impersonate law officers and investigate the fence cutting. In doing so, these people had intimidated and harassed a number of Mexican-origin people, compelling them to give false testimony about the fence cutting, testimony that county courts later rejected.[51] Cipriano Baca's arrival seemed to calm the situation and the fence cutting as well as the fake police all stopped.[52]

White Americans saw the events in Anton Chico as illegal fence cutting by a group that acted as had Las Gorras Blancas. Mexican Americans in Anton Chico who followed the White Caps' example had made clear that their efforts were in response to land dispossession and problematic law enforcement. The use of law enforcement to achieve local investigations, either in the form of pretend law officers, such as Jose Sosteno Baca, or real law enforcement, such as Cipriano Baca, also show the ways in which individuals manipulated policing to keep local people in check. Like the Salt War, the development of Las Gorras Blancas represented Mexican and Mexican American resistance to greed and abusive law enforcement. White people across the Southwest viewed that resistance negatively, however, and they found one word that could accurately and easily convey their fear and apprehension: bandit.

White people often confused outlaw activity, whether legitimate bandits such as Joaquin Murrieta or groups that resisted White encroachment like Las Gorras Blancas, with everyday Mexican-origin people. The problem with a term such as "bandit" is that anyone could be a bandit. The case of Gregorio Cortéz in Texas underscores this problem.[53] Like other so-called bandits, Gregorio Cortéz had a bad encounter with a White Texas law officer and while many White people regarded him as a bandit, that term simply does not fit Cortéz. But the casual way in which White folks could label him a bandit demonstrates the problematic use of that term.

Cortéz was born in Mexico but moved to Texas as a youth in 1887. In the 1890s his family had settled in Gonzales County. As an adult Cortéz relocated to nearby Karnes County. In June of 1901, Karnes County sheriff William Morris went to the Cortéz homestead to question him about the theft of a horse from a nearby ranch. Two deputies, John Trimmell and Boone Choate, accompanied Sheriff Morris. Choate served as an interpreter. According to almost all accounts of this encounter, Choate was a poor translator and the results proved horrific.[54]

The sheriff and deputies arrived late in the afternoon and found Cortéz, his wife Leonor, his brother Romaldo, and the Cortéz children relaxing on the porch of their farmhouse after work. Choate asked Cortéz whether he had sold a horse to another man named Andrés Villarreal. In fact, Cortéz had traded a horse to Villarreal, a mare, but Choate asked about "un caballo," or a male horse, and so Cortéz responded by saying, "No, era una yegua." (No, it was a mare.) Choate allegedly called him a liar and Sheriff Morris said he was going to arrest Cortéz. Hearing the word "arrest," Cortéz protested by saying, "¿Por que? No me puede arrestar por nada." (Why? You can't arrest me for nothing.) Choate mistranslated that statement to "no White man can arrest me," which Sheriff Morris took as an affront to his authority. He withdrew his sidearm and approached Cortéz. Romaldo intervened, placing himself between the two men. Morris shot him. He also fired at Gregorio but missed. Cortéz then fired at Morris several times, mortally wounding the sheriff. Morris died a short time later at the scene. Romaldo Cortéz survived for about a month but died in jail from his injuries. The deputies ran for their lives.[55]

Cortéz knew the potential fate that awaited him, so he fled to his friend Martin Robledo's house. He rode and walked close to one hundred miles to get there. Another sheriff named Robert Glover, a friend of William Morris, organized a posse and pursued Cortéz to Robledo's home. The posse arrived at night and proceeded to shoot up the house. Cortéz attempted to flee but ran into Sheriff Glover. The two men exchanged fire. Glover was hit and died. One drunken posse member accidentally killed another posse member named Henry Schnabel. The posse reported that Cortéz killed Schnabel, so now authorities wanted him for killing three men. Cortéz escaped again.[56]

The multiple shoot-outs and deaths prompted involvement from the Texas Rangers. To them, and White Texans more broadly, Cortéz was a "bandit." Ranger captain John Rogers, a decent and effective law officer, took charge of the posse, which now included close to 300 men. Cortéz eluded this massive posse for nearly two weeks and rode over 400 miles. At the end of that period, Rogers tracked Cortéz to a ranch near the border. He and another man found Cortéz asleep. They took him into custody without incident.[57]

The Rangers transported Gregorio Cortéz to jail in San Antonio.[58] He awaited trial for only a short time, but while he did, Mexicans and Mexican Americans from across the state launched a legal defense effort to try to ensure that he received a fair trial.[59] That defense network proved key in garnering financial and political support for Cortéz's defense. Both individuals and entire newspapers participated in this network. For example, one letter writer named Frederick Opp railed against the posse that pursued Cortéz, acknowledged that they "ruthlessly slaughtered a number of innocent citizens of this state simply because they had the misfortune of being of the same blood as the alleged Mexican murderer," and demanded Cortéz receive a fair trial.[60] In several instances, newspapers such as San Antonio's *El Regidor* devoted extended coverage of these events to garner support for Cortéz.[61]

Gregorio Cortéz's first trial began in late July 1901 for the death of posse member Henry Schnabel.[62] Despite the fact that another posse member had killed Schnabel in a somewhat classic friendly fire incident, the jury convicted Cortéz of second-degree murder and sentenced him to a fifty-year prison term.[63] Meanwhile, a mob had gathered to lynch Cortéz, but they did not succeed in their effort.[64] The state also tried and convicted Cortéz for horse theft, the original reason Sheriff Morris had gone to his homestead.[65] Another trial for the death of Sheriff Glover resulted in another conviction and a life sentence.[66]

The trials for the death of Sheriff Morris were perhaps the most interesting. The first resulted in a quick conviction and death sentence.[67] Upon appeal, however, the Texas Court of Criminal Appeals found a number of irregularities in that trial. It had taken place in Karnes City, where Morris worked and had many friends. The appeals court also questioned Morris's warrantless attempted arrest of Cortéz, the fact that Morris had not announced himself as a law officer to Cortéz, and the fact that Morris had not informed Cortéz as to the reason for his arrest. In short, the appeals court deemed the attempted arrest improper. The Texas Court of Criminal Appeals overturned the conviction in June 1902, almost a year to the day after the initial incident.[68] So, the state tried again, but that trial resulted in a hung jury.[69] The appeals court also determined that Cortéz owned the mare he had sold, so he had not sold stolen property. As a result, the appeals court overturned his conviction for horse theft. The court also overturned Cortéz's conviction for the death of Schnabel.[70]

Another trial for Morris's death took place in 1904. That trial, presided over by Rio Grande City District Court judge Stanley Welch in Corpus Christi, proceeded with a great deal more professionalism than the other trials. The jury heard evidence about the poor translations offered by Deputy Sheriff Choate and deduced based on the totality of the evidence that Cortéz had acted in self-defense. The all-male, all-White jury found Cortéz not guilty of murdering Sheriff Morris, a conclusion that for the time was exceedingly unusual.[71] Cortéz began serving his life sentence for the death of Sheriff Glover shortly thereafter.[72]

The defense committee formed on Cortéz's behalf did not give up. They acquired the assistance of several law firms in Texas. These firms had handled the appeals of the various Cortéz cases and continued to work on his behalf afterward. In particular, they petitioned several different state governors to pardon Gregorio Cortéz. These efforts finally produced results in 1913 when Governor Oscar Colquitt granted Cortéz a conditional pardon.[73] The state released him that same year. He died of an undisclosed sickness, possibly pneumonia, only three years after his release in 1916.[74]

Gregorio Cortéz was no bandit. He had not stolen horses, nor had he sold stolen horses. When Morris attempted to arrest him for a crime he did not commit, Cortéz shot Morris in self-defense only after the sheriff had shot Romaldo and after Morris had attempted to shoot him. That Cortéz fled seems hardly surprising given the fate that awaited Mexican-origin people who killed White people, and White law officers more specifically. When the posse confronted him at Martin Robledo's house, posse member Henry Schnabel and Sheriff Robert Glover both died after a violent shoot-out. But Cortéz did not kill Schnabel and he again acted in self-defense when he killed Glover. Ranger Rogers did a commendable job in arresting Cortéz without incident. The Cortéz defense committee and the results of his various trials and ultimate release demarcate some of the successful strategies the Mexican-origin community used to defend someone in need. The Cortéz case also serves as a good example of the ways in which terms like "bandit" became negatively discursive. That word was all White folks needed to hear to try and convict an innocent individual of any crime in the Southwest. The result for Cortéz proved atypical given that the state actually put him on trial for his alleged crimes. But for others, no trial was needed. In fact, White people murdered an untold number of Mexican-origin people during the manhunt for Cortéz.[75]

The extralegal killing of Mexicans and Mexican Americans became much more extreme in the twentieth century. The 1905 killing of Carlos Muñoz, called Atanasio López in the Spanish-language press, outside the small central Texas town of Dale, serves as a useful example. Muñoz, "a middle-aged, one eyed Mexican," according to one newspaper, had allegedly attempted to sexually assault "Mrs. John Miers." A deputy sheriff and a town constable had quickly located Muñoz and placed him under arrest. But while transporting him to jail in nearby Lockhart, a mob of at least forty men opened fire on them. The law officers returned fire, but when their ammunition ran out, they fled, leaving Muñoz behind. The mob then captured Muñoz and shot him dead. He was allegedly shot fifty times and hanged.[76] Local authorities investigating the lynching of a Black man happened to discover Muñoz's body.[77] Despite the fact that Muñoz died extralegally and the mob also assaulted the officers, no investigation followed.

Fear and violence continued in the border region. In November of 1906, someone killed Judge Stanley Welch, who had presided over the 1904 trial of Gregorio Cortéz.[78] Suspicion quickly fell on the Mexican community, although years later in 1909 it became clear that Welch's political rivals had paid assassins of Mexican ancestry to murder the judge.[79] That didn't really matter at the time, though. What mattered was that Mexicans seemed involved.[80]

Governor Samuel Lanham dispatched the Texas Rangers under the command of Captain William McDonald to investigate the Welch killing.[81] McDonald formed a posse of four men, whom the press referred to as "rangers" with a lowercase "r." As they neared Rio Grande City, they had a shoot-out with some Mexican men. The press hyped this story dramatically as a bandit ambush, but the actual situation was more mundane.[82] The Rangers had encountered a covered wagon with several men inside on the outskirts of Rio Grande City. These men had attended a party and were headed home intoxicated. When McDonald announced himself as a Ranger, Juan Garcia Perez jumped out of the hack excitedly and started shooting. The Rangers returned fire and killed four men: Juan Garcia Perez, Candelario Garcia Farias, Gaspar Osuna, and Jose Vaneca. They wounded Manuel Osuna, who later gave testimony in the case.[83]

The press detailed the political intrigue of the time, the Gregorio Cortéz trial, and the killing of Judge Welch as the causes of this incident. But the fact of the matter is simpler than any of that. Juan Garcia Perez heard "Rangers" and panicked. It was not a "premeditated attack," as the *Brownsville Herald* termed it.[84] The press greatly inflamed the tension and fear White people had about this situation in other ways. The *Houston Post* warned, "It is now considered probable that much more bloodshed will follow."[85] The *Palestine Daily Herald* reported that "rioting continues" after the Rangers killed the four Mexicans, but that was sheer hyperbole.[86] Police eventually nabbed two Mexican men for the murder of Judge Welch and the state convicted them. The augmented Ranger presence in Starr County then began to ease.[87]

And then in May 1909, Texas Ranger Levi Davis killed Severo Lopez at Rio Grande City. Lopez and a number of his friends were enjoying a farewell dinner before departing Rio Grande City for Falfurrias. Ranger Davis and two other Rangers hearing the celebration said they thought a fight had broken out. They tried to disperse the crowd violently by pushing people around with the barrels of their shotguns. Lopez evidently pushed Davis's gun away and Davis shot him in the stomach. Lopez was not armed.[88] Police arrested

Davis for killing Lopez, but only a few days later the Rangers had already crafted a story of self-defense that would exonerate Davis. Captain Frank Johnson, Davis's superior, explained in a report to Ranger adjutant general James Newton that Lopez had attempted to wrestle the shotgun away from Davis. Johnson also claimed that Davis had seen something shiny in Lopez's pocket, which he believed was a pistol, although it turned out to be a flask.[89] The Starr County grand jury indicted Davis for murder.[90] His trial began late June 1909.[91] It ended in early July with an acquittal.[92]

The killings perpetrated by the Texas Rangers in 1906 and 1909 followed a pattern that began long before and persisted well after. While such police murders continued, extralegal lynchings did as well. Like the lynchings of unknown Mexicans, the lynching of Francisco Quiñones Jr., and the near lynching of Manuel Mejía, among others discussed in chapter 2, the case of Antonio Rodríguez elicited considerable attention from the Mexican government. Rodríguez, a twenty-year-old ranch hand from Central Mexico, allegedly shot and killed the wife of rancher Lemuel Henderson (her first name was Effie, but the press referred to her as Mrs. Lem Henderson) near Rocksprings, Texas, in November of 1910. The accounts vary, but what seems to have happened is that a Mexican-origin individual rode up to the Henderson ranch house and asked for food or water. Shortly thereafter this person shot Henderson several times. One of the Henderson children reported that "a bad Mexican had killed mama."[93] Lemuel Henderson alerted authorities, the press picked up the story, and a posse soon formed to apprehend this "unknown Mexican." The press went on to warn, the suspect "may be lynched if he is caught by the posse now in pursuit."[94]

As word of the killing spread, another rancher named Jim Hunter came to believe that his newly employed hand, Antonio Rodríguez, might have killed Effie Henderson. Hunter drew his gun on Rodríguez and then took him to the police station in Rocksprings. Rodríguez allegedly confessed to the killing after an interrogation. A mob composed of White Americans and Mexican Americans then overpowered the single guard, broke Rodríguez out of his cell, and took him outside of the town. They tied him to a mesquite tree, doused him in kerosene, and burned him alive.[95] The coroner reported that "un mexicano desconocido habia sido quemado vivo por personas desconocidos." (an unknown Mexican man had been burned alive by persons unknown.) No investigation to determine the identity of these unknown persons ever occurred.[96]

Once Rodríguez was dead, local papers began to pen accounts to exonerate his killers. A week after the killing, the *Brownsville Herald* reported that the perpetrator, a "fiend," had "violated and ruthlessly shot to death" Henderson. Such language implied that Rodríguez had sexually assaulted Effie Henderson and, as such, the resulting lynching had more in common with Southern spectacle lynchings of Black people than it did with the usual types of lynching Mexican-origin people experienced. It is unclear whether the mob believed Rodríguez had "violated" Henderson or the paper invented this as a justification a week after the fact.[97]

News of Rodríguez's lynching spread quickly. While the Mexican diplomatic offices began work on the case, the turmoil of the Mexican Revolution slowed their efforts. This frustrated people in Mexico. In Mexico City people rioted in anger. Mexicans attacked Americans, burned American businesses, and drove the U.S. consul in Piedras Negras (then called Ciudad Porfirio Díaz) across the border. While Mexicans and Mexican Americans hoped the Mexican diplomatic corps would make the lynching an international incident, the American diplomatic corps made more of an issue of the harassment Americans faced in Mexico.[98]

The lynching of Antonio Gómez also incensed Mexican-origin people in Texas. A mob murdered Gómez in Thorndale, Texas, in June of 1911. Fourteen-year-old Gómez was walking home, whittling a wood shingle with a pocketknife. As he passed a saloon owned by William Stephens, who evidently knew the youth, Stephens jokingly complained that Gómez's whittling slivers were litter and he allegedly grabbed Gómez playfully. Another man, Charles Zieschang, then intervened, aggressively grabbed Gómez, swiftly wrestled the shingle away from him, and said, "If that son-of-a-bitch did that in front of my store, I would paddle his ass with it." Gómez responded by slashing at Zieschang with his whittling knife. A bystander noticed blood, but Zieschang stated, "No, he hasn't stabbed me," as blood began to gush from his chest. Constable Robert McCoy collared Gómez as Zieschang fell to the ground. He died shortly thereafter.[99]

Constable McCoy attempted to do his duty and took Gómez to the calaboose. But as a mob began to form outside the jail, McCoy worried that they would lynch Gómez. To protect the youth, McCoy and another man named Wilford Wilson secreted Gómez from the jail to a nearby cotton gin building. McCoy decided to secure his prisoner by attaching a chain to Gómez's neck; the same chain would later hang him. After debating about how to proceed, McCoy and Wilson decided to take Gómez to the home of G. W. Penny, McCoy's friend. McCoy left Gómez in the protection of Wilson and Penny while he attempted to find transportation to take Gómez out of town. While Constable McCoy was away, the mob appeared at the Penny home. Wilson fled out the back door with Gómez and down an alley. Unfortunately, they ran directly into a group of White men walking to join the mob. This group took Gómez from Wilson and then joined up with the lynch mob. The mob dragged Gómez by the chain around his neck to downtown Thorndale, beating him along the way. By some accounts Gómez was near death when the mob arrived downtown. They hanged him from the underside of a ladder, and he died.[100]

As in the Antonio Rodríguez case, the Mexican-origin community was outraged. *La Crónica* ran several lengthy articles sternly rebuking lynch law and demanding justice for Antonio Gómez. The paper wanted the Mexican consul to look into the lynching and for the state government to prosecute the attackers.[101] Mexico, still mired in the revolution, could do very little. But the State of Texas could. Governor Oscar Colquitt probably did not want to intervene, but he received considerable pressure from San Antonio City Council member Francisco A. Chapa. As one of the few Mexican American elected officials in Texas, Chapa wielded some influence. Colquitt ordered an investigation into the lynching. Even though an estimated one hundred people observed the murder, the state singled out the main culprits quickly: Ezra Stephens (the son of saloon-owner William Stephens), Garrett Noack, Harry Wuensche, and Z. T. Gore. All four men stood trial for Gómez's murder. Alas, in separate trials, juries acquitted Gore, Stephens, and Noack. The state dropped the charges against Wuensche.[102] An inspector for the Mexican consulate also visited Texas and the governor again promised the state would take action, but nothing more came from the case.[103]

Both the Antonio Rodríguez and Antonio Gómez cases once again demonstrate certain aspects about the criminal justice system and extralegal justice in the Southwest. The Rodríguez case seems perhaps the more typical of the two: someone killed Effie Henderson, suspicion fell on a person of Mexican ancestry, Rodríguez was Mexican, and after an interrogation he allegedly confessed and was murdered. The legitimate criminal justice system at least initially worked, but once suspicion had fallen on Rodríguez, and perhaps because the victim was a White woman, the mob took over and exercised extralegal justice. The criminal justice system then wiped its hands of the case because "justice" had been done for Henderson, whether or not Rodríguez had committed the crime. Of course, because no trial occurred Rodríguez was not guilty, since only a trial confers guilt.

The Antonio Gómez case was more troubling. In some versions, Zieschang had not only verbally accosted Gómez and taken the shingle away from him but he had also physically accosted the youth. Whether true or not, Zieschang had initiated the confrontation by assaulting Gómez, and Gómez defended himself. Since Gómez used a knife, a disparity of force certainly existed, but such an argument would have come at his trial. There was, of course, no trial. Instead, locals took the law into their own hands, even though the established police agents did their duty. Constable McCoy should receive credit for attempting to protect Gómez, although he ultimately failed in this effort. As in other cases, the determination of the Mexican American population forced the trial of the mob. That they stood trial at all is surprising; that they got off is not.

These cases also generated civil rights activism. The violence in 1910s Texas proved so bad that in San Antonio Mexicans and Mexican Americans formed an anti-lynching society, La Agrupación Protectora Mexicana (Mexican Protective Group). They specifically hoped to raise funds to help prosecute lynchers who killed Mexicans and Mexican Americans. They professed the following: "To defend their lives and interests when our unfair enemies, with no other right than the rabid hatred they profess, try to impose their capricious and unhealthy will." While the group seemed primarily legalistic, it also challenged lynchers in a more confrontational manner.[104] A few years later, the group morphed into La Liga Protectora Mexicana (Mexican Protective League) and wrote to Governor Oscar Colquitt commending him for investigating the Gómez lynching and stating that in a mass meeting the group had passed resolutions "condemning and protesting against these lynchings of our countrymen ... signed by 300 citizens of this city."[105]

Other Mexican Americans resisted individually. Perhaps the most famous was Jovita Idar. She worked for her father's newspaper, *La Crónica*, and later founded *El Progreso* newspaper. Idar had published a number of accounts opposing lynching. The paper also published editorials from Mexican revolutionaries. The Texas Rangers appreciated neither of those two things and went to the offices of *El Progreso* to destroy the press in 1914. Idar, the only person at the press, stood down the Rangers and held them off. The Rangers had killed for lesser offenses and Idar knew it, magnifying her bravery. Alas, the Rangers returned the next morning when no one was at work and burned the newspaper offices to the ground.[106]

Mexican Americans attempted to counter the negativity they encountered in a number of ways, from contacting the Mexican government to forming groups like La Agrupación, later La Liga. They also celebrated bandits. In the cases of numerous bandits, Mexican-origin people wrote corridos, heroic folk songs, which detailed the exploits of the bandido. One of the most famous corridos was that of Gregorio Cortéz. For the most part, White people tended to want to forget about bandits. But some authors penned accounts that became highly popular, serialized, and mass-marketed. John Rollin Ridge, for example, an author of Indigenous ancestry, wrote one of the first accounts of Joaquin Murrieta as well as an account of Tiburcio Vásquez.[107] These popular, and often largely fictional, accounts had the effect of further rationalizing the problem with so-called bandits because they aroused and confirmed the fears that White people had about Mexicans and Mexican Americans. In short, they propagandized banditry in an overly racist fashion.

A perfect example of this propaganda came in 1913 with the publication of the book *Utah's Greatest Manhunt: The True Story of the Hunt for Lopez*. The book's author, listed as "an Eyewitness" although writer Bertrand Gallagher penned the book (it's unclear whether Gallagher is the "Eyewitness"), recounted the exploits of "Rafael Lopez, the Mexican" in the mining district of Bingham Canyon, Utah. "An Eyewitness" labeled Lopez especially vicious, so much so that the author promised to give a percentage of the book's sales to the "widows and orphans of Lopez's victims."[108] But "an Eyewitness" also described how White law enforcement wronged Lopez, acknowledging that this negative interaction with police led Lopez to become a "murderer and outlaw."[109] The author also mentioned a story about Lopez's brother, whom a man named Juan Valdez allegedly murdered. According to "an Eyewitness," Rafael Lopez became a bandit to avenge his brother.

While the author of *Utah's Greatest Manhunt* took great pangs to distance the book's version of Lopez with policing issues, the policing story remained central to the account. "An Eyewitness" offers two versions of the troubling encounter Lopez had with law enforcement. The first came when Lopez somewhat heroically intervened on behalf of two Mexican women on the outskirts of Bingham Canyon. A couple of Greek miners had attempted to accost the women and Lopez defended them. A fight ensued and Lopez beat the Greek men badly. The two women then went to fetch a Salt Lake County deputy sheriff named Julius Sorenson. When Sorenson arrived, he arrested Lopez and let the Greek men go.[110] A jury convicted Lopez of undisclosed charges, which "an Eyewitness" called "a case of railroading."[111] Upon his release, the police continued to arrest Lopez for "trivial things."[112] "An Eyewitness" therefore described a common form of police harassment and explained that the officers "just showed him [Lopez] that they and their wishes were law and it was no use for him to try to even get justice."[113] Lopez evidently grew weary of this treatment and told Deputy Sorenson that if he "ever interfered with him again or tried to arrest him that he would kill him or anyone with him."[114]

The title page for *Utah's Greatest Manhunt*, which was also used as the book's cover. Here a heavily armed, menacing looking Rafael Lopez or more simply the "bandit Lopez," as "An Eyewitness" calls him throughout the book, leers at readers. Books like this helped to exacerbate White fears about so-called bandits in the Southwest. Like other social bandits of Mexican ancestry, Lopez's life as a desperado only began after an ugly encounter with White law enforcement. *Chávez Library Vertical File Collection. Fray Angélico Chávez History Library, New Mexico History Museum, Santa Fe.*

The second story "an Eyewitness" told about police came after these authorities discovered the body of Juan Valdez. The "Eyewitness" speculated that Lopez killed Valdez for the death of his brother.[115] The death of Valdez has entered the record as what actually precipitated the manhunt for Lopez.[116] Whether he killed Juan Valdez or not, Sorenson decided to arrest Lopez. Several officers, including Sorenson, Bingham chief marshal John Grant, and Salt Lake County deputy sheriffs George Witbeck and Nephi Jensen, accompanied Sorenson to a house where Lopez was staying. Lopez fled, the officers gave chase, and Lopez opened fire from a distance. He killed Grant, Witbeck, and Jensen. Only Sorenson survived the encounter.[117]

The deaths of these law officers triggered the hunt for Lopez. Salt Lake County sheriff Andrew Smith organized a massive 200-person posse to track Lopez, but they failed to locate him. "An Eyewitness" actually lambasted the sheriff as "ludicrous" and full of "incompetence." He is pictured in one of the book's illustrations, lounging in the back of a car smoking. Perhaps because of this incompetence, the manhunt proceeded as a comedy of errors.[118] The posse seemed to see Lopez behind every rock or bush. They shot wildly at anything and only proceeded to injure themselves. When they did actually encounter Lopez, he taunted them from a distance and succeeded in further arousing their fears. This continued for several days. Finally, on the tenth day of the manhunt, the posse learned that Lopez had taken refuge in a mine. Now the search became more daunting as Lopez could be anywhere underground. "He had hundreds of places to hide," "an Eyewitness" explained.[119]

Soon the posse, in its frustration, began to turn on the officers and in particular Sheriff Smith. "The faith of the people in the county officers was dead," the author commented.[120] Here we see the classic pattern of lynch justice come into view: the officers had failed, and it thus fell to the mob to become the enforcers of justice. But according to "an Eyewitness," the mob proved just as ineffective. From Lopez's perspective, they were probably all the same. Eventually the search ended and "an Eyewitness" speculated that somewhere in the mine laid "the body of the Bandit Lopez, the man who, singlehandedly and alone, defied the officers of Salt Lake County and over two hundred citizens for fourteen days."[121]

For the individuals involved in the search, once Rafael Lopez disappeared in the mine, the story more or less ended. They never saw him again. For "an Eyewitness," the events surrounding the Lopez affair merited more grandstanding. For instance, the author alluded to the power of the lynch mob: "If interfered with by the officers, they [the lynch mob] resent it to such an extent as to threaten the lives of those who arrest them, and they are seldom interfered with by the majority."[122] Here the mob also failed, but of course in hundreds of other cases the so-called bandit would have been killed.

It took until 2003 for officials in Utah to learn the truth about Rafael Lopez. He did not die in the mine. Instead, he escaped to Texas, where he became an actual bandit known as Red Lopez. In 1921 Texas Ranger Frank Hamer received a tip that Lopez would be meeting with others in South Texas. Hamer and a group of Rangers ambushed the men. Lopez managed to shoot Hamer, grazing his face with a bullet before Hamer shot him dead. The Rangers killed nearly a dozen other Mexican-origin people in this encounter, another large group of victims.[123] The connection between Texas's Red Lopez and Utah's Rafael Lopez went unnoticed for nearly one hundred years. In the 1990s, Salt Lake County deputy sheriff Randy Lish began investigating the case after reading Hamer's autobiography. Lish had noticed similarities between the Texas Lopez and the Utah Lopez. He concluded that the two men were the same. In 2003 the state agreed, and Utah closed the case. The hunt for Lopez had ended.[124]

If Gregorio Cortéz and Rafael Lopez entered and then left the historical record, other so-called bandits had a longer-lasting legacy. Chico Cano was one of these individuals. Cano, like Joaquin Murrieta, provoked so much fear in the minds of White Americans that they attributed just about every "bandit" act in the 1910s to him. Cano was a product of the border region. Born in Mexico in the 1880s, he came up in poverty with four brothers, Manuel, José, Antonio, and Robelardo. He and several of his brothers eventually acquired a small farm near San Antonio del Bravo, Mexico, a community across the river from Candelaria, Texas. While they broke wild horses and raised cattle, Texans in Candelaria suspected the brothers of livestock theft. When the Mexican Revolution broke out, Cano originally joined the army of Venustiano Carranza and later formed his own revolutionary militia.[125]

Customs inspector Joe Sitter took special offense at the alleged thefts attributed to Chico Cano. Sitter owned a ranch near Valentine, Texas, and even though Cano's property was over one hundred miles away, Sitter blamed Cano for every raid in the region.[126] So, in late January 1913, he set out to apprehend Cano. Another U.S. customs inspector named Jack Howard and a member of the Texas Cattle Raisers Association named J. A. Harvis accompanied Sitter. They located Cano at the wake of a family friend on the U.S. side of the border. Cano probably could have escaped, but according to several accounts he feared what the posse might do to the people at the wake. Cano surrendered to Sitter, who allegedly planned to take him to the jailhouse in Marfa.[127]

Now, law enforcement officers frequently disposed of suspects such as Cano as they transported them to jail. Whether a ley fuga killing or something

Chico Cano (*wearing a sombrero*) appears with Major John Arthur Considine (*far left*), Captain Leonard Matlack, and two of Cano's brothers, José and Manuel, near Candelaria, Texas. Like other figures, Cano only became a "bandit" after an incident with White law enforcement. This photograph also demonstrates that the U.S. military continued to serve as police force in the border region. Matlack allegedly attempted to have Cano killed shortly after this picture was taken circa 1918–19. This photograph probably captured a meeting designed to ease tensions between American military forces and Mexican revolutionaries after Cano had become a leader in the Mexican Revolution.
Harry Ransom Center, University of Texas at Austin.

else, the Rangers' captives didn't seem to make it to jail and instead wound up dead. Surely Cano considered this. His brothers certainly had. Robelardo and Manuel gathered a group of men and rode out to intercept Sitter and rescue their brother. They ambushed Sitter and his posse. Sitter received a bullet wound to the head, but he survived. A bullet pierced Howard in the abdomen, and he died several days later. Harvis was shot in the leg and lived. Cano escaped. These events magnified Cano's bravery in the minds of many Mexican-origin people, while also raising White people's anxieties even further. More "bandit" raids occurred after Cano's escape and every one of them, White people believed, had to be the work of Chico Cano. Ranger captain James M. Fox investigated and tried to track Cano, but law enforcement would never capture him again. Police and members of the military also attempted to assassinate Cano on over a dozen occasions. One account says he had been wounded by gunfire fourteen times, ten of those from Texas Rangers. They failed to kill him. He outlived all of his enemies and died in 1943.[128]

Joe Sitter provides a good example of a law enforcement official who abused his authority to punish a Mexican opponent. He turned Cano into a bandit. As historian Miguel Antonio Levario explained, "Cano violently engaged law enforcement officials and ranchmen as a result of the ill repute Joe Sitters fostered on him."[129] Sitter died in a shoot-out in 1915 with other so-called Mexican bandits. The state indicted Chico Cano for this killing but he never stood trial.[130]

Chico Cano, of course, was not the only person to receive such treatment. As historian Walter Prescott Webb analyzed, "Not only were the Mexicans bamboozled by the political factions, but they were victimized by the law. One law applied to them and another, far less rigorous, to the political leaders and to the prominent Americans." Webb viewed this situation starkly, "Here, indeed, was rich soil in which to plant the seed of revolution and a race war."[131] White folks sowed that seed in the nineteenth century; the Cart War and Salt War in Texas, as well as land depredations and the White Caps in New Mexico, are good examples of its early flowering. But in the 1910s, as Mexicans fled the Mexican Revolution, "the seed of revolution and race war" once again suggested that there were "bandits" everywhere. The Texas government knew exactly what to do: augment law enforcement. Governor Oscar Colquitt dispatched over 1,000 Texas Army National Guard soldiers to the border in 1913. In 1915, Governor James "Pa" Ferguson expanded the Texas Rangers from a force of 13 men to nearly 1,500. These included 150 new regular Rangers, 400 specialty Rangers, and 800 loyalty Rangers, the latter two received no pay and training but had the full legal authority of a regular Ranger.[132]

If a "seed of revolution" existed, the *Plan de San Diego* and its follow up *Manifiesto ¡A los Pueblos Oprimidos de America!* (Manifesto to the Oppressed Peoples of America) seemed to be it. Both caused much tension in South Texas. A number of individuals drafted the *Plan* in January of 1915, allegedly in the small town of San Diego, Texas, sixty miles to the west of Corpus Christi. The basic contours of the plot proved fairly simple: it called for an uprising of

Mexicans, Mexican Americans, African Americans, and Indigenous groups who would form a "Liberating Army of Races & Peoples" that would drive White Americans from the region and then found an independent republic that Mexico might one day annex. Parts of the idea seemed pretty extreme. For instance, section 6 stated, "Every foreigner who shall be found armed and cannot prove his right to carry arms, shall be summarily executed, regardless of his race or nationality." Section 7 dictated, "Every North American over sixteen years of age shall be put to death."[133]

The *Plan* was hyperradical. So much so that many observers at the time and historians today doubt the *Plan*'s provenance, the intent of its writers, and the ability of anyone to actually carry out its goals.[134] But at the time the *Plan* increased tensions. White people across the Southwest already feared the increasing population of Mexicans in the region and the violence of the Mexican Revolution. Moreover, White people had long, and speciously, suspected that Mexicans and Mexican Americans desired to retake lands acquired by the United States from Mexico. The *Plan de San Diego*, much like the Zimmermann Telegram of January 1917—which proposed that if Mexico backed Germany in the Great War, Germany would help Mexico reconquer its lost territories—confirmed White people's erroneous fears that there really were bandits everywhere.

These fears only increased after the arrest of Basilio Ramos, whom the writers of the *Plan de San Diego* had allegedly sent to Texas to foment the rebellion. Ramos seemed a bad choice: authorities quickly arrested him, and he allegedly revealed the plot, which once again illustrates how law enforcement effectively did its job. For Ramos these events became somewhat of a comedy of errors, since he basically bumbled around looking for support and instead got himself arrested.[135] The bloody results that followed were anything but funny. When more "bandits" crossed the Rio Grande into Texas, this reconquista seemed to White people a reality. They proved so malevolent that historians call the violence of this period the Bandit Wars.

Now, as noted, there were some bandits in the Southwest. In July of 1915, for example, a group raided several ranches near Harlingen. They stole horses, mounts, and then disappeared. Later that month bandits robbed one farmer and allegedly killed another. When someone burned a railroad trestle, White folks knew it had to be Mexican "bandits." Bandits may have committed this act, but it may also be the case that local people simply blamed banditry out of fear.[136]

Other bandit raids may have been about something else. In August 1915, for instance, a group of bandits robbed the town of Sebastian, Texas, and then went to the ranch of Alfred Austin. They quickly found Alfred and his son Charles and executed the two men. But the choice of the Austin ranch was hardly coincidental; the family, composed of prominent segregationists, had helped found the Law and Order League, a vigilante group that had harassed and brutalized local Mexican-origin people.[137] While their deaths further aroused White people's anxiety about Mexican banditry, they also reveal how Mexican-origin people resisted an abusive extralegal vigilante group. A raid on a ranch was one thing, a raid on White supremacist vigilantes, I would suggest, is something else entirely.

Alas, vigilante attacks on vigilantes only spawned more vigilantes. In fact, the murders of Mexican-origin people at the hands of White law officers and vigilante groups increased markedly at this time. One case that aroused considerable attention in 1915 was that of Adolfo Muñoz. As noted in chapter 3, Deputy Sheriff Daniel Hinojosa and Town Marshal Frank Carr arrested Muñoz in August of that year, but a group of ranchers either took him from the officers or they turned him over to the ranchers, and they lynched him. The South Texas press, as in other parts of the Southwest, excused and justified the lynching. As one paper noted, "Lynch law is never a pleasant thing to contemplate, but it is not to be denied that it is sometimes the only means of administering justice." The paper demanded that law enforcement do its job, again raising the fiction that vigilantes had to step in because of a weakness in the criminal justice system, even though, of course, Carr and Hinojosa had arrested Muñoz. Other killings followed. A few days after the Muñoz lynching, a group of Rangers murdered Desiderio Flores and his son, also named Desiderio. The Rangers returned the following day to kill the final Flores son, Antonio. It remains unclear why the Rangers targeted the Flores men. It seems likely the Rangers simply wanted to kill some Mexicans since Mexicans were "bandits."[138]

A raid on the Norias section headquarters of the King Ranch in August of 1915 had some similarities to the raid on the Austin ranch. Norias was located seventy miles north of Brownsville. A group of about sixty Mexican revolutionaries attacked the ranch house. Around fifteen men defended the ranch, many of whom were law enforcement, including Cameron County deputy sheriff Gordon Hill, several U.S. cavalry officers, and several Texas Rangers. They repulsed the Mexican attack and killed at least six.[139] The size of this battle suggested to many White Americans that it resulted from the *Plan de San Diego*, but as historian Benjamin Johnson has observed, whether the Mexicans raiders "were either directly inspired by the Plan de San Diego or responsible for drafting it remained unclear." The presence of so many law enforcement officers may have motivated Mexicans to attack the ranch given the unstable law enforcement situation at the time, but the revolutionaries were probably searching for supplies. After the attack, unknown assailants, possibly Texas Rangers, executed three individuals, Juan Tobar, Eusebio Hernández, and Abraham Salinas, for their alleged participation in the Norias Ranch Raid. Like other killings, we don't know whether these men had anything to do with the raid.[140]

Both legal and extralegal executions continued throughout 1915 as White fears of Mexican "bandits" reached a critical mass. For their part, the Rangers had the legal power to kill people—and they did—and then to successfully justify it after the fact. Many accounts of the Rangers read like this one from Ranger James M. Fox regarding the killing of Tomas Aguilar: "Of course he tried to make his escape but we killed him." Like other ley fuga cases, Fox had already somehow deduced Aguilar's guilt of robbing a train depot and also of killing the owners of the Austin ranch, which further helped excuse the killing.[141]

In addition to these killings, large-scale massacres of Mexicans and Mexican Americans also took place. The Texas Rangers, for example, clashed with a group of "bandits" near Ebenoza in September of 1915. Little is known about this incident, but according to a report from an army officer, the Rangers captured a dozen or more men and hanged them. The next month the Rangers found nearly a dozen Mexicans dead outside of the small town of Lyford. The Rangers likely killed these Mexicans and then "found" their bodies.[142] A similar massacre occurred two years later. The owner of the Indio Ranch near Eagle Pass complained that Mexicans had stolen his cattle. So, a group of Rangers and army soldiers crossed into Mexico to find the alleged thieves. The citizens of the small Mexican town of San Jose defended themselves. The townspeople had all but won the battle when a late-arriving machine gun platoon reinforced the Americans. The machine gun cut the townsfolk down, although the Americans "did not take the trouble to count the bandit dead, but six bodies were seen and officers say there were probably several others in the brush." For the Americans, all these people were "bandits." Interestingly, the U.S. government seemed little troubled about Americans crossing into Mexico and seemed shocked the Mexicans would defend themselves.[143]

September of 1915 also witnessed the murders of Jesus Bazán and Antonio Longoria. Outlaws had raided their ranch and stolen horses and supplies. Bazán and Longoria reported the robbery to local authorities and wound up dead because of it. The two men had travelled to a nearby ranch to report the crime to several Texas Rangers who had bivouacked there. When they departed, Texas Ranger captain Henry Ransom and two civilians followed in their Model T. As they passed Longoria and Bazán, one of the men leaned out the window and opened fire, killing the two men. Captain Ransom refused to allow the families to bury the men; their bodies remained on the side of the rode until late October.[144]

Several exceptional cases exist in which the Rangers killed someone and later faced charges. The case of Florencio García serves as a good example. García went missing in April 1918. After his father made numerous inquiries, authorities in Brownsville revealed they had located the skeletal remains of Florencio. Someone had shot him in the back at least three times. The Mexican government pressed the state for an investigation, which discovered that Texas Rangers George Sadler, John Sittre, and Alfred Locke had taken García into custody. Florencio García's parents filed civil charges against the Rangers. Justice of the Peace Henry J. Kirk convened a grand jury. The all-White, all-male grand jury no-billed the Rangers.[145] Hearings such as this were rare, and in most cases the justice system excused the Rangers because the victim was Mexican, or because the Rangers had broad authority to kill, or both.

And then came the Porvenir Massacre, or matanza, an altogether senseless slaughter of fifteen innocent boys and men. Porvenir, a small farming village in West Texas, had a population of about 150 people. The village became enmeshed in the brutality of the period for rather idiotic reasons. The first was a raid by a group of Mexicans on the nearby Brite Ranch in December 1917. The circumstances of that raid remain murky: a group of about forty Mexican soldiers seeking supplies for the Mexican Revolution besieged the ranch and robbed the ranch store. A White postal employee and two Mexican-origin individuals died in the raid. In response, Army Colonel George T. Langhorne mobilized about 200 men, including soldiers and Texas Rangers, to chase the Mexicans into Mexico. They killed twenty-five "bandits," another large-scale massacre that only momentarily satisfied their bloodlust.[146]

For these law enforcement officials, more than twenty-five people needed to pay for the raid on the Brite Ranch. They singled out Porvenir, a dozen miles to the west of the Brite Ranch, for punishment. While they probably selected Porvenir because of the racism of the period—Mexicans and Mexican Americans inhabited the village, any of them could be "bandits"—their actual justification was Chico Cano. When the Rangers, under the direction Captain James M. Fox, went to Porvenir on January 28, 1918, they allegedly asked a number of men "are you Chico Cano?"[147] Fox had tracked Cano and he knew well enough that Cano wasn't there. In fact, it seems unlikely that Cano had ever visited Porvenir. Chico Cano was merely an excuse for them to exercise their authority. In fact, a few days before the massacre, on January 23, the Rangers had already visited Porvenir, ostensibly to search for "loot" taken from the Brite Ranch. In reality, they went to disarm the villagers.[148] When they returned the night of January 28, Ranger Fox, his men, four additional local ranchers, and a contingent of U.S. Army soldiers need not worry about the residents of Porvenir defending themselves. The soldiers roused the sleeping residents, gathered families together, and separated fifteen men and boys, who ranged in age from sixteen to sixty-four.[149]

The Rangers at this point led the fifteen men and boys to a bluff just outside of Porvenir. Ranger Fox dismissed the army soldiers, who remained in the town itself. And then the Rangers and the four ranchers simply opened fire on these fifteen innocents, executing them all in cold blood. Historian Monica Muñoz Martinez commented on the violence, she wrote, "The entire bluff was stained with blood and human tissue."[150] Upon hearing gunfire, the soldiers ran to investigate. They encountered several Rangers who exclaimed, "We got him, Captain, we got him," as they rode off. The "him," obviously, was Chico Cano.[151]

The Rangers had in fact not gotten Chico Cano, but the Cano story gave the press the proof it needed to claim that the Rangers had taken care of some "bandits." But others saw things differently. Harry Warren, who interviewed some of the survivors, saw the scene of the massacre the following day and with the help of an eleven-year-old boy, Juan Flores, whose father had died in the massacre, identified the dead. They were Antonio Castañeda, Longino Flores (Juan's father), Alberto García, Eutimio González, Ambrosio Hernández, Pedro Herrera, Severiano Herrera, Vivian Herrera, Macedonio Huerta, Tiburcio Jácquez, Juan Jiménez, Pedro Jiménez, Serapio Jiménez, Manuel Morales, and Román Niéves. Warren later wrote about the sadness and defeat of the survivors. He stated, "The Rangers and the four cowmen made 42 orphans that night."[152]

The Porvenir Massacre might have been forgotten but for the families of the murdered, who rallied on both sides of the border for justice. Captain Fox's report suggested he thought the incident would hardly trouble him. As he had with the twenty-five individuals killed in the Brite Ranch retribution, he commented simply that he had killed fifteen more "bandits" at Porvenir. The families, however, appealed to authorities in Mexico and the United States for aid. So, Fox started making excuses, forgetting the Chico Cano story and instead claiming that the Porvenir residents—all "bandits"—had fired first, that the Rangers had returned fire into the dark only in self-defense, and that they had accidentally killed the men and boys. Several of his Rangers and three of the ranchers repeated these lies. All these reports referred to the residents of Porvenir and the men killed as "bandits," "bandit gangs," and "thieves, informers, spies, and murderers."[153]

Despite the disarray in the Mexican government because of the Mexican Revolution, acting consul Cosme Bengoechea took testimony from several of the survivors and demanded that American authorities investigate. The Rangers themselves investigated the incident and, despite this obvious conflict of interest, uncovered some of the information that we now know demonstrated their guilt. They recommended charges, but a grand jury failed to indict any of the men. The grand jury no-billed Captain Fox. The Rangers reassigned him, dissolved his company (Company B), and fired five other Rangers. This punishment was small recompense for the relatives of the victims. But given the time period, the fact that the Rangers received any punishment at all was unusual. Usually, they got away with murder.[154]

The surviving Porvenir family members continued to fight for justice and filed claims with the General Claims Commission. The commission, designed to adjudicate claims between citizens of Mexico and the United States, rarely ruled in favor of Mexican nationals. The U.S. attorneys responding to the case dismissed the charges and argued that the families making claims were American citizens, not Mexican nationals; that they were not actually related to the victims at Porvenir; and that the Rangers were justified in killing the fifteen boys and men in self-defense. The attorneys not only excused the massacre but also ridiculed the claimants and the dead, mocked the claimants' imperfect English, and stated yet again that the dead men and boys were probably "bandits." Such a response demonstrates how the criminal justice system insulated itself from responsibility.[155]

This massacre, along with the other mass killings in Texas, shows just how hard-boiled anti-Mexican racism was in the state and how easily law enforcement could commit murder and get away with it. The matanza further demonstrates the problem with the "banditization" of Mexican-origin people in the Southwest since law enforcement could use that label so easily to justify killing innocent people. The result was that, bandit or not, hundreds and possibly thousands of Mexicans and Mexican Americans lost their lives during this period.[156]

Texas was not alone in its racist response to Mexican refugees fleeing the Mexican Revolution. Arizona and New Mexico in particular experienced a similar level of apprehension, although the level of violence there differed from the violence in Texas. The Columbus Raid of 1916 in New Mexico actually exacerbated American anxieties in both New Mexico and Arizona. That year,

Mexican revolutionary Francisco "Pancho" Villa attacked the small town of Columbus. The raid eventually turned into an outright battle. The U.S. Army successfully repelled Villa's attack and later began the Punitive Expedition to rid the world of Villa, a campaign that failed.[157]

The Columbus Raid further intensified American fears that Mexican "bandits" were everywhere. Americans responded with violence, such as when White people murdered Mexicans arriving to Columbus by train shortly after the raid.[158] In Arizona, White folks responded by forming vigilante committees that they called home guards. These home guards operated as local militias to prevent another Columbus-style raid. They were also supported by the government. For instance, Arizona governor George W. P. Hunt asked the War Department to send 3,000 rifles and 30,000 rounds of ammunition for the defense of the state. The War Department denied this request. Local military recruiters and National Guard officers also recruited individuals into home guards, demonstrating a clear connection between vigilante justice and the military.[159] Phoenix went so far as to form a home guard with an additional 300 "special policemen" to serve in this role. The Phoenix police force also purchased 300 rifles and 90,000 rounds of ammunition for these new police, demonstrating a clear connection between vigilante justice and local law enforcement.[160] Additional towns, including Tucson, Bisbee, and Glendale, formed home guards.[161] New Mexico also formed a series of home guards in Las Cruces, Deming, Silver City, Lordsburg, Tyrone, Hurley, and Santa Rita in 1917.[162] By 1917, with the failure of the Punitive Expedition and a period of calm in the borderlands, along with U.S. entry into the Great War, many home guards shifted focus to border protection against German encroachment. Having no Mexicans to fight, the home guards also shifted to anti-union organizing and basically made war on the Industrial Workers of the World (IWW).[163]

Now, labor unrest associated with Mexican-origin people and the IWW has a long history. For example, during a short recession in 1913, labor activists gathered on Christmas Day to protest unemployment in Los Angeles. Los Angeles Police Department officers attacked the gathering, brutally beat a number of Mexican American Wobblies, killed one, and arrested seventy-three individuals, mainly Mexican Americans. About forty of those people later stood trial for a variety of charges, of whom the jury convicted ten, all Mexican Americans. Police and the local press dubbed these activists "agitators," "gangsters," and "unworthy foreigners" in order to discredit them.[164]

In Arizona, the 1917 Bisbee Deportation saw similar unrest. Bisbee, a mining town largely controlled by the Phelps Dodge Corporation, had experienced a growing level of labor unrest because of the poor working conditions in the mines. The IWW brought the power of a strong union to Bisbee. The local government and law enforcement decided to act. The Bisbee Home Guard and the Cochise County Sheriff's Office deputized 2,000 men and then arrested over 1,300 mine workers, imprisoning them at a baseball park. This posse hoped to deport the primarily Mexican and Mexican American people they had arrested to Mexico, but fearing international reprisals, they instead deported them to New Mexico.[165]

The Bisbee Deportation spawned a congressional investigation and a trial of nearly two dozen Phelps Dodge managers and law enforcement officials in Cochise County. The congressional investigation castigated local leaders and declared their actions illegal, but the subsequent trial went nowhere because the judge decided that those responsible for the deportation had violated no federal laws.[166]

The home guard movement was a fairly short-lived phenomenon. In Arizona and New Mexico, these groups formed rapidly to stop "bandits" after Pancho Villa's raid on Columbus but then quickly pivoted to other things such as the fear of a German invasion and halting the IWW. In short, while the home guards formed because of the fear of bandits everywhere, they found that in fact there weren't bandits anywhere. Still, it is important to remember that this was yet another extralegal policing enterprise organized out of fear of Mexicans, one that culminated in the very ugly Bisbee Deportation.

Mexican-origin people in Arizona did work to combat the racism they experienced. Along with labor unrest in Bisbee, cotton workers in the Salt River Valley south of Phoenix organized La Liga Protectora Latina (Latin Protective League) to challenge the abuse and neglect workers experienced. The cotton workers in particular experienced brutal working and living conditions. La Liga helped them organize a strike and appealed to Arizona governor Thomas E. Campbell for support.[167] While La Liga operated like a labor union, it also specifically focused on law enforcement issues. Article 5 of its incorporation document spelled out that the group would advocate for "Protection, Equality, and Justice."[168] La Liga suffered devastating losses, though. The government red-baited it, Mexican workers in the cotton fields were, as in Bisbee, deported, and the group fell apart in the early 1920s.[169]

La Liga Protectora Latina, Las Gorras Blancas, La Agrupación Protectora Mexicana, and other similar groups represented Mexican American resistance to the violence of this period. Also, individuals such as Jovita Idar, and even some of the bandits mentioned above, all fought against anti-Mexican violence. These groups and individuals tried to halt the killings, although they stood against a far more powerful group and their results were, at best, mixed. But that resistance would not soon dissipate and would continue into the 1920s and beyond.

The early twentieth century represented a nadir in Mexican and Mexican American relations with local, state, and national law enforcement. White Americans, motivated by fear of bandits, which translated into a generalized fear of all Mexican-origin people, used police agencies and extralegal law enforcement in an attempt to control Mexicans and Mexican Americans. Their fears that bandits were everywhere were overblown and misplaced. When combined with anti-Mexican racism, the larger culprit for all the murders and massacres, White people's anxieties resulted in the killing, harassment, and intimidation of Mexican-origin people across the region, but especially in Texas. The level of violence was far out of step with the actual threat bandits posed.

Many White people accepted and even promoted this violence and the need for both legally codified law enforcement as well as lynch justice. Lynching basically continued unabated from the nineteenth and into the twentieth century. The overpolicing of Mexican-origin people also continued unabated. But some White people saw things as they were. Reporter George Marvin explained honestly in 1917, "The killing of Mexicans . . . along the border in these last four years is almost incredible. . . . Some rangers have degenerated into common mankillers. There is no penalty for killing, no jury along the border would ever convict a White man for shooting a Mexican. . . . Reading over Secret Service records makes you feel as though it was open gun season on Mexicans along the border."[170] But the George Marvins of the world were largely in the minority. Only in the 1920s, with some major reform efforts and attempts at police professionalization, would things change, if slightly. While reform took place, anti-Mexican racism and violence continued.

6

THE PENDULUM OF CHANGE

Mexican Americans and Law Enforcement in a Time of Transition

In 1919, Texas representative José Tomás "J. T." Canales, the only Mexican American in the Texas Legislature, put the Texas Rangers on trial for the border massacres and murders they had committed over the previous five years. Canales convened a special legislative inquiry, The Joint Committee of the Senate and the House in the Investigation of the Texas Ranger Force, known more simply as the Canales Investigation. He made nineteen charges against the Rangers, the investigation took nearly two weeks, the committee heard testimony from eighty-three witnesses (including Representative Canales himself, who gave some of the most compelling testimony in the investigation), and the final report was 1,600 pages long. While he commented on his early respect for the Rangers, Canales explained that by 1915 something had changed. "In 1915, so far as my recollection goes," he stated, "is when the first general outrages perpetrated by the Rangers began."[1] He went on to describe in detail the various murders and lynchings committed by the Rangers, from Adolfo Muñoz to the murders after the Norias Ranch Raid, from Florencio García to the Porvenir Massacre. In speaking the names of the dead, he not only breathed them into the historical record but also simultaneously issued a demand for justice, making sure the state would not simply ignore and forget the victims and the survivors.

In the end the investigation exonerated the Rangers. But that should not diminish what Representative Canales did. The weeks of testimony and the massive investigative report detailed with great clarity the violent and lawless nature of the Rangers. That a person of Mexican ancestry could bring this data to light, daring to use his political power against such a powerful group, was itself important. Moreover, the state government began a series of reforms in the 1920s that effectively curtailed the power of the Texas Rangers. Canales had asked for many of these reforms during the investigation. Ranger violence, however, had always occurred simultaneously with the violence of local police and individuals, and that violence did not end in the 1910s. Instead, a new wave of murders and lynchings occurred in Texas in the 1920s. In other words, while Canales could push an activist agenda that demonstrated the growing political power of the Mexican American community, the violence and abuse Mexican-origin people had experienced during the previous decade nonetheless persisted into the next.

The Canales Investigation and the subsequent violence in the 1920s serve as good examples of the oscillatory nature of progress and stagnation, of change and business as usual that characterized this period. The 1920s and early 1930s witnessed the beginning of an evolution in the relationship between Mexican Americans and law enforcement in the border region. Police agencies began to modernize their practices. The early twentieth century saw a new focus on police professionalization across the region and across the United States more broadly.[2] This professionalization included new data collection techniques, new investigative tools such as fingerprinting, the use of new technologies from radio call boxes to squad cars, and in cities such as Albuquerque, a focus on hiring Mexican American police officers. In Texas, the reforming of the Texas Rangers perhaps best represents the transformation of policing at this time. Police professionalization and modernization went lockstep with other Progressive Era reforms in the borderlands.

But many problems remained. Police agencies continued to target Mexican-origin people with violence and intimidation. A series of murders in the Texas border region reminded many Mexican Americans that law enforcement did not exist to protect and serve them. While New Mexico inaugurated many reforms, local police agencies also continued to vilify Mexican Americans as bandits and target them as criminals. New Mexico also witnessed the last lynching of a Mexican-origin person in the Southwest. While some police agencies initiated reforms, others, such as the police force in Miami, Arizona, led by racist police chief John Welch, continued to treat Mexican-origin people with brutality. Additionally, the actions of the U.S. government, particularly the formation of the Border Patrol in 1924, which probably changed little in the day-to-day lives of Mexican folks, and a new "unlawful entry" law in 1929, which did change the lives of thousands of Mexicans, exacerbated problems at the local level.[3]

As the number of Mexican-origin people increased in the teens and twenties, mainly due to refugees fleeing the revolution, this new larger population gave people of Mexican ancestry a necessary power base that helped them push local authorities to inaugurate change. Many transitional figures supported these transitional moments: new Mexican American police officers, new civic and political leaders, new appeals to the Mexican government, new reforms pushed by Mexican Americans. As such the 1920s and 1930s were decades of transition and change.

The investigation into the Texas Rangers symbolized this evolution. Representative J. T. Canales had served in the Texas House from 1905 to 1911 and had only recently begun a new term in 1917. He had sought elected office to protect Mexican-origin people, especially after all the violence in the border region, violence that culminated in the Porvenir Massacre. Canales had experienced this violence himself; first when Ranger Frank Hamer and others had beaten his relative Santiago Tijerina for alleged horse theft in October 1918 and second when Hamer had threatened Canales for looking into Tijerina's case in December of 1918. Hamer had a long history of anti-Mexican violence and had killed an untold number of Mexicans (such as Rafael "Red" Lopez, discussed in the last chapter). Hamer disapproved of Canales's inquiries into the Tijerina case and confronted the representative on the streets of San Benito, warning him, "If you don't stop that you are going to get hurt."[4]

Representative Canales did not stop. On January 15, 1919, he introduced House Bill No. 5, "An Act reorganizing the State Ranger force, prescribing the pay, qualifications and duties of State Rangers, and declaring an emergency."[5]

Part of his reform idea focused on the professionalization of the Rangers, including a measure that would have required minimum educational standards and previous law enforcement experience for new recruits. He also proposed a pay increase for the Rangers. He wanted the number of Rangers reduced to twenty-four (eighty during times of emergency), which was basically the size of the Ranger force before 1915. His boldest proposal came in section 10 of House Bill No. 5 wherein he declared a state of emergency because of the lack of laws detailing the duties and qualifications of Rangers, which had in his view led to all the Ranger violence. Such a state of emergency would also allow the House to pass Canales's bill after one reading (bills are usually read three times). Instead, the House postponed the bill in late January and again in late February.[6]

While House Bill No. 5 lingered, Canales proposed House Concurrent Resolution 20, asking for a congressional investigation of the Rangers.[7] The Canales Investigation officially convened on January 31, 1919. Of the nineteen charges Canales made, the most serious included charge 5, the murder of Florencio García; charges 9 and 10, both of which dealt with corruption in Ranger leadership (specifically in charge 9 which stated that Ranger captain William Hanson, the adjutant general's chief investigative officer, was unfit for office because he conducted "most, if not all, of the investigations against Rangers with the idea of justifying the actions of the Rangers in committing the offenses charged"); and charge 11, that Rangers under the command of Captain James Fox had murdered fifteen Mexican men and boys at Porvenir the previous January.[8] The investigation heard testimony from a variety of people from the border region. Some noted honestly that the Mexican Revolution had created an atmosphere where police violence was not just tolerated but expected. Others commented that both the extralegal violence in the form of lynch mobs and state-sanctioned violence in the form of the Texas Rangers grew out of the same type of White racist anxiety, one that saw "bandits" hiding around every corner.[9]

The state's response to these charges shows yet again how the criminal justice system protects itself from attack.[10] Representative Canales testified at the hearing and the state's primary attorney, Robert E. Lee Knight, turned the proceedings from an investigation of the Rangers into an investigation of Canales.[11] For instance, in addition to bringing up Mexican bandit raids as a justification for the Ranger presence in the border region, Knight castigated Canales as sympathetic to bandits. Knight's argument hinged on two basic assumptions: that the threat of bandits was real and therefore the violence to stop them necessary and that as a Mexican American Canales had a racial or ethnic predisposition to siding with bandits because they were Mexican. While Canales ably deflected these charges, such assertions showed clearly that the government would not only side with the Rangers but would do so by openly casting racist aspersions on a witness's character.[12]

This strategy worked. The post-investigation report, for instance, absolved the adjutant general and investigator Hanson of any wrongdoing. In fact, the report declared that Hanson had worked "under the most trying circumstances [and had] endeavored in every way to faithfully, efficiently and impartially discharge the duties resting upon him."[13] While the report noted that some Rangers had acted improperly in the discharge of their duties, especially when dealing with Mexican-origin people, it also found that many of those violations had occurred under a different administration and that many of those charged in the investigation had already left the Ranger force.[14] The report specifically mentioned the murder of Florencio García but found only that the explanation for the killing made "by the rangers was wholly unsatisfactory."[15] The report barely mentioned the most egregious act of violence brought into the record by Representative Canales: the Porvenir Massacre. Instead, it simply swept the massacre under the rug. The state, via the report, did nothing to really change the culture of violence in the Rangers at this time. Canales called it "whitewashed" and demanded, to no avail, a revised report.[16]

While the Canales Investigation and the state's post-investigation report changed little in the day-to-day operations of the Texas Rangers, Canales was far from finished. In fact, his House Bill No. 5, which had lingered since February 1919, finally saw the light of day in March 1919.[17] It generated some political intrigue in that Representative William Bledsoe offered a revised version of Canales's bill, one that eliminated some of Canales's reforms, most notably the minimum educational standards for new Ranger recruits. The House subsequently adopted this revised bill. Perhaps somewhat surprisingly, after its third reading the bill passed by a very large margin in the House, 95 to 5.[18] Surely the bill would die in the Senate. But no, the Senate adopted the bill, renumbered it Senate Bill No. 331, which also amended the appropriate Texas statutes that actually gave the bill its power, and then passed the bill by a vote of 28 to 1 on March 17, 1919.[19] The House then passed the Senate's amended bill by a vote of 113 to 1.[20]

When Governor William Hobby signed the bill into law on March 31, 1919, he assisted Representative Canales in the most significant overhaul of the Texas Rangers to date.[21] While the legislature had stripped some of Canales's original provisions from the new law, it actually went quite far in reforming the Rangers. The reforms have come to be known as the Canales Reforms.

The new law amended a number of Texas statutes, including Article 6755, which officially reduced the Ranger force to seventy-four men (sixty-eight mounted Rangers and a headquarters staff of six). That number, three times higher than what Canales had proposed, still represented an exceedingly high reduction of the Ranger force, which stood at nearly 1,000 men at the start of the Canales Investigation. Article 6756 augmented the pay of the Rangers, a positive step in the professionalization of the organization. Article 6764 prescribed the duties and authority of the Rangers and stated specifically that they were "clothed with powers of peace officers." That language was important because before this bill, as noted by Canales, "no sufficient law prescribing the duties, pay and qualifications of State Rangers" existed. Article 6764, therefore, enumerated the extent and limits of the Rangers' authority.[22] Article 6765 specified that Rangers had to transport individuals they had arrested to the county jail where they were wanted, an important revision given the number of people who never made it to jail or who suffered a *ley fuga* death. Article 6766 detailed revisions to the investigative powers of the adjutant general, dictating specific parameters by which the adjutant general could exercise those powers, which would seem to vindicate Canales's charge that the Adjutant General's Office needed reforming.[23]

These reforms continued into the 1920s. In 1923, for example, Governor Pat Neff signed into law Senate Bill No. 8, an act that provided that if any "sheriff, deputy sheriff, constable, ranger, city marshal, chief of police, policeman or any other public officer" tortured a person to secure a confession, that officer would "be deemed guilty of a misdemeanor."[24] Known colloquially as the "third degree" law, this measure responded to the practices of the Rangers, but also law enforcement in general, in using violence to coerce an individual to confess to a crime, which often then also resulted in the individual's death. Governor Neff supported further reducing the number of Rangers. That number had hovered around fifty men since 1919 but dropped to thirty after Neff's request for a reduction.[25] The Senate reformed other police procedures in 1925 when it declared illegal search and seizure a crime. Senate Bill No. 174, "An Act making the people secure in their persons, houses, papers and possessions from all unlawful and unreasonable seizures or searches," made it unlawful for courts to use illegally obtained evidence. "Any peace officer, State ranger, or any other person" who obtained such evidence would be guilty of a misdemeanor punishable by a fine up to $500 or a six-month jail sentence.[26]

Finally, in 1935 the legislature put the Rangers under the purview of the newly created Texas Department of Public Safety. This represented the culmination of more than a decade of reforms. A director of public safety would preside over the Rangers, which created an additional level of accountability for the organization. The Texas Highway Patrol, which the legislature had founded in 1929, joined the Rangers in the Department of Public Safety. The legislature also added several new bureaus to round out the department: Intelligence, Communications, Identification and Records, and Education. This basically brought state-level law enforcement into compliance with modern policing practices. In sum, the state in this series of far reaching moves transformed the Texas Rangers.[27]

While J. T. Canales left office in 1920, and as such had no direct role in the reforms of 1923, 1925, and 1935, his attempts to reform the Rangers through the Canales Investigation and via the Canales Reforms inspired these latter reforms. Canales's efforts represented an important moment in the history of Mexican Americans and policing. They showed the nascent power of the Mexican American community in Texas. Canales conscientiously acted in defense of a wounded people because it was the right thing to do. His efforts demonstrated that Mexican Americans would not sit idly by and allow racial terrorism to masquerade as law enforcement. But more importantly, Canales succeeded in his bid to reform the Rangers. The investigation aired the Rangers' dirty laundry, allowing anyone who would look the chance to see the dangers of the Ranger force. House Bill No. 5 then engineered specific, well-thought-out reforms. In fact, just about everything Canales had demanded in the investigation he got in the new law that reorganized the Texas Rangers and in the subsequent reforms in 1923, 1925, and 1935. And while many legislators had demonstrated their racist bona fides during the 1919 investigation, a surprisingly large number of lawmakers fell in line to vote for Canales's bill and the other measures that followed. Even after he left office in 1920, Canales continued his work. He remained an important civic leader, helped to found the League of United Latin American Citizens, and served as its national president.

With all the reforms of the Texas Rangers in the 1920s, and of Texas law enforcement more broadly in the 1930s, the pendulum eventually swung in the other direction. The 1920s also saw an alarming number of border killings, again raising the ire of Mexican American leaders and community, and of the Mexican government. Part of this violence stemmed from the deteriorating economic environment following the end of the Great War, which resulted in a postwar recession. This in turn caused an informal Mexican repatriation campaign in the early 1920s.[28] Part of the violence also stemmed from the continuation of anti-Mexican racism. The Texas Rangers participated in none of these border killings, perhaps a sign that the reforms had worked.

Things began to go awry in the Rio Grande Valley when someone murdered Marie Schroeder, a seventeen-year-old White girl, in the town of Rio Hondo in February of 1921. Cameron County authorities almost from the get-go sought "four strange Mexicans, said by school children to have acted strangely in the neighborhood of the school" that Schroeder attended.[29] Mobs and posses engaged in a massive manhunt and rounded up dozens of Mexican-origin men. They captured one promising suspect named Teodoro Ortega, whom police arrested but then had to quickly ferry out of town to San Antonio after a mob threatened to lynch him.[30] Eventually the mobs and police simply began to raid the Mexican section of Rio Hondo and take into custody any man of Mexican ancestry.[31] One of these men, Salvador Saucedo, evidently acted too suspiciously for the mob. He allegedly attempted to flee, and the mob shot him dead. White locals vilified Saucedo as a murderer, while Mexican Americans knew him to be a hardworking, well-liked American of Mexican ancestry. White folks eventually conceded that Saucedo didn't kill Marie Schroeder. As in other cases, the Mexican government intervened on Saucedo's behalf, and while the State of Texas investigated the case, nothing came of that investigation.[32]

The Saucedo family continued to suffer. A few months after the mob murdered Salvador Saucedo, his uncle Pedro Saucedo died horribly. He was plowing a field when an eleven-year-old White girl passed by. Saucedo spoke to her, which evidently frightened the child. She ran to her nearby home and alerted her brother, Sam Graham. He retrieved his rifle, went outside, and confronted Saucedo. The two men exchanged words and then Graham viciously beat Saucedo to death with the butt of his gun. A jury later acquitted Graham of murder.[33]

Meanwhile authorities eventually settled on Teodoro Ortega, also known as Federico Ortega, and Guadalupe Rincones as the killers of Marie Schroeder. The mobs had picked up these men early on in their rush to gather suspects. Their trial began in November of 1921. It ended quickly when the judge suspended the trial after an outlaw named Alfredo Luna confessed to killing Schroeder.[34] It took until 1923 for this case to come to an end, though. In April of that year, Luna had bragged about killing Schroeder. He had also kidnapped another youth, the sixteen-year-old spouse of Guadalupe Moreno (whom the press referred to only as Mrs. Moreno) in March 1923, in the same fashion as Schroeder. Luna ultimately faced down a sheriff's posse and lost. Deputy Sheriff Ortega (first name unknown) had formed the posse to track Luna. They surrounded Luna, he tried to escape, and the posse shot him dead. The state released Teodoro Ortega and Guadalupe Rincones, who had nothing to do with the killing of Marie Schroeder.[35]

Another senseless murder occurred in 1922. That February a White mob killed Manuel Duarte in Harlingen, also in Cameron County. This case smacks of the vigilance committees of previous decades. A group of at least twenty-five White men had met in late January to make plans to force Duarte from the area and off his land. Men from this vigilante group went to Duarte's farm to run him off several times but could not locate him. Finally, on the last visit to his ranch house they spotted Duarte and, instead of running him off, they shot him dead.[36] The Cameron County Sheriff's Office swore out warrants for the arrest of twenty of the men who had participated in the meeting and subsequent murder of Manuel Duarte. The grand jury indicted them all.[37] Their trial finally began in October of 1923, but what happened after that is not clear.[38]

The killing of Virginia Becerra serves as a final example of the senselessness of many of these murders in the 1920s. Her death came in the aftermath of another killing, that of customs inspector Jot Jones in Mercedes in Hidalgo County on September 30, 1922. Jones had attempted to apprehend Jose Garza for liquor smuggling, but Garza had resisted arrest and killed Jones. In the aftermath of his death, as had occurred in Rio Hondo the year before, White posses went out searching for Garza, who unbeknownst to law enforcement had escaped to Mexico and was never apprehended. Authorities told posse members to "shoot first." They abused and assaulted a number of Mexican-origin people, and they murdered Becerra. A posse searching for Garza went to the Becerra home and broke down the front door. Virginia fled out the back door in fear. The posse members gunned her down in her own backyard. Virginia Becerra was fourteen years old. Her death seemed to cause little sympathy, although the Mexican government demanded justice.[39]

The extralegal murder that caused the most attention in the 1920s was that of Elías Villareal Zárate, a Mexican national in his twenties who did construction work in Weslaco.[40] He had gotten into a fistfight with J. F. Sullivan, one of his White coworkers. Local police had taken Villareal into custody for the fight on November 11, 1922. That night, an angry mob of about ten White men broke him out of jail and beat him. They then drove him about five miles outside of town, beat him some more, and finally executed Villareal by shooting him in the heart. Authorities found his body discarded on the side of the road later that same day. To justify the lynching, White folks in Weslaco circulated rumors that Villareal had killed a White man ten days before, a charge the state press picked up. That charge was wholly fictional. The press also disclaimed any law enforcement culpability in the jailbreak and killing.[41] Mexicans in Guadalajara protested the murder of Villareal.[42]

Mexican Americans also gathered in Weslaco to protest Villareal's murder. In response a day or so later, a mob of angry White people randomly targeted Enrique Olivares and nearly beat him to death. The details of the incident have been lost, but the Mexican government made numerous mentions of Olivares's beating.[43]

While South Texas continued to resort to mob violence and murder, the oil boomtown of Breckenridge in North Texas, adjacent to Dallas and Fort Worth, went the Klan route to harass and intimidate Mexican Americans and African Americans. Breckenridge had seen its status as a boomtown diminish in 1922. As the oil dried up, competition for jobs became stiff. A group of White men, 300 strong, formed the "White Owls," a KKK-esque organization, to prevent African Americans and Mexican Americans from acquiring jobs in town.[44] They also organized a campaign of terror and demanded that Black and Mexican-origin people leave Breckenridge. Allegedly hundreds fled "due to threats from a gang of close to 300 individuals who threatened to burn them out if they did not leave their homes."[45] Governor Pat Neff ultimately sent in Texas Ranger Frank Hamer to quell the situation.[46]

The murder of Virginia Becerra, the lynching of Elías Villareal Zárate, the beating of Enrique Olivares, and the mob action in Breckenridge occurred basically simultaneously in late 1922. So when the Mexican government got involved in these cases, they treated them as a group and called on the U.S. government and the State of Texas to protect citizens of Mexican ancestry. Mexican consul Enrique D. Ruíz demanded that the state prosecute the lynchers of Villareal. He also asserted that Villareal's murder, like so many others, had occurred with the "complicity of the authorities."[47] Mexican ambassador Manuel C. Téllez likewise called for an investigation. The mob also threatened the life of Consul Ruíz, and Téllez requested that state authorities investigate that threat as well.[48] U.S. secretary of state Charles Evans Hughes petitioned Texas governor Neff to launch an official investigation. Neff had already sent the Rangers to Breckinridge, and he dispatched Rangers to Weslaco to investigate as well.[49]

Ranger William Lee Wright arrived in Weslaco in late November 1922. Surely the Rangers gave the Mexican government and Mexican-origin people living in the border region pause, especially after the previous decade's violence and massacres. Ranger Wright discovered very little, and authorities arrested no one for the killing.[50] Similarly, in Breckenridge the Rangers determined that the White Owls had in fact terrorized the African American and Mexican American communities, but they somehow had trouble determining who led the group (even though the local press had published the names of the group's officers). All the investigations ended having basically achieved nothing.[51]

While the White Owls disbanded in Breckenridge, they inspired new versions elsewhere. A copycat group in San Antonio formed in December of 1922. Six White men in the group beat and robbed Almando Rodriguez on the night of December 13, 1922. The press explained that the men had "white owled" Rodriguez.[52] After Rodriguez reported the incident to Sheriff Alphonse Newman, the sheriff's office quickly located the main perpetrator, Oscar Rawlinson. Competition for local jobs, as in Breckenridge, seems to have sparked this beating.[53]

The Mexican press also picked up these stories. *El Heraldo de México* focused on all the violence but called the lynch mob that murdered Elías Villareal Zárate "savage Texas lynchers" and noted, that the killing was "solely based on racial prejudice and a spirit of savagery on the part of local elements that differs widely with the consonance of the civilization under which this great nation presides."[54] Even in the 1920s, Mexican-origin people understood that the delusion of the "civilizing mission" that Americans labored under was a fiction and that Whites could easily manipulate the concept of law and order. Mexican American leader Alonso Perales also argued, "We would like when an individual of Mexican origin violates the laws of the country, he be judged before a competent Court of Justice and not be lynched, like they did to the unfortunate young man Elías Villareal Zárate in Weslaco, Texas, on November 1921 [*sic*, 1922].... In one word, we ask for justice and the opportunity to prosper."[55] Perales's statement was logical in the extreme.

The Mexican government protested almost all the 1920s murders. According to the consular officials, the list of 1921 murders included additional killings we know almost nothing about, such as Alego Quintanilla, murdered by three White men, and Jose de Jesus Puente and Adolfo Galvan, simply listed as murdered. In 1922, in addition to Villareal and Virginia Becerra, Jose (last name unknown), Cesario Garcia, Macario Martinez, German Martinez, Manuel Arevalo, Anastacio Ortega, and Manuel Zapata all died under questionable circumstances.[56] The Mexican government concluded, "No matter how convincing the evidence might be and no matter how horrible might have been the circumstances under which the crime was committed, the guilty parties are invariably set free by local juries." They also averred that in only one or two of these cases did an investigation and trial occur, which resulted in not guilty verdicts. Another probe by the Texas Rangers went nowhere.[57]

The Mexican consulate also intervened when several Mexican nationals were killed mysteriously in Raymondville, Texas, a few years after the Valley killings. That case generated not only a murder trial but also simultaneously exposed how Willacy County used Black and Mexican-origin people as prison labor. The killings occurred in September of 1926. Someone fired a gun in the Mexican section of Raymondville and several law officers went to investigate. Additional shooting, from an unknown source and location, broke out, killing Deputy Sheriff Leslie Shaw and Deputy Constable Louis May.[58] This incensed Raymondville sheriff Raymond Teller and he quickly sought out the killers. He found his suspects in the form of four men: brothers Jose and Delancio Nuñez and Inocencio González, all American citizens, as well as an Austrian named Matt Zaller (sometimes Haller or Zauder).[59] According to the sheriff, these men confessed and promised to reveal the location of the weapons used in the attack that led to the deaths of the deputy sheriff and constable. Tomás Nuñez, the father of Jose and Delancio, joined this group at the request of his two sons. Upon arriving at the supposed location of the stash of weapons, someone allegedly ambushed the sheriff, the several deputies, and the five civilians from a distance. Tomás, Jose, and Delancio Nuñez, Inocencio González, and Matt Zaller all died, while the sheriff and deputies were unharmed.[60]

This sequence of events aroused the suspicions of Mexican American leaders and the Mexican consulate. Alonso Perales hoped the Texas government would investigate. He pleaded with Governor Miriam Ferguson to intervene, telling her, "I hardly need to indicate to your Excellency that the murder of these defenseless citizens constitutes a disgrace for our own state and for our nation in general." The officers, Perales alleged, "failed in their duty to provide them with the equal protection of the laws granted by the Fourteenth Amendment of the Constitution of the United States of America." He asked that the governor remove the officers from duty and try them for these injustices.[61]

In early 1927, Perales wrote to President Calvin Coolidge about the case. Perales noted that he had never received a response from Governor Ferguson and hoped Coolidge would be more receptive. Perales's main request to the president proved incredibly forward thinking and something that would become much more commonplace in the 1960s and 1970s: he asked the president to order the Department of Justice to investigate the case. "I trust," Perales wrote, "therefore, that the President of the United States of America, order the Department of Justice to do a thorough and impartial investigation of the murder of those defenseless (and, it appears, innocent) American citizens, whose death has caused their respective households sadness and misery."[62] Perales evidently received no response or the response he received was unsatisfactory, because he wrote President Coolidge a second time a month later.[63]

The Mexican ambassador, Manuel C. Téllez, also demanded justice in the case.⁶⁴ He instigated his own investigation and employed the services of San Antonio attorney and civil rights leader Manuel C. Gonzales. Téllez was wise to do so. Gonzales's investigation revealed that the sheriff's story was largely fictitious. No one knew who had killed Deputy Sheriff Shaw and Deputy Constable May; Sheriff Teller evidently decided that the Nuñezes, González, and Zaller could serve as the culprits. Tomás Nuñez had only come to the jail at the request of his sons. Zaller was already in jail for an unrelated crime at the time of the shooting of the deputy sheriff and constable. It is unclear how Inocencio González got involved in this situation. The Mexican government claimed that a mob broke into the jail and killed the men, but it seems more likely that the sheriff and several deputies beat them, escorted them to the field, and murdered them. Four of the men had been shot in the head at close range, one in the heart. Authorities later exhumed the body of Tomás Nuñez; his body showed massive bruising inconsistent with the sheriff's story and consistent with the subsequent investigation. According to one account, someone had beheaded Tomás.⁶⁵ The exhumation quickly disproved that rumor but also showed that Tomás had died from a close range gunshot wound to the chest.⁶⁶ With this new information, Ambassador Téllez demanded the state prosecute Sheriff Teller for murder.⁶⁷

In December of 1926, the Willacy County grand jury indicted Sheriff Teller and fourteen other individuals, including the county attorney R. F. Robinson and several other law enforcement officers, *not* for the murders, but for conspiracy to enforce peonage, a federal offense.⁶⁸ In addition to the types of abuses that the murders brought to light, the sheriff evidently had made a habit of rounding up Mexican-origin people and African Americans for vagrancy and then doling out these individuals to local landowners for farm labor. While Black people experienced this common practice across the South, so too did Mexican-origin people in the Southwest.

The following month the state did arrest Sheriff Teller, Deputy Sheriffs Frank Brandt and Leon Gill, the county jailor Arturo Flores, and four other men for the murders of Tomás, Delancio, and Jose Nuñez, Inocencio González, and Matt Zaller. The state charged these officials with accessory to first-degree murder.⁶⁹ While credit for the arrests surely goes to the efforts of Alonso Perales, Manuel Gonzales, Manuel Téllez, and others, Teresa Nuñez, Tomas's widow and the mother of Jose and Delancio, actually swore out the complaint against the officers that led to the arrests.⁷⁰ As had occurred in other cases, the circumstances of her husband and children's deaths gave Teresa Nuñez cause to come forward to push for justice. After hearing testimony and reviewing the investigation material, the grand jury decided not to indict the officers for the murders of the five men. All the charges relating to the killings were dismissed.[71]

While justice for the five murdered men certainly did not occur at this time, the peonage case went forward. A number of men the sheriff had arrested for vagrancy and forced into farm work testified in the case. One of the witnesses explained that he had never seen a judge, the sheriff simply arrested him and sent him to work.[72] Another stated that a guard had warned him that if he tried to escape from the cotton fields he would be executed.[73] Interestingly, one of the officers in the trial gave testimony for the defense that benefited the prosecution. Deputy Sheriff Frank Brandt testified that he saw a local farmer bring Sheriff Teller an envelope full of money. The money allegedly paid the fines of the individuals the sheriff had arrested to pick cotton for the farmer. Brandt also disclosed that on several occasions he had arrested men only to later find that they had vanished from jail, presumably because the sheriff had doled them out to local farmers.[74] The jury found Teller, Brandt, and three other men guilty of enforcing peonage. Teller received the harshest sentence of eighteen months in prison and a $1,000 fine. Brandt received a sentence of one year and one day.[75] After these convictions, the state arrested and prosecuted several others for intimidating witnesses, including Deputy Sheriffs John Swanner and Jesse Rose, as well as two farmers involved in the peonage scheme. The state later added County Judge A. B. Crane to the list of those indicted.[76] A jury convicted Swanner and Rose a year later and Judge Joseph Hutcheson sentenced them to a five-year probated sentence. The jury acquitted Judge Crane and one of the farmers, while the state dropped the charges against the other farmer.[77]

Despite his conviction and the nasty business Teller was clearly associated with, White people rallied behind him. The Willacy County Commissioners Court accepted his resignation only with "great reluctance" and praised the former sheriff for standing "for the enforcement of the law." A conviction for a crime would seem to negate such a point, but evidently not for the commissioners.[78] Moreover, Teller ran again for sheriff even while still in prison.[79] He lost the election to Sheriff Luther Snow and served his eighteen months at the U.S. Penitentiary Leavenworth.[80]

The level of violence in South Texas and elsewhere remains difficult to fathom. While it pales in comparison to the violence of the 1910s, the fact that the violence of one decade continued into the next was deeply troubling. The circumstances differed, of course. In the 1910s the border angst over "bandits" led to murder and wholesale massacres. In the 1920s a deteriorating economic environment and competition for jobs spawned the violence. While Mexican officials and Mexican American leaders attempted to secure justice for the victims, the state responded lackadaisically. But while this violence occurred, many southwestern police agencies began looking internally to reform themselves. They understood that part of the problem with policing at this time revolved around the negative treatment that Mexican-origin people received from law enforcement (and from extralegal mobs too, as the cases mentioned above make clear). With police reform, the pendulum swung back in the other direction.

The recruitment of Mexican American officers and police professionalization provided two methods that demonstrate some of the broader law enforcement transitions during this period, especially in New Mexico. For example, the Albuquerque Police Department made hiring Mexican American officers a priority beginning in the 1910s. Albuquerque officials had founded the police department much later than most other city police forces. The city had for generations relied on a force of town marshals, the first of which, Milton Yarberry, had started work in 1880. As noted in chapter 3, Yarberry's career ended ignobly and at the end of a rope. Albuquerque also used the Bernalillo County Sheriff's Office for their policing needs. By the early twentieth century, Albuquerque began work to organize its police department. As police departments across the country began to engage in programs of professionalization, from the use of squad cars and radio to the recruitment of officers who had some college education, Albuquerque was at the forefront of these changes in the Southwest.

The Albuquerque government implemented police reform and ultimately founded the Albuquerque Police Department in 1916 after several major controversies in the early twentieth century. The history of the Albuquerque Police Department is a little confusing because local people and the press frequently referred to the town marshal's office as "police" and even the chief marshal as the "chief of police" before 1916. In 1905, the Albuquerque Marshal's Office became involved in a scandal for allegedly usurping the power of the local court system by arresting and fining individuals without the involvement of a judge or a jury trial.[81] The city council initiated minor reforms by reaffirming the role of the police judge in handling petty cases and establishing a new position of "police sergeant" who would handle police collection of cash.[82] The Albuquerque City Council followed this minor reform with the hiring of a new probation officer in 1907.[83]

The minor reforms in the marshal's office proved ineffective. That office got into more serious trouble in 1909 over these same issues. This time, though, the procedural problems ended up before the Bernalillo County grand jury. While Chief Marshal Thomas McMillen explained that Albuquerque operated like other cities, the grand jury critiqued its policies as "a reproach to the administration of the law." The grand jury issued a report recommending new reforms. Again, the city responded with minor reforms that strengthened police procedures.[84] In fact, real reforms wouldn't occur until 1916, when the city officially founded the Albuquerque Police Department and in 1917 when the city adopted a new charter.

The individual who would modernize the Albuquerque Police Department was Jandon "J. R." Galusha, Albuquerque's first chief of police. He arrived in the city in 1910 as a "special police officer" for the Atchison, Topeka & Santa Fe Railway.[85] In 1912 Galusha began filling in for officers in the marshal's office.[86] Also in 1912, he had evidently earned such a degree of respect that the city council put his name forward as a candidate for chief marshal, although they hired Thomas McMillen instead.[87] Galusha also began working for the Albuquerque U.S. Marshal's Office, in addition to the Santa Fe Railway.[88] In 1913 he became deputy U.S. marshal for the region.[89] In April of 1916, the city formally established the Albuquerque Police Department and the city government again floated Galusha's name for chief. This time he got the job.[90]

Chief Galusha went about reforming police policies and procedures throughout 1916. Some of this was mundane: public safety measures, for instance, requiring all motorists to install taillights on their automobiles to reduce accidents or supporting the city's efforts to make Albuquerque "dry" on Sundays so as to cut down on drinking-related crimes.[91] He also began to rid the department of problematic patrol officers and began hiring new officers.[92] In 1922 he employed new technology to aid police work by purchasing a wireless broadcasting system that would allow Albuquerque police to receive quick communication about criminal activity.[93] But one of his most important early successes came when he derailed local plans for a vigilance committee. In March of 1916, Mexican revolutionary Pancho Villa had raided the town of Columbus, New Mexico. That raid had caused tensions to rise dramatically and, as noted in the previous chapter, White people living in the border area began forming home guards to protect themselves. In Albuquerque, White residents met in an attempt to do the same thing, but Galusha shot down their idea as unnecessary vigilante justice. He had a corps of officers and had already begun planning with Bernalillo County sheriff Jesus Romero in case Mexican revolutionaries should attack. But such an attack seemed highly unlikely given that Albuquerque is nearly 300 miles away from the border. Moreover, according to a deputy sheriff, Mexicans came to the city to escape conflict, not to start it. The men who had gathered to form a home guard agreed to leave the protection of the city in the hands of the police force and sheriff's office.[94]

Chief Galusha continued to professionalize Albuquerque police by attempting to remove problematic officers. In January of 1917, the city council authorized him to remove Sergeant Nathanial Miller for abusing Mexican-origin people. Miller had badly beaten two men, Fernando Garcia and Nestor Hernandez, while processing their arrests. He beat Garcia with his nightstick, an attack witnessed by several city council members who described it as "entirely unnecessary and uncalled for and not required to maintain the peace or dignity of the city or law, or to handle the said prisoner."[95] The city council brought him up on a charge of "cruelty to prisoners" a few weeks later.[96] Despite much evidence and the wishes of Galusha that the city remove Miller from the force, the trial exonerated the officer.[97] Such circumstances have seemingly always dogged police departments; city policies and hiring regulations often prevent authorities from terminating troubled officers.

Chief Galusha had already begun developing other strategies to address policing inequities as they related to the Mexican-origin community. To his credit, Galusha understood the importance of employing Mexican American police officers. It was no coincidence that Galusha hired Dennis Chavez as a police officer in 1917, shortly after the problems with Sergeant Miller surfaced. Officer Chavez, who wore "Badge #1" from 1917 to 1966, not only had a long career on the Albuquerque police force but he also represented a transitional figure who understood the importance of good, modern police work. And he approached law enforcement without fear or trepidation. "A good policeman," Chavez noted, "can't be afraid."[98]

Like many others, Dennis Chavez had witnessed some of the extralegal violence of the late nineteenth and early twentieth centuries, noting for instance that he found the body of a lynching victim hanging from a cottonwood tree in Old Town. He despised such practices, which he rightly saw as an affront to good policing. His overall outlook toward policing was fairness within the color of law. A police officer, he believed, needed to walk a beat and "stop, look and listen."[99] Chavez was well regarded for patrolling "skid row." He got beat up a lot but always responded with proportional force and rarely drew his gun. He allegedly only used his firearm once to wound an individual. He claimed, "I don't like to hurt anyone if I can help it."[100] This example came in 1919 when Chavez intercepted a bootlegger named Fred Luna. Luna broke away from Chavez. During a lengthy chase, Chavez fired two shots at the ground. When those shots failed to stop Luna, Chavez wounded him in the shoulder, bringing the chase to an end. Chavez then took Luna, who received only a slight flesh wound, into custody. Now, police departments would not condone such a practice today, but it worked for Officer Chavez. It was allegedly the only time he used his gun in the line of duty.[101]

In many ways Officer Chavez viewed policing as both enforcing the law and as a kind of public service. His method of policing was more personal than we might expect today. He knew everyone on his beat. "They all know me. They don't give me any trouble," he said. He walked that beat for forty-seven years. He often dealt with children as a patrol officer, so it's no surprise that he went on to become a beloved crossing guard for school children near his home after his retirement.[102] Chief Galusha said, "Dennis Chavez was the bravest policeman I ever saw."[103]

Chief Galusha initiated many reforms in the Albuquerque Police Department and brought a number of qualified Mexican American officers into policing. But he was not alone in such efforts. Many communities across the Southwest attempted to do similar things. In 1920 Austin police hired José Acevedo and Miguel Oyervides as the first members of the force of Mexican ancestry.[104] While Dallas did not hire its first police officer of Mexican ancestry, Gabriel Macias, until 1956, the city began to attempt to smooth relations with Mexican-origin residents in the 1930s. This effort was important after the large-scale arrests of Mexican refugees in Dallas and other cities in the period between 1900 and 1930. While Dallas's reforms stayed at the level of the individual officer, they still mattered. Some officers remained hostile to Mexicans and Mexican Americans, but others sought to build bridges to better relations.

A number of examples bear this point out. In one anonymous account from the early 1930s, two Dallas officers encountered an individual named Mike Martinez, who stood beside his vehicle late on a very cold night. The officers asked Martinez why he was out in the cold. He explained that another police officer had stopped him for a traffic violation and told him to wait by his vehicle until he returned from city hall with a traffic ticket. The two officers knew something was amiss: they were the only ones patrolling the area and no officer would detain a person in this manner. They escorted Martinez home and one of the officers later wrote about this incident. He ended his account of these events with this: "Yes, Mike Martinez was an American—perhaps a better American citizen than you or I. Would you have waited in below-zero weather to get a traffic ticket? Sometimes, our so-called minority citizens are not so minor—sometimes they are the best citizens. In my work with them as a policeman, I have enjoyed going into their homes, churches, and businesses. We should get acquainted with them—learn about their culture, philosophy and desires. If we did this, perhaps we could understand and respect each other better."[105]

This unknown officer knew his stuff. He well understood that a little bit of knowledge about culture, language, or family could go a long way when interacting with any ethnic community in the city and in this case the Mexican-origin community specifically. This was a perfectly sensible concept of community service, one that members of the Mexican American community, in Dallas and across the Southwest, would call for in the 1960s and 1970s. And to their credit, law enforcement in many southwestern communities adopted these calls.

The Dallas Police Department engaged in other efforts aimed at outreach and maintaining professionalism. For instance, in 1931 the department began administering intelligence tests to all officers. Such examinations became a hallmark of police professionalization in the 1930s.[106] In 1932 Dallas police utilized undercover operatives known as the "Secret Twelve" to observe patrol officers. The department leaders tasked the "Secret Twelve" to especially monitor officers who were "fractious or hard-boiled with the public." While the "Secret Twelve," a kind of informal internal affairs, looked for troubled officers, we can assume the rank and file more than likely did not appreciate this spying.[107] Dallas police officers also heard lectures in 1939 from the chief of police of Mexico City about differences in police procedures in Mexico. Such information was important because recent immigrants familiar only with policing in Mexico might not act or respond to police in ways that Dallas officers expected.[108]

Corpus Christi also attempted to expand its officer corps by bringing Mexican Americans into the force. But its first attempt ended badly. Rafael Galvan Sr. became Corpus Christi's first officer of Mexican ancestry in 1928, but later that same year Galvan got into trouble when he attempted to bribe a fellow officer to change the charge against an arrested individual from a felony to a misdemeanor.[109] While he awaited trial, Galvan evidently also ran afoul of the law when he violated prohibition laws. He, Police Chief C. B. Shaw, and others were all arrested for prohibition violations.[110] Galvan's trial for the bribery attempt began in May of 1929.[111] The jury deadlocked, though, and the judge sent the case from Nueces County to Cameron County for a retrial.[112] A retrial began, but then ended when the district attorney and Galvan's defense agreed to postpone the trial, which did not resume.[113] It's unclear what happened with the prohibition charge. Galvan never worked in law enforcement again, although he had a long career as a musician and even helped to found the League of United Latin American Citizens.[114]

While police forces in Albuquerque, Dallas, or Corpus Christi attempted to professionalize and modify how they treated Mexican-origin people, other law enforcement agencies in other parts of the Southwest continued to abuse Mexicans and Mexican Americans. Thus, the pendulum swung back in the other direction. The mining districts of Arizona remained exceedingly violent well into the twentieth century. While the practice of extralegal lynching had dissipated in these areas, local police sometimes acted just as violently as lynch mobs. In Miami, Arizona, the face of that violence was John Welch. He was born in Mexico in the late 1890s but moved to Miami in the mid-1910s. His father, Barney Welch, got a job with the Miami Police Department and eventually became chief. In 1919, Chief Welch offered his son a position. This nepotism initiated a long rise up the ranks for John Welch. Despite his time in Mexico, the only thing Welch seemed to have gained from the experience was disdain for Mexican people. He killed a number of suspects, most importantly Martin Lopez, another victim in a long line of "accidental" police shootings.[115]

Officer Welch apprehended Lopez, a Mexican national, on the night of July 4, 1930. According to many accounts, this was a simple drunk and disorderly case—Lopez had spent the night celebrating Fourth of July and police found him inebriated. But as Welch processed Lopez into the city jail, Lopez evidently did not move fast enough for Welch. So Welch began beating him with the butt of his service revolver. While he was beating Lopez with his gun, the firearm discharged. The bullet hit Lopez in the head, killing him instantly.[116] A coroner's jury cleared Welch of wrongdoing and declared the shooting an accident.[117]

Martin Lopez's family was angered by the lack of justice shown to their son. His mother, Eululotia de la Torres, much like Teresa Nuñez in Texas, came forward to demand the district attorney file murder charges against Welch.[118] The district attorney, after this pressure, filed both aggravated assault and manslaughter charges against Welch. Judge H. P. Wilson dismissed those charges, though, asserting that Welch had acted in self-defense because Lopez had attacked him with a knife. This was a lie. He further declared that Lopez died while Welch was in the process of legally doing his duty.[119] Eululotia de la Torres's action also brought the case to the attention of the Mexican government. The Mexican embassy took a keen interest in the case both because Lopez was a Mexican citizen and because of the circumstances of his death. Mexican consul Manuel Payno lodged a formal protest with Arizona governor John Phillips. When nothing happened, Ambassador Manuel C. Téllez delivered an official note expressing his dissatisfaction with the handling of the case and demanding that Governor Phillips reopen the case.[120]

Finally in October of 1930, Governor Phillips reopened the case. Authorities arrested Welch a second time and charged him this time with first-degree murder.[121] At his 1931 trial, Welch's defense again alleged that Martin Lopez attacked him with a knife and that he defended himself by beating the prisoner with his revolver, which accidentally discharged. He had several witnesses, all fellow White police officers, who corroborated this story. Welch basically asserted that Lopez caused his own death. The state, however, produced a number of witnesses, all Mexican-origin people, who testified that Lopez was handcuffed, inebriated, and simply moved too lethargically for Officer Welch. Lopez had no knife, and the officers concocted the story of Lopez attacking Welch after the fact to turn an example of police brutality into an act of self-defense. Authorities never located a knife. In an interesting twist, Chief Barney Welch testified on behalf of his son, even though he had not witnessed the incident.[122] An all-White jury deliberated for ten minutes before finding Welch not guilty.[123]

The outcome of this case is perhaps unsurprising. But the case itself is important. It demonstrates another example of how Mexican-origin people pushed for rights. First, Martin Lopez's mother came forward. Like Teresa Nuñez in Texas, the circumstances of her son's death caused Eululotia de la Torres to demand justice for her son. Second, the work of the consul's office proved important. Mexican officials still constituted a force of advocacy for Mexican nationals like Lopez. Without Eululotia de la Torres or the Mexican government, it seems likely that Welch would have not been tried at all.

Mexican Americans also found other ways to reject the ascension of John Welch to chief of police in Miami. When the city initially promoted him to acting chief in 1933, the Mexican American community objected.[124] Welch did succeed his father as police chief in 1934. As chief he also killed Mexican-origin people or was present when other officers did. When Special Deputy Sheriff T. F. Russell shot and killed Arnulfo Robles in December 1935, Welch was there.[125] In April 1937, Chief Welch shot Juan Lugo to death. It is unclear what Lugo did specifically to warrant attention from the police. He was simply a "crazed killer" and a "crazed Mexican" according to the state press. Such language justified the killing. In one article on the Lugo shooting, Chief Welch received most of the media coverage, not Lugo.[126] The fact that these killing all seemed to occur under odd circumstances, and always with Welch present, remains exceedingly unusual.

In 1940 Welch ran for the position of sheriff of Gila County. Mexican Americans again made their dislike of Welch apparent. The community opposed his run for sheriff by destroying campaign signs and other campaign material and by voting heavily against him. He called this group an "organized gang of saboteurs." Chief Welch disliked this opposition and called for an investigation into the tampering with his campaign. He also labelled these opponents "fifth-columnists" and "Communist fronts."[127] Instead of Welch, his opponent, Deputy Sheriff William Richardson, won the race for sheriff.[128] Mexican American agency cost Welch the election. Their political activism, one of several tools that Mexican Americans would use in their quest for civil rights in the middle to late twentieth century, worked to keep Welch out of the sheriff's office. Welch nonetheless served as chief of police until his death in 1961.

Part of the way law enforcement continued to justify its abuse of Mexican-origin people was via the terminology it used to describe them, as the Juan Lugo case demonstrated. Local law enforcement and the media reminded the public about the dangers posed by people of Mexican ancestry by publicly tarnishing individuals as "bandits" or as "crazed." Lugo was, of course, a "crazed Mexican." In a similar way, authorities continued to refer to them as "bandits" even though social banditry by the 1920s no longer really existed. In Los Angeles, the police department often termed Mexican-origin suspects as "bandits." For example, Detective E. J. Long interviewed a man named Louis Castro about his son, Sam, in December of 1929. As Long explained, "We had info that his son Sam Castro was a bandit."[129] Detective Long also frequently referred to subjects only as "Mex." For instance, on December 27, 1929, he reported that he had visited the "County Jail to see Capt Brooks regarding two mex they have in custody[,] a mex and white man charged with robbery and rape."[130]

In addition to terming Mexican-origin people "bandits," law enforcement and the media also gave them outlaw nicknames. A good example of this phenomenon was the case of Henrico "Henry" Gallegos of New Mexico, whom law enforcement in Albuquerque dubbed "the Lonesome Kid." Despite his moniker, Gallegos rarely worked alone, and police usually caught him with at least one accomplice. Gallegos, a run-of-the-mill petty criminal, had been in and out of jail since the early 1920s. His criminal activity did not merit the media attention that he received, but he had a cool nickname and the local press seemed to delight in reporting about this latter-day bandido. And so he went from an average criminal to a legend in his own time. Gallegos provides a good example of the pendulum in Albuquerque swinging back in the other direction. Albuquerque had done much to change policing practices, but the way law enforcement treated the Lonesome Kid shows that it had much more work to do.

This posed photograph, titled "El Bandolero," of an unidentified Mexican-origin man was taken by Arizona artist Thomas Bate in 1937 as part of a photography contest for which Bate won a certificate of merit. Photos such as this one can be viewed in several ways. First, it is a highly stylized image that does not seem to mock or stereotypically portray a bandit. Second, it was taken in a period long after social banditry in the Southwest had come to an end. As such, like the example of Henry "Lonesome Kid" Gallegos, it utilized the trope of the bandido, which often worked to sensationalize banditry in a manner that negatively impacted Mexican-origin people.
Arizona State Library, Archives and Public Records, History and Archives Division, Phoenix, #01–9368.

The Lonesome Kid's first media appearance came in February of 1923. The *Albuquerque Morning Journal* reported that police had arrested Gallegos in connection with several minor thefts.[131] A few days later, police arrested him for stealing two suitcases.[132] The grand jury indicted him for larceny.[133] Gallegos spent a short amount of time in jail but was then released, possibly due to some irregularity in the trial. Police arrested him again in December of 1923 for stealing a purse. For that crime he received a thirty-day jail sentence.[134] Gallegos disappears from the record for the next few years, a common and, for researchers, frustrating occurrence. But the Lonesome Kid was back in the news in 1927. While police suspected him of robbing a corsetiere, the only crime they could pin in on him was vagrancy. He spent fifteen days in jail.[135]

And then 1928 rolled around and all hell broke loose. Gallegos found himself in the center of a storm that had little to do with him and instead involved some serious law enforcement infighting. The Albuquerque Police Department and the Bernalillo County Sheriff's Office were engaged in a nasty battle for recognition and supremacy in the city. Each side schemed to show that it represented the finest form of law enforcement in Albuquerque. The Lonesome Kid unwittingly got caught up in this police squabble.

So here's what happened. On the night of January 2, 1928, Albuquerque police officer Russell C. Charlton (who would go on to become chief of police in Albuquerque) collared Gallegos after police spotted him near a Piggly Wiggly grocery store. The police alleged that he had attempted to rob the safe at the store, or "loot" as the local press dubbed the attempted robbery. The case might have quickly gone away; Gallegos pleaded guilty to the charge of conspiracy to commit a burglary and the judge was prepared to sentence him. Instead, the case brought the conflict between the sheriff's office and the police force into the light of day.[136]

Shortly after police arrested Gallegos, his accomplice, Harlow Haas, confessed to the Albuquerque police that he worked for the Bernalillo County Sheriff's Office as a "stool pigeon," or what we would today call a confidential informant. The sheriff's office had tasked Haas with orchestrating the Piggly Wiggly safe robbery so that Sheriff Philip Hubbell could capture the Lonesome Kid. In fact, Sheriff Hubbell suspected Gallegos of a number of safe burglaries in Albuquerque, so he had set up a sting at the Piggly Wiggly using Haas and hoping to entrap Gallegos. According to Haas, the Lonesome Kid was somewhat deranged and had made statements about wanting to "take in all over the world."[137] Alas, Albuquerque police, unaware of the scheme, botched the sheriff's plan when they arrested the Lonesome Kid *before* he had actually robbed the store![138] The mayor of Albuquerque, Clyde Tingley, decided to publicly praise the police and simultaneously accuse Sheriff Hubbell of orchestrating the robbery so that he could make arrests and look good. For the mayor, the attempted robbery was "a plot of sheriff officers to discredit the police department" so that the sheriff could lay claim to being the most effective law enforcement agency in the city.[139]

To his credit, Sheriff Hubbell responded with equanimity and asserted that "he was only interested in catching criminals and it made no difference to him who caught them, just so they were caught."[140] When Mayor Tingley intimated that the sheriff was jealous of the police, Sheriff Hubbell again responded with composure, explaining, "We're not jealous of the police department by any means. We have no reason to be that I know of. If they should arrest 500 criminals tomorrow we would be tickled to death." He did, however, refer to the idea of a frame-up or plot as a method of garnering recognition as "an absolute joke."[141] But the mayor was basically right. The sheriff had initiated the sting to capture the Lonesome Kid and raise the stature of the sheriff's office. And, of course, the police had botched the whole thing.

While this war of words continued, Gallegos recanted his confession. It seems that in the confusion caused by the sheriff and police bickering and because Officer Charlton had arrested him before he actually committed a crime, the Lonesome Kid suspected that he could possibly avoid a conviction. Indeed, the evidence against him came exclusively from Haas and from a search of his apartment, which yielded a screwdriver, some postcards, nutpicks, pens and pencils, and witch hazel, among other sundry goods. Police decided these goods were all stolen, making the Lonesome Kid a poor thief indeed.[142]

Unfortunately, it is unclear what happened with the Lonesome Kid as the story ends here. Albuquerque police arrested someone named Henry Gallegos for possession of marijuana in April 1928, but it's not clear this was the Lonesome Kid.[143] He disappears from the available record in 1928 and never reappears. It's possible he left town, halted his criminal activity, or that he died. The record doesn't allow for a determination.

In some ways, perhaps, Henrico Gallegos was lucky. Other individuals in New Mexico received far harsher treatment. Rafael Benavides, allegedly the last Mexican-origin person lynched in the United States, offers a good example. Benavides, a sheepherder by trade, had allegedly attempted to assault two minor Mexican girls and Mrs. Charles Lewis (whose first name is never listed in the sources) in the small New Mexico town of Farmington in November of 1928. Although the sixty-year-old Lewis defended herself, Benavides overpowered her, beat her, and possibly sexually assaulted her.

She lived and reported the incident to Sheriff George Blancett, who formed a posse to apprehend Benavides. They caught up with him and Blancett ordered Benavides to surrender. He refused and the posse shot him, wounding him in the stomach. They took Benavides into custody and transported him to the hospital in Farmington.[144]

Despite his legally authorized arrest, a mob of men gathered to lynch Benavides. At least ten masked men entered the hospital and removed him. They took him to the outskirts of town and quickly hanged him. Later that day police located Benavides's still hanging body. Local authorities and the state government initiated a search for the lynchers. While the press largely praised the lynch mob, New Mexico authorities seemed embarrassed by the murder. Yet law enforcement could locate none of the lynch mob.[145] A grand jury convened in December of 1928, but after hearing testimony and without anyone to prosecute, the grand jury issued no indictments. Later, in early 1929, the state authorized a $1,000 reward ($17,000 in 2022) for any information about the case. No one came forward to give information.[146]

No one was ever punished for the murder of Rafael Benavides. Like other lynchings, it seems that for many people in New Mexico his murder was justice done. This lynching followed the pattern of lynchings of Black people in the South for alleged transgressions of sexual mores, but without an investigation or trial, Benavides's crimes remain alleged. It is interesting that the final lynching of a Mexican person occurred in New Mexico. Given some of the police reforms that took place there, New Mexico remained a violent state.

While an individual such as the Lonesome Kid became the focus of legitimate police agencies and an individual such as Rafael Benavides experienced mob justice, it is important to note that the policing of Mexican-origin people through extralegal forms of law enforcement that occurred throughout the nineteenth century continued well into the twentieth century. Not only did law enforcement arrest and jail Mexican-origin people, as it had with the Lonesome Kid, but also did nonpolice entities. Maria de Jesus Jimenez Serrano offers an important example. She recounted her family's experience migrating to Texas as refugees from the Mexican Revolution in about 1920. The family originally settled in Gaston, a small farming community in Rusk County east of Dallas, where they worked on a large cotton plantation. Jimenez Serrano recalled that the foremen of the plantation carried guns and that they "were like Rangers or Sheriffs." If workers got into fights or drank too much, she stated, "There was a long jail house there and those that committed problems were put there." To express this succinctly, the plantation had its own jail. Large plantations in the South occasionally had a plantation jail in the nineteenth century, although such structures became less common after the Civil War.[147] Jimenez Serrano also noted that if workers committed more serious offenses, the foremen, even though they had no legal authority to do so, took them to the jail in Dallas. "The foremen were the authority there," she remembered, and "they might put the guilty one in jail for about a week, fine him, and reprimand him so he would not misbehave again." As such, the foremen, who were all White men, became the police, jury, judges, and jailers of the plantation.[148]

In about 1921 the members of Jimenez Serrano's family relocated to the Houston area, settling in the boundary region between Houston and Sugar Land. They experienced the same intrusive "law enforcement" situation here. Jimenez Serrano's father, for instance, found work at a ranch that bordered the Texas Department of Corrections' Central Unit Prison, or "El Gran Centro" as the Mexican-origin community called it. There, two men, a Mr. Bull and a Mr. Gingguy patrolled the workers like the foremen had in Gaston. Jimenez Serrano remembered Gingguy, who was also known by the nickname "Pata de Hule," or "Wooden [really rubber] Leg," as particularly mean spirited. "He rode around in his horse with his rifle, his gun and a whip," she remembered, "those that stood up to him got whipped." She also remembered that in some cases individuals who disobeyed Bull or Gingguy "were put in the penitentiary and would be taken out to work in the fields." Such an act was a violation of the law and the civil rights of those jailed, but in scenarios such as this, Gingguy and Bull were the law. Jimenez Serrano also related rumors she and other Mexican immigrants had heard that Gingguy had "killed some [Mexicans] and dumped the bodies in the bayou because they had disobeyed him or had stood up to him." As such, on the ranch lands around the Central Unit Prison, and even in the town of Sugar Land itself, White foremen such as Bull and Gingguy constituted a powerful form of unsanctioned law enforcement, and in the case of Gingguy that meant police officer, jury, judge, and allegedly executioner. "There was no law that protected the Mexicans and no one really knew what was going on there. There they [Bull and Gingguy] were the authority and no other authority entered here. In Sugar Land, they had their own laws and authority," Jimenez Serrano stated.[149]

It is interesting, and probably far more common than we might think today, that plantations had forepersons that acted like police. It was also common for plantations to have jails, for plantation workers to be incarcerated in city jails, and even for them to be imprisoned in a state facility like the Central Unit Prison even though they had not been arrested or tried. Such practices, paired with Sheriff Raymond Teller's peonage schemes, demonstrate that

White people controlled the lives of Mexican-origin people, and African Americans too, via work and the criminal justice system. Human caging, both the unofficial kind that Maria de Jesus Jimenez Serrano described as well as legitimate jails and prisons, had long been a part of the southwestern history.[150]

The rise of the prison industrial complex, usually thought of as a late twentieth century phenomenon, began in the 1930s in the Southwest. New Mexico, for example, had begun expanding its prison system at the turn of the century, but the most significant expansion came in the 1930s. The Board of Penitentiary Commissioners focused particular attention on female prisoners. They noted the dangerous conditions in the overcrowded women's quarters of the Penitentiary of New Mexico: because of "the danger of fire, an emergency exists, requiring the immediate construction of suitable quarters for women prisoners." Thus, at a time when the Great Depression put state budgets under considerable constraints, the board authorized a $15,000 budget for constructing a new facility for female prisoners ($288,000 in 2022 dollars). That money would come from those incarcerated in the prison, specifically the Construction Earnings Fund, which held monies incarcerated individuals earned from various construction projects around the state.[151] Later that year the board authorized the superintendent to hire additional guards "owing to the increase of the population of the institution."[152] A new prison wing meant more room for more incarcerated people, which meant the prison needed more guards. That is how the prison industrial complex works.[153]

Here's another example of how the carceral system operates. In August 1931, the Board of Penitentiary Commissioners heard a report from Superintendent Edwin Swope about "the absolute necessity for the purchase of new generators for furnishing light and power to the institution." The penitentiary's single generator was twenty-five years old and overloaded. The cost of new generators amounted to about $12,000. This time the board balked and refused to authorize the expense. While it would spend money to build new facilities to expand the prison and to pay for additional staff, it did not want to spend on the necessary infrastructure to provide for the individuals incarcerated in the facility.[154]

The Depression also saw an increase in the number of cases of parole at the penitentiary. So while the state incarcerated more people, it also released more. It also tended to release Spanish-surnamed people and those with non-Spanish surnames fairly equally. In April 1931, prison staff reported that forty individuals were eligible for parole. Of those, seventeen had Spanish surnames, a little less than half the total number of parolees.[155] In June of 1931, there were thirty individuals up for parole, nine with Spanish surnames and twenty-one with English surnames. The board recommended all for parole.[156] In August of 1932, the board reviewed thirty-six cases eligible for parole. That month, prison staff paroled twenty individuals with Spanish surnames and sixteen with English surnames, one of the first instances where Mexican-origin parolees exceeded the number of White parolees.[157] These examples demonstrate that individuals with Spanish surnames, most likely Mexican-origin people, continued to receive similar treatment as other incarcerated people.

The June 1931 Board of Penitentiary Commissioners meeting also considered the case of Guadalupe Rodriguez, who was serving time for an undisclosed crime. The board recommended a conditional pardon to Rodriguez "on account of the serious illness of her baby and the general destitution and lack of care that the rest of her family was receiving on the representations of the Child's Welfare Bureau." While no additional information exists, the penitentiary board's compassion in her case is notable. Like Manuela Fimbrez (discussed in chapter 4), Rodriguez represents another incarcerated woman who gave birth in prison and was then released. Prison births remain a common occurrence today; releases similar to Rodriguez's are not.[158]

California also saw an expansion of its prisons and jails in the 1930s. In the Los Angeles area, as in other parts of the Southwest, the arrest and confinement of Mexicans and Mexican Americans increased dramatically at this time. While arrests of Mexican-origin people had spiked in the 1910s because of the number of immigrants fleeing the revolution in Mexico, in the 1930s the numbers spiked again because of the Depression and a new law that criminalized unlawfully entering the United States. Mexicans often had difficulty proving they had entered the United States lawfully since border security remained lax, and this gave local authorities carte blanche to arrest Mexican people. This overtaxed the federal prison system and Congress responded by allocating funds for the construction of new facilities, including La Tuna Detention Farm (known also as the El Paso Detention Farm) in 1932 and the Tucson Federal Prison Camp No. 10 in 1933. As in New Mexico, the federal government spent additional dollars from an already strained federal budget on prisons.[159] In fact, in 1930 the Department of Justice saw its budget increase by nearly $4 million, from just under $28 million to just under $32 million (that's over $560 million in 2022). Sanford Bates, the superintendent of the federal prison system, asked for an additional $8 million for new prison construction that same year. He got it.[160] To put this in perspective, the federal government at the beginning of the Depression increased federal spending on the prison system by nearly 43 percent.

This situation proved deeply problematic. First, local governments used the new "unlawful entry" law to arrest Mexican-origin people they deemed undesirable. Federal authorities then deported these individuals. Second, when federal authorities conducted immigrant raids, local police often did the arresting, and then federal officials housed the arrested individuals in city or county jail facilities. There existed, in short, a great deal of collusion between local and federal authorities that resulted in the arrest and incarceration of tens of thousands of Mexican-origin people. In Southern California this equated to a massive increase in the incarceration of Mexicans and Mexican Americans in city and county jail facilities.[161] Add to this a massive increase in the number of "public order" arrests in the LA area, which could be anything from vagrancy to fighting, and the carceral population exploded. According to historian Kelly Lytle Hernández, between 1928 and 1939 the number of Mexican-origin people arrested for public order violations doubled from 4,455 to 9,729.[162]

The Great Depression, then, ushered in the final pendulum swing in this period. The massive increase in the population of incarcerated Mexican-origin people and the subsequent repatriation (i.e., deportation) campaign begun by the Herbert Hoover administration to rid the Southwest of Mexicans had a chilling effect on the region and its people. Hoover, and his labor secretary William Doak, both racists who disliked Mexicans, also believed that removing Mexican workers might alleviate labor shortages. Repatriation began in 1929 with some Mexicans voluntarily returning to Mexico when they lost their jobs or could not find work. The federal government then followed with a forcible deportation campaign beginning in 1930, which continued well into the administration of Franklin D. Roosevelt. Doak expanded the number of Border Patrol agents adding 245 new agents to assist in deporting a planned 400,000 Mexicans (a number invented by Doak).[163] Here again local law enforcement colluded with the federal government. The Border Patrol did not have enough agents to accomplish its task, so local police filled in. Immigrant raids by city police and county sheriff's office, usually approved and guided by the Border Patrol, did much of the apprehending of Mexican-origin people.[164] Los Angeles police proved particularly adept at this task, and by the mid-1930s some residents of East Los Angeles and other heavily Mexican parts of Los Angeles County such as Pacoima and San Fernando reported that the raids basically depopulated the region of Mexicans and Mexican Americans.[165] In total, the government forcibly repatriated between 400,000 and 2 million Mexican-origin people. About 60 percent of these deportees were citizens of the United States.[166]

Historians have well analyzed the 1930s repatriation campaigns. What I want to make clear is the way the federal government utilized law enforcement, whether a national police body such as the Border Patrol or local police such as the Los Angeles Police Department, to accomplish this task. Punitive policing, always a problem in the Southwest, now joined forces with draconian immigration laws. This potent combination still exists today. And the fact that the government deported hundreds of thousands of Americans of Mexican descent remains an ugly stain on the history of this country.

The 1920s and 1930s represented important moments in the history of Mexican-origin people and policing. While a nadir in relations between Mexican folks and police had characterized the early twentieth century, especially with the problematic focus on bandits, the lynchings, and the massacres that occurred between 1900 and 1920, the 1920s seemed to usher in some auspicious alterations in southwestern law enforcement. The Canales Investigation and Canales Reforms brought the Texas Rangers under greater scrutiny and control. These were clear victories for Mexican American leaders such as J. T. Canales. Alas, those reforms occurred simultaneously with more murders of Mexican-origin people in Texas. The pendulum always swings in two directions.

The same was true for New Mexico. There, local police agencies such as the Albuquerque Police Department inaugurated many reforms designed to professionalize the police force. The Albuquerque Police Department also worked to hire Mexican American officers such as Dennis Chavez. At about the same time, of course, Albuquerque police got into some serious trouble after arresting Henrico "Lonesome Kid" Gallegos and engaging in a war of words with the Bernalillo County sheriff. Other parts of New Mexico had worse policing problems, as the lynching of Rafael Benavides makes clear. Arizona was similar to New Mexico, with some locales working to modernize police while other cities such as Miami clung to a racist form of policing as evidenced by the actions of Police Chief John Welch. All southwestern states, but especially California, New Mexico, and Texas, also augmented jails and prisons, which tended to also harm the Mexican-origin community.

Mexican Americans did much to initiate reforms, oppose racist policing, and stand up for themselves, either individually or with the assistance of the Mexican government. There were some important examples that set the stage for the kind of activism that would become common in the middle to late twentieth century. They politically opposed racist individuals such as John Welch. They pushed and won reforms from state governments. They demanded local and state governments investigate and prosecute lynchers and murderers. They urged the Mexican government to assist in the investigation and prosecution of cases. They became police officers. Their examples significantly helped modernize southwestern policing.

The 1920s and 1930s were decades of transition and change. That period of change and transition persisted into the 1940s and early 1950s. Mexican Americans in the 1940s and 1950s would continue to experience many of the things described in this chapter. Violence and degradation—for example, in the so-called Zoot Suit Riots of 1943—would be followed by change and reform—for example, in the 1954 *Pete Hernandez v. Texas* case, which outlawed the exclusion of Mexican Americans on juries. In that period, Mexican Americans laid the foundation for a sustained civil rights movement, a struggle that focused heavily on policing problems such as police harassment, brutality, and murder.

CONCLUSION

According to the many accounts examining the exploits of Elfego Baca, he ventured to Frisco and challenged the Texas Cowboys there because he was angry. The abuse that Mexican-origin people endured, the castration of El Burro, the shooting of Epitacio Martinez, the fact that the Cowboys operated as "a notorious lynching gang" that was "hanging all the mexicans they could," all these things infuriated Baca. Moreover, the weak response from local law officers such as Deputy Sheriff Pedro Saracino further angered him. Baca didn't simply get angry and walk away. He stepped into the role of police officer and halted the violence of the Texas Cowboys. As Baca himself stated, "I went up there and pacified them."[1] Given the bloody history examined in this book, Baca's anger is understandable, and his efforts are a unique solution to the violence Mexicans and Mexican Americans experienced from the 1830s to the 1930s.

Elfego Baca's actions serve as a useful example of some of the creative adaptations Mexican-origin people utilized when addressing racist violence masquerading as law enforcement. He understood that someone needed to confront lawless groups like the Texas Cowboys and that law enforcement should be the entity to engage in that confrontation. When that didn't happen, he pinned a badge to his chest and did it himself. Baca thus used law enforcement to effectively challenge and ultimately halt the extralegal violence that groups such as the Texas Cowboys meted out on the Mexican-origin population in New Mexico. He continued to do the same thing during a lengthy career in the field of criminal justice. And Elfego Baca wasn't the only Mexican American to exercise police authority in this way.

Baca's example also shows the senseless, brutal violence that Mexican-origin people endured at the hands of White people in the border region. Violence characterized this period. While Mexican-origin people certainly challenged it—and they found unique ways to do so—they could not escape or avoid it. Law enforcement frequently instigated these violent encounters or allowed them to happen. Lynch mobs, pretending to be law enforcement, also proved willing to engage in violence. We'll never know the exact number of deaths that resulted from this bloody period but given the numbers of lynchings and massacres and ley fuga killings and other deaths discussed throughout this book, that number was surely thousands of people. If nothing else, I hope *Borders of Violence and Justice* made clear why so much violence occurred and how Mexicans and Mexican Americans dealt with it.

The bloodiness of this history began with American ventures into Mexico's northern territories. First in Texas and then in the rest of the Southwest, military personnel, both in the form of the Texas Army and U.S. Army, operated as a conquering force as well as a law enforcement body. The military laid the groundwork for the colonization of the Southwest. The 1846 Kearny Code of Law remains the best example of this process. It established a code of justice in the Territory of New Mexico. It created the first iterations of criminal justice institutions necessary to control Mexicans. It allowed the military to illegally try Mexicans for treason because they fought against the United States. And then the military gave way to formally established police agencies as well as extralegal lynch mobs. In every part of the Southwest, state and territorial governments made founding the criminal justice system a priority; it was one of the first institutional bodies developed during and after the war. They then used the justice system to control Mexican-origin people.

Mexicans fought back against this newly created colonial regime. They actively opposed the Americans during the Mexican-American War, engaging in full-scale resistance and insurrectionary movements. When Americans tried Mexicans who rebelled, a number prevailed in court. Some Mexican

Americans who served in newly formed state and territorial governments attempted to make the developing criminal justice system fairer. But for the most part, Mexican-origin people did not have the requisite power to halt the violence they experienced.

While southwestern governments worked hard to establish criminal justice systems, mob violence masquerading as justice occurred as well. The actions of mobs show that White Americans considered extralegal justice a legitimate form of justice, even though legally established law enforcement existed. This fictional viewpoint allowed vigilantes to assert that the violence they resorted to was justice. Mexican-origin people responded to lynching in a variety of ways. Like other people in the region, they owned guns and defended themselves. They also demanded protection from legitimate law enforcement. While police did participate in mob violence, many White and Mexican American law officers either attempted to protect or did successfully protect Mexican-origin people from mobs. Mexicans and Mexican Americans also pushed criminal justice authorities to punish vigilantes. They also fled mobs, a type of resistance that shows they understood they probably wouldn't live through a lynching. The Mexican government also aided those people mistreated or killed by mobs. This strategy of resistance proved unique for Mexican-origin people. And of course, Mexican folks also occasionally engaged in lynch justice, a fact that complicates the history of mob law in the Southwest.

Mexican Americans frequently served in law enforcement. This also worked as a kind of resistance. Some interesting features emerge from this history. First, a number of Mexican American police began their careers as bandits, only to became law enforcement later on. Second, most Mexican American police exercised their authority without limits on their power. Third, early Mexican American police officers inspired those who came after them. Finally, while some Mexican American officers chose this profession because they needed a job or they were they only ones to want it, others, like Elfego Baca, became police because they wanted to protect people of Mexican ancestry. Their service represented an early civil rights strategy to help the Mexican-origin community.

Law enforcement, by design, is tasked with addressing criminality. But White people had some strange, problematic views about Mexican and Mexican American criminality. They tended to stereotypically believe that Mexican-origin people were criminally prone to stealing, sex work, or murder. These racist viewpoints drove the heavy-handed type of policing Mexicans and Mexican Americans experienced. While police tended to treat them poorly, others in the criminal justice system, including attorneys, judges, or prison wardens, tended to treat them more justly. The onset of the Mexican Revolution and the migration of millions of Mexican refugees from 1900 to 1930 also saw an evolution in policing. Law enforcement cracked down on refugees by augmenting fines for vagrancy and by arresting more Mexicans for a variety of crimes. This was an ugly, racist response to the in-migration of Mexican people and a clumsy attempt to control them.

The racist opinions that White law enforcement had about Mexicans and Mexican Americans were particularly visible during the so-called Bandit Wars. Especially in the late nineteenth and early twentieth centuries, White folks tended to think Mexican bandits overran the borderlands. In fact, White Americans tagged just about anyone of Mexican ancestry, and others as well, with the label "bandit" so that they could expel or kill those people. Now, there were bandit raids and thus some Mexican-origin people were outlaws, but many so-called bandits weren't bandits, or they only became desperados after a problematic encounter with a White law officer. White people used extralegal and legal justice to try to control and kill these people, too. And therein lay the problem. Fear and hatred and violence only drove more violence, even in the twentieth century as some law enforcement agencies attempted to professionalize and diversify their staff. The massacres and other killings in the early twentieth century remain an ugly blot on borderlands history today. Mexican Americans have historically viewed the Texas Rangers as anti-Mexican; the violence committed by the Rangers in this period in part explains why.

For some in the Mexican American community, bandits were heroic. They stood up to abusive law enforcement, another form of resistance. Mexicans and Mexican Americans for instance adored Chico Cano. They considered him a hero and friend and regarded him as an important leader during the Mexican Revolution. Mexican Americans also founded anti-lynching groups and legal aid societies that challenged this abusive situation. While those challenges didn't—and really couldn't—stop or diminish the level of violence Mexican-origin people experienced, they remain still an important example of community agency and activism. They helped Gregorio Cortéz, for example. Although he had to endure multiple trials and a system that railroaded him, the defense group created on his behalf succeeded in securing his pardon.

Interestingly enough, change was afoot after the border violence of the 1910s. The 1920s and 1930s witnessed the beginning of police professionalization, as law enforcement agencies began to modernize their practices. It also meant the curtailment of the power of some law enforcement agencies.

The best example of this, the Canales Investigation and Reforms of the Texas Rangers as well as subsequent legislative action restraining the power of the Rangers, resulted in a significant transformation of the Ranger force. In other locales, the political power of the Mexican American community successfully kept abusive law officers from advancement. The Mexican American rejection of John Welch for sheriff in Miami, Arizona, represents a notable example of this type of activism.

Police professionalization was a major component of the Progressive Era, but that professionalization proved incremental and oscillatory. Moments of positive reform were punctuated by moments of violence. Border killings in Texas continued. The final verifiable lynching of a Mexican-origin person occurred in New Mexico in 1928. The persistence of violence certainly suggests that the police reforms of the 1920s and 1930s needed to continue beyond that period. Even police departments that engaged in reforms, such as the Albuquerque Police Department, fell prey to the racism of the time when they helped elevate Henry "the Lonesome Kid" Gallegos to the status of criminal mastermind that he in no way deserved.

The 1920s and 1930s represented something else: the growth and thereby the concomitant increase in power of the Mexican American population. As the number of Mexican-origin people expanded through the teen years and into the twenties, that larger population base laid the groundwork for better resistance to abusive policing and for the political clout to begin pushing authorities to inaugurate change. And Mexican Americans demonstrated that growth in power in a number of ways: by demanding reforms such as the ones J. T. Canales implemented in Texas; by helping to improve policing by becoming police officers such as Dennis Chavez in Albuquerque; and by utilizing political processes to demand justice for those abused by law enforcement such as Alonso Perales did through his activism. The conscientious reforms begun in the 1920s and 1930s—the product, mind you, of Mexican Americans *and* law enforcement—set the stage for a new, modern Southwest.

Demarcating the borders of violence and justice reveals a troubling history. For most of the Southwest's history, the boundary between the two was very fine. Although White people argued for justice, vocally supported justice, said they revered justice, they simultaneously acted in unconstitutional, unconscionable, and unjust ways. Perhaps mob law best underscores this point. Extralegal justice occurred alongside legal justice. In many cases the authorities in the criminal justice system joined lynch mobs. Members of mobs also professed to respect justice, yet those vigilantes operated contrary to the law. Despite what they said, lynching was not justice. It was the opposite, and it represented an abrogation of duty, principle, and morality for those who claimed to revere justice. The vigilante lie that mob law was justice did not allow justice to happen, it allowed wanton killing, violence, and the satisfying of bloodlust to happen.

The development of police agencies, from sheriff's offices to constabularies to police departments, as well as the broader criminal justice system, represented the seriousness of American ambitions to control the border region. This was not haphazard or poorly executed. Instead, White leaders knew exactly what they were doing, and they crafted the institutions they knew would work. The system they created was the system they intended to create, and it operated as they wanted it to. And it was built on racism that equated Mexican-origin people with barbarity and criminality; that pigeonholed them as foreigners and second-class citizens; and that demanded that they be controlled or accommodate themselves to the system or die. When scholars and activists speak of the institutionalization of racism within the criminal justice system, this is what they are talking about. That system remains with us today.

Systems often overlap. The criminal justice system is, of course, not one but multiple closely connected institutions. These overlapping systems reinforce one another in a variety of ways. Take, for example, the large number of senseless murders of Mexican-origin people by police. This was one of the most atrocious aspects of the criminal justice system. Law enforcement seemingly could kill with impunity. State governments and city ordinances of course gave law officers the legal power to kill people. As the numerous examples of this type of abuse make clear, police rarely received any kind of punishment for these deaths. Grand juries no-billed their actions and district attorneys refused to prosecute them for their killing. That further demarcates how police murder was a state-sanctioned police practice in all parts of the Southwest. And it exemplifies a serious problem in law enforcement in that excused killings seemed to prompt more killings.

The different layers of the system also worked to excuse officers accused of wrongdoing in other ways. The concept of ley fuga allowed for unchecked killing, but the aftermath also saw this system work to exonerate officers. When police victimized or killed Mexican-origin people, authorities often trotted out a laundry list of excuses as to why the officers were justified in their actions. They published the criminal record of the victims (if they had one), labelled them a "bandit," made them into an aggressor, all with the goal of absolving the officers. Similarly, city hiring procedures meant that police authorities often had difficulty getting rid of troubled officers that they wanted to fire. That problem remains with us today.

The criminal justice system at multiple levels also tended to harass Mexicans and Mexican Americans. This was especially true during the Mexican Revolution, when authorities arrested greater numbers of Mexican-origin people for vagrancy and increased the fines for that offense substantially. Arresting people only to release them a day later or arresting them and courts throwing out their cases, these were common forms of harassment. While credit goes to those court officers who dismissed such cases, a sign of the fair operating of the system, police probably should never have arrested those individuals in the first place. Of course, law enforcement found other ways to harass Mexican-origin people; by closely monitoring them, by holding them in jail unlawfully, and by killing them. Again, the various aspects of the system overlapped to treat them in this way.

Another aspect of this system merits additional scrutiny: incarceration. White authorities fixated on erecting jails, prisons, penitentiaries, juvenile facilities, prison camps, immigrant detention facilities, and other forms of human caging going back to the first days of American control in the border region. While there was a certain unfortunate logic to incarceration—if you're going to adjudicate people in a court of law and find them guilty of a crime then you have to do something with them—the overwhelming focus on building these facilities, the huge expenditures governments spent on them, and the lives they damaged meant incarceration was anything but logical. Today we see the problem with this logic (or illogic); prisons are a trillion-dollar industry, the United States incarcerates more people than any other nation on the globe, and incarceration disproportionately affects communities of color. While the rise of the carceral state is largely viewed as a 1960s and 1970s phenomenon, its antecedents go back much further than that in the Southwest.

One of the interesting examples of overlapping systems visible throughout this period is the intersection between capitalism and law enforcement. The United States took over Mexico's territories because the United States wanted those lands for the expansion of markets and the creation of new ones. Many of the early documents, the Kearny Code in New Mexico or Stockton's proclamation and the Capitulation of Cahuenga in California, made explicit references to capital and criminal justice. The land wars in California and New Mexico, the Cart and Salt Wars in Texas, the labor unrest in Arizona and New Mexico, all those things were about the acquisition, control, or expansion of markets, and almost all had some form of participation from law enforcement and the criminal justice system. That linkage of systems, often hidden from view, is important to our understanding of why criminal justice works the way it does.

One of the interesting things about the criminal justice system is that Mexican-origin people actively participated in it. When they pinned a star or a shield to their chest they, like their White counterparts, took an oath to uphold the system. When they won election as sheriffs or district attorneys or justices of the peace they actively participated in the system. When the state accused Mexican-origin people of a crime and they hired attorneys to represent them, whether successfully or not, they participated in the system. When they wrote letters to elected officials or joined advocacy groups that put pressure on state agencies to halt abuses in law enforcement, they were participating in the system. Why? Because like other people, Mexicans and Mexican Americans understood that the criminal justice system and all its facets represented, or at least should have represented, everyone. For much of this history, they attempted to make the system work fairly. That history should effectively counter the narratives about the supposed criminality, inferiority, and foreignness of Mexican-origin people.

The problem with the institutional issues mentioned above is that members of the criminal justice system who wanted to engage in fair, effective policing had to operate within a system designed to treat Mexican-origin people, and others too, poorly. This book is full of examples of decent, fair-minded individuals in the criminal justice system, White and Mexican American. Sheriff Perfecto Armijo or Marshal Henry Garfias serve as good examples of effective Mexican American law officers. The number of White individuals who acted conscientiously and fairly is equally as long. For example, Maricopa County district attorney Frank Cox and Yavapai County sheriff William J. Mulvenon both assisted Manuel Mejía. While the Texas Rangers did a lot of damage, some Rangers such as Captain John Rogers, who captured Gregorio Cortéz without incident, operated with decency. Or recall the example of Constable Robert McCoy, who attempted to protect Antonio Gómez from the lynch mob. Last, there were the countless officers in the criminal justice system who dismissed charges against Mexican-origin defendants or exercised compassion in their jurisprudence. All these people demonstrate the existence of impartial, just, and effective White members of the justice system. The problem with the institutionalization of racism within the criminal justice system is that these people did not have the requisite power to alter the system. Their individual actions, while they helped, did little to change the operation of the justice system. They should still receive credit for their work and actions. Their examples remain worthy of honor.

The modern history of the Southwest, from the 1930s to the present day, reveals the ongoing importance of many of the issues detailed in *Borders of*

Violence and Justice. Like the 1920s and 1930s, the 1930s–1950s was also a period of transition and stagnation. Reforms took place, change happened, but then violence also occurred, which set back change and reform. Mexican Americans in Houston, for example, continued to think up new, creative adaptations to law enforcement problems. After several instances of violence in the late 1930s, Mexican American leaders proposed that Houston authorities establish a "Latin Squad," or a group of Spanish-speaking officers, to help police when they interacted with Mexican-origin people. That idea set the stage for similar programs in the 1960s and 1970s, especially cultural sensitivity training, Spanish-language instruction, and officer recruitment programs.

Other events marred the World War II period. While Mexicans and Mexican Americans volunteered their service in the military and war industries or the military drafted them into service, at home they continued to experience violence at the hands of law enforcement as well as the military. The so-called Zoot Suit Riots, wherein White service members and police officers brutalized Mexican-origin people and other individuals in Los Angeles and other cities, best demonstrates this fact. The way law enforcement treated zoot suiters during the Second World War communicated clearly that Mexican Americans would not receive equal treatment from the criminal justice system. But Mexican Americans resisted this treatment as well. They fought back during the riots. Mexican American leaders joined several investigations of the Zoot Suit Riots that called for greater scrutiny of police practices. These examples reveal the beginning of a nascent civil rights movement that sought to redress police violence and reform American policing.

Those early civil rights efforts ultimately transformed into a distinct Mexican American civil rights movement in the 1960s. The Chicano Movement, the activist phase of the Mexican American struggle for freedom, sought changes to school segregation patterns, the desegregation of public accommodations, increased voting and political participation, and reforms in how law enforcement treated Mexican-origin people. That latter focus on police reform characterized much of the Chicano Movement period, from the 1960s to the 1980s. Mexican Americans waged a concerted effort to curb police violence, especially police murder, which resulted in several noteworthy reforms. They protested and demonstrated against police abuse, while they simultaneously worked with law enforcement for reforms such as the development of internal affairs departments, the creation of police civilian review boards, increased training of officers, and community outreach. While there was no universal police reaction to this activism, in many locales law enforcement responded positively and proactively to these reform efforts.

But Chicano activists suffered horribly from police harassment and abuse during the Chicano Movement. The number of police killings of movement participants such as Luis "Junior" Martinez, Rito Canales, and Antonio Cordova, among many others, as well as the murders of nonmovement participants like Santos Rodriguez, Jose H. Sinohui Jr., Jose "Joe" Campos Torres, and too many more to name, show how police violence really persisted unabated during the Chicano era. And yet Mexican Americans continued to approach law enforcement with smart, well-crafted ideas about how to reform police. It is a strange irony that law enforcement could act with such violence toward Chicanos while they still conscientiously engaged in reform at the same time.

The late twentieth century represented a new evolution in American policing, much of it negative. In the 1980s, with economic recessions and tightened budgets, many communities began to roll back the reforms of the 1960s and 1970s. In the 1990s, new legislation such as the 1994 Violent Crime Control and Law Enforcement Act, otherwise known as the Clinton Crime Law, greatly augmented the number of police in the United States while also expanding jail and prison facilities throughout the country. Coupled with the War on Drugs and the more ubiquitous War on Crime, police forces launched massive new crime control techniques that disproportionately impacted communities of color. In the Southwest, Mexican-origin and other Latino/a/x people were especially affected. The late twentieth century thus gave the American public massive, militarized police forces that have largely characterized policing in the twenty-first century.

The new, twenty-first-century model of policing has been particularly brutal in its treatment of people of color. While many Americans may be familiar with the cases of police killings that helped spawn a Movement for Black Lives, across the Southwest Mexican Americans have similarly felt the sting of this modern-day version of policing. Many of the twenty-first century's victims of police abuse and murder have been Mexicans and Mexican Americans. Like Black people, Mexican Americans have protested such abuses and have waited anxiously for the outcomes of trials of officers accused of murder. Like Black people, Mexican Americans have often been disappointed with the outcomes of those trials. While the nineteenth and twentieth centuries were marred by bloodshed, the late twentieth and early twenty-first centuries have also been a borderland of violence.

There is much to say about the history of Mexican American and police interactions from the mid-twentieth to the early twenty-first century. I fully explore this history in *Brown and Blue*, the book that follows *Borders of Violence and Justice*. This book details the violence mentioned above, but also pays close attention to the civil rights efforts of Mexican Americans. Since the 1940s, the Southwest has witnessed a sustained civil rights struggle among Mexican Americans, one that has conscientiously fought for better, more just, and less violent law enforcement.

Notes

ABBREVIATIONS

ABCPL	Special Collections Library, Albuquerque and Bernalillo County Public Library, Albuquerque, N.Mex.
APL	Austin History Center, Austin Public Library, Tex.
ASL	Arizona State Library Archives, Phoenix
BC	Dolph Briscoe Center for American History, University of Texas at Austin
DPL	Texas/Dallas History and Archives Division, Dallas Public Library
FACHL	Fray Angélico Chávez History Library, Santa Fe, N.Mex.
HL	Huntington Library, San Marino, Calif.
NMSRCA	New Mexico State Records Center and Archives, Santa Fe
SAMAR	San Antonio Municipal Archives and Records, Tex.
SAPL	Texana/Genealogy Collection, San Antonio Public Library
TANM microfilm	Territorial Archives of New Mexico (microfilm), Santa Fe
UCSD	Special Collections and Archives, University of California, San Diego

UNM Center for Southwest Research and Special Collections, University of New Mexico, Albuquerque
UTA Special Collections, University of Texas, Arlington

INTRODUCTION

1. Chas. P. Stanton to His Excellency M. Romero, September 13, 1886, Secretary of the Territory Papers, 1864–1912, ASL; "An Outrage by a Mob," *Daily Alta California*, September 19, 1886; "Ultrajes a un Mejicano" (Outrages to a Mexican), *El Fronterizo*, March 22, 1890.

2. On the linkage between racial violence and criminal justice, see Pfeifer, *Rough Justice*; Berg, *Popular Justice*; Carrigan and Webb, *Forgotten Dead*.

3. For a few general studies that focus on the Mexican-origin community and law enforcement in this period, see Morales, *Ando Sangrando (I Am Bleeding)*; Escobar, *Race, Police, and the Making of a Political Identity*; Rosales, *¡Pobre Raza!*. See also Graybill, *Policing the Great Plains*.

4. On Manifest Destiny and its racial baggage, see Horsman, *Race and Manifest Destiny*; Hietala, *Manifest Design*.

5. See Hixson, *American Settler Colonialism*; Goldstein, *Formations of United States Colonialism*; Gonzales, *Política*; Saito, *Settler Colonialism, Race, and the Law*; Dunbar-Ortiz, *Not "a Nation of Immigrants."*

6. For background, see Behnken, *Fighting Their Own Battles*.

7. For example, Phoenix had a population of three Black people in 1870, five in 1880, and zero in 1890. See Luckingham, *Minorities in Phoenix*, 1. See also Glasrud, *African American History in New Mexico*, 1–8; Sides, *L.A. City Limits*, 15–16.

8. My thinking has been especially influenced by the work of DeLay, *War of a Thousand Deserts*. Also, a 2019 Forum in the journal *William and Mary Quarterly* offered much needed nuance on the issue of settler colonialism in early American history. For important sources that more fully flesh out and complicate what I described above, see Glassburn, "Settler Standpoints"; Smallwood, "Reflections on Settler Colonialism"; Miles, "Beyond a Boundary"; Spear, "Beyond the Native/Settler Divide"; Truett, "Settler Colonialism and the Borderlands." See also Wolfe, "Settler Colonialism and the Elimination of the Native"; Anderson, *Ethnic Cleansing and the Indian*.

9. On the issue of colonialism as experienced by Mexican-origin people, see Sánchez and Pita, "Rethinking Settler Colonialism"; Gratton and Merchant, "An Immigrant's Tale." For an excellent discussion that situates colonization as a process done by Mexico itself, see Hernández, *Mexican American Colonization During the Nineteenth Century*.

10. See, for example, De León, *They Called Them Greasers*, 32, 33, 41–43, 70–71; Menchaca, *The Mexican Outsiders*, chap. 2; Telles and Ortiz, *Generations of Exclusion*, 76–78.

11. See, for example, Roberts and Roberts, *New Mexico*, 129–30; Sánchez, Spude, and Gómez, *New Mexico*, 139, 159–60; and Raspa, *Bloody Bay*, 219.

12. Miller, *The Social History of Crime and Punishment*, 1592, 1663–65.

13. On the development of local law enforcement, see Griffin, *Policing Las Vegas*; Rubenser and Priddy, *Constables, Marshals, and More*; Roth and Kennedy, *Houston Blue*.

14. On these Ranger forces, see DeSoucy, *Arizona Rangers*; Hornung, *New Mexico's Rangers*; Hornung, *Fullerton's Rangers*; Glasrud and Weiss, *Tracking the Texas Rangers*.

15. On federal law enforcement, see Hernández, *Migra!*; Kang, *The INS on the Line*; Turk, *Forging the Star*.

16. See Gardiner and Fiber-Ostrow, *California's Criminal Justice System*; Frantzen and Lloyd, *Texas's Criminal Justice System*.

17. Perkinson, *Texas Tough*; Secrest, *Behind San Quentin's Walls*; Hernández, *City of Inmates*.

18. Population demographics for Mexican-origin people in the United States are imprecise before about 1960. For some work focusing on the period from 1850 to 1930, see Haverluk, "The Changing Geography of U.S. Hispanics"; Gratton and Merchant, "An Immigrant's Tale"; Gutiérrez, "Mexican Immigration to the United States."

19. The concept of "ley fuga" originated in Mexico. For background, see Kloppe-Santamaría, *In the Vortex of Violence*.

20. On Porvenir, see Martinez, *The Injustice Never Leaves You*.

21. Orozco, *No Mexicans, Women, or Dogs Allowed*, 69. Chico Cano's first name is something of a mystery. Many scholars concur that his first name was Francisco, but he seems to have almost exclusively used Chico.

22. For background, see Weiss, "The Texas Rangers Revisited," 637–38.

23. Regarding borderlands history, I have been particularly influenced by the work of: Truett and Young, "Introduction: Making Transnational History"; Johnson, "The Plan de San Diego Uprising"; Blackhawk, *Violence over the Land*; Benton-Cohen, *Borderline Americans*; Johnson and Graybill, "Introduction: Borders and Their Historians"; Lim, *Porous Borders*; Grandin, *The End of the Myth*. See also Weber, *The Mexican Frontier*; Behnken and Wendt, *Crossing Boundaries*. On violence, see especially Guidotti-Hernández, *Unspeakable Violence*.

24. See Feagin and Cobas, *Latinos Facing Racism*; Zack, *White Privilege and Black Rights*; Taylor, *From #BlackLivesMatter to Black Liberation*; Schrader, *Badges without Borders*.

CHAPTER 1

1. "Art. 139," *Early Laws of Texas, Volume 1*, 193. Article 139 established the Rangers; Article 140 raised a regular army.

2. Deverell, *Whitewashed Adobe*, 14.

3. "The War," *Democratic Review*, February 1847.

4. See "John O'Sullivan Declares America's Manifest Destiny."

5. For works that explore the development of local police agencies, see, for example, Rousey, *Policing the Southern City*; Crongeyer, *Six Gun Sound*; Roth and Kennedy, *Houston Blue*; Mitrani, *The Rise of the Chicago Police Department*; Chadwick, *Law & Disorder*; Jett, *Race, Crime, and Policing in the Jim Crow South*. See also Behnken, "Controlling Los Hombres."

6. Hopkins, *American Empire*; Immerwahr, *How to Hide an Empire*; Deverell, *Whitewashed Adobe*; Hietala, *Manifest Design*; Horsman, *Race and Manifest Destiny*.

7. de la Teja, *A Revolution Remembered*.

8. Blake, "Córdova, Vicente." See also Haynes and Saxon, *Contested Empire*; Lack, *The Texas Revolutionary Experience*; Ramos, *Beyond the Alamo*.

9. "Art. 139," *Early Laws of Texas, Volume 1*, 193.

10. "Art. 212," *Early Laws of Texas, Volume 1*, 202–4.

11. "Art. 269," *Early Laws of Texas, Volume 1*, 223–24.
12. "Art. 275," *Early Laws of Texas, Volume 1*, 225–30.
13. "Art. 483," *Early Laws of Texas, Volume 1*, 285.
14. "Art. 509," *Early Laws of Texas, Volume 1*, 287.
15. "Art. 580," *Early Laws of Texas, Volume 1*, 300.
16. "Art. 768," *Early Laws of Texas, Volume 1*, 405.
17. "Art. 1145," *Early Laws of Texas, Volume 1*, 493.
18. See, for instance, "Art. 4254," *Early Laws of Texas, Volume 3*, 485–88.
19. "Art. 1973," *Early Laws of Texas, Volume 2*, 228.
20. "Art. 374," *Early Laws of Texas, Volume 1*, 254.
21. "Art. 632," *Early Laws of Texas, Volume 1*, 305.
22. *The Penal Code of the State of Texas*; "An Act to Amend an Act Entitled an Act to Adopt and Establish a Penal Code for the State of Texas," *Early Laws of Texas, Volume 1*, 84–85.
23. Article IV, Section 12, of the Constitution of the Republic of Texas stated that "there shall be appointed, for each county, a convenient number of justices of the peace, one sheriff, one coroner, and a sufficient number of constables." Under the General Provisions, Section 7 stated that "so soon as convenience will permit, there shall be a penal code formed on principles of reformation, and not of vindictive justice." The first counties were established in late 1836, the first official penal code was not established until 1856. See "Article IV, Section 12" and "General Provisions, Section 7" of the *Constitution of the Republic of Texas*.
24. "Article 9," *Treaty of Velasco* (public). See also the *Treaty of Velasco* (private).
25. De León, *Ethnicity in the Sunbelt*, 4–5. See also Allen, *The City of Houston*.
26. See Roth and Kennedy, *Houston Blue*, 5–12.
27. As quoted in De León, *Ethnicity in the Sunbelt*, 5.
28. "City Marshals and Chiefs of Police, San Antonio, Texas, 1845–1983," Police Department Vertical File, SAPL.
29. *Austin Police Department Guide*, 3.
30. "Hispanic Beginnings of Dallas," 11.
31. "History of the Dallas Police Department," compiled by Lieutenant Cantrell, February 24, 1940, State Fair Grounds (Fair Park) Folder, Dallas Police Archives, DPL.
32. For good histories of the war, see Bauer, *The Mexican War*; Levinson, *Wars within War*; Chávez, *The U.S. War with Mexico*; Greenberg, *A Wicked War*; Guardino, *The Dead March*.
33. See Beyreis, *Blood in the Borderlands*, chap. 3 and 4.
34. Fred Lambert, "The Long H Rancho," 5–6, Emma Moya Collection, UNM.
35. Manuel Armijo proclamation, January 10, 1846, Maria G. Duran Collection, NMSRCA.
36. Mariano Lucero circular, January 28, 1846, Maria G. Duran Collection, NMSRCA.
37. Jose Pablo Gallegos circular, April 7, 1846; Jose Pablo Gallegos circular, April 30, 1846; Jose Pablo Gallegos Circular, June 18, 1846; Maria G. Duran Collection, NMSRCA.
38. Manuel Armijo proclamation, August 8, 1846; Manuel Armijo letter to the Department for Appropriations, August 10, 1846, Benjamin M. Read Collection, NMSRCA. I am using Read's translation here.
39. Loyola, "The American Occupation of New Mexico," 160–63.
40. Some reports indicate that American agents convinced Armijo to flee. One account even suggests he was bribed. I discount these reports in favor of the more logical

conclusion that Armijo knew he and his soldiers would be decimated. See Mora, *Border Dilemmas*, 23.

41. See Bancroft, *History of Arizona and New Mexico*, 324; Magoffin, *Down the Santa Fe Trail*, 96–97; Van Ness, *Spanish & Mexican Land Grants*, 53. Ray John de Aragón and Brian DeLay both succinctly countered this viewpoint. See de Aragón, *New Mexico in the Mexican American War*, 76; DeLay, *War of a Thousand Deserts*, 255.

42. By the Order of Don Antonio Maria Trujillo circa January 1847, "1847 Treason Trials," Lucien A. File Papers, NMSRCA.

43. Jesus Tafolla to the defenders of their country, January 20, 1847, "1847 Treason Trials," Lucien A. File Papers, NMSRCA.

44. On the Kearny Code of Law, see Smith, *The New Mexico State Constitution*, 5–7. On the code as a form of law enforcement, see Wadman and Allison, *To Protect and to Serve*, 46–47.

45. "Laws for the Government of the Territory of New Mexico," *Kearny Code of Law*.

46. Loyola, "The American Occupation of New Mexico," 234.

47. Loyola, "The American Occupation of New Mexico," 154.

48. "The President's Secret Emissary," *Golden West*, July 1970. See also "The Capture of New Mexico," *New York Herald*, October 3, 1846.

49. Ligon de Ita, "Taos Rebellion Revisited," 2–3; S. W. Kearny, "Aviso," September 22, 1846, Stephen Watts Kearny, 1846 Papers, TANM microfilm, Roll 98.

50. Charles Bent to Manuel Alvarez, May 3, 1846, Benjamin M. Read Collection, NMSRCA.

51. Bent elaborated on the attacks in another letter to Manuel Alvarez, also dated May 3, 1846, Benjamin M. Read Collection, NMSRCA.

52. Charles Bent to Manuel Alvarez, February 24, 1846, Benjamin M. Read Collection, NMSRCA.

53. Lavender, *Bent's Fort*, 293. See also Herrera, "New Mexico Resistance to U.S. Occupation"; Reséndez, *Changing National Identities at the Frontier*.

54. Lavender, *Bent's Fort*, 273.

55. Loyola, "The American Occupation of New Mexico," 167.

56. Ligon de Ita, "Taos Rebellion Revisited," 3–6.

57. Ligon de Ita, "Taos Rebellion Revisited," 5.

58. Ligon de Ita, "Taos Rebellion Revisited," 6.

59. "Details of the Insurrection in New Mexico," *Niles National Register*, April 3, 1847; Gómez, *Manifest Destinies*, 27–29.

60. Tórrez, "A Deceptive Silence."

61. Tórrez, "A Ruthless Suppression of the Insurrection."

62. Gómez, *Manifest Destinies*, 15–16, 28–31; Tórrez, "A Short History of New Mexico"; Rulska, "Taos Revolt."

63. "Triunfo de los Principios Contra la Torpeza!" (Triumph of Principles against Stupidity), January 25, 1847, Donaciano Vigil, 1847–1848 Papers, TANM microfilm, Roll 98.

64. Tórrez, "Tragedy at Los Valles."

65. Hughes, *Doniphan's Expedition*, 200.

66. For an overview of these events, see Gómez, *Manifest Destinies*, chap. 1; Wroth, "1847 Taos Rebellion."

67. Tórrez, "Tragedy at Los Valles."

68. Turner, *The Massacre of Gov. Bent*, 35.

69. Grand Jury Proceedings, *United States v. Antonio Ma Trujillo*, treason; *United States v. Trinidad Barcelo*, treason; *United States v. Pantaleon Archuleta*, treason, "1847 Treason Trials," History Files, folders no. 158–70, NMSRCA.

70. *United States v. Archuleta*, plea; *United States v. Barcelo*, plea, "1847 Treason Trials," History Files, folders no. 158–70, NMSRCA.

71. *United States v. Barcelo*, nolle prosequi; *United States v. Archuleta*, nolle prosequi, "1847 Treason Trials," History Files, folders no. 158–70, NMSRCA.

72. *United States v. Vigil*, indictment; *United States v. Vigil*, plea; *United States v. Vigil*, nolle prosequi, "1847 Treason Trials," History Files, folders no. 158–70, NMSRCA.

73. Tórrez, "The Trials at Taos."

74. Tórrez, "The 'Treason Trials' of 1847."

75. "The True Story," unknown newspaper clipping, n.d., "General History," Lucien A. File Papers, NMSRCA.

76. *United States v. Antonio Maria Trujillo*, True Bill, "1847 Treason Trials," History Files, folders no. 158–70, NMSRCA. See also *United States v. Trujillo*, plea; *United States v. Trujillo*, verdict, "1847 Treason Trials," History Files, folders no. 158–70, NMSRCA.

77. *United States v. Antonio Maria Trujillo*, True Bill, "1847 Treason Trials," History Files, folders no. 158–70, NMSRCA.

78. *United States v. Antonio Maria Trujillo*, Sentence of the Court, "1847 Treason Trials," History Files, folders no. 158–70, NMSRCA.

79. *United States v. Trujillo*, appeal, "1847 Treason Trials," History Files, folders no. 158–70, NMSRCA.

80. Tórrez, "Rebellion of 1847 Treason Trials."

81. Jones, "New Mexico Massacre."

82. Ligon de Ita, "Taos Rebellion Revisited," 9.

83. "Trail Dust: Vicious Fighting Marked Taos Revolt," *Santa Fe New Mexican*, April 24, 2009.

84. Tórrez, "Tragedy at Los Valles" (quotation); Twitchell, *The History of the Military Occupation of the Territory of New Mexico*, 162–66, 178–202.

85. See Walker, *Bear Flag Rising*.

86. Pio Pico to Excellent Sir, May 25, 1846, Tays, "Pio Pico's Correspondence," 103–4.

87. Pio Pico to Excellent Sir, July 13, 1846, Tays, "Pio Pico's Correspondence," 109–10.

88. Sloat, *The Sloat Proclamation*; Faragher, *Eternity Street*, 97–99.

89. José Castro to Fellow Citizens, August 9, 1846, Tays, "Pio Pico's Correspondence with the Mexican Government," 117–18; Harlow, *California Conquered*, 149.

90. José Castro to Excellent Sir, August 8, 1846, Tays, "Pio Pico's Correspondence with the Mexican Government," 116–17.

91. José Castro to Most Excellent Sir, August 9, 1846, Tays, "Pio Pico's Correspondence with the Mexican Government," 118–19.

92. Pio Pico to the people under his rule, August 10, 1846, Tays, "Pio Pico's Correspondence with the Mexican Government," 122–23.

93. Bauer, *The Mexican War*, 174–76.

94. Singletary, *The Mexican War*, 66.

95. Stockton, *The Stockton Proclamation*.

96. As quoted in Harlow, *California Conquered*, 159.

97. Harlow, *California Conquered*, 161.

98. Faragher, *Eternity Street*, 109–13, chap. 7.
99. Faragher, *Eternity Street*, 113–14.
100. Walker, *Bear Flag Rising*, 193–200.
101. Walker, *Bear Flag Rising*, 201–5.
102. Bauer, *The Mexican War*, 185.
103. Bauer, *The Mexican War*, 186.
104. Bauer, *The Mexican War*, 188.
105. Bauer, *The Mexican War*, 191–93.
106. *Treaty of Cahuenga*.
107. *Treaty of Guadalupe Hidalgo*.
108. For the fullest account of slavery and Mexican-origin people in Texas, see Campbell, *An Empire for Slavery*; Torget, *Seeds of Empire*; Baumgartner, *South to Freedom*. See also de la Teja, *A Revolution Remembered*.
109. See, for example, Tyler, "The Callahan Expedition of 1855."
110. "Mexicans in Texas," *Texas State Gazette*, September 2, 1854; "Public Meeting in Seguin—Vagrant Mexicans," *Texas State Gazette*, September 9, 1854. See also "Runaways to Mexico," *Texas State Gazette*, September 9, 1854; "Mexicans Aiding Negroes," *Texas State Gazette*, September 30, 1854.
111. Campbell, *An Empire for Slavery*, 218, 219; Montejano, *Anglos and Mexicans in the Making of Texas*, 25–30. These conventions and vigilante groups always referred to "Mexicans" even though some of the people they targeted may have been American citizens of Mexican ancestry.
112. "Gonzales Convention," *Texas State Gazette*, October 14, 1854.
113. "Peons," n.d., Mexican "Peons" 1854–1855 Folder, Camacho Family Papers, APL.
114. "Resolution," *Texas State Gazette*, October 14, 1854. See also "Editorial," *Texas State Times*, October 21, 1854.
115. "The Meeting of Last Saturday," *Texas State Times*, October 21, 1854.
116. "Peons," n.d., Mexican "Peons" 1854–1855 Folder, Camacho Family Papers, APL; "Resolution," *Texas State Gazette*, October 14, 1854; "Gonzales Convention," *Texas State Gazette*, October 14, 1854; "The Meeting of Last Saturday," *Texas State Times*, October 21, 1854; "Editorial," *Texas State Times*, October 21, 1854.
117. "Grand Ratification Meeting," *Texas State Times*, October 21, 1854.
118. "Gonzales Convention," *Texas State Gazette*, October 14, 1854; "Meeting of Last Saturday," *Texas State Times*, October 21, 1854.
119. Title unknown, *Texas State Times*, October 28, 1854, Camacho Family Papers, APL.
120. "Peons," *Annals of Travis County*, 1854.
121. "Proceedings of the Gonzales Convention," *Texas State Gazette*, November 14, 1854.
122. "Two O'clock PM (Gonzales convention resumes)," *Texas State Gazette*, November 14, 1854.
123. "Worthy of Notice," *Texas State Gazette*, February 24, 1855.
124. See for instance Jacoby, *The Strange Career of William Ellis*, 21–23; Torget, *Seeds of Empire*, 233–35.
125. "Sheriff Makes Arrest of Three Idle Mexicans," *Austin American*, September 1, 1918.
126. Sumner Proclamation, June 29, 1852, James S. Calhoun, 1851–1852 Papers, TANM microfilm, Roll 98.
127. William Carr Lane Message to the Legislative Assembly of the Territory, December 7, 1852, William Carr Lane, 1852–1853 Papers, TANM microfilm, Roll 98. While Lane

mentioned "Red thieves" and "White thieves," and probably meant Indigenous and White people, either of those terms could have meant Mexican-origin people too.

128. Second Annual Message of W. F. N. Arny, Acting Governor, to the Legislative Assembly, December 1866, Henry Connelly, 1861–1866 Papers, TANM microfilm, Roll 98.

129. Charles De Gaslon? (last name illegible) to David Meriwether, July 10, 1856, David Meriwether, 1853–1857 Papers, TANM microfilm, Roll 98. See also Hornung, *Fullerton's Rangers*.

130. Chapter XV, "An Act Creating Police Officers in Settlements Distant from the Residence of the Justice of the Peace," *New Mexico Territorial Laws*, 33.

131. Benjamin M. Read, "Vigilantes of Santa Fe," 1866 Murder of Foster Folder, Benjamin M. Read Collection, NMSRCA. Foster's first name is not known.

132. Johnson O'Kock, et al. to H. H. Heath, May 27, 1868, Robert B. Mitchell, 1866–1869 Papers, TANM microfilm, Roll 98.

133. Judge Antonio Ortiz y Salazar, "Police Regulations," May 27, 1868, Robert B. Mitchell, 1866–1869 Papers, TANM microfilm, Roll 98.

134. "Chapter IV, An Act with Reference to County Warrants," *Acts of the Legislative Assembly of the Territory of New Mexico, Twenty-First Session*, 23–24.

135. "Chapter IX, An Act Putting in Force the Police Law Passed at the Session 1871–72," *Acts of the Legislative Assembly of the Territory of New Mexico, Twenty-First Session*, 27–28.

136. "Chapter XII, An Act to Authorize the Governor to Offer Rewards for the Apprehension of Persons Accused of Crime," *Acts of the Legislative Assembly of the Territory of New Mexico, Twenty-First Session*, 30.

137. "Chapter VII, An Act Giving Additional Jurisdiction to Justices of the Peace in Certain Cases," *Acts of the Legislative Assembly of the Territory of New Mexico, Twenty-First Session*, 26.

138. "Orders Establishing the San Juan Guards," April 1881, Campaign Against Outlaws in Rio Arriba County, 1881 Papers, TANM microfilm, Roll 73.

139. Blew, "Vigilantism in Los Angeles, 1835–1874," 20–25.

140. John Franklin Burns, "Reminiscences," in James Franklin Burns Reminiscences Folder, HL.

141. Griswold Del Castillo, *The Los Angeles Barrio*, 109; Faragher, *Eternity Street*, chap. 17.

142. Horace Bell, draft of chapter 24, "On the Old West Coast," Bell (Horace) Collection, HL.

143. As quoted in Deverell, *Whitewashed Adobe*, 14.

144. Hernández, *City of Inmates*, 35.

145. See *The Statutes of California Passed at the First Session*, 57–59.

146. "Chapter 24," *The Statutes of California Passed at the First Session*, 81–83.

147. "Chapter 40," *The Statutes of California Passed at the First Session*, 112–13.

148. "Chapter 44," *The Statutes of California Passed at the First Session*, 118.

149. "Chapter 106," *The Statutes of California Passed at the First Session*, 258–59.

150. "Chapter 112," *The Statutes of California Passed at the First Session*, 263–64.

151. "Chapter 119," *The Statutes of California Passed at the First Session*, 275–332; *The Penal Code of California: Enacted in 1872; as Amended in 1881*.

152. "Chapter II, III, VII, and VIII," *The Howell Code*, 25, 28–29, 31, 40–41, 41–42. For background, see Goff, "William T. Howell"; Wagoner, *Arizona Territory*.

153. "Chapter VII–XII," *The Howell Code*, 40–145.

154. "Chapter XLIV and XLV," *The Howell Code*, 286–87, 287–91.

155. "Police in Cities and Towns and their Attendance at exposed Places," "Chapter XI," *The Howell Code*, 77.

156. "No. 8, No. 20, and No. 24," *Acts, Resolutions and Memorials of the Fifteenth Legislative Assembly*, 23–24, 45–46, 50.

157. "Chapter 4," *The Revised Statutes of Arizona Territory*, 1304.

158. "Un Asunto Internacional" (An International Issue), *El Horizonte*, November 29, 1879; *Correspondencia Diplomática Cambiada entre el Gobierno de los Estados Unidos y los de Varias Potencias Extranjeras*, 33–34, 43–48. The del Valle incident proved far more typical than we might think, and similar incidents happen today, such as the 2010 case of Border Patrol agent Jesus Mesa who shot and killed Sergio Adrián Hernández Güereca.

CHAPTER 2

1. Benjamin M. Read, "Vigilantes of Santa Fe," 1866 Murder of Foster Folder, Benjamin M. Read Collection, NMSRCA.

2. Johnson O'Kock et al. to H. H. Heath, May 27, 1868; Judge Antonio Ortiz y Salazar, "Police Regulations," May 27, 1868, Robert B. Mitchell, 1866–1869 Papers, TANM microfilm, Roll 98.

3. "A Most Horrible Crime—Brutal Murder of Dr. J. P. Courtier," *Santa Fe Daily New Mexican*, June 26, 1876.

4. "Two more arrests . . . ," *Santa Fe Daily New Mexican*, June 28, 1876. See also "Local," *Santa Fe Daily New Mexican*, June 27, 1876. Winters was initially reported to be Ramon Guanter, later updated to Winters.

5. "Four of the five persons arrested . . . ," *Santa Fe Weekly New Mexican*, July 4, 1876; "The Grand Jury made a report," *Santa Fe Daily New Mexican*, July 14, 1871.

6. "Yesterday the District Court," *Santa Fe Daily New Mexican*, February 24, 1877; "The Trial . . . ," *Santa Fe Weekly New Mexican*, February 27, 1877.

7. "In the District Court . . . ," *Las Vegas Gazette*, March 3, 1877.

8. "Killing No Murder," *Santa Fe New Mexican*, March 12, 1877.

9. Flora Spiegelberg, "A Lynching Party in Santa Fe in 1877," Spiegelberg, Flora Papers, 1919–1939, UNM.

10. Flora Spiegelberg, "A Lynching Party in Santa Fe in 1877," Spiegelberg, Flora Papers, 1919–1939, UNM.

11. The phenomenon of extralegal violence, especially lynching, has been well explored. For accounts on the Southwest, see Carrigan and Webb, "The Lynching of Persons of Mexican Origin"; Gonzales-Day, *Lynching in the West*; Carrigan and Webb, "Mexican Perspectives on Mob Violence"; Carrigan and Webb, "'This Community Will Not in the Future Be Disgraced'"; Carrigan and Webb, "The Rise and Fall of Mob Violence"; Carrigan and Webb, *Forgotten Dead*. The scholarship on lynching outside of the Southwest is voluminous. The works that have influenced my thinking on mob violence include, Campney, *This Is Not Dixie*; Hill, *Beyond the Rope*; Hobbs, *Democracy Abroad, Lynching at Home*; Ore, *Lynching*; Waldrep, *The Many Faces of Judge Lynch*.

12. This assertion stands in contrast to the work of W. Fitzhugh Brundage who detailed four types of lynching in the South: terroristic mobs, private mobs, posses, and mass mobs. While I focus on some of these types, in the Southwest lynching was more fluid and

not always reducible to any distinct typology. Mob violence there, of course, involved a different ethnoracial community and region, which explains some of these differences. See Brundage, *Lynching in the New South*, 18–19. For works that comment on the multifacetedness of lynching, see Waldrep, *The Many Faces of Judge Lynch*; Wright, *Racial Violence in Kentucky*; Pfeifer, *Roots of Rough Justice*; Campney, *This Is Not Dixie*.

13. Some lynching scholars have detailed a "lynching era" that stretched from the 1880s to the 1920s. My research shows that numerous lynchings and massacres occurred before the 1880s and continued relatively unabated into the twentieth century. For examples of this "lynching era," see Brundage, *Lynching in the New South*; Tolnay and Beck, *A Festival of Violence*.

14. Hill, *Beyond the Rope*, chap. 1.

15. See, for example, "A Black Day in San Patricio When Chipita Was Hanged," *Corpus Christi Caller Times*, April 6, 2017; Underwood, "Rodriguez, Josefa [Chipita]"; De León, *They Called Them Greasers*, 80–81. Some also suggest that the judge acted improperly by changing the punishment recommended by jury, but in 1836 judges had the power to do that. See Hurt, "Determination of the Penalty."

16. Carrigan and Webb, *Forgotten Dead*, 68.

17. Hertzog, *A Directory of New Mexico Desperados*, 4, 8, 25, 30.

18. As quoted in Deverell, *Whitewashed Adobe*, 13–14.

19. Horace Bell, original manuscript of "On the Old West Coast," Bell (Horace) Collection, HL.

20. Some accounts unfortunately refer to Segovia as a sex worker, a common way of disparaging Mexican women, which also provided additional cover for her lynchers. See Krazmien, "Gold-Rush Era Prostitutes." For an accurate account of her murder, see especially Guidotti-Hernández, *Unspeakable Violence*, chap. 1.

21. Carrigan and Webb, *Forgotten Dead*, 69–70; Gonzales-Day, *Lynching in the West*, 185–87; Segrave, *Lynchings of Women in the United States*, 21–22.

22. Carrigan and Webb, *Forgotten Dead*, 69–71.

23. "Dastardly Outrages," *Sacramento Daily Union*, August 8, 1855 (quotations); "Particulars of the Rancheria Tragedy," *Sacramento Daily Union*, August 9, 1855; "Rancheria Massacre," *Sacramento Daily Union*, August 11, 1855.

24. "The Rancheria Tragedy," *Daily Alta California*, August 11, 1855.

25. Carrigan and Webb, *Forgotten Dead*, 40; Gonzales-Day, *Lynching in the West*, 36; "Dastardly Outrages," *Sacramento Daily Union*, August 8, 1855; "The Fortnights' News," *Daily Alta California*, August 18, 1855; "The Rancheria Tragedy," *Daily Alta California*, August 11, 1855; "Rancheria Tragedy," *Placer Herald*, August 11, 1855; "Rancheria Massacre," *Sacramento Daily Union*, August 11, 1855.

26. "The Rancheria Tragedy," *Daily Alta California*, August 11, 1855.

27. Gonzales-Day, *Lynching in the West*, 36–37; "The Tuolumne Calamity," *Sacramento Daily Union*, August 15, 1855.

28. "The Rancheria Tragedy Breeding More Murders," *Los Angeles Star*, August 25, 1855; "The Murders at Rancheria," *Los Angeles Star*, August 25, 1855.

29. "The Reign of Violence," *Daily Alta California*, August 31, 1855.

30. "Dastardly Outrages," *Sacramento Daily Union*, August 8, 1855; "Particulars of the Rancheria Tragedy," *Sacramento Daily Union*, August 9, 1855.

31. "The Tuolumne Calamity," *Sacramento Daily Union*, August 15, 1855.

32. "Mexican Difficulties in Amador and Tuolumne, The Murder of Sheriff Phoenix," *Sacramento Daily Union*, August 14, 1855.

33. Faragher, *Eternity Street*, 266 (quotation), 263–76.

34. Horace Bell, original manuscript of "On the Old West Coast," Bell (Horace) Collection, HL.

35. Horace Bell, original manuscript of "On the Old West Coast," Bell (Horace) Collection, HL.

36. As quoted in Deverell, *Whitewashed Adobe*, 13–14.

37. John Franklin Burns, "Reminiscences," in James Franklin Burns Reminiscences Folder, HL.

38. Griswold del Castillo, *The Los Angeles Barrio*, 108–9; Guillow, "The Origins of Race Relations in Los Angeles," 98–108.

39. Carrigan and Webb, "The Lynching of Persons of Mexican Origin," 416.

40. "Lynching at Bakersfield," *Los Angeles Evening Express*, December 24, 1877; "The Caliente Raiders," *San Francisco Daily Examiner*, December 24, 1877; Pfeifer, *Rough Justice*, 85–86.

41. "Lynching at Bakersfield," *Los Angeles Evening Express*, December 24, 1877; "The Caliente Raiders," *San Francisco Daily Examiner*, December 24, 1877.

42. Chapman, "Lynching in Texas."

43. Jesse Sumpter, *Life of Jesse Sumpter*, 52–53; De León, *They Called Them Greasers*, 91.

44. Jesse Sumpter, *Life of Jesse Sumpter*, 53–54.

45. "Murdered and Burned," *Austin Weekly Statesman*, February 6, 1896.

46. Carrigan and Webb, "The Lynching of Persons of Mexican Origin," 420.

47. "Local News and Views," *Galveston Daily News*, March 16, 1870; "The live oaks . . . ," *Dallas Daily Herald*, May 28, 1870.

48. "Nueces County," *Galveston Daily News*, January 28, 1875.

49. "Cameron County," *Galveston Daily News*, December 7, 1875.

50. "A Mexican Murdered by a Mob," *Dallas Daily Herald*, September 30, 1880.

51. Carrigan and Webb, "The Lynching of Persons of Mexican Origin," 417.

52. "Horrible Murder Discovered," *Houston Daily Post*, December 16, 1893.

53. New Mexico's history of extralegal violence was matched only by its legal violence. Historian Robert Tórrez tabulated a total of forty-nine legal executions carried out by territorial courts between 1849 and 1908. All these executions except for one were punishment for murder. See Tórrez, "Crime and Punishment," 2–3.

54. Lester Raines, "The Old Windmill, Las Vegas Plaza," WPA 5-5-50 #27, WPA New Mexico Collection, FACHL.

55. "Notice," n.d., Mauro Montoya Collection, FACHL. Montoya also identified another group known only as the Good Government League as a "vigilante group." See signed pledge sheet, Good Government League, Mauro Montoya Collection, FACHL.

56. "Fred Lambert," unknown newspaper, probably *Santa Fe New Mexican*, July 9, 1967, Emma Moya Collection, UNM.

57. "1870 . . . 1880 St. James Hotel . . . Own & Builder Henry Lambert . . . Cimarron, Territory of New Mexico, List of Those Killed in Lambert's Saloon," Emma Moya Collection, UNM. Henry Lambert struck Tomas Rodriguez, who died after falling and hitting his head. Juan Borrego accused David Crockett of cheating at monte and Crockett murdered him.

58. On the Ring, see Caffey, *Chasing the Santa Fe Ring*.

59. "Who Killed Parson Tolby," *Pueblo Chieftain*, December 4, 1875.

60. "Cimarron, Nov. 4," *Santa Fe Daily New Mexican*, n.d. (quotations), Clay Allison and Francisco "Pancho" Griego Folder, Philip J. Rasch Collection, FACHL; Caffey, *Chasing the Santa Fe Ring*, 44–46; Carrigan and Webb, *Forgotten Dead*, 100–102.

61. Drawing and Narrative of Griego murder, "1870 . . . 1880 St. James Hotel. . . . ," Emma Moya Collection, UNM. See also June 6, 1875, Pancho Griego story, "1870 . . . 1880 St. James Hotel. . . . ," Emma Moya Collection, UNM.

62. *Pueblo Chieftain* as quoted in Rasch, "Taking a Closer Look at Cimarron Murders," 8–9.

63. "Anarchy at Cimarron," *Santa Fe Daily New Mexican*, November 9, 1875; "Nuevo Mejicano Diario," *Santa Fe Daily New Mexican*, November 12, 1875; "From Wednesday's Daily," *Santa Fe Weekly New Mexican*, November 16, 1875.

64. "Who Killed Parson Tolby," *Pueblo Chieftain*, December 4, 1875.

65. As quoted in Carrigan and Webb, *Forgotten Dead*, 101.

66. "The Taos Court," *Santa Fe Daily New Mexican*, September 13, 1876; "Corte en Taos," *Santa Fe Daily New Mexican*, September 14, 1876; Carrigan and Webb, *Forgotten Dead*, 101. See also untitled article, *Santa Fe New Mexican*, May 1, 1876.

67. Drawing and Narrative of Butaras murder, "1870 . . . 1880 St. James Hotel. . . . ," Emma Moya Collection, UNM.

68. "Clay Allison and Pancho Griego," unknown newspaper clipping, n.d. (circa 1960), Emma Moya Collection, UNM; see also "Cimarron's Clay Allison Lived the Law of the Gun," *Raton Daily Range*, June 16, 1954.

69. "Private Letter," *Santa Fe Daily New Mexican*, November 9, 1875.

70. Abney, "Capital Punishment in Arizona," 41–42 (quotations).

71. "Editorial Notes," *Arizona Weekly Journal-Miner*, July 8, 1888.

72. "Summary Proceeding," *Weekly Arizona Miner*, September 16, 1871.

73. "Letter from Phoenix," *Weekly Arizona Miner*, June 1, 1872.

74. "Local Intelligence," *Weekly Arizona Miner*, December 13, 1878.

75. "Murder and Retribution," *Arizona Citizen*, August 9, 1873. The *Arizona Weekly Citizen* reprinted the 1873 story in full in 1895, see "Murder and Retribution," *Arizona Weekly Citizen*, August 31, 1895.

76. "Murder and Retribution," *Arizona Citizen*, August 9, 1873; "Double Murder in Tucson," *Prescott Arizona Miner*, August 16, 1873; Carrigan and Webb, "The Rise and Fall of Mob Violence," 113–14; Sonnichsen, *Tucson*, 83–84. In some accounts Leocardo Cordova is listed as "Leonardo."

77. "Murder and Retribution," *Arizona Weekly Citizen*, August 9, 1873.

78. "Double Murder in Tucson," *Prescott Arizona Miner*, August 16, 1873; "Murder and Retribution," *Arizona Weekly Citizen*, August 31, 1895 (reprinted version of the August 9, 1873, story).

79. Sonnichsen, *Tucson*, 84. Certainly some White people in Tucson spoke Spanish, but it seems unlikely that they would have answered a question posed by Zeckendorf in English with an answer in Spanish.

80. "Chronological Events of the Past Year," *Weekly Arizona Miner*, January 22, 1875.

81. "Editor Star," *Arizona Weekly Citizen*, December 11, 1881; "A Galeyville 'Dogberry': How Justice is Sometimes Dispensed on the Border," a version of the "Editor Star" article from "Clipper," Secretary of the Territory Papers, 1864–1912, ASL. See also Hayes, *A Portal*

to Paradise, chap. 6. Hayes repeated the concerns about justice and Judge Ellingwood aired by "Clipper," but there is no evidence that Ellingwood had done anything improper.

82. Boessenecker, *When Law Was in the Holster*, 184–86.

83. M. de Zamacona to Mr. Secretary (James Blaine), August 8, 1881, Secretary of the Territory Papers, 1864–1912, ASL.

84. James G. Blaine to His Excellency, John C. Fremont, August 29, 1881, Secretary of the Territory Papers, 1864–1912, ASL.

85. As quoted in Carrigan and Webb, *Forgotten Dead*, 132.

86. "An Interrupted Breakfast," *Arizona Weekly Citizen*, August 7, 1881; M. de Zamacona to Mr. Secretary (James Blaine), August 18, 1881, Secretary of the Territory Papers, 1864–1912, ASL. See also "Cow-boys," *Arizona Weekly Citizen*, December 11, 1881.

87. James G. Blaine to His Excellency, John C. Fremont, August 29, 1881, Secretary of the Territory Papers, 1864–1912, ASL.

88. Others also wanted to see a more vigorous exercising of the criminal justice system. The U.S. marshal in the Arizona territory, C. P. Dake, wrote to acting territorial governor John Gosper asking him to take "some steps to stop the raiding and lawlessness on our borders by the desperadoes called 'Cowboys.'" Gosper again filled in for Frémont, but as before he proved unwilling to assist Dake. C. P. Dake to Hon. J. J. Gosper, November 28, 1881, Secretary of the Territory Papers, 1864–1912, ASL.

89. "Cow-Boys," letter from John Gosper to U.S. Attorney General Wayne McVeagh (reprinted in full), *Arizona Weekly Citizen*, December 11, 1881.

90. Quiñones's age is not clear, but various sources referred to him as "youth" and "boy," indicating he was probably in his midteens.

91. Boessenecker, *When Law Was in the Holster*, 280.

92. "Star Editor," *Arizona Daily Star*, October 8, 1884; M[atías] Romero to Mr. Secretary (Thomas F. Bayard), March 22, 1887, Secretary of the Territory Papers, 1864–1912, ASL.

93. "Triple Murder," *Arizona Daily Star*, October 7, 1884; "The Tragedy in the Huachucas," *Arizona Daily Star*, October 8, 1884; and especially "Full Particulars of the Tragedy, in the Mountain, West Huachucas," *Arizona Daily Star*, October 12, 1884; "The Huachuca Butchery," *Arizona Daily Star*, October 12, 1884.

94. "Proclamation," *Arizona Daily Star*, October 11, 1884; "Governor Acts Quickly," *Arizona Weekly Citizen*, October 11, 1884. See also "Territorial News," *Mohave County Miner*, December 14, 1884.

95. "Full Particulars of the Tragedy, in the Mountain, West Huachucas," *Arizona Daily Star*, October 12, 1884.

96. "A Mexican Hanged," *Arizona Daily Star*, July 24, 1884.

97. See for instance "Small Talk," *Arizona Weekly Citizen*, January 31, 1885; "Small Talk," *Arizona Weekly Citizen*, February 7, 1885.

98. "The Huachuca Tragedy," *Arizona Weekly Citizen*, October 11, 1884.

99. Sadly, Duncan and the rest weren't wrong. For example, a "Mexican found hanging to a tree," a crime committed by "unknown parties" earlier in 1884, and others like it got one paragraph write-ups in newspapers and were usually quickly forgotten. See "Graham County Troubles," *Arizona Weekly Republican*, January 3, 1884; "Outlaws Killed," *Arizona Weekly Citizen*, March 29, 1884.

100. "Local News," *Arizona Daily Star*, November 25, 1884; "Telegraph," *Arizona Weekly Citizen*, December 6, 1884; "A Bad State of Affairs," *Arizona Daily Star*, December 6, 1884;

"Outlawry and Border Relations," *Journals of the Thirteenth Legislative Assembly of the Territory of Arizona*, 125–26.

101. "On Habeas Corpus," *Arizona Daily Star*, January 8, 1885; "Territorial Topics," *Arizona Silver Belt*, January 17, 1885.

102. "Local News," *Arizona Daily Star*, December 4, 1884; "Mysterious Disappearance," *Arizona Daily Star*, December 7, 1884; "Local News," *Arizona Daily Star*, December 11, 1884.

103. "Territorial Topics," *Arizona Silver Belt*, May 30, 1885.

104. "False Report," *Tombstone Daily Epitaph*, March 23, 1887; "Lively Corpses," *San Francisco Chronicle*, March 25, 1887; "Only an Arizona Canard," *Los Angeles Times*, March 25, 1887 (quotations); "Territorial," *Arizona Champion*, April 2, 1887.

105. T. F. Bayard to the Honorable C. Meyer Zulick, March 19, 1888, Secretary of the Territory Papers, 1864–1912, ASL.

106. "Horrible Murder," *Arizona Weekly Citizen*, February 1, 1890; "Stabbed in Bed," *St. Johns Herald*, February 6, 1890.

107. "A Tough Neighborhood," *Arizona Daily Star*, March 24, 1896.

108. Affidavit of Manuel Mejía, October 26, 1886, Secretary of the Territory Papers, 1864–1912, ASL; Correspondence with the Legation of Mexico at Washington, no. 838, *Papers Relating to the Foreign Relations of the United States*, 1253–54, 1301–2.

109. Chas. P. Stanton to His Excellency M. Romero, September 13, 1886, Secretary of the Territory Papers, 1864–1912, ASL; "An Outrage by a Mob," *Daily Alta California*, September 19, 1886; "Ultrajes a un Mejicano" (Insults to a Mexican), *El Fronterizo*, March 22, 1890. Stanton's letter to Envoy Romero is factually correct, but he has a bad reputation and is generally considered an unsavory character by Arizona historians. Stanton in a sworn deposition stated that Blankenship had asked Mejía to secure a horse for the trip to Phoenix, only to take Mejía into custody for stealing the horse he had just been commanded to acquire. Stanton of course likely instigated the murder of the Martin family. He was murdered a few months after these events. See Hanchett, *Catch the Stage to Phoenix*, 99–104; Anderson, *Arizona Gold Gangster*, chap. 10.

110. Chas. P. Stanton to M. Romero, November 6, 1886, Secretary of the Territory Papers, 1864–1912, ASL.

111. Testimony of Frank Cox, November 1886; Enrique Garfias to his Excellency Señor Matías Romero, October 10, 1886; Enrique Garfias to Señor Don Rufino Velez (Mexican Vice Consul in Tucson), October 25, 1886; Affidavit of J. W. Blankenship, October 26, 1886, Secretary of the Territory Papers, 1864–1912, ASL.

112. M. Romero to Mr. Secretary (Thomas F. Bayard), September 30, 1886, Secretary of the Territory Papers, 1864–1912, ASL.

113. M. Romero to Mr. Secretary (T. F. Bayard) October 26, 1886, Secretary of the Territory Papers, 1864–1912, ASL.

114. Enrique Garfias to his Excellency Señor Matías Romero, October 10, 1886, Secretary of the Territory Papers, 1864–1912, ASL.

115. Enrique Garfias to Señor Don Rufino Velez, October 2, 1886, Secretary of the Territory Papers, 1864–1912, ASL.

116. Alvey A. Adee to the Honorable C. Meyer Zulick, October 6, 1886, Secretary of the Territory Papers, 1864–1912, ASL.

117. T. F. Bayard to the Honorable C. Meyer Zulick, November 3, 1886, Secretary of the Territory Papers, 1864–1912, ASL.

118. "$250 Reward!" *Arizona Weekly Journal-Miner*, August 11, 1886; "Proclamation of Reward," *Arizona Daily Star*, August 21, 1886. The second article mentioned the $1,000 reward.

119. Testimony of Frank Cox, November 1886; Frank Cox to Dear Sir (Rufino Velez), September 16, 1886, Secretary of the Territory Papers, 1864–1912, ASL.

120. Affidavit of Manuel Mejía, October 26, 1886, Secretary of the Territory Papers, 1864–1912, ASL.

121. M. Romero to Mr. Secretary (T. F. Bayard), January 18, 1887, Secretary of the Territory Papers, 1864–1912, ASL. Romero's letter, translated into English for Bayard, uses the word "reclamation" for "reclamación." "Claim" or "complaint" is a more accurate translation.

122. T. F. Bayard to the Honorable C. Meyer Zulick, February 16, 1887, Secretary of the Territory Papers, 1864–1912, ASL.

123. "Barney Martin," *Arizona Daily Star*, September 20, 1889; "Can't Exchange Prisoners," *Arizona Daily Star*, October 16, 1889.

124. Carrigan and Webb, *Forgotten Dead*, 180–218, 133–34.

125. Carrigan and Webb, *Forgotten Dead*, 5.

CHAPTER 3

1. Crichton, *Law and Order, Ltd.*, 34.
2. Zarbin, "Henry Garfias," 56–57.
3. Zarbin, "Henry Garfias," 57–58.
4. "Fight with Cowboys at Phoenix," *Arizona Daily Star*, August 3, 1892; Zarbin, "Henry Garfias," 61–64.
5. "A Year's Hunt Ends with the Capture of a Desperado," *Arizona Republic*, July 11, 1895.
6. "A Brave Officer Gone," *Arizona Republic*, May 9, 1896; "Death of Henry Garfias," *Arizona Weekly Republican*, May 14, 1896.
7. "Doña Ana County Republican Convention," *Santa Fe New Mexican*, June 17, 1871.
8. "De El Fronterizo de Las Cruces" (From the Las Cruces Frontier), *La Gaceta de las Vegas*, December 7, 1872; Mora, *Border Dilemmas*, 118.
9. "Republican Convention," *Santa Fe Weekly New Mexican*, November 2, 1878; "Bueno, Bueno, Bueno," *Las Vegas Gazette*, October 19, 1880. In this article Armijo is listed as "sheriff."
10. "A Stout Rope," *Santa Fe New Mexican*, December 30, 1880.
11. "Colonel Potter's Murder," *Santa Fe New Mexican*, February 1, 1881; Bryan, *Albuquerque Remembered*, 112.
12. "1880s Murder in Sandias Led to Lynchings, Shootout," *Santa Fe New Mexican*, April 26, 2016. See also transcripts of *Santa Fe Daily New Mexican*, January 30, 1881, February 2, 1881, February 4, 1881 (quotations), Philip J. Rasch Collection, FACHL; "Perfecto Armijo: Effective Lawman," *Visions of the West Side*, March 22, 1989.
13. Polston, *Wicked Albuquerque*, 11; Trimble, "Vigilante Committees," (this issue defined "601").
14. "Territorial Jottings," *Las Vegas Gazette*, February 15, 1881; "Rincon," *Las Vegas Gazette*, March 20, 1881.
15. Transcripts of *Las Vegas Daily Optic*, February 24, 1881, March 18, 1881, March 21, 1881, April 5, 1882, April 6, 1881, Philip J. Rasch Collection, FACHL; "District Court," *Las Vegas Gazette*, March 21, 1881.

16. "Murdered and Burned," *Albuquerque Morning Democrat*, March 8, 1887; "The Lackey Murder," *Albuquerque Morning Democrat*, March 9, 1887; "Tracked and Caught," *Las Vegas Daily Optic*, March 21, 1887; "Tracked to Las Vegas," *Santa Fe Daily New Mexican*, March 24, 1887.

17. "Manzano Valley," *Santa Fe Daily New Mexican*, March 24, 1887.

18. "Local Laconics," *Albuquerque Journal*, March 27, 1887; "Leyba's Last Shot," *Santa Fe New Mexican*, March 30, 1887.

19. "Leyba's Last Shot," *Santa Fe Daily New Mexican*, March 30, 1887; "Bit the Dust," *Albuquerque Journal*, March 31, 1887.

20. "Death of Harry Brown," *Public Ledger*, March 31, 1881; "Ex-Governor Brown's Son Killed in New Mexico," *Clarksville Weekly Chronicle*, March 31, 1881.

21. "Gazette Gleanings," *Las Vegas Gazette*, May 19, 1881.

22. "Yarberry's Crime," *Santa Fe New Mexican*, June 22, 1881; "Milton's Murder," *Santa Fe New Mexican*, January 26, 1883; "Yarberry," *Las Vegas Gazette*, February 10, 1883; DeArment, *Deadly Dozen*, 57–58.

23. This altercation has been recounted with slight variation in several sources. The quotation comes from Crichton, *Law and Order, Ltd.*, 18. Baca offered a slightly different account of this event in "Political Record of Elfego Baca and a Brief History of His Life," circa 1944, Goddard Collection of Elfego Baca Papers, UNM. In this source, he recounts how he and Billy the Kid witnessed a "policeman" kill a man who was soon arrested by Perfecto Armijo and later hanged. After an exhaustive search, I could find no other examples of a police officer killing a man in this fashion, getting arrested by Armijo, and later being hanged, which makes me believe this "policeman" was Milton Yarberry. See also Woods, "Señor Americano," 62–63; Ball, *Elfego Baca in Life and Legend*, 4.

24. As quoted in Ball, *Desert Lawmen*, 156. See also "Perfecto Armijo: Effective Lawman," *Visions of the West Side*, March 22, 1989.

25. "Enclosure No. 2," details the sentencing of Yarberry. See "Enclosure No. 2," *Report of the Governor of New Mexico*, 105–6; "Political Record of Elfego Baca and a Brief History of His Life," circa 1944, Goddard Collection of Elfego Baca Papers, UNM; Ball, *Desert Lawmen*, 155–56; Groves, "Jerked to Jesus."

26. Armijo, Perfecto biography, n.d., Donald Cline Collection, NMSRCA.

27. "An Albuquerque Muddle," *Santa Fe New Mexican*, February 22, 1884; "The Sheriff Matter," *Albuquerque Journal*, February 24, 1884; "Perfecto's Trouble," *Albuquerque Evening Democrat*, March 7, 1884. The *New Mexican Review* reported Armijo's paper deficit at $5,171.99 after an audit of his records. See "Bernalillo Shrievalty," *New Mexican Review*, March 20, 1884. The *Albuquerque Weekly Journal* reported that Governor Sheldon confirmed the Board of Commissioners' decision and removed Armijo from office, "The Revolutionary Policy of the Governor," *Albuquerque Weekly Journal*, April 28, 1884.

28. "Campaign Echoes," *New Mexican Review*, November 13, 1884.

29. "County Commissioners," *Albuquerque Journal*, June 20, 1885.

30. "Webb Gets There," *Weekly New Mexican Review*, August 27, 1885.

31. "Round about Town," *Santa Fe New Mexican*, July 2, 1890; "Territorial Tips," *Santa Fe New Mexican*, October 9, 1891; "October," *Albuquerque Journal*, January 1, 1892.

32. "Three Official Heads Fall for Cause," *Santa Fe New Mexican*, August 31, 1905; "Gov. Otero Today Removed Accused Officials from Office," *Albuquerque Evening Citizen*, August 31, 1905; "Case of Hubbells and Vigil," *Las Vegas Daily Optic*, September 1, 1905;

"Decision en las Causas de Bernalillo" (Decision in Bernalillo Cases), *La Voz del Pueblo*, September 2, 1905; Ball, *Desert Lawmen*, 21; Bryan, *Albuquerque Remembered*, 175.

33. "Bernalillo Shrievalty," *Santa Fe New Mexican*, September 7, 1905; "Complaint of Sheriff Hubbell against Perfecto Armijo, Governor's Appointee," *Albuquerque Evening Citizen*, September 8, 1905; "Judge Abbott Recognizes Perfecto Armijo as Sheriff," *Albuquerque Weekly Citizen*, September 9, 1905; "County has Two Jails to Support," *Albuquerque Evening Citizen*, September 12, 1905; "Judge Abbott Denies Position for Mandamus," *Albuquerque Morning Journal*, September 27, 1905; "Hubbell Must Vacate by Tomorrow Morning," *Albuquerque Evening Citizen*, September 28, 1905; "Hubbell Committed to Jail for Contempt of Court," *Albuquerque Evening Citizen*, September 19, 1905.

34. "Supreme Court Decides for Hubbells," *Albuquerque Morning Journal*, December 29, 1906; "Armijos Want Rehearing in Hubbell Cases," *Roswell Daily Record*, January 3, 1907.

35. "The People's Ticket," *Albuquerque Morning Journal*, October 14, 1906.

36. "Legislation and County Ticket of People's Party Elected," *Albuquerque Evening Citizen*, November 7, 1906.

37. "New County Officers Begin Work," *Albuquerque Citizen*, January 1, 1909.

38. "Col. Perfecto Armijo Dead," *Carlsbad Current-Argus*, September 26, 1913.

39. "Don Perfecto Armijo, de Albuquerque, Pasa a Mejor Vida" (Don Perfecto Armijo, of Albuquerque, Passes Away), *La Revista Popular de Nuevo Mexico*, October 3, 1913.

40. Crichton, *Law and Order, Ltd.*, 7–10.

41. Ross, "The Bad Man of Socorro," 54. Some authors speculate that Marshal Baca had killed two Mexican men, not White men.

42. Crichton, *Law and Order, Ltd.*, 10–11; Sager, *¡Viva Elfego!*, 93–94. Francisco Baca eventually returned to New Mexico and lived a quiet life.

43. Crichton, *Law and Order, Ltd.*, 11–14.

44. On their relationship, see Crichton, *Law and Order, Ltd.*, chap. II and VII; "Old Town Was Big Enough for Elfego and the Kid," *Albuquerque Tribune*, February 8, 1995; Emma Moya, "Elfego Baca: El Bastoñero" and "When 'El Chamaco' Met Elfego Baca," *La Herencia del Norte*, Spring 1995, 25, 37.

45. "Political Record of Elfego Baca and a Brief History of His Life," circa 1944, Goddard Collection of Elfego Baca Papers, UNM; Woods, "Señor Americano," 62–63. As noted above in footnote 23, the details of this killing as described by Baca are sketchy.

46. The Town of Frisco was in far western Socorro County, but today Reserve is located in Catron County.

47. "Political Record of Elfego Baca and a Brief History of His Life," circa 1944, Goddard Collection of Elfego Baca Papers, UNM; Woods, "Señor Americano," 63; Crichton, *Law and Order, Ltd.*, 28.

48. "Speech to the Rio Grande Conservancy District," n.d., Goddard Collection of Elfego Baca Papers, UNM.

49. "Political Record of Elfego Baca and a Brief History of His Life," circa 1944, Goddard Collection of Elfego Baca Papers, UNM.

50. "Speech to the Rio Grande Conservancy District," n.d., Goddard Collection of Elfego Baca Papers, UNM.

51. "Political Record of Elfego Baca and a Brief History of His Life," circa 1944, Goddard Collection of Elfego Baca Papers, UNM.

52. This encounter was detailed in, Woods, "Señor Americano," 63. Other documents reveal a similar, yet slightly less detailed, version of this story.

53. See Ross, "The Bad Man of Socorro," 55; Ball, *Elfego Baca in Life and Legend*, 40; Groves, *When Outlaws Wore Badges*, 116; "Political Record of Elfego Baca and a Brief History of His Life," circa 1944, Goddard Collection of Elfego Baca Papers, UNM.

54. "Speech to the Rio Grande Conservancy District," n.d., Goddard Collection of Elfego Baca Papers, UNM.

55. Lopez's first name was not disclosed by Baca or apparent in any other source.

56. Crichton, *Law and Order, Ltd.*, 29.

57. "Political Record of Elfego Baca and a Brief History of His Life," circa 1944, Goddard Collection of Elfego Baca Papers, UNM.

58. "New Mexico Standoff," *Valencia County News-Bulletin*, January 15, 2005.

59. Woods, "Señor Americano," 64.

60. Ross, "The Bad Man of Socorro," 55. See also Brayer, "Could Gunfighters Really Shoot," 14–17, 48–50.

61. "Elfego Baca Shot His Way into History Defending Village Alone," *New Mexico Independent*, October 7, 1977; Sager, *¡Viva Elfego!*, 28. See also Bio—Baca, Elfego Folder, ABCPL.

62. Cook, *Fifty Years on the Old Frontier*, 221.

63. Woods, "Señor Americano," 64–65.

64. Woods, "Señor Americano," 65.

65. "Political Record of Elfego Baca and a Brief History of His Life," circa 1944, Goddard Collection of Elfego Baca Papers, UNM; Crichton, *Law and Order, Ltd.*, 34.

66. Trimble, "The Legend of Elfego Baca."

67. "Elfego Baca vs. The 80 Cowboys," *Albuquerque Journal*, October 8, 2000.

68. Crichton, *Law and Order, Ltd.*, 42–47.

69. Crichton, *Law and Order, Ltd.*, 64–68.

70. *Territory v. Elfego Baca*, Case no. 694, trial transcript; *Territory v. Elfego Baca*, Case no. 526, grand jury indictment; *Territory v. Elfego Baca*, Case no. 743, true bill, NMSRCA.

71. Sager, *¡Viva Elfego!*, 38.

72. Crichton, *Law and Order, Ltd.*, 32.

73. Woods, "Señor Americano," 64.

74. Trimble, "The Legend of Elfego Baca."

75. Cook, *Fifty Years on the Old Frontier*, 224.

76. Sager, *¡Viva Elfego!*, 35–36.

77. "Local Laconics," *Albuquerque Morning Democrat*, August 15, 1886; Mrs. William C. Heacock, interview by Janet Smith. This event was also chronicled in Crichton, *Law and Order, Ltd.*, chap. 19.

78. Baca Detective Agency Advertisement Card, n.d., Goddard Collection of Elfego Baca Papers, UNM.

79. Crichton, *Law and Order, Ltd.*, 49–53; Woods, "Señor Americano," 68.

80. Crichton, *Law and Order, Ltd.*, 84; Elfego Baca, interview by Janet Smith.

81. Crichton, *Law and Order, Ltd.*, 86.

82. "Man Held Up and Shot by Robbers Near Home," *Albuquerque Morning Journal*, November 25, 1919; "Abran Contreras Shot by Robbers at La Joya," *Mountainair Independent*, November 27, 1919.

83. "Officers Trail and Capture the Socorro Holdups," *Albuquerque Journal*, November 29, 1919.

84. "Had to Await Action of Grand Jury," *Mountainair Independent*, December 11, 1919; "Southwest News," *Spanish American*, December 13, 1919; "Alleged Slayers of Contreras Indicted," *Santa Fe New Mexican*, January 13, 1920; "Five Bandits Sentenced for Killing Contreras," *Santa Fe New Mexican*, February 16, 1920; "Five Bandits Are Sentenced to State Prison," *Albuquerque Journal*, February 16, 1920; Elfego Baca, interview by Janet Smith; Jonathan A. Ortega, "Legendary Lawman Elfego Baca Tracks Down 'Manzano Gang' after 1919 Murder of Los Ranchos de La Joya Businessman Abran Contreras," unpublished manuscript in Bio—Baca, Elfego Folder, ABCPL; "Sheriff Made History in Torrance County as Well," *Mountain View Telegraph*, October 22, 2009.

85. "Really Good Sheriff Should Be a Little Bad; Jailer Should Be a Lockup Graduate, Says Elfego," probably *New Mexico State Tribune*, circa 1932, Goddard Collection of Elfego Baca Papers, UNM.

86. "El Roosevelt Neo-Mexicano" (The New Mexican Roosevelt), *La Opinión Publica*, circa July 1928, Goddard Collection of Elfego Baca Papers, UNM. See also "No Suena Bien El Nombre" (The Name Doesn't Sound Right), *La Aurora*, May 11, 1928; "Elfego Baca Anuncia sus Manifiestos" (Elfego Baca Announces His Intentions), *La Opinión Publica*, July, 26 1928; "Elfego Baca to Throw County Ticket in the Field . . . ," *New Mexico State Tribune*, September 15, 1928; "Baca to Organize Independent Slate," *New Mexico State Tribune*, October 2, 1928.

87. "Elfego Baca Trompea a Fred Otero" (Elfego Baca Punches Fred Otero), *La Aurora*, May 31, 1928; "Almost Fight Ends with No Decision," *Albuquerque Journal*, May 31, 1928; "Elfego Baca is Fined for Fight," *Santa Fe New Mexican*, June 1, 1928; "Aquellas Trampadas" (Those Punches), *La Aurora*, June 14, 1928; "Elfego Baca Fined $15 for Fight with Fred Otero . . ." unknown newspaper, n.d., Goddard Collection of Elfego Baca Papers, UNM. The Spanish language press sided with Baca and reveled in the fact that he had punched Otero, called Otero a "pocho" (an Americanized Mexican), and *La Victoria* called people such as Otero "the curse of our people in New Mexico because of the mere fact that they themselves serve nothing [and] give the impression to the world that there is no Hispano who serves," untitled article, *La Victoria*, June 8, 1928.

88. "Political Record of Elfego Baca and a Brief History of His Life," circa 1944, Goddard Collection of Elfego Baca Papers, UNM.

89. "Baca's Visit So Different," unknown newspaper, circa 1939; "Old-time Law Officer Here," unknown newspaper, circa 1939; "Fighter Drew Bead on Fame in West's 'Greatest Battle,'" unknown newspaper, n.d., Goddard Collection of Elfego Baca Papers, UNM.

90. See Szasz, "A New Mexican 'Davy Crockett.'"

91. "Really Good Sheriff Should Be a Little Bad; Jailer Should Be a Lockup Graduate, Says Elfego," probably *New Mexico State Tribune*, circa 1932, Goddard Collection of Elfego Baca Papers, UNM.

92. Guy Franklin Kelsey, "Elfego Baca Paniological Reading," circa August 1939, Goddard Collection of Elfego Baca Papers, UNM.

93. Guy Franklin Kelsey to Elfego Baca, August 30, 1939, Goddard Collection of Elfego Baca Papers, UNM.

94. Elfego Baca, interview by Janet Smith.

95. "Rusty .45 Uncovered at Federal Bldg. Site Probably Baca's Gun," *Albuquerque Journal*, May 2, 1958.

96. For an interesting discussion of Chavez y Chavez's time as a Regulator and member of the Mounted Rifles, see "Testimony of Jose Chavez y Chavez, Member of the McSween

Party, Dudley Court of Inquiry, Fort Stanton, New Mexico, May 19, 1879," transcript and copies of original documents prepared by R. M. Barron, Southwestern Historical Research Group, El Paso, Tex., Donald Cline Collection, NMSRCA.

97. For background, see Johnson, *The Horrell Wars*, especially chap. 5–7.

98. Boardman, "The First Lincoln County War."

99. Donald Cline, "Jose Chavez y Chavez—Lincoln County Warrior," draft paper in Donald Cline Collection, NMSRCA.

100. Donald Cline, "Jose Chavez y Chavez—Lincoln County Warrior," draft paper in Donald Cline Collection, NMSRCA; Tsompanas, *Juan Patron*, 28–32; Fulton, *History of the Lincoln County War*, 22–24; Wilson, *Merchants, Guns, & Money*, 44. An early account of this violence mislabels the Horrells as the Harrolds but is still a useful source. See Anderson, *History of New Mexico*, 232–33.

101. "New Light on Jose Chavez y Chavez," draft paper credited to research done by Bill C. Cummings, September 30, 1992, Donald Cline Collection, NMSRCA; Nolan, *The West of Billy the Kid*, 134.

102. "New Light on Jose Chavez y Chavez," draft paper credited to research done by Bill C. Cummings, September 30, 1992, Donald Cline Collection, NMSRCA.

103. Caldwell, *Dead Right*, 115–18. See also "Testimony of Jose Chavez y Chavez, Member of the McSween Party, Dudley Court of Inquiry, Fort Stanton, New Mexico, May 19, 1879," transcript and copies of original documents prepared by R. M. Barron, Southwestern Historical Research Group, El Paso, Texas, Donald Cline Collection, NMSRCA.

104. "Jose Chavez y Chavez: Outlaw - Hombre Muy Malo," DesertUSA, n.d.; Eustis and Morsberger, *Lew Wallace*, 149.

105. See Yeatman, *Frank and Jesse James*, 291–92; Lowe, *Speaking Ill of the Dead*, 101–2.

106. Rasch, "A Mention of Jose Chavez y Chavez," 27, 30; Donald Cline, "Jose Chavez y Chavez—Lincoln County Warrior," draft paper, Donald Cline Collection, NMSRCA.

107. There was always some measure of suspicion that Silva's Gorras Blancas and Sociedad de Bandidos were really just one group. Recent work has demonstrated they were separate groups. See, for example, Correia, "'Retribution Will Be Their Reward,'" 68; Meléndez, *Spanish-language Newspapers in New Mexico*, 79. Manuel C. de Baca wrote the earliest account of Silva, which some consider flawed: *Historia de Vincente Silva*.

108. McGrath, "Vicente Silva and his Forty Thieves," essay, Donald Cline Collection, NMSRCA.

109. "Las Vegas Crime Notes," *Santa Fe New Mexican*, April 19, 1894; "¡¡Retribucion!!," *La Voz del Pueblo*, May 5, 1894; "Getting in the Gang," *Santa Fe New Mexican*, May 5, 1894; "Vida por Vida" (Life for a Life), *La Voz del Pueblo*, May 26, 1894. The Territory eventually tried Manuel Gonzales y Blea, Ramijio Sandoval, and Librado Polanco for Maes's murder. They changed their initial not guilty pleas to guilty and received lengthy jail sentences. See also *Territory v. Chavez* (8 N.M. 528); *The Pacific Reporter, Volume 45*, 1107–10; "Silva's Gang," list of members, Donald Cline Collection, NMSRCA. Chavez y Chavez is not listed as a member of Silva's Gang. But in a similar document, also entitled "Silva's Gang," probably prepared by author Tom McGrath, Chavez y Chavez is listed as a member of the gang. See "-2- Silva's Gang," Donald Cline Collection, NMSRCA.

110. "Chief of Assassins," *Santa Fe New Mexican*, March 18, 1895; "Desperado Captured," *Santa Fe New Mexican*, July 15, 1895; "Was One of Silva's Gang," *Albuquerque Journal*, May 29, 1896; McGrath, "Vicente Silva and his Forty Thieves," 30–40; "Silva Cuts Up His Wife, Leaves Body in Arroyo," *Southwesterner*, May 1963; "Las Vegas Killer," draft paper, author

unknown, n.d., Donald Cline Collection, NMSRCA. New Mexico sought Silva for some time before his body was discovered. See chapter XXXVI, "An Act to Appropriate Money to Pay [A] Certain Reward Offered by the Governor," May 17, 1894, *Acts of the Legislative Assembly of the Territory of New Mexico, Thirty-Second Session*, 63.

111. "Official Budget," *Santa Fe New Mexican*, May 11, 1894; "Maestas the Murderer," *Santa Fe New Mexican*, May 25, 1894; "New Mexico News," *Santa Fe New Mexican*, June 1, 1895.

112. "Socorro County," *Sierra County Advocate*, June 7, 1895; Jerry Padilla, "Quien a Hierro Vive a Hierro Muere" (He Who Lives by the Sword Dies by the Sword), *La Herencia del Norte*, Summer 1996.

113. "Chavez Murder Trial" *Las Vegas Daily Optic*, May 27, 1896; "Court Items," *Las Vegas Daily Optic*, June 3, 1896; "To Be Sentenced Tomorrow," *Las Vegas Daily Optic*, June 12, 1896; "New Mexico News," *Santa Fe Daily New Mexican*, June 15, 1896; "Convicted of Murder," *Santa Fe Daily New Mexican*, December 2, 1896; "Court Matters," *Las Vegas Daily Optic*, October 4, 1897; "The Chavez Case," *Las Vegas Daily Optic*, October 27, 1897; "Local News," *Rio Grande Republican*, November 26, 1897. See also Donald Cline, "Jose Chavez y Chavez—Lincoln County Warrior," draft paper, Donald Cline Collection, NMSRCA; and related Jose Chavez y Chavez material, including trial transcripts and prison data, "Research File-Person-Chavez y Chavez, Jose," Donald Cline Collection, NMSRCA.

114. Ball, *The United States Marshals*, 153.

115. Council Bill No. 122, February 6, 1891, Special Reports and Issues, Investigation of Shooting of J. A. Ancheta 1891–92 file, L. Bradford Prince, 1889–1893 Papers, TANM microfilm, Roll 121.

116. Jas. McParland to Hon. L. Bradford Prince, February 10, 1891, Special Reports and Issues, Investigation of Shooting of J. A. Ancheta 1891–92 file, L. Bradford Prince, 1889–1893 Papers, TANM microfilm, Roll 121.

117. Chas. Leon to Mr. B., March 10, 1891, Special Reports and Issues, Investigation of Shooting of J. A. Ancheta 1891–92 file, L. Bradford Prince, 1889–1893 Papers, TANM microfilm, Roll 121.

118. Deputy Sheriff Cade Selvy to Gov. L. Bradford Prince, telegram, February 12, 1891; Deputy Sheriff Cade Selvy to Gov. L. Bradford Prince, telegram, February 13, 1891, Special Reports and Issues, Investigation of Shooting of J. A. Ancheta 1891–92 file, L. Bradford Prince, 1889–1893 Papers, TANM microfilm, Roll 121.

119. C. A. Siringo to Gov. Prince, March 18, 1891, Special Reports and Issues, Investigation of Shooting of J. A. Ancheta 1891–92 file, L. Bradford Prince, 1889–1893 Papers, TANM microfilm, Roll 121. For information on Siringo, see Siringo, *A Cowboy Detective*; Lamar, *Charlie Siringo's West*.

120. C. A. S. to Gov. B. L. Prince, July 8, 1891; Jas. McParland to Hon. L. Bradford Prince, July 15, 1891, Special Reports and Issues, Investigation of Shooting of J. A. Ancheta 1891–92 file, L. Bradford Prince, 1889–1893 Papers, TANM microfilm, Roll 121.

121. Gov. L. Bradford Prince Proclamation, May 31, 1892, Penal Papers, L. Bradford Prince, 1889–1893 Papers, TANM microfilm, Roll 121.

122. "Four Lives Taken to Pay for One," *San Francisco Call*, April 3, 1897; "Borrego Gang," *Los Angeles Herald*, April 3, 1897.

123. "Terrible Crimen" (Terrible Crime), *La Voz del Pueblo*, July 6, 1895; "Los Asesinos de Chavez" (The Murderers of Chavez), *La Voz del Pueblo*, July 6, 1895; "Learned, Luminous, Able," *Santa Fe Daily New Mexican*, September 2, 1896. See also L. A. Hughes to E. L.

Bartlett, n.d., Edward L. Bartlett Papers, NMSRCA; Ike Nowell, direct examination testimony, n.d.; Ike Nowell, cross examination testimony, n.d.; In the Matter of the Territory vs. Thomas Hughes for Contempt, n.d., Laughlin, N. B. Collection, NMSRCA.

124. G. F. Murray to Capt. Fred Fornoff, September 30, 1907, Arrests and Investigations, TANM microfilm, Roll 93; Mora, *Border Dilemmas*, 167–69 (quotation 168).

125. G. F. Murray to Capt. Fred Fornoff, telegram, October 17, 1907; G. F. Murray to Capt. Fred Fornoff, October 18, 1907, Arrests and Investigations, TANM microfilm, Roll 93.

126. R. L. Baca to Honorable George Curry, January 1, 1908, Arrests and Investigations, TANM microfilm, Roll 93. Baca confused Murray's name, referring to him as Morris.

127. Superintendent (name illegible) to Captain Fred Fornoff, January 22, 1909, Arrests and Investigations, TANM microfilm, Roll 93.

128. Unnamed lieutenant N.M.M.P. to Mr. T. J. Sawyer, January 24, 1909, Arrests and Investigations, TANM microfilm, Roll 93.

129. In the Matter of the Alleged Misconduct of G. F. Murray, circa 1908, Arrests and Investigations, TANM microfilm, Roll 93; "Investigates Charges Against Ranger," *Albuquerque Citizen*, January 29, 1908. Today San Rafael is in Cibola County.

130. "Fred Murray Here on Way to the Penitentiary," *Albuquerque Morning Journal*, June 10, 1908; "New Mexico Territorial News," *Fort Sumner Review*, July 17, 1909.

131. "Both Grand Juries Continue Work Today," *Albuquerque Citizen*, March 16, 1909.

132. "Murray Indicted by Jury," *Albuquerque Journal*, March 17, 1909; "Murray Pleads Guilty to One Charge," *Albuquerque Citizen*, March 18, 1909; "Lee Como Un Romance," (Reads like a Romance), *La Voz del Pueblo*, June 12, 1909.

133. "Nominees for the House," *Albuquerque Journal*, November 2, 1911; "House of Representatives," *Sierra County Advocate*, March 8, 1912.

134. City Payroll, City Clerk's Office, 1904, Santa Fe, New Mexico Records, 1822–1934, UNM.

135. Santa Fe City Council meeting minutes, April 20, 1914, Santa Fe, New Mexico Records, 1822–1934, UNM.

136. Santa Fe City Council meeting minutes, December 18, 1922, Santa Fe, New Mexico Records, 1822–1934, UNM.

137. Office of Tomas P. Delgado, Sheriff, appointment of Deputy Sheriff Harold R. Holcomb, July 7, 1923, Santa Fe, New Mexico Records, 1822–1934, UNM.

138. *La Ciudad de Santa Fe vs. Nicolas Maes*, Case no. 676, UNM. Many thanks to my friend Dr. José Angel Hernández for his help in deciphering Ortiz's Spanish.

139. Rafael Gomez report to the City of Santa Fe, July 1, 1912, Santa Fe, New Mexico Records, 1822–1934, UNM.

140. Albert Garcia report to the City of Santa Fe, July 1915, Santa Fe, New Mexico Records, 1822–1934, UNM.

141. *Territory of New Mexico vs. Juan Antonio Ortega, Emilio Gutierrez, and Cleofas Jimenez*, witness testimony, NMSRCA.

142. Parra, "Tomás A. Sanchez."

143. "Los Angeles County Sheriff's Office California History 20th C.," 40–41, Murrieta Family Materials, 1848–1990, HL.

144. "Los Angeles County Sheriff's Office California History 20th C.," 39–40, Murrieta Family Materials, 1848–1990, HL. See also Sheriff Sherman Block to Mrs. William M. Smith, May 6, 1983, Murrieta Family Materials, 1848–1990, HL. Murrieta was Spanish, but

because he came to the United States through Mexico and spoke Spanish many people assumed he was of Mexican descent.

145. "Mentions," *El Paso Times*, January 18, 1889.

146. "Krakauer's Recklessness," *El Paso Times*, April 9, 1889.

147. "A Breezy Session," *El Paso Times*, April 13, 1889. Interestingly Krakauer won the election, but because he had never finalized his citizenship papers (he had immigrated to Texas from Germany), his election was disqualified.

148. García, *Desert Immigrants*, 73.

149. "Arrested for Horse Stealing," *El Paso Times*, November 21, 1890 (quotations); "The Courts," *El Paso Times*, February 28, 1891. Special thanks to Dr. Monica Perales for her assistance in helping me determine that the smelter was the ASARCO smelter. For more on this, see Perales, *Smeltertown*.

150. "A Would-be Murderer," *El Paso Times*, March 6, 1891; "Mentions," *El Paso Times*, Match 7, 1891.

151. Peck, "Divided Loyalties," 53. See also "Arrested on Suspicion of Being a Burglar," *El Paso Herald*, July 24, 1903; "Three Changes in the Police Force," *El Paso Herald*, April 21, 1905; "About Railroad People," *El Paso Herald*, September 5, 1905.

152. García, *Desert Immigrants*, 73.

153. "History of El Paso, Texas."

154. "New Deputy Sheriff," *El Paso Herald*, June 1, 1900.

155. "Beat an Officer," *El Paso Times*, September 29, 1895.

156. "In the District Court," *El Paso Times*, October 22, 1895; "On Trial for Murder," *El Paso Times*, October 31, 1895; "In the District Court," *El Paso Times*, November 1, 1895; "Around Town," *El Paso Times*, November 3, 1895; "Two Convictions Yesterday," *El Paso Times*, November 10, 1895.

157. "Pitched Battle Near San Elizario," *El Paso Times*, April 18, 1899.

158. "Three Outlaws Captured," *El Paso Times*, December 2, 1899; "Grand Jury in Session," *El Paso Times*, January 28, 1900; "Grand Jury Indictments," *El Paso Herald*, January 27, 1900; Unterman, *Uncle Sam's Policemen*, 140–41.

159. "Blas Will Fight," *El Paso Herald*, February 17, 1900; "Blas Aguirre Case," *El Paso Herald*, May 2, 1900; "To Be Shot to Death," *El Paso Herald*, December 10, 1900; "Blas Aguirre," *El Paso Herald*, December 15, 1900.

160. "Another Aguirre Case on Trial," *El Paso Times*, January 30, 1900; "Fighting to a Finish," *El Paso Herald*, March 7, 1900.

161. "First American Doomed to Die by Mexican Law," *St. Louis Post-Dispatch*, January 27, 1901.

162. "Surgical Operation," *El Paso Herald*, July 29, 1899; "Application for an Extradition," *El Paso Times*, March 6, 1900.

163. "On the Trail of the Murderer of Ex-Constable Leon Chavez," *El Paso Times*, December 13, 1894.

164. "Shot by an Officer," *El Paso Times*, June 29, 1893.

165. "Accused of Cutting Aged Man," *El Paso Herald*, June 9, 1906.

166. "Indicted Liquor Dealers Give Bond," *El Paso Herald*, May 30, 1908.

167. "Man Wanted for Murder Captured," *El Paso Times*, October 29, 1909.

168. For background, see Perez, "Tejano Rangers."

169. Jesse Perez Reminiscences, 1870–1927, BC, 3–4, 12, 25–26. Special thanks to Dr. Bill Carrigan for recommending the Perez account to me.

170. Jesse Perez Reminiscences, 1870–1927, BC, 32. See also "Arrested on Charge of Horse Theft," *Brownsville Herald*, July 8, 1908.

171. Jesse Perez Reminiscences, 1870–1927, BC, 141; "Local News," *Laredo Weekly Times*, July 31, 1921.

172. Jesse Perez Reminiscences, 1870–1927, BC, 95, 96–100.

173. Jesse Perez Reminiscences, 1870–1927, BC, 37–41, 56–58. Perez offered no real judgement on banditry, he simply mentioned that it existed. He also seems to have confused some of the details. For instance, on page 37 he began discussing the *Plan de San Diego* but attached it to the efforts of the Flores Magon brothers, a connection that seems unlikely. See Harris III and Sadler, *The Plan de San Diego*.

174. "Threat against Sanchez?" *El Paso Herald*, February 6, 1919; Ventura R. Sanchez testimony, *Proceedings of the Joint Committee of the Senate and the House, Volume I*, 337–52; "Denies Charges Against Rangers," *El Paso Herald*, February 3, 1919.

175. "10 Masked Men Hang Mexican; Fear Violence," *Austin American*, July 30, 1915; "Capture Mexican Prisoner; Kill Him," *Austin American Statesman*, July 29, 1915. Muñoz's name was widely misspelled as "Muniz," "Munzo," "Muenoz," etc. The *Austin American* speculated that the lynch mob was mainly composed of Mexican-origin people.

176. "Daniel Hinojosa Mexiquito Deputy," *Valley Morning Star*, January 11, 1931 (quotation); "Hinojosa Claimed by Death," *Valley Morning Star*, August 12, 1932.

CHAPTER 4

1. The Territory of Arizona against Valerio Garcia, A True Bill, March 24, 1886, Secretary of the Territory Papers, 1866–1902, ASL.

2. C. L. Gutterson to His Excellency C. Meyer Zulick (letter no. 2), January 18, 1886; C. L. Gutterson to Honorable C. Meyer Zulick, May 30, 1886, Secretary of the Territory Papers, 1866–1902, ASL.

3. Bench Warrant, Arthur Ashton, clerk, February 8, 1890; Executive Department, Territory of New Mexico, order of Governor Lewis Wolfley, signed by Acting Governor Nathan O. Murphy, February 17, 1890, Secretary of the Territory Papers, 1866–1902, ASL.

4. St. George Greaghe to Governor Lewis Wolfley, May 7, 1890; St. George Greaghe, statement of claims, March 1890, Secretary of the Territory Papers, 1866–1902, ASL.

5. F. L. Bunch to Hon. John N. Irwin, February 19, 1891, Secretary of the Territory Papers, 1866–1902, ASL.

6. See, for example, De León, *They Called Them Greasers*, 32, 33, 41–43, 70–71.

7. In the Territory of Arizona, for example, sex work was legal unless it occurred within a certain distance from a school or courthouse. See *Acts, Resolutions and Memorials of the Seventeenth Legislative Assembly*, 30–31. See also MacKell, *Red Light Women*. In New Mexico, sex work was similarly legal unless such work was connected to vagrancy. See *Laws of the Territory of New Mexico*, 102–3. Texas largely left the legality of sex work to local municipalities, most of which found ways to criminalize "disorderly houses," usually as a misdemeanor. See *The Laws of Texas*, 251, 525, 780, 1061–62. The 1872 California Penal Code addressed prostitution as a criminal offense if individuals forced women into sex work. See *The Penal Code of California: Enacted in 1872; as Amended Up to and Including 1905*, 112–20b.

8. See Hernández, *City of Inmates*, 36.

9. The Spanish-language press commented on the differential treatment that Mexican-origin people and Whites experienced in the criminal justice system. In 1879, *El Horizonte* in Corpus Christi, Texas, decried the double justice system and explained there were judges who "would like to see all Mexicans on the edge of a precipice and be able to throw them all over." The paper also documented the cases of Pedro Ramirez and William Miller, noting that they were both criminals who had committed the same crime, assault and attempted murder, in the same location, but Ramirez was sentenced to two years in the penitentiary while Miller was fined and released. For *El Horizonte*, this outcome was the result of not only a dual justice system but also of a biased jury selection, which excluded Mexican Americans and allowed only Whites to serve. See, for example, "La Justicia en Texas" (Justice in Texas), *El Horizonte*, November 19, 1879. Much of the scholarship on criminality in the Southwest has focused on homicide. This scholarship has shown less disproportionality in sentencing. See especially, Abney, "Capital Punishment in Arizona"; McKanna, *Race and Homicide*, chap. 3; Wilson, *Legal Executions in the Western Territories*.

10. Williams et al., "Balancing Punishment and Compassion," 122–26; Bandes, "Compassion and the Rule of Law"; Hueston and Hutchins, "The Power of Compassion"; May et al., *Corrections and the Criminal Justice System*, 379–412.

11. *People vs. Antonio Garcia*, Case no. 536½, HL. A note on these records: the case file jackets have case numbers that differ from the paperwork contained within the jacket. In Garcia's case, the jacket has the case number as 536½, but the case number on court documents inside the jacket is 227. I am using the case file numbers on the case jackets, which is also what the Huntington Library uses.

12. *The People vs. Juan N. Padilla*, Case no. 343, motion to set aside indictment, HL.

13. *People vs. Juan N. Padilla*, Case no. 537, HL.

14. Nolle prosequi cases include *People vs. Vicente Ochoa*, Case no. 557; *People vs. Serrapio Navarro, Ramon Navarro, and Jesus Lopez*, Case no. 561; *People vs. Mariano Villa*, Case no. 563, HL.

15. *People vs. Jose Machado*, Case no. 565, HL.

16. *People vs. Ramon Carrillo*, Case no. 622, HL.

17. *People vs. Gabriel Rodriguez*, Case no. 632, HL.

18. For an excellent starting place for women and crime, see Chesney-Lind and Pasko, *The Female Offender*.

19. See Phelan, "The Evolution of Rape Law Reform."

20. *People vs. Epifano Valdez*, Case no. 670, HL.

21. *People vs. Polonia Acosta and Josefa Ybarra*, Case no. 568, HL.

22. *People vs. Isabella Esquerer*, Case no. 604, HL.

23. "Territorial News," *Arizona Sentinel*, May 24, 1873.

24. "Phenix, May 12," *Arizona Citizen*, May 24, 1873.

25. F. L. Hayes to Gov. A. P. K. Safford, May 16, 1873, Secretary of the Territory Papers, 1864–1912, ASL.

26. C. L. Gutterson to His Excellency C. Meyer Zulick (letter no. 1), January 18, 1886, Secretary of the Territory Papers, 1866–1902, ASL.

27. "Local News," *St. Johns Herald*, June 10, 1886.

28. C. L. Gutterson to Hon. C. Meyer Zulick, July 19, 1886, Secretary of the Territory Papers, 1866–1902, ASL.

29. *Territory of Arizona v. Francisco Yanez*, Case no. 71, ASL; *Territory of Arizona v. John Doe*, Tiburcio Ruiz, Case no. 247, ASL. Some of these cases are interesting in that they were tried in criminal court but presided over by a justice of the peace.

30. *People of the Territory of Arizona vs. Manuela Cruz*, Case no. 1, ASL.

31. *The People of the Territory of Arizona vs. Guadalupe Corrales*, Case no. 89, ASL.

32. *The People of the Territory of Arizona vs. Luz Miranda*, Case no. 108; *The People of the Territory of Arizona vs. Manuela Pesquiera*, Case no. 109, ASL.

33. F. L. Bunch to Hon. John N. Irwin, February 19, 1891, Secretary of the Territory Papers, 1866–1902, ASL; Grand Jury Inquest into the murder of Matias Analla [sic], February 13, 1891, Secretary of the Territory Papers, 1866–1902, ASL.

34. "Proclamation of Reward," *Arizona Silver Belt*, March 14, 1891; "Local News," *St. Johns Herald*, March 19, 1891.

35. "From Tuesday's Daily," *Tombstone Weekly Epitaph*, March 29, 1891; "List of Territorial Warrants," *Arizona Republic*, October 23, 1891.

36. Domingo Laguna arrest warrant, signed by Sheriff C. B. Kelton, February 6, 1891; Justice's Court Warrant for Domingo Laguna, February 9, 1891, Secretary of the Territory Papers, 1866–1902, ASL.

37. "Local Notes," *Tombstone Weekly Epitaph*, June 7, 1893; "Executive Clemency," *Arizona Republic*, November 30, 1893.

38. Sheriff E. O. Shaw to C. Meyer Zulick, March 6, 1887; Sheriff E. O. Shaw to Sir (A. Meyer Zulick), March 6; 1887, Secretary of the Territory Papers, 1866–1899, ASL; "$500 Reward!," *Clifton Clarion*, April 6, 1887, April 13, 1887, and April 27, 1887.

39. "Local Matters," *Arizona Champion*, September 24, 1887.

40. Martina Gonzales testimony, *Territory of Arizona versus Martin Duran*, trial transcript, 8, ASL.

41. Antonio Camperantio testimony, *Territory of Arizona versus Martin Duran*, trial transcript, 25, ASL.

42. Jose Lujan testimony, *Territory of Arizona versus Martin Duran*, trial transcript, 5, ASL.

43. David Trujillo testimony, *Territory of Arizona versus Martin Duran*, trial transcript, 21, ASL.

44. Harry Fulton testimony, *Territory of Arizona versus Martin Duran*, trial transcript, 13, ASL.

45. Sandy Donahue testimony, *Territory of Arizona versus Martin Duran*, trial transcript, 15, ASL.

46. Martin Duran testimony, *Territory of Arizona versus Martin Duran*, trial transcript, 29–31, ASL.

47. "Local Brevities," *Mohave County Miner*, September 24, 1887.

48. "Local Matters," *Arizona Champion*, November 19, 1887. This kind of intimate partner homicide is still, unfortunately, common today. See "Intimate Partner Homicide."

49. Today Flagstaff is located in Coconino County.

50. John Howard et al. to His Excellency, the Governor of Arizona, December 29, 1887, Secretary of the Territory Papers, 1866–1902, ASL.

51. L. F. Eggers to His Excellency C. Meyer Zulick, n.d., Secretary of the Territory Papers, 1866–1902, ASL. See also D. F. Sullivan to Hon J. A. Bayard (acting governor), January 18, 1888, Secretary of the Territory Papers, 1866–1902, ASL.

52. "Dead Duran," *Arizona Weekly Champion*, March 3, 1888.

53. "Hempen Cordage...," *Arizona Silver Belt*, March 10, 1888.

54. These records and others like them do not always identify a person's ethnic identity or national attachment. I am therefore relying on surnames to make determinations about ethnicity.

55. Commitment Number 235, Bernardo Martin, Name of Convicts in the Territorial Prison at Yuma, April 27, 1884, Secretary of the Territory Papers, 1873–1901, ASL.

56. Commitment Number 254, Crecentio Barrila, Name of Convicts in the Territorial Prison at Yuma, September 19, 1884, Secretary of the Territory Papers, 1873–1901, ASL.

57. Commitment Number 355, Francisco Yanez, Name of Convicts in the Territorial Prison at Yuma, December 17, 1885, Secretary of the Territory Papers, 1873–1901, ASL.

58. Commitment Number 495, Santiago Pedia, Name of Convicts in the Territorial Prison at Yuma, December 11, 1887, Secretary of the Territory Papers, 1873–1901, ASL.

59. Commitment Number 547, Miguel Chicon, Name of Convicts in the Territorial Prison at Yuma, November 26, 1888, Secretary of the Territory Papers, 1873–1901, ASL.

60. Commitment Number 571, Juan Marquez, Name of Convicts in the Territorial Prison at Yuma, March 30, 1889, Secretary of the Territory Papers, 1873–1901, ASL.

61. Commitment Number 386, Albino Villa, Name of Convicts in the Territorial Prison at Yuma, March 19, 1886, Secretary of the Territory Papers, 1873–1901, ASL.

62. Commitment Number 514, A. Lopez, Name of Convicts in the Territorial Prison at Yuma, April 20, 1888; Commitment Number 540, Isadore Lopez, Name of Convicts in the Territorial Prison at Yuma, October 13, 1884, Secretary of the Territory Papers, 1873–1901, ASL.

63. Commitment Number 584, H. Salazar Martin, Name of Convicts in the Territorial Prison at Yuma, May 28, 1889, Secretary of the Territory Papers, 1873–1901, ASL.

64. Commitment Number 526, Rich Downing, Name of Convicts in the Territorial Prison at Yuma, July 24, 1888, Secretary of the Territory Papers, 1873–1901, ASL.

65. Commitment Number 554, James Henrickson, Name of Convicts in the Territorial Prison at Yuma, December 14, 1888; Commitment Number 581, Wm. M. Hall, Name of Convicts in the Territorial Prison at Yuma, April 15 (probably 25), 1889, Secretary of the Territory Papers, 1873–1901, ASL.

66. Commitment Number 314, Fred Glover, Name of Convicts in the Territorial Prison at Yuma, June 30, 1885, Secretary of the Territory Papers, 1873–1901, ASL.

67. Commitment Number 419, Wilson Douglass, Name of Convicts in the Territorial Prison at Yuma, December 3, 1886, Secretary of the Territory Papers, 1873–1901, ASL.

68. Commitment Number 533, L. W. Davis, Name of Convicts in the Territorial Prison at Yuma, October 2, 1888; Commitment Number 552, W. D. Harper, Name of Convicts in the Territorial Prison at Yuma, December 14, 1888, Secretary of the Territory Papers, 1873–1901, ASL.

69. Commitment Number 332, James E. Williams, Name of Convicts in the Territorial Prison at Yuma, November 1, 1885, Secretary of the Territory Papers, 1873–1901, ASL.

70. Commitment Number 443, B. F. Thornton, Name of Convicts in the Territorial Prison at Yuma, May 25, 1887, Secretary of the Territory Papers, 1873–1901, ASL.

71. Report of Prisoners, Date of Receipt at Prison September 29, 1883–August 8, 1890, p. 1–4, Secretary of the Territory Papers, 1873–1901, ASL.

72. See, for example, Report of Prisoners Received and Discharged and Conduct for 1st Quarter Ending March 31, 1892; Report of Prisoners Received, Discharged and Conduct, Etc., for the Quarter Ending June 30, 1892, Secretary of the Territory Papers, 1886–1892,

ASL; Names of Convicts in the Territorial Prison at Yuma, March 1893, Secretary of the Territory Papers, 1865–1901, ASL.

73. Names of Convicts in the Territorial Prison at Yuma, 3rd Quarter, 1890, Secretary of the Territory Papers, 1873–1901, ASL.

74. Names of Convicts in the Territorial Prison at Yuma, 4th Quarter, 1890, Secretary of the Territory Papers, 1873–1901, ASL.

75. Names of Convicts in the Territorial Prison at Yuma, 1st Quarter, 1891, Secretary of the Territory Papers, 1873–1901, ASL.

76. Commitment Number 614, Ramon Flores, November 17, 1889, Report of Prisoners Received, Discharged and Conduct, Etc. for Quarter Ending September 30, 1891, Secretary of the Territory Papers, 1873–1901, ASL.

77. Names of Convicts in the Territorial Prison at Yuma, 2nd Quarter, 1892, Secretary of the Territory Papers, 1886–1892, ASL.

78. Discharges for Third Quarter 1892, Secretary of the Territory Papers, 1886–1892, ASL.

79. "Wednesday's Edition"; "From Thursday's Daily," *Arizona Weekly Journal-Miner*, March 25, 1891; Lauterio Aguilar, Application for Pardon, December 31, 1893; Lauterio Aguilar to the Hon. Board of Prison Commissioners (this is a statement from Aguilar that accompanied his application for pardon), December 31, 1893, Secretary of the Territory Papers, 1864–1912, ASL (quotation). Court records and newspaper accounts spell McRae's name differently: "McRae," "McRay," and "McRea." The most consistent spelling is "McRae," which is the spelling I am using.

80. "District Court," *Arizona Weekly Journal-Miner*, June 17, 1891.

81. "District Court," *Arizona Weekly Journal-Miner*, June 24, 1891.

82. Thomas Gates to Hon. L. C. Hughes, May 10, 1894 (quotation), and M. J. Shaw (assistant superintendent) to Hon. L. C. Hughes, May 11, 1894, Secretary of the Territory Papers, 1864–1912, ASL.

83. Deposition of Charles E. McGarr, December 31, 1893, Secretary of the Territory Papers, 1864–1912, ASL.

84. Lauterio Aguilar to the Hon. Board of Prison Commissioners (this is a statement from Aguilar that accompanied his application for pardon), December 31, 1893, Secretary of the Territory Papers, 1864–1912, ASL.

85. See L. Aguilar to Dear Sir, April 3, 1894, Secretary of the Territory Papers, 1864–1912, ASL.

86. Geo[rge] Merwin to Hon. L. C. Hughes, April 1894; Richard L. Tea to Hon L. C. Hughes, April 4, 1894; James M. Dobson, April 1894, Secretary of the Territory Papers, 1864–1912, ASL. An additional individual named Henry Spaulding also wrote on Aguilar's behalf. Spaulding claimed to have been a member of the jury, although he is not listed as a juror in the original jury list. He may have been an alternate juror. See Henry Spaulding to Hon L C Hughes, April 11, 1894, Secretary of the Territory Papers, 1864–1912, ASL.

87. Proclamation of Commutation of Sentence for Lauterio Aguilar, June 6, 1894, and Commutation of Sentence of Lauterio Aguilar, June 11, 1894, Secretary of the Territory Papers, 1864–1912, ASL; "Yuma Arizona April 4th, 1894," *Arizona Sentinel*, April 14, 1894.

88. Table no. 6, Biennial Report of the Board of Control of Arizona from January 1, 1899, to June 30, 1900, Secretary of the Territory Papers, 1877–1902, ASL. I am unsure why there is an error in the math in the report.

89. Table no. 12, 13, 14, 15, Biennial Report of the Board of Control of Arizona from January 1, 1899, to June 30, 1900, Secretary of the Territory Papers, 1877–1902, ASL.

90. Commitment Number 1525, Francisco (last name unknown), Biennial Report of the Board of Control of Arizona from January 1, 1899, to June 30, 1900, Secretary of the Territory Papers, 1877–1902, ASL.

91. Table no. 20 and 21, Biennial Report of the Board of Control of Arizona from January 1, 1899, to June 30, 1900, Secretary of the Territory Papers, 1877–1902, ASL. The expenditures included in the report were for the third and fourth quarters of the 1888–99 fiscal year, $11,258 and $12,616 respectively. Data for the previous two quarters are missing. I am therefore using an average amount of $10,000 for each missing quarter to provide a speculative projection of what the prison cost that year. The expenditure reports for fiscal year 1899–1900 are missing.

92. Statistical and Sex and Nationality, p. 1, Biennial Report of the Superintendent Territorial Prison for July 1, 1900, to June 30, 1902, Secretary of the Territory Papers, 1865–1901, ASL.

93. Financial, p. 2, Biennial Report of the Superintendent Territorial Prison for July 1, 1900, to June 30, 1902, Secretary of the Territory Papers, 1865–1901, ASL.

94. Paroles and Pardons, pp. 4–9, Biennial Report of the Superintendent Territorial Prison for July 1, 1900, to June 30, 1902, Secretary of the Territory Papers, 1865–1901, ASL.

95. Commitment Number 572, Manuela Fimbrez, Name of Convicts in the Territorial Prison at Yuma, March 30, 1889, Secretary of the Territory Papers, 1873–1901, ASL. Fimbrez's name was frequently listed as "Fimbres."

96. Case no. 572, Manuela Fimbrez, Report of Prisoners, Date of Receipt at Prison March 29, 1889, p. 2, Secretary of the Territory Papers, 1873–1901, ASL.

97. "The Murderers of Sullivan," *Arizona Daily Star*, March 27, 1889; "Local News," *Arizona Daily Star*, March 29, 1889.

98. "In Self Defense," *Arizona Daily Star*, December 22, 1888; "Arizona News," *Tombstone Weekly Epitaph*, December 22, 1888.

99. "Local Notes," *Arizona Sentinel*, November 2, 1889.

100. For an excellent overview of this issue, see "Babies behind Bars."

101. "The Prison at Yuma," *Arizona Republic*, August 24, 1890.

102. "Para la Prisión de Yuma" (For the Yuma Prison), *El Fronterizo*, April 3, 1889; "Territorial News," *Arizona Weekly Citizen*, March 29, 1890.

103. "Local Notes," *Arizona Sentinel*, October 3, 1891. See also Butler, *Gendered Justice in the American West* and *Daughters of Joy, Sisters of Misery*. Butler claimed that Fimbrez was a sex worker and Enriquez her pimp. She also claimed Fimbrez had an eight-year-old child, which means she would have gotten pregnant at twelve or thirteen (which seems unlikely). I found no evidence to support any of these claims. See *Daughters of Joy, Sisters of Misery*, 80.

104. "Local Notes," *Arizona Sentinel*, October 3, 1891.

105. Commitment Number 692, Matilda Garcia, October 19, 1890; Commitment Number 689, Antonia (last name unknown), October 2, 1890; Commitment Number 701, Guadalupe (last name unknown), November 8, 1890, Report of Prisoners, Date of Receipt at Prison May 21, 1890—November 6, 1890, Secretary of the Territory Papers, 1873–1901, ASL. "Guadalupe" is also a male first name, so this person could have been a man. "Antonia" was more than likely a misspelling of "Antonio."

106. Biennial Report of the Superintendent Territorial Prison, June 30, 1902, Secretary of the Territory Papers, 1865–1901, ASL. See also Roberts, "'The Women Was Too Tough.'"

107. See Cardoso, *Mexican Emigration to the United States*; Henderson, *Beyond Borders*; Gonzales, *Mexicanos*.

108. *Territory of Arizona v. John Doe (a Mexican)*, ASL.

109. *Territory of Arizona v. John Doe unknown Mexican*; *Territory of Arizona v. John Doe Mex.* (aka Ferdinand Rivera); *Territory of Arizona v. John Doe Mex.* (aka Refugio Bernal), ASL.

110. *Territory of Arizona v. John Doe—Mexican, true name unknown*, ASL.

111. *Territory of Arizona v. John Doe*, Case no. 61, ASL.

112. *Territory of Arizona v. John Doe, a Mexican*, Case no. 175, ASL.

113. For background on criminal law in New Mexico, see Gómez, "Race, Colonialism, and Criminal Law."

114. *Territory of New Mexico v. Juan Villegas*, Case no. 102, NMSRCA.

115. *Territory of New Mexico v. Juan Villegas*, Case no. 118, NMSRCA.

116. *Territory of New Mexico v. Albino Gomez and Juan Benavides*, Case no. 112, NMSRCA.

117. Placido Trujillo arrested on September 8, 1907, Arrest Book, June 21, 1907–January 5, 1912, TANM microfilm, Roll 93.

118. Juan Barquello arrested on February 15, 1911, Arrest Book, June 21, 1907–January 5, 1912, TANM microfilm, Roll 93.

119. Placido Trujillo arrested on September 8, 1907, Arrest Book, June 21, 1907–January 5, 1912, TANM microfilm, Roll 93.

120. City of Santa Fe to Charles C. Closson, Sheriff, for keeping and feeding city prisoners for the quarter ending December 31, 1908, Santa Fe, New Mexico Records, 1822–1934, UNM.

121. City of Santa Fe to Chas C. Cosson [sic], Sheriff, for feeding city prisoners for the quarter ending Dec. 31, 1912, Santa Fe, New Mexico Records, 1822–1934, UNM.

122. Superintendent D. B. Abraham certification, December 13, 1889; Jesus Acosta pardon, December 16, 1889, Pardons file, Penal Papers, L. Bradford Prince, 1889–1893 Papers, TANM microfilm, Roll 121.

123. Meeting of the Board of Penitentiary Commissioners, March 28, 1919, "Reports-Special Investigations," Governor Octaviano A. Larrazolo Papers, NMSRCA.

124. Meeting of the Board of Penitentiary Commissioners, January 20, 1920, "Reports-Special Investigations," Governor Octaviano A. Larrazolo Papers, NMSRCA.

125. No. 2078, Eliseo Valles, Penitentiary Report, February 26, 1919, "Federal Documents-Penal Papers," Governor Octaviano A. Larrazolo Papers, NMSRCA.

126. No. 4322, Agapito Nunez, Penitentiary Report, February 26, 1919, "Federal Documents-Penal Papers," Governor Octaviano A. Larrazolo Papers, NMSRCA.

127. Record of Arrests, January 30, 1876, January 1, 1876 to January 1, 1879 (logbook), APL.

128. Record of Arrests, February 12, 1876, January 1, 1876 to January 1, 1879 (logbook), APL.

129. Record of Arrests, November 26, 1876, January 1, 1876 to January 1, 1879 (logbook), APL.

130. Record of Arrests, April 28, 1877, January 1, 1876 to January 1, 1879 (logbook), APL.

131. Record of Arrests, November 30, 1878, January 1, 1876 to January 1, 1879 (logbook), APL.

132. Record of Arrests, March 1, 1876; Record of Arrests, February 4, 1878, January 1, 1876, to January 1, 1879 (logbook), APL. The logbook shifted from referring to police as "marshal" to "police" at this time.

133. "Rabbit," December 26, 1885, AR Record of Arrests, June 1885–May 1891 (logbook), APL. There was another Rabbit arrested on January 20, 1886, AR Record of Arrests, June 1885–May 1891 (logbook) APL.

134. AR Record of Arrests, January 11, 1886, June 1885–May 1891 (logbook), APL.

135. On how people of color were viewed as similar to animals, see Behnken and Smithers, *Racism in American Popular Media*.

136. See Juana Ruiz, November 22, 1886, arrest; Jose Maria, February 2, 1887, arrest, AR Record of Arrests, June 1885–May 1891 (logbook), APL.

137. AR Record of Arrests, July 30, 1885, June 1885–May 1891 (logbook), APL.

138. AR Record of Arrests, February 24, 1877, June 1885–May 1891 (logbook), APL.

139. *State of Texas v. "Mexican Antone,"* Case no. 3488, UTA.

140. See Criminal Docket, Tarrant County Court, 1876–79; Sheriff Acct. Bk. 1876–1885; Tarrant County Criminal Minutes, County Court, 1886–1887; Tarrant County Criminal Minutes, County Court, 1893–1895, UTA.

141. *State of Texas v. L. Reno*, Case no. 10737, UTA.

142. *State of Texas v. L. Reno*, Case no. 11334–11338, UTA.

143. *State of Texas v. Raul Orozco*, Case no. 37696, UTA.

144. No. 80, Luis Hernandez, October 14, 1905, Tarrant County—List of Convicts—1905–1907, UTA.

145. No. 112, Santiago Mendoza, May 17, 1907, Tarrant County—List of Convicts—1905–1907, UTA.

146. See Tarrant County Criminal Minutes, County Court, 1902–1909, UTA Archives and Tarrant County—List of Convicts—1905–1907, UTA.

147. P. P. Martinez, March 11, 1891, Calaboose Logbook, DPL.

148. "Mexican," September 7, 1891, Calaboose Logbook, DPL.

149. "Mexican," September 19, 1901, Calaboose Logbook, DPL. The following day the Calaboose admitted another "Mexican laborer" for drunk and disorderly conduct who was twenty-eight. See "Mexican," September 20, 1901, Calaboose Logbook, DPL.

150. Frank Mercado arrest, September 29, 1901, Calaboose Logbook, DPL.

151. "Mexican" and "Mexican," February 3, 1902; Frank Lopez arrest, March 1, 1902; Joe Gonzales, March 23, 1902, Calaboose Logbook, DPL.

152. "Mexican," July 12, 1920, Dallas City Jail Records, DPL.

153. "Mexican," July 24, 1920, Dallas City Jail Records, DPL.

154. "Unknown Mexica," June 24, 1922, Dallas City Jail Records, DPL.

155. "Unknown—Mex. Man," June 9, 1923, Dallas City Jail Records, DPL.

156. Complaint by Frank Wright, City of Dallas, Police Department, February 13, 1913, Wanted Posters and Bulletins, 1913–1914, DPL.

157. C. Gomez, Jose Galindo, and Severo Romediaz, March 7, 1921, Dallas City Jail Records, DPL.

158. Carlos Tellez, May 21, 1926, Dallas City Jail Records, DPL.

159. L. Vasquez, May 26, 1926, Dallas City Jail Records, DPL.

160. M. Martinez, May 29, 1926, Dallas City Jail Records, DPL.

161. Belen Peralez [sic], May 19, 1926, Dallas City Jail Records, DPL.

162. Mary Garcia, July 27, 1931, Dallas City Jail Records, DPL.

163. Perfidos Amiora et al., March 10, 1921, Dallas City Jail Records, DPL.

164. Anita Gomez, Esperanza Aldana, Annie Lopez, Abel Martinez, and Jesucila Bravo, July 1, 1922, Dallas City Jail Records, DPL.

165. *State of Texas vs. Rafael Garza*, Case no. 5114; *State of Texas vs. Andreas Coy, Jr.*, Case no. 5115, SAMAR.

166. *State of Texas vs. Jose Martinez*, Case no. 3796; *State of Texas vs. Jose Martinez*, Case no. 3800, SAMAR.

167. Almost every page of the Recorder's Court Docket makes this clear. For example, see the cases for September 25, 1899.

168. *State of Texas vs. Joe Sarromar and Jose Dan Ramon*, Case no. 514; *State of Texas vs. Andres Casteneda*, Case no. 515; *State of Texas vs. Victor Sanchez*, Case no. 516, SAMAR.

169. *State of Texas vs. Louisa Garcia*, Case no. 5276; *State of Texas vs. Julia Martinez*, Case no. 5277, SAMAR.

170. *State of Texas vs. Stella Ramirez*, Case no. 6202; *State of Texas vs. Josephine Gomez*, Case no. 6203, SAMAR.

171. *State of Texas vs. Valentina Puente*, Case no. 850, SAMAR.

172. *State of Texas vs. Maria Ruiz*, Case no. 2333, SAMAR.

173. *State of Texas vs. Isabela Rodriguez*, Case no. 3000, SAMAR.

174. *State of Texas vs. Maria D. Trevino*, Case no. 502, SAMAR.

175. *State of Texas vs. Guillermo Rodriguez*, Case no. 19018, SAMAR.

176. *State of Texas vs. Antonio Jesus Lopez*, Case no. 19070, SAMAR.

177. *State of Texas vs. Andres Pena*, Case no. 19479, SAMAR. Pena was probably Peña.

178. *State of Texas vs. Louis Ramos*, Case no. 18958, SAMAR.

179. *State of Texas vs. Juan Gutierrez*, Case no. 19503, SAMAR.

180. *State of Texas vs. Antonio Torres*, Case no. 21915, SAMAR.

181. *State of Texas vs. Antonio Bernal*, Case no. 21944, SAMAR.

182. *State of Texas vs. Jesus Garcia*, Case no. 21679, SAMAR.

183. *State of Texas vs. P. G. Garza*, Case no. 24517, SAMAR.

184. *State of Texas vs. mex*, Case no. 2245, SAMAR. See also *State of Texas vs. unknown mex*, Case no. 4013, SAMAR.

185. Jake Giles to Chief of Police, Dallas, October 25, 1911, Wanted Persons Letters from Other Cities to Dallas, 1910–1912, DPL.

186. 7:30pm, message from Sheriff—Tom Whitson, n.d., Wanted Persons Letters from Other Cities to Dallas, 1910–1912, DPL.

187. William Young to J. W. Ryan, August 28, 1912, Wanted Persons Letters from Other Cities to Dallas, 1910–1912, DPL.

188. "Yellow Mexican" letter, unsigned (on City of Dallas stationary), n.d., Wanted Posters and Bulletins, 1913–1914, DPL. See also Paige, "'To Get Their Labor for Nothing.'"

CHAPTER 5

1. "Chico Cano's Band of 100 Outlaws Terrorizes Border," *El Paso Herald*, May 31, 1915.

2. "Hundred Men in Gang," *Austin Daily Statesman*, May 29, 1915.

3. "Chico Cano's Band of 100 Outlaws Terrorizes Border," *El Paso Herald*, May 31, 1915.

4. "Una Supercheria que Causa Panico" (A Fraud that Causes Panic), *El Paso Times*, August 3, 1916.

5. "U.S. Soldier Killed by Villistas," *Austin Statesman*, December 3, 1917.

6. Some newspapers emphasized border issues, the problems with bandits, and called for vigilante justice going back to the 1870s. For a few examples, see "More Trouble on the Mexican Border," *San Francisco Examiner*, August 4, 1873; "Mexican Border Troubles," *Galveston Daily News*, January 13, 1875; "Mexican Border Troubles," *Austin Daily Statesman*, March 14, 1875; "Mexican Outrages," *Dallas Daily Herald*, April 27, 1875; "The Mexican Border Depredations," *San Francisco Examiner*, May 9, 1877; "Telegraphic," *Santa Fe Daily New Mexican*, May 10, 1877; "Latest News Regarding Mexican Border Trouble," *Albuquerque Morning Democrat*, August 12, 1886; "Mexican Border Troubles," *Los Angeles Herald*, December 25, 1892.

7. Hobsbawm, *Primitive Rebels*; Hobsbawm, *Bandits*; Baker, *Revolutionaries, Rebels and Robbers*.

8. On Mexican-origin bandits as folk heroes, see Paredes, *"With His Pistol in His Hand"*; Castro, *Chicano Folklore*; Gurza, "The Mexican Corrido," parts 1–4.

9. On the gold rush and Mexicans, see Boessenecker, *Gold Dust and Gunsmoke*. On Mexican American land dispossession in the Southwest, see Roybal, *Archives of Dispossession*; Correia, *Properties of Violence*.

10. That story came from the highly fictionalized account of John Rollin Ridge, *Life and Adventures of Joaquin Murieta*.

11. Wilson, *The Joaquín Band*, x.

12. Author Ireneo Paz also notes that the killing of Bean may have been done by another, *The Life & Adventures of the Celebrated Bandit Joaquin Murrieta*, xvi.

13. Wilson, *The Joaquín Band*, 4–5. This part of the Murrieta story is also in dispute.

14. Boessenecker, *Bandido*, 28–30.

15. Boessenecker, *Bandido*, 42, 48.

16. Boessenecker, *Bandido*, 71–73.

17. Weber, *Foreigners in Their Native Land*, 231–33.

18. Perales, *"Juan N. Cortina, Bandit or Patriot?,"* 6–7.

19. Quoted in De León, *They Called Them Greasers*, 54.

20. Thompson, *Cortina*, 37–38. Cortina's viewpoints on Anglo governance in the borderlands were captured in "Difficulties on Southwestern Frontier," in *Executive Documents Printed by the Order of the House of Representatives*, 78–82.

21. Thompson, *Cortina*, 41–44.

22. Thompson, *Cortina*, 45, 48–49, 50–57, 78–81; De León, *They Called Them Greasers*, 53–55; Montejano, *Anglos and Mexicans in the Making of Texas*, 35–37, 47–49. See also Thompson, "Cortina, Juan Nepomuceno"; Goldfinch and Canales, *Juan N. Cortina*.

23. "The Border," *Dallas Weekly Herald*, April 3, 1875; "Our Border Affairs," *Dallas Weekly Herald*, April 3, 1875; "Our Frontier," *Dallas Daily Herald*, April 3, 1875; "Mexican Marauders," *Dallas Daily Herald*, April 8, 1875; "From Brownsville," *Galveston Daily News*, April 17, 1875; "From Corpus Christi," *Galveston Daily News*, April 20, 1875.

24. "Cortina says . . ." *Austin Weekly Statesman*, April 15, 1875; "Feeling on the Frontier," *Galveston Daily News*, April 16, 1875.

25. "The Border," *Dallas Weekly Herald*, April 3, 1875; "Live Oak County," *Galveston Daily News*, April 13, 1875; *Texas Frontier Troubles, Report No. 343*, xii–xiii, xxi, 5–6, 9–10, 110; "Three Men Were Lynched after Nuecestown Raid," *Corpus Christi Caller-Times*, April 6, 2017; Taylor, *An American-Mexican Frontier*, 56–58; González-Quiroga, *War and Peace on the Rio Grande Frontier*, 262–63.

26. See Orozco, "The Nuecestown Raid of 1875."

27. "'A Little Standing Army in Himself.'"

28. Knight, "The Cart War," 318–35.

29. Cool, *Salt Warriors*, 1–3.

30. Cool, *Salt Warriors*, 3, 129.

31. Cool, *Salt Warriors*, 83.

32. Cool, *Salt Warriors*, 126–27.

33. Cool, *Salt Warriors*, 119, 133–34, 159–61.

34. Cool, *Salt Warriors*, 128–33, 168–76.

35. Levario, *Militarizing the Border*, 20–23; Shipman, "The Salt War of San Elizario," 1933; "The Salt War of San Elizario," 1934, 198–206.

36. See especially, Romero, "Class Struggle and Resistance," 87–109; Correia, "'Retribution Will Be Their Reward,'" 49–68; Correia, "Las Gorras Blancas of San Miguel County."

37. Some of the initial scholarship on the White Caps focused on their fence cutting and ranch burning, downplaying their activities to maintain law and order. See Graham, "Have You Ever Heard of the White Caps?"

38. "Las Gorras Blancas," unknown newspaper clipping, n.d., Gloria Montoya Chavez Papers, UNM.

39. Report to Hon. John W. Noble, Secretary of the Interior, August 12, 1890, L. Bradford Prince, 1889–1893 Papers, TANM microfilm, Roll 121.

40. E. W. Wynkoop to Gov. L. B. Prince, December 13, 1889, L. Bradford Prince, 1889–1893 Papers, TANM microfilm, Roll 121.

41. Lorenzo Lopez to Gov. Prince, telegram, December 11, 1889; E. V. Long to Gov. Prince, December 11, 1889, L. Bradford Prince, 1889–1893 Papers, TANM microfilm, Roll 121.

42. Joseph Trumbly to Governor Prince, March 29, 1890, L. Bradford Prince, 1889–1893 Papers, TANM microfilm, Roll 121.

43. Manuel C. de Baca to L. Bradford Prince, April 15, 1890, L. Bradford Prince, 1889–1893 Papers, TANM microfilm, Roll 121.

44. Miguel Salazar to Hon. L. Bradford Prince, July 25, 1890, L. Bradford Prince, 1889–1893 Papers, TANM microfilm, Roll 121.

45. Miguel Salazar to Hon. L. Bradford Prince, January 12, 1891, L. Bradford Prince, 1889–1893 Papers, TANM microfilm, Roll 121.

46. Manuel C. de Baca to L. Bradford Prince, April 15, 1890, L. Bradford Prince, 1889–1893 Papers, TANM microfilm, Roll 121.

47. Las Vegas, New Mexico, June 26, 1890, a report to Governor Prince, L. Bradford Prince, 1889–1893 Papers, TANM microfilm, Roll 121.

48. S. E. Booth to Hon. Bradford Prince, August 9, 1890, L. Bradford Prince, 1889–1893 Papers, TANM microfilm, Roll 121.

49. Reyes Martinez, "Societies—Severity Corruption," WPA 5-5-2 #33, WPA New Mexico Collection, FACHL.

50. C. M. O'Donel to Hon. Herbert J. Hagerman, February 12, 1906, Special Investigation Case Files, TANM microfilm, Roll 93. See also Hornung, *Cipriano Baca*, 162–63.

51. (Name illegible) to Hon. J. F. Fullerton, February 13, 1906, Special Investigation Case Files, TANM microfilm, Roll 93.

52. C. M. O'Donel to Captain Fred Fornoff, April 17, 1906, Special Investigation Case Files, TANM microfilm, Roll 93.

53. The classic account of Cortéz remains Paredes, *"With His Pistol in His Hand."*

54. Mertz, "No One Can Arrest Me."

55. Paredes, *"With His Pistol in His Hand,"* 61–62; "Renoldo [sic] Cortez Dead," *Austin Daily Statesman*, August 10, 1901.

56. Paredes, *"With His Pistol in His Hand,"* 67–71; "Still At Large," *Austin Daily Statesman*, June 17, 1901.

57. "That Urbiquitous [sic] Mexican," *Austin Daily Statesman*, June 19, 1901; "The Mexican Murderers Still At Large," *Austin Daily Statesman*, June 22, 1901; "They Have the Right Man," *Austin Daily Statesman*, June 24, 1901; "Captured at Last," *El Paso Herald*, June 24, 1901; "Caught in Webb County," *Brownsville Herald*, June 24, 1901; Spellman, *Captain John H. Rogers*, 113–16.

58. "In Bexar County Jail," *Austin Daily Statesman*, June 25, 1901.

59. Orozco, *No Mexicans, Women, or Dogs Allowed*, 69.

60. "Breezy Open Letter," *Austin Daily Statesman*, June 30, 1901.

61. Orozco, *No Mexicans, Women, or Dogs Allowed*, 69.

62. "Gregorio Cortez," *Austin Daily Statesman*, July 7, 1901; "Cortez to Be Tried," *Shiner Gazette*, July 10, 1901.

63. "Texas Notes," *Brownsville Herald*, August 5, 1901.

64. "Three Cheers for Brave Sheriff Fly," *Brownsville Herald*, August 15, 1901.

65. "Texas Items," *Brownsville Herald*, March 25, 1903; "Story of One of Texas' Most Famous Criminals," *Brownsville Herald*, March 28, 1903; "The Cortez Case," *Austin Statesman*, June 4, 1903.

66. "Cortez Case Remanded," *Brownsville Herald*, January 21, 1902.

67. "Taken to Karnes County," *El Paso Herald*, September 16, 1901; "Cortez to Be Tried Again," *El Paso Herald*, October 1, 1901; "Will Try Cortez Case," *Brownsville Herald*, October 11, 1901; "The Sheriff Murderer," *El Paso Herald*, October 11, 1901; "For Two Murders," *Fort Worth Register*, October 12, 1901; "Given Death Penalty," *Brownsville Herald*, October 15, 1901.

68. *Cortez v. State*, 69 S.W. 536; "Court Criminal Appeals," *Austin Daily Statesman*, May 1, 1902; "Not Murder to Kill Sheriff," *El Paso Herald*, June 24, 1902; "The Gregorio Cortez Case," *Houston Post*, June 29, 1902.

69. "Gregorio Cortez on Trial," *Austin Statesman*, April 2, 1903; "The Trial of Gregorio Cortez," *Brownsville Herald*, April 8, 1903; "The Jury That Sat in the Case of Gregorio Cortez . . . ," *Brownsville Herald*, April 13, 1903.

70. "Reversed and Remanded," *Austin Daily Statesman*, January 16, 1902; "Cortez Case Remanded," *Brownsville Herald*, January 21, 1902.

71. "Gregorio Cortez Found Not Guilty," *Refugio Review*, May 6, 1904.

72. "The Court of Criminal Appeals Has Affirmed . . . ," *State Herald*, June 23, 1904; "Cortez Taken to the Pen," *Galveston Daily News*, January 2, 1905.

73. Paredes, *"With His Pistol in His Hand,"* 97–99.

74. Paredes, *"With His Pistol in His Hand,"* 103–4.

75. "Fight with Mexicans," *Cuero Daily Record*, June 17, 1901; "Still at Large," *Austin Daily Statesman*, June 17, 1901; "More Bloodshed," *Alpine Avalanche*, June 21, 1901; "Breezy Open Letter," *Austin Daily Statesman*, June 30, 1901.

76. "Mob Lynched Mexican Near Dale, Texas," *Lockhart Daily Post*, February 17, 1905 (quotation); "In Hands of Mob," *Houston Post*, February 17, 1905.

77. "Two Men Lynched in Texas in Same Section," *El Paso Herald*, February 17, 1905; "Atanasio López Linchado" (Atanasio López Lynched), *El Regidor*, February 23, 1905;

"Reo Mexicano Asesinado por un Motin" (Accused Mexican Murdered by a Riot), *La Voz del Pueblo*, March 4, 1905.

78. "Judge Welch Murdered, Governor Sends Rangers," *Austin Daily Statesman*, November 7, 1906; "A Judge Murdered," *Houston Post*, November 7, 1906.

79. *The Texas Criminal Reports*, 141–88.

80. Special thanks to Dr. Brent Campney, who shared with me some of the resources he located about these events.

81. See Paine, *Captain Bill McDonald*, 357–72; Weiss, *Yours to Command*, 277–82.

82. See "May This Forever End It," *Corpus Christi Caller*, November 16, 1906; "Ambushed by Mexican Band," *Jefferson Jimplecute*, November 17, 1906.

83. "Fight on the Border," *Palestine Daily Herald*, November 9, 1906; "Armed and Drunk," *Palestine Daily Herald*, November 10, 1906; "Rangers Attacked Near Rio Grande," *Brownsville Herald*, November 10, 1906; "Attempt Made to Assassinate Captain M'Donald and Rangers," *Houston Post*, November 10, 1906.

84. "Situation at Rio Grande," *Brownsville Herald*, November 13, 1906.

85. "Attempt Made to Assassinate Captain M'Donald and Rangers," *Houston Post*, November 10, 1906.

86. "Fight on the Border," *Palestine Daily Herald*, November 9, 1906.

87. *The Texas Criminal Reports*, 141–88.

88. "Killing at Rio Grande City," *Houston Post*, May 5, 1909; "Mexican Killed by Ranger," *Brownsville Herald*, May 6, 1909; "Killing at Rio Grande City," *Victoria Daily Advocate*, May 6, 1909.

89. "Report is Received from Capt. Johnson," *Austin Daily Statesman*, May 8, 1909.

90. "Ranger Davis Was Indicted," *Palestine Daily Herald*, May 11, 1909.

91. "Ranger Davis's Trial," *Victoria Daily Advocate*, July 2, 1909.

92. "Ranger," *Victoria Daily Advocate*, July 5, 1909; "Ranger Davis Acquitted," *Brownsville Herald*, July 6, 1909.

93. Caldwell and DeLord, *Eternity at the End of a Rope*, 502.

94. Taylor, "Lynching on the Border," 38.

95. Taylor, "Lynching on the Border," 39.

96. "Barbarismos," *La Crónica*, November 12, 1910; Carrigan and Webb, *Forgotten Dead*, 142–43.

97. Martinez, *The Injustice Never Leaves You*, 46–47; Villanueva, *The Lynching of Mexicans*, chap. 2.

98. Carrigan and Webb, *Forgotten Dead*, 142; Taylor, "Lynching on the Border," 40–44, chap. IV.

99. "Mass Meeting in Thorndale," *Galveston Daily News*, June 26, 1911; Nielson, *Vengeance in a Small Town*, 2–3; Villanueva, *The Lynching of Mexicans*, chap. 2.

100. "Death of Boy," *Houston Daily Post*, June 25, 1911; "The Thorndale Lynching," *San Antonio Express*, July 28, 1911; Nielson, *Vengeance in a Small Town*, 2–6.

101. "Cobarde, Infame e Inhumano Lynchamiento de un Jovencito Mexicano en Thorndale, Milam Co., Texas" (Cowardly, Infamous, and Inhuman Lynching of a Mexican Youngster in Thorndale, Milam Co., Texas), *La Crónica*, June 29, 1911; "Valiente Cobardia de los Linchadores de Thorndale" (Brave Cowardice of the Thorndale Lynchers), *La Crónica*, July 13, 1911.

102. "Probe Thorndale Lynching," *San Antonio Express*, June, 23, 1911; "Four Men Arrested for Thorndale Lynching," *El Paso Morning Times*, June 24, 1911; "Lynching Case

is Begun," *San Antonio Express*, July 4, 1911; "Defendants Denied Bail," *Houston Daily Post*, July 4, 1911; "Ban on Lynching," *Alpine Avalanche*, July 6, 1911; "Will Be Given Hearing," *Houston Daily Post*, July 31, 1911; "Granted Bail," *Rockdale Reporter*, August 3, 1911; "Four Were Indicted," *Houston Daily Post*, October 26, 1911; "Thorndale Cases," *Houston Post*, November 7, 1911; Villanueva, *The Lynching of Mexicans*, 72–76.

103. "Consul Will Investigate," *Houston Post*, June 22, 1911; "Brief Austin Locals and Personal Notes," *San Antonio Express*, August 15, 1911.

104. "Agrupacion Protectora Mexicana," *La Crónica*, July 13, 1911.

105. "Colquitt Commended," *San Antonio Express*, July 6, 1911.

106. González, *Redeeming La Raza*, 24–26.

107. Ridge, *Life and Adventures of Joaquin Murieta*; Ridge, *The Lives of Joaquin Murieta and Tiburcio Vasquez*.

108. Gallagher, *Utah's Greatest Manhunt*, frontispiece.

109. Gallagher, *Utah's Greatest Manhunt*, 15.

110. Gallagher, *Utah's Greatest Manhunt*, 36–38.

111. Gallagher, *Utah's Greatest Manhunt*, 39.

112. Gallagher, *Utah's Greatest Manhunt*, 39.

113. Gallagher, *Utah's Greatest Manhunt*, 39.

114. Gallagher, *Utah's Greatest Manhunt*, 40.

115. Gallagher, *Utah's Greatest Manhunt*, 27–33.

116. See, for example, Rickard, *The Utah Copper Enterprise*, 42–44; Van Leer, "Where'd He Go?"

117. Gallagher, *Utah's Greatest Manhunt*, 43–47.

118. Gallagher, *Utah's Greatest Manhunt*, 47–50, illustration 55.

119. Gallagher, *Utah's Greatest Manhunt*, 57–77, 84 (quotation), "Lopez is Surrounded-Battle in Progress," *Deseret Evening News*, November 24, 1913; "Believe Lopez is Dead, Body in Mountains," *Salt Lake Telegram*, November 25, 1913; "Believe Lopez is Dead in Gas-filled Mine," *San Francisco Examiner*, December 3, 193. Speculation that Lopez escaped the mine began in December of 1913. See "Believe Bandit Lopez has Escaped," *San Francisco Call*, December 3, 1913.

120. Gallagher, *Utah's Greatest Manhunt*, 94.

121. Gallagher, *Utah's Greatest Manhunt*, 141.

122. Gallagher, *Utah's Greatest Manhunt*, 7–8 (quotation), 9–18.

123. According to John Boessenecker, Lopez was little more than a "notorious" bandit who had "murdered five Utah lawmen." Boessenecker's hagiographic *Texas Ranger* makes no attempt to critically examine Lopez or Hamer. Boessenecker, *Texas Ranger*, 241.

124. Kirby, "Kirby," *Salt Lake Tribune*, November 20, 2013; "Salt Lake County Deputy Killed in 1913 Gets Marker," *Daily Herald* (Chicago), November 4, 2009.

125. *Investigation of Mexican Affairs*, 1531–58, 1638–55.

126. Levario, *Militarizing the Border*, 28. Joe Sitter began his service in the Rangers in about 1894. By 1899 he had joined the U.S. Customs Service as a mounted inspector. It also appears that he served as a sheriff for some time before his time in the Rangers. Sitter's name was often referred to as "Sitters" in the press, a spelling often used today.

127. Jameson, *Border Bandits, Border Raids*, 63; Levario, *Militarizing the Border*, 28.

128. Jameson, *Border Bandits, Border Raids*, 63, 70–72; Levario, *Militarizing the Border*, 28–29; *Investigation of Mexican Affairs*, 1638, 1655. On the fourteen wounds, see the caption of the picture of Chico Cano with military men in Zakharova, "Throwback Thursday."

129. Most accounts of Cano simply refer to him as a bandit. Others offer a more sympathetic assessment. Levario notes that Cano was blamed for the Brite Ranch raid, for example, but that patriarch Lucas Brite doubted it and requested a meeting with Cano. The two men met, Cano professed his innocence, and Brite believed him. Levario, *Militarizing the Border*, 28, 31–32. There were those who believed Cano committed few of the crimes attributed to him. See Miles, *More Tales of the Big Bend*, 117–18, 143. One army officer mentioned that at one point Cano actually offered to help American soldiers "capture some bandits." See *Investigation of Mexican Affairs*, 1637–38.

130. "Two Americans, Missing, Are Believed to Have Been Captured or Killed," *El Paso Herald*, May 25, 1915; "Rover Guard and Ranger Killed," *El Paso Herald*, May 25, 1915; "Chico Cano Is Sought Here for Old Charge," *Austin Statesman*, August 22, 1919; "Bandit Under Indictment," *Corsicana Daily Sun*, August 28, 1919.

131. Webb, *The Texas Rangers*, 175–76.

132. Martinez, *The Injustice Never Leaves You*, 83, 87, 88.

133. "Plan de San Diego"; Johnson, *Revolution in Texas*, 79–82. See also Harris and Sadler, *The Plan de San Diego*.

134. Johnson, *Revolution in Texas*, 81–82.

135. Johnson, *Revolution in Texas*, 71–73.

136. Johnson, *Revolution in Texas*, 75–76.

137. Johnson, *Revolution in Texas*, 77–78.

138. Johnson, *Revolution in Texas*, 86–87; *Investigation of Mexican Affairs*, 1243–50. Jesse Perez detailed these and many other killings in 1915. See Jesse Perez Reminiscences, 1870–1927, BC, 57–58.

139. "6 Mexicans Killed in Battle Sunday at Norrias Ranch," *Wichita Daily Times*, August 9, 1915; "American Civilians and Soldiers Saved from Annihilation," *Denton Record-Chronicle*, August 9, 1915; "Five Outlaws Killed in Attack on Norrias Ranch," *Houston Post*, August 10, 1915.

140. Johnson, *Revolution in Texas*, 93 (quotation), 113.

141. Johnson, *Revolution in Texas*, 113.

142. Johnson, *Revolution in Texas*, 115.

143. "Mexican Bandits Are Killed by Soldiers," *Galveston Daily News*, December 31, 1917.

144. Testimony of James B. Wells, *Proceedings of the Joint Committee of the Senate and the House, Volume II*, 678; Martinez, *The Injustice Never Leaves You*, 76–79.

145. Martinez, *The Injustice Never Leaves You*, 1–5.

146. Martinez, *The Injustice Never Leaves You*, 130–31.

147. Martinez, *The Injustice Never Leaves You*, 122–23.

148. Levario, *Militarizing the Border*, 32–34.

149. Martinez, *The Injustice Never Leaves You*, 122.

150. Martinez, *The Injustice Never Leaves You*, 123.

151. Martinez, *The Injustice Never Leaves You*, 122.

152. Martinez, *The Injustice Never Leaves You*, 124. The Canales Investigation offered particularly compelling testimony about the massacre. See the testimony of James B. Wells, *Proceedings of the Joint Committee of the Senate and the House, Volume II*, 676–722.

153. Martinez, *The Injustice Never Leaves You*, 132–33.

154. Martinez, *The Injustice Never Leaves You*, 136.

155. Martinez, *The Injustice Never Leaves You*, 135–51.

156. See Hernández and González, *Reverberations of Racial Violence*.

157. See Welsome, *The General and the Jaguar*; Monticone, "Revolutionary Mexico"; Levario, *Militarizing the Border*.

158. Levario, *Militarizing the Border*, 74.

159. "House Votes on Hay Army Bill Today," *Arizona Daily Star*, March 23, 1916; "Hunt Wants Rifles," *Arizona Daily Star*, March 24, 1916; "Company D Is After Recruits," *Arizona Republic*, March 25, 1916; "Phoenix to Have Home Guard Company," *Tucson Citizen*, March 25, 1916; "Department Refuses Rifles," *Arizona Republican*, March 30, 1916.

160. "Phoenix Swears in 300 Extra Policemen for Duty," *Tombstone Weekly Epitaph*, March 26, 1916; "Home Guards Are Formed," *Arizona Republican*, May 14, 1916; "Home Guard Grows," *Arizona Republican*, May 24, 1916.

161. "Home Guard is Formed for City's Protection," *Arizona Daily Star*, May 16, 1916; "Support Given Home Guards in City of Bisbee," *Bisbee Daily Review*, June 24, 1916; "Glendale to Have Own Home Guards," *Arizona Republican*, April 20, 1917.

162. "New Mexico Towns Form Home Guards," *Tucson Citizen*, April 12, 1917; "Las Cruces Forms Home Guards Companies," *Arizona Republican*, May 12, 1916.

163. "Go After the I.W.W.," *Arizona Republican*, July 11, 1917; "Yavapai Decides to Wipe Out I.W.W.; Home Guard Acts," *Tucson Citizen*, July 12, 1917; "Douglas Man Relates Story of Smelter City's Part in I.W.W. Clean-up," *Arizona Daily Star*, July 13, 1917.

164. Escobar, *Race, Police, and the Making of a Political Identity*, 42–49; "Unworthy Foreigners," *Los Angeles Times*, December 27, 1913.

165. "Douglas Man Relates Story of Smelter City's Part in I.W.W. Clean-up," *Arizona Daily Star*, July 13, 1917; Benton-Cohen, *Borderline Americans*, chap. 7; Byrkit, *Forging the Copper Collar*, 1–3.

166. See President's Mediation Committee, *Report of the Bisbee Deportation*; *United States v. Wheeler*, 254 U.S. 281.

167. Meeks, *Border Citizens*, 93–96.

168. See Rosales, *Testimonio*, 114–15.

169. McBride, "The Liga Protectora Latina."

170. George Marvin quoted in *World Work Magazine*, January 1917, found in "1993/1994 INS/Customs/Border Patrol Complaints San Diego," American Friends Service Committee Papers, Roberto Martinez Papers, UCSD.

CHAPTER 6

1. Testimony of J. T. Canales, *Proceedings of the Joint Committee of the Senate and the House, Volume II*, 856–57 (quotation 857).

2. See, for instance, Walker, *A Critical History of Police Reform*; Palombo, *Academic Professionalism in Law Enforcement*; Cooper, *Twentieth-Century Influences on Twenty-First-Century Policing*. Many of these reform efforts followed, or borrowed from, the work of August Vollmer. An early twentieth century proponent of modernizing police forces, Vollmer also utilized eugenics theories, believed nonwhite people committed more crime, and in some ways viewed policing as akin to a colonial militia, which reinforced nineteenth century notions of policing. See Moffitt, "Weighing August Vollmer's Tarnished Legacy."

3. See, for instance, Hernández, *Migra!*; Hernández, *City of Inmates*; Kang, *The INS on the Line*.

4. J. T. Canales to Gov. W. P. Hobby, December 12, 1918, *Proceedings of the Joint Committee of the Senate and the House, Volume II*, 888–90; "Report Favorably on Suffrage and

Prohibition," *Houston Post*, January 17, 1919; "Ranger Force Bill is Under Consideration," *Galveston Daily News*, January 24, 1919. Santiago Tijerina may have been a relative of New Mexico activist Reis Lopez Tijerina. Oropeza, *The King of Adobe*, 21.

5. "H. B. No. 5," *Journal of the House of Representatives of the First Regular Session of the Thirty-Sixth Legislature*, 37.

6. "House Bill No. 5 on Second Reading," 163–64; "House Bill No. 5 on Second Reading," 608, *Journal of the House of Representatives of the First Regular Session of the Thirty-Sixth Legislature*.

7. "Relating to Ranger Force," *Journal of the House of Representatives of the First Regular Session of the Thirty-Sixth Legislature*, 211; "Ranger Probe is Started Today," *Austin Statesman*, January 30, 1919.

8. "Charges 6–10," *Proceedings of the Joint Committee of the Senate and the House, Volume I*, 125; "Specific Charges Against Rangers Are Submitted by Canales," *Austin Statesman*, January 31, 1919.

9. "Witnesses Relate Rangers' Conduct in Border Towns," *Houston Post*, February 8, 1919; Harris III and Sadler, *The Texas Rangers and the Mexican Revolution*, 427–40; Cox, *Time of the Rangers*, 86–99; Martinez, *The Injustice Never Leaves You*, 183.

10. "New Light Thrown Upon Daily Doings Along Rio Grande," *Houston Post*, February 1, 1919; "Texas Ranger Hearing Shows Smoke but No Fire and Brings Out Praise," *Austin American*, February 1, 1919.

11. "Representative Canales Steps Before Public in Fight Against Rangers," *Marshall Messenger*, February 3, 1919; "Rep. Canales Will Testify This Morning," *Austin American*, February 10, 1919; "Canales on Stand in Ranger Inquiry," *Galveston Daily News*, February 11, 1919.

12. Martinez, *The Injustice Never Leaves You*, 183–91, 208–11.

13. "Report of Ranger Investigating Committee," *Journal of the House of Representatives of the First Regular Session of the Thirty-Sixth Legislature*, 537; "Report on Ranger Investigation Read," *Galveston Daily News*, February 20, 1919; "Ranger Service Found Necessary for Regulation," *Houston Post*, February 20, 1919.

14. "Report of Ranger Investigating Committee," *Journal of the House of Representatives of the First Regular Session of the Thirty-Sixth Legislature*, 537–38.

15. "Report of Ranger Investigating Committee," *Journal of the House of Representatives of the First Regular Session of the Thirty-Sixth Legislature*, 538.

16. "Charges Adjutant General Whitewashed," *Corsicana Daily Sun*, March 1, 1919; "Canales After Rangers Again," *Marshall Messenger*, March 3, 1919.

17. "Texas Rangers to Get New Chance on Bledsoe Measure," *Austin American*, March 4, 1919; "Canales Talks of His Bill; Opposes the Substitute," *Austin Statesman*, March 6, 1919.

18. "House Bill No. 5 on Third Reading," *Journal of the House of Representatives of the First Regular Session of the Thirty-Sixth Legislature*, 866–67; "Texas Ranger Bill Engrossed Friday After Big Debate," *Austin American*, March 8, 1919; "Reorganization of Ranger Force Seems Assured," *Houston Post*, March 8, 1919.

19. "By Canales, H. B. No. 5, A Bill," *Journal of the Senate of Texas, Regular Session, Thirty-Sixth Legislature*, 816–19; "House Bill No. 5," *Journal of the Senate of Texas, Regular Session, Thirty-Sixth Legislature*, 1000–1001; "Message from the Senate," *Journal of the House of Representatives of the First Regular Session of the Thirty-Sixth Legislature*, 1064; "Ranger Bill Passes," *El Paso Times*, March 18, 1919.

20. "House Bill No. 5 with Senate Amendments," *Journal of the House of Representatives of the First Regular Session of the Thirty-Sixth Legislature*, 1093–94. Canales was displeased with the modifications to his original bill. He did not vote on the House bill and abstained from voting on the revised Senate bill.

21. "State Rangers' Bill and Many Others Become Law," *Liberty Vindicator*, April 4, 1919.

22. "By Canales, H. B. No. 5, A Bill," *Journal of the Senate of Texas, Regular Session, Thirty-Sixth Legislature*, 816–19 (quotations 818, 819).

23. "By Canales, H. B. No. 5, A Bill," *Journal of the Senate of Texas, Regular Session, Thirty-Sixth Legislature*, 816–19 (quotation 818); "State 'Rangers' Bill and Many Others Become Law," *Liberty Vindicator*, April 4, 1919.

24. "Bills and Resolutions Signed by the Speaker," *Journal of the House of Representatives of the Regular Session of the Thirty-Eighth Legislature*, 1679; "Changes in Medical Act Made Law by Gov. Neff," *El Paso Herald*, March 24, 1923.

25. For reference to fifty Rangers, see "Ranger Force," *Journal of the House of Representatives of the Regular Session of the Thirty-Seventh Legislature*, 542; "Ranger Force," *Journal of the House of Representatives of the Regular Session of the Thirty-Eighth Legislature*, 488–89. For Neff's reductions, see "Message from the Governor" and "Ranger Force," *Journal of the House of Representatives of the Regular Session of the Thirty-Ninth Legislature*, 107, 1474.

26. "Bills and Resolutions Signed by the Speaker," *Journal of the House of Representatives of the Regular Session of the Thirty-Ninth Legislature*, 1888; "Search and Seizure Bill is Approved," *Victoria Advocate*, March 15, 1925.

27. "Conference Committee Report on Senate Bill No. 146," *Journal of the House of Representatives of the Regular Session of the Forty-Fourth Legislature*, 2189–96; Harris and Sadler, *The Texas Rangers in Transition*, chap. 36.

28. See Rosales, *¡Pobre Raza!*, 99–100.

29. "Texas Mobs Hunt Slayer of Girl on Mexico Border," *Austin American*, February 28, 1921.

30. "Mexican Held Relative to Rio Hondo Murder," *Corpus Christi Caller*, March 9, 1921; "Ortega is Rushed to San Antonio," *Taylor Daily Press*, March 11, 1921; "Arrested for Murder of Rio Hondo Girl," *Mercedes Tribune*, March 11, 1921; "Mexicano Acusado de Asesinato en Brownsville" (Mexican Accused of Murder in Brownsville), *La Prensa*, March 11, 1921; "Se Investiga el Caso de Teodoro Ortega" (The Case of Teodoro Ortega Is Investigated), *La Prensa*, March 13, 1921; "Se Rinde un Informe Sobre la Muerte de Salvador Saucedo" (Report about the Death of Salvador Saucedo), *La Prensa*, April 9, 1921.

31. "Excitement Runs High When Hundreds Take Part in Hunt in Murder Clues," *San Benito Light*, February 28, 1921.

32. "Se Pone en Claro Como Fue Asesinado S. Saucedo Cerca de Rio Hondo" (Clarification that S. Saucedo Was Murdered Near Rio Hondo), *La Prensa*, March 9, 1921; "Neff Requested to Probe Death," *Marshall News Messenger*, March 23, 1921; "Killing of Mexican at Rio Hondo is Being Investigated," *Austin Statesman*, April 28, 1921.

33. "Fue Absuelto un Acusado de la Muerte de un Mexicano" (Defendant Was Acquitted of the Death of a Mexican), *La Prensa*, October 16, 1922; Rosales, *¡Pobre Raza!*, 102–3.

34. "Men Charged with Killing Rio Hondo Girl Granted Venue Change," *Austin Statesman*, September 19, 1921; "Comezo el Jurado por la Muerte de la Jovencita Schroeder" (Jury into the Death of the Shroeder Youth Begins), *La Prensa*, November 9, 1921; "Jurado Pospuesto" (Jury Postponed), *La Prensa*, November 10, 1921.

35. "Sheriff's Bullet Ends Career of Alleged Murderer Who Had Terrorized Rio Grande Area," *Galveston Daily News*, April 2, 1923; "Alleged Double Murderer Killed by Texas Deputy," *Austin American*, April 2, 1923; "Alleged Kidnapper and Murderer is Killed by Posse," *El Paso Times*, April 2, 1923; "Suspect's Death May Clear Up Series of Rio Hondo Mysteries," *El Paso Times*, April 3, 1923; "Alfredo Luna, Brutal Killer, Slain by Posse," *Mercedes Tribune*, April 4, 1923. Deputy Sheriff Ortega's first name is not used in this reporting.

36. "Grand Jury Probes Death of Mexican," *San Benito Light*, February 4, 1922; "Begin Investigation of Murder at Brownsville," *Waco News-Tribune*, February 5, 1922. Special thanks to Dr. Brent Campney for sharing some of his clippings from the *San Benito Light*.

37. "20 Men Indicted for Murder of Mexican in Cameron County," *Austin Statesman*, February 28, 1922; "Indict 20 for Slaying," *El Paso Herald*, February 28, 1922; "Twenty Indicted for Killing," *Houston Post*, March 1, 1922; "Farmers Surrender on Bills Charging Murder," *Temple Daily Telegram*, March 2, 1922; "Thirteen Held in Cameron County on Murder Charge," *Galveston Daily News*, March 3, 1922; "Son Aprehendidos Catorce Vecinos Prominentes" (Fourteen Prominent Residents Are Apprehended), *La Prensa*, March 3, 1922; "Twenty Indicted in Death of Mexican," *Winnsboro Weekly News*, March 3, 1922.

38. "Judge Boone Will Hear Murder Trial," *Willacy County News*, September 20, 1923.

39. "Customs Officer Slain at Mercedes, His Slayer Escapes," *Austin Statesman*, October 2, 1922; "Slayer of Customs Officer Arrested," *Austin American*, October 4, 1922; "Orders Border Men to 'Shoot First,'" *San Antonio Light*, October 2, 1922 (quotation); "Mayor Proteccion Reclaman los Mexicanos Residentes en el Condado de Hidalgo, Texas" (Mexicans Demand Better Protection in Hidalgo County, Texas), *La Prensa*, November 7, 1922.

40. Villareal's last name is occasionally spelled "Villarreal" in newspaper reports. He was also referred to as "Zárate."

41. "Texas Lynching Stirs Mexican Officials," *Austin Statesman*, November 15, 1922; "El Secuestro de Villarreal Zarate en Weslaco, Texas, Fue Realizado por un Grupo de Dies Individuos" (The Kidnapping of Villarreal Zarate in Weslaco, Texas Was Accomplished by a Group of Ten Individuals), *La Prensa*, November 15, 1922; "Appeal to Gov. Neff for Aid in Protecting Mexican Born Ordered from Town in Texas," *El Paso Herald*, November 16, 1922; "Mexican Killed After Being in Jail at Weslaco," *Marshall Morning News*, November 16, 1922.

42. Powers, "Settlement Colonialism," 129–31.

43. "Mexico Protesting Attack on Mexican Near Texas Border," *San Antonio Evening News*, November 24, 1922; "Nuevas Representaciones de la Embajada Mexicana a la Secretaría de Estado" (New Representations/Petitions from the Mexican Embassy to the Secretary of State), *La Prensa*, November 24, 1922; "Cuentan Ya con la Debida Proteccion los Mexicanos en el Condado de Hidalgo" (Mexicans Say They Are Already Due Protection in Hidalgo County), *La Prensa*, November 26, 1922; Villanueva, *The Lynching of Mexicans*, 170. Special thanks to my friend Kristin MacDonald York for helping me translate some of the newspaper article titles in this chapter.

44. "Big Crowd Attends 'White Owls' Meet," *Breckenridge Daily News*, November 6, 1922; "'White Owls' Organize; to Meet Thursday," *Breckenridge Daily News*, November 8, 1922; "White Owls to Parade Next Tuesday," *Breckenridge Daily News*, November 10, 1922; "The White Owls Parade Through the Business and Negro Districts," *Breckenridge Daily News*, November 15, 1922.

45. "Neff Confers on Breckenridge Situation," *Taylor Daily Press*, November 16, 1922; "Consuls of Mexico Are Appealing for Action," *San Antonio Evening News*, November 16,

1922; "Appeal to Gov. Neff for Aid in Protecting Mexican Born Ordered from Town in Texas," *El Paso Herald*, November 16, 1922.

46. "Breckenridge Under Control of Officers," *Daily Herald* (Weatherford, Tex.), November 17, 1922.

47. "Mexican Embassy Has Made Representations against an Alleged Mexican Lynching," *Corsicana Daily Sun*, November 15, 1922; "Fue Asesinado un Mexicano en Texas" (A Mexican Was Murdered in Texas), *El Tucsonense*, November 16, 1922; "Mexico Protests Against Alleged Lynching in Texas," *Houston Post*, November 16, 1922; "Demands U.S. Protect Mexicans," *El Paso Times*, November 16, 1922; "No Han Sufrido Perjuicios los Mexicanos de Breckenridge (Breckenridge Mexicans Have Not Suffered Damages)," *La Prensa*, November 20, 1922; Carrigan and Webb, *Forgotten Dead*, 151.

48. "State Investigates Weslaco Lynching," *Austin Statesman*, November 23, 1922.

49. "Rangers Will Probe Killing in Texas City," *El Paso Herald*, November 23, 1922; "Ranger Captain Expects to Complete Probe," *El Paso Herald*, November 27, 1922.

50. "Barton Receives Report on Mexican Lynching," *Houston Post*, December 6, 1922.

51. "Officials Begin Probe of Purpose of 'White Owls,'" *Houston Post*, November 18, 1922; "Federal Agents in Probe of Parade at Breckenridge," *Waco News-Tribune*, November 19, 1922.

52. "Mexican is Victim of Santone 'White Owls,'" *Waco News-Tribune*, December 14, 1922.

53. "Man Held in Oil Field 'White Owl' Case at Somerset," *San Antonio Evening News*, December 16, 1922.

54. As quoted in Urbina, Vela, and Sánchez, *Ethnic Realities of Mexican Americans*, 110.

55. "El Ideal de los Mexico-Americanos," in Perales, *En Defensa de mi Raza*, 29.

56. "Consul General Makes Public List of Mexicans Killed in Texas," *Corsicana Daily Sun*, November 18, 1922; "Twelve Mexicans Killed on Border in Eleven Months," *Austin Statesman*, November 18, 1922; "Mexicans Killed in Past Eleven Months in Texas," *Daily Herald* (Weatherford, Tex.), November 20, 1922. See also Urbina, Vela, and Sánchez, *Ethnic Realities of Mexican Americans*, 110; Villanueva, *The Lynching of Mexicans*, 170.

57. "Twelve Mexicans Killed on Border in Eleven Months," *Austin Statesman*, November 18, 1922 (quotation); "Rangers Will Probe Killing in Texas City," *El Paso Herald*, November 23, 1922.

58. "Foreign Official Probes Slaying of Mexicans in Texas," *Austin Statesman*, September 8, 1926; "Funeral is Held for Two Officers," *Galveston Daily News*, September 7, 1926.

59. "Slain Mexicans Held U.S. Citizenship, 'Ma' Tells Secretary," *Austin Statesman*, October 23, 1926.

60. "Prisoners Killed in Ambush," *El Paso Times*, September 8, 1926; "Five Killed as Officers Battle Ambuscaders," *Galveston Daily News*, September 8, 1926; "Officers Cleared in Ambuscade," *Abilene Morning News*, September 18, 1926.

61. Alonso S. Perales to Su Excelencia Miriam Ferguson, October 24, 1926, A. S. Perales, *En Defensa de mi Raza*, 32–33.

62. Alonso S. Perales to Su Excelencia Calvin Coolidge, February 14, 1927, A. S. Perales, *En Defensa de mi Raza*, 37.

63. Alonso S. Perales to Su Excelencia Calvin Coolidge, April 30, 1927, A. S. Perales, *En Defensa de mi Raza*, 41–43.

64. "Mexico Protests Willacy County Killings," *Corsicana Daily Sun*, September 14, 1926.

65. "Alleged Mexican Citizens Tortured After Their Arrest," *Corsicana Daily Sun*, September 14, 1926; "Sheriff Denies Mob Killed Mexicans," *Austin Statesman*, September 14, 1926; "Victim of Alleged Attack on Officers Will be Exhumed," *Corsicana Daily Sun*, September 17, 1926. Alonso Perales wrote to President Coolidge explaining the facts in this way as well. See Alonso S. Perales to Su Excelencia Calvin Coolidge, February 14, 1927, A. S. Perales, *En Defensa de mi Raza*, 35–38.

66. "Grand Jury Makes Report on Killing," *Galveston Daily News*, September 18, 1926.

67. "Slain Mexicans Held U.S. Citizenship, 'Ma' Tells Secretary," *Austin Statesman*, October 23, 1926.

68. "Texans Charged in Peonage Conspiracy," *Austin Statesman*, December 13, 1926; "Willacy Officers Indicted by Grand Jury," *McAllen Daily Press*, December 13, 1926; "County Officials in Custody Under Peonage Charges," *Waco News-Tribune*, December 14, 1926. See also Taylor, *An American-Mexican Frontier*, 325–29.

69. "Officers Charged in Connection with Mexicans' Slaying," *Corsicana Daily Sun*, January 8, 1927; "Willacy Sheriff Held for Nunez Killing," *Lubbock Morning Avalanche*, January 8, 1927; "Sheriff, Seven Others Held," *Fort Worth Press*, January 8, 1927.

70. Some accounts state that Teresa was Tomás Nuñez's daughter and Jose and Delancio were her brothers.

71. "Grand Jury No Bills Willacy County Posse," *Austin American*, January 25, 1927; "Willacy County Officers Absolved," *Marshall News Messenger*, January 25, 1927.

72. "Washington Youth Tells of Peonage in Willacy County," *Corsicana Daily Sun*, February 1, 1927; "Factional Politics Ruled Out Peonage Case at Corpus," *Corsicana Daily Sun*, February 2, 1927.

73. "Guard Threatened to Kill Cotton Pickers," *Brownwood Bulletin*, February 2, 1927.

74. "Defense Offering Testimony in Case of Alleged Peonage," *Corsicana Daily Sun*, February 4, 1927.

75. "Sheriff and 4 Others Guilty of Peonage," *Austin American Statesman*, February 6, 1927; "Sentences in Peonage Case May be Heavy," *Brownwood Bulletin*, February 7, 1927; "Willacy Co. Officials Sentenced," *Waxahachie Daily Light*, March 12, 1927; "Willacy Sheriff Sentenced," *Press*, March 12, 1927.

76. "Four More Arrests in Willacy Peonage Case," *Borger Daily Herald*, March 23, 1927; "Four Men Were Indicted for Intimidation," *Marshall Messenger*, May 14, 1927.

77. "Two Defendants Are Acquitted," *Abilene Reporter-News*, May 27, 1928.

78. "Commissioners of Willacy County are for Convicted Men," *Corsicana Daily Sun*, March 14, 1927; "Willacy County Sheriff Resigns," *Galveston Daily News*, March 15, 1927.

79. "Prison Inmate Runs for Sheriff," *Austin American*, June 19, 1928; "Runs for Sheriff While in Prison," *Victoria Advocate*, June 24, 1928.

80. "'Jailbird' Sheriff Gets Big Welcome," *Austin Statesman*, July 12, 1928.

81. "The Albuquerque Police Department," *Santa Fe New Mexican*, August 7, 1905; "Albuquerque Police Department," *Albuquerque Citizen*, August 8, 1905; "All Poppycock," *Albuquerque Journal*, August 9, 1905; "Interesting Sidelights on 'Canard Branding,'" *Albuquerque Journal*, August 11, 1905.

82. "Albuquerque Police Investigation," *Las Vegas Daily Optic*, August 17, 1905.

83. "Want Probation Officer," *Albuquerque Citizen*, February 14, 1907.

84. "Grand Jury Finds Grave Abuses in Police Department," *Albuquerque Morning Journal*, October 7, 1909; "Mayor Lester May Probe Police," *Albuquerque Journal*, October 9, 1909.

85. "Local News of Interest," *Albuquerque Journal*, February 8, 1910.
86. "Local News of Interest," *Albuquerque Journal*, April 17, 1912.
87. "Regular Meeting of the City Council, April 15, 1912," *Albuquerque Evening Herald*, April 25, 1912.
88. "Officer Galusha Resigns from the Police Department," *Albuquerque Journal*, November 17, 1912.
89. "Deputy U.S. Marshal Galusha to Maintain Office in This City," *Albuquerque Journal*, June 11, 1913.
90. "Slate of City Offices Made When Mayor and Aldermen Meet," *Albuquerque Morning Journal*, April 17, 1916; "Galusha Becomes Albuquerque Chief; Kelcher Attorney," *Santa Fe New Mexican*, April 18, 1916.
91. "Galusha Starts His First Real Crusade," *Albuquerque Evening Herald*, April 28, 1916; "Sunday Will Be a Little Mojave in Albuquerque," *Albuquerque Morning Journal*, June 21, 1916.
92. "Policeman is Suspended to Await Hearing," *Albuquerque Morning Journal*, December 7, 1916; "Council Ready for Negotiations with M'Millen," *Albuquerque Morning Journal*, December 12, 1916.
93. "Police News to be Received by Wireless Here," *Albuquerque Morning Journal*, November 15, 1922.
94. "Chief Galusha Knocks Idea of Guard in Head," *Albuquerque Evening Herald*, June 27, 1916.
95. "Chief is Requested to File Charges Against Sergeant Miller," *Albuquerque Morning Journal*, January 21, 1917.
96. "Council Will Try Miller on Cruelty Charge," *Albuquerque Evening Herald*, February 20, 1917.
97. "Police Sergeant is Told to Report for Duty by the Mayor," *Albuquerque Morning Journal*, February 28, 1917.
98. "Those Were Tough First Days," *Albuquerque Tribune*, August 7, 1968 (quotation); "Guard Recalls Crime Fighting Days," *Albuquerque Tribune*, December 6, 1974. Officer Chavez was a cousin of Senator Dennis Chávez (D-N.Mex.).
99. "First Street Won't Seem Same When Officer Chavez Retires," *Albuquerque Tribune*, April 6, 1966.
100. "After 47 Years on 'Skid Row,' Patrolman to Retire," *Valley News*, March 3, 1966; see also Bio—Chavez, Dennis A. (policeman) file, ABCPL.
101. "Prisoner, Trying to Escape, Shot by Patrolman," *Albuquerque Morning Journal*, April 1, 1919; "First Street Won't Seem Same When Officer Chavez Retires," *Albuquerque Tribune*, April 6, 1966.
102. On kids, see "Newsies Trick Boy Janitor and Rifle Register," *Albuquerque Morning Journal*, September 1, 1919; "Hearing Postponed," *Albuquerque Journal*, March 30, 1948. On his retirement see "After 47 Years on 'Skid Row,' Patrolman to Retire," *Valley News*, March 3, 1966.
103. "First Street Won't Seem Same When Officer Chavez Retires," *Albuquerque Tribune*, April 6, 1966.
104. McDonald, *Racial Dynamics in Early Twentieth-Century Austin*, 209; "New Austin Patrolman Starts Walking Beat," *Austin American*, June 2, 1920.
105. "Lesson to Learn," author unknown, dated "The Early Thirties," A Lesson to Learn (The Early 1930's) Folder, Dallas Police Archives, DPL.

106. "Dallas Police Given Test on Intelligence," *Marshall News Messenger*, August 19, 1931.

107. "Secret Twelve to Observe Conduct of Dallas Police," *Tyler Morning Telegraph*, September 17, 1932.

108. "State Officers Hear from Mexico City Chief," *Valley Morning Star*, June 16, 1939.

109. "Officer Held on Bribe Attempt Charge," *Austin American*, May 19, 1928.

110. "Policeman Jailed," *Austin American*, August 17, 1928; "Release Cop on Bond," *Waco News-Tribune*, August 18, 1928; "2 Officers Face Liquor Charges," *Fort Worth Star-Telegram*, September 17, 1928.

111. "Corpus Christi Cop Denies He Offered Bride to Prober," *Corsicana Daily Sun*, May 21, 1929.

112. "Bribery Case Jurors Disagree, Dismissed," *Fort Worth Star-Telegram*, May 23, 1929; "Jury Disagrees in Case of Policeman," *Corsicana Daily Sun*, May 23, 1929.

113. "May Postpone Galvan Trial," *Corpus Christi Times*, September 12, 1930.

114. Louzon, "Corpus Christi's Galvan Ballroom."

115. Some of this background is covered in Rosales, ¡*Pobre Raza!*, 81.

116. "Mexican is Killed in Arrest Attempt," *Arizona Daily Star*, July 5, 1930; "Mexican Dies as Weapon Explodes," *Arizona Silver Belt*, July 5, 1930; "Miami Officer Kills Mexican Who Uses Knife," *Arizona Republic*, July 5, 1930.

117. "Lopez Death Accidental," *Arizona Silver Belt*, Jul 10, 1930; "Coroner's Jury Frees Welch of Blame in Death," *Arizona Republic*, July 10, 1930.

118. "Miami Patrolman Accused of Killing," *Arizona Daily Star*, July 12, 1930.

119. "Miami Police Officer Freed in Lopez Case," *Arizona Republic*, August 6, 1930; "Welch Exonerated," *Arizona Daily Star*, August 8, 1930.

120. "Torre Slaying Probe Reopened by U.S. Order," *Arizona Daily Star*, September 21, 1930.

121. "Torre Slaying Probe Reopened by U.S. Order," *Arizona Daily Star*, September 21, 1930; "Welch is Arrested Second Time," *Arizona Silver Belt*, October 30, 1930; "Reopen Miami Killing Probe," *Arizona Republic*, October 31, 1930; "John Welch Released on Bond Today," *Arizona Silver Belt*, November 3, 1930.

122. "Murder Case Trial Started at Globe," *Arizona Daily Star*, February 17, 1931; "Chief Takes Stand in Defense of Son," *Arizona Daily Star*, February 18, 1931.

123. "Jury Frees Welch," *Arizona Silver Belt*, February 19, 1931; "Welch Free After Trial for Murder," *Arizona Daily Star*, February 19, 1931.

124. "Miami Police Chief is Granted Leave," *Arizona Republic*, July 8, 1933; "Miami," *Arizona Daily Star*, September 27, 1934; "Barney Welch, of Miami Police, Dies," *Arizona Daily Star*, October 11, 1934.

125. "Globe Slaying Blame Placed," *Arizona Republic*, December 31, 1935.

126. "Crazed Killer 'Shoots it Out,'" *Arizona Officers*, April 1937.

127. "John Welch to be Candidate for Sheriff of Gila County," *Arizona Silver Belt*, May 3, 1940; "Fifth Columnist Report Asked," *Arizona Republic*, August 3, 1940; "An Organized Gang of Saboteurs," *Arizona Silver Belt*, August 23, 1940.

128. "Safe Margins Are Attained," *Arizona Republic*, November 6, 1940. It is unclear if Welch withdrew from the election or lost to Richardson. This article states that Richardson was unopposed.

129. Edward J. Long, Daily Report, Detective Officer, Los Angeles Police Department, December 12, 1929, 269, HL.

130. Edward J. Long, Daily Report, Detective Officer, Los Angeles Police Department, December 27, 1929, 279, HL.

131. "Henry Gallegos and Alleged Marihuana Peddler to be Tried," *Albuquerque Morning Journal*, February 20, 1923.

132. "Henry Gallegos Held to Grand Jury for Theft," *Albuquerque Morning Journal*, February 24, 1923. See also "Eight Indicted by Grand Jury," *Albuquerque Morning Journal*, March 29, 1923; "Four Criminal Cases Ready to Go to Trial," *Albuquerque Morning Journal*, April 3, 1923.

133. "Old Indictments are Dismissed in Court in Favor of New Ones," *Albuquerque Morning Journal*, October 13, 1923. Police arrested Gallegos again in November for robbery, "Henry 'The Lonesome Kid' in Jail Again," *Albuquerque Morning Journal*, November 17, 1923.

134. "'Lonesome Kid' is Once More in Jail," *Albuquerque Morning Journal*, December 21, 1923; "Alleged Robber of Cycle Shop Sent to Juvenile Court," *Albuquerque Morning Journal*, December 22, 1923.

135. "'Lonesome Kid' Gets 15 Days Jail Sentence on Vagrancy Charge," *Albuquerque Journal*, June 12, 1927.

136. "'Lonesome Kid' in Jail Charged with Burglary," *Albuquerque Journal*, January 2, 1928.

137. "Conspiracy Charge is Filed Against 'Lonesome Kid' Who Takes up Abode in County Jail," *Albuquerque Journal*, January 3, 1928.

138. "'Lonesome Kid' in Jail Charged with Burglary," *Albuquerque Journal*, January 2, 1928.

139. "Police and Sheriff War is Still On," *Albuquerque Tribune*, January 3, 1928.

140. "City Police Blocked Plans to Catch 'Kid,'" *Albuquerque Tribune*, January 2, 1928; "Police and Sheriff War is Still On," *Albuquerque Tribune*, January 3, 1928 (quotation); "Mayor of City and Sheriff in a Controversy," *Albuquerque Tribune*, January 3, 1928.

141. "Frame-up Talk Absolute Joke Sheriff Says," *Albuquerque Journal*, January 3, 1928.

142. The inventory of Gallegos's belongings was reported in "'Lonesome Kid' in Jail Charged with Burglary," *Albuquerque Journal*, January 2, 1928; "Lone Kid Case is Postponed," *Albuquerque Tribune*, January 4, 1928; "Gallegos Hearing in Duran's Court at 2 P.M. Friday," *Albuquerque Journal*, January 6, 1928.

143. "Faces Charges of Having Marijuana; Autoist Arrested," *Albuquerque Journal*, April 30, 1928.

144. Carrigan and Webb, *Forgotten Dead*, 160–61; Tórrez, *Myth of the Hanging Tree*, 9–10; Carrigan and Webb, "A Dangerous Experiment."

145. "Benavides Lynched at Farmington," *Santa Fe New Mexican*, November 16, 1928; "'Judge Lynch' Law Takes Life at Farmington," *Santa Fe New Mexican*, November 17, 1928; "Farmington Lynchers Are Sought," *Albuquerque Journal*, November 17, 1928; "N.M. Lynchers Got Right," *Carlsbad Current-Argus*, November 23, 1928.

146. "Booze Cleanup at Farmington, Aztec, Ordered by the Court," *Albuquerque Journal*, December 5, 1928; "Grand Jury Can't Find Lynchers," *Albuquerque Journal*, December 6, 1928; "New Bills," *Santa Fe New Mexican*, February 9, 1929.

147. See Schweninger, *Families in Crisis in the Old South*, 106; Taylor, *Negro Slavery in Arkansas*, 211–17; Jordan, *Tumult and Silence at Second Creek*, 41.

148. Maria de Jesus Jimenez Serrano, "Immigration of the Domingo Serrano Family, Ameca, Jalisco, Mexico to Houston, Texas, 1920's–1930's," interview by Isabel S. Perales.

149. Maria de Jesus Jimenez Serrano, "Immigration of the Domingo Serrano Family, Ameca, Jalisco, Mexico to Houston, Texas, 1920's–1930's," interview by Isabel S. Perales.

150. Special thanks to Dr. John K. Bardes for helping me understand the history of plantation policing and jailhouses. For information on this practice in Texas, see the Federal Writers' Project, *Slave Narrative*.

151. Meeting of the Board of Penitentiary Commissioners, April 22, 1931, "Speeches, Petitions, Reports," Governor Arthur Seligman Papers, NMSRCA.

152. Meeting of the Board of Penitentiary Commissioners, October 9, 1931, "Speeches, Petitions, Reports," Governor Arthur Seligman Papers, NMSRCA.

153. See, for example, Perkinson, *Texas Tough*; Hinton, *From the War on Poverty to the War on Crime*; Alexander, *The New Jim Crow*.

154. Meeting of the Board of Penitentiary Commissioners, August 19, 1932, "Speeches, Petitions, Reports," Governor Arthur Seligman Papers, NMSRCA.

155. Meeting of the Board of Penitentiary Commissioners, April 22, 1931, "Speeches, Petitions, Reports," Governor Arthur Seligman Papers, NMSRCA.

156. Meeting of the Board of Penitentiary Commissioners, June 17–18, 1931, "Speeches, Petitions, Reports," Governor Arthur Seligman Papers, NMSRCA.

157. Meeting of the Board of Penitentiary Commissioners, August 19, 1932, "Speeches, Petitions, Reports," Governor Arthur Seligman Papers, NMSRCA.

158. Meeting of the Board of Penitentiary Commissioners, June 17–18, 1931, "Speeches, Petitions, Reports," Governor Arthur Seligman Papers, NMSRCA.

159. Hernández, *City of Inmates*, 138–40.

160. "More Money to Justice," *Santa Fe New Mexican*, January 22, 1930; "Federal Prison Plans Outlined," *Los Angeles Times*, May 26, 1930; "Federal Prison Plans Speeded," *Los Angeles Times*, March 22, 1931.

161. Hernández, *City of Inmates*, 145–46.

162. Hernández, *City of Inmates*, 148–49.

163. Balderrama and Rodriguez, *Decade of Betrayal*, 74–75.

164. Balderrama and Rodriguez, *Decade of Betrayal*, 71.

165. Balderrama and Rodriguez, *Decade of Betrayal*, 71–75.

166. Balderrama and Rodriguez, *Decade of Betrayal*, 330. The exact number of people deported is unknown.

CONCLUSION

1. "Speech to the Rio Grande Conservancy District," n.d., Goddard Collection of Elfego Baca Papers, UNM.

Bibliography

MANUSCRIPT AND ARCHIVAL COLLECTIONS

Arizona
  Phoenix
    Arizona State Library Archives
      Maricopa County, Phoenix Precinct, Criminal Docket, 6–12/1885
      Maricopa County, Phoenix Precinct, Criminal Docket, 12/14/1885–12/30/1886
      Maricopa County, Phoenix Precinct, Criminal Docket, 1893–1895
      Secretary of the Territory Papers, 1864–1912
      Secretary of the Territory Papers, 1865–1901
      Secretary of the Territory Papers, 1866–1899
      Secretary of the Territory Papers, 1866–1902
      Secretary of the Territory Papers, 1873–1901
      Secretary of the Territory Papers, 1877–1902
      Secretary of the Territory Papers, 1886–1892
      Tombstone Courthouse, Justice Court Register of Actions, 1889–1893
      Tombstone Courthouse, Justice Court Register of Actions, 1893–1898

California
   San Diego
      Special Collections and Archives, University of California, San Diego
         Roberto Martinez Papers
   San Marino
      Huntington Library
         Bell (Horace) Collection
         Edward J. Long, Daily Report manuscript
         James Franklin Burns Reminiscences Folder
         Los Angeles Area Court Records, Criminal
         Murrieta Family Materials, 1848–1990

New Mexico
   Albuquerque
      Center for Southwest Research and Special Collections, University of New Mexico
         Emma Moya Collection
         Gloria Montoya Chavez Papers
         Goddard Collection of Elfego Baca Papers
         Santa Fe, New Mexico Records, 1822–1934
         Spiegelberg, Flora Papers, 1919–1939
      Special Collections Library, Albuquerque and Bernalillo County Public Library
         Bio—Baca, Elfego Folder
         Bio—Chavez, Dennis A. (policeman) Folder
         City Clerk Scrapbooks
         Clipping Files
   Santa Fe
      Fray Angélico Chávez History Library
         Clipping Files
         Mauro Montoya Collection
         Phillip J. Rasch Collection
         WPA New Mexico Collection
      New Mexico State Records Center and Archives
         Benjamin M. Read Collection
         Donald Cline Collection
         Edward L. Bartlett Papers
         Governor Arthur Seligman Papers
         Governor Octaviano A. Larrazolo Papers
         History Files, folders no. 158–70
         Justice of the Peace Criminal Docket Book (1893–1894),
            Doña Ana County Records
         Laughlin, N. B. Collection
         Lucien A. File Papers
         Maria G. Duran Collection
         Santa Fe County Records, Justice of the Peace
      Territorial Archives of New Mexico (microfilm)
         Arrests and Investigations, Roll 93
         Arrest Book, June 21, 1907–January 5, 1912, Roll 93

    Campaign Against Outlaws in Rio Arriba County, 1881 Papers, Roll 73
    David Meriwether, 1853–1857 Papers, Roll 98
    Donaciano Vigil, 1847–1848 Papers, Roll 98
    Henry Connelly, 1861–1866 Papers, Roll 98
    James S. Calhoun, 1851–1852 Papers, Roll 98
    L. Bradford Prince, 1889–1893 Papers, Roll 121
    Robert B. Mitchell, 1866–1869 Papers, Roll 98
    Special Investigation Case Files, Roll 93
    Stephen Watts Kearny, 1846 Papers, Roll 98
    William Carr Lane, 1852–1853 Papers, Roll 98

Texas
  Arlington
    Special Collections, University of Texas, Arlington
      Criminal Docket, Tarrant County Court, 1876–79
      Sheriff Acct. Bk. 1876–1885
      Tarrant County Criminal Minutes, County Court, 1886–1887
      Tarrant County Criminal Minutes, County Court, 1893–1895
      Tarrant County Criminal Minutes, County Court, 1902–1909
      Tarrant County—List of Convicts—1905–1907
  Austin
    Austin History Center, Austin Public Library
      AR Record of Arrests, June 1885–May 1891 (logbook)
      Camacho Family Papers
      Clipping Files
      Record of Arrests, January 1, 1876, to January 1, 1879 (logbook)
    Dolph Briscoe Center for American History, University of Texas at Austin
      Jesse Perez Reminiscences, 1870–1927
  Dallas
    Texas/Dallas History and Archives Division, Dallas Public Library
      Calaboose Logbook
      Dallas City Jail Records
      Dallas Police Archives
      Wanted Persons Letters from Other Cities to Dallas, 1910–1912
      Wanted Posters and Bulletins, 1913–1914
  San Antonio
    Texana/Genealogy Collection, San Antonio Public Library
      Clipping Files
      Police Department Vertical File
    San Antonio Municipal Archives and Records
      37th District Court Case Files
      Recorder's Court Docket, San Antonio, Texas
      San Antonio Corporation Court Docket, 1914
      San Antonio Corporation Court Docket, 1920
      San Antonio Corporation Court Docket, 1924
      San Antonio Corporation Court Docket, March 1902–1903
      San Antonio Corporation Court Docket, November 25, 1915–February 7, 1916

COURT CASES

United States
- U.S. District Court for the New Mexico Territory, First Judicial District, Taos and Santa Fe (military tribunal)
  - *United States v. Antonio Maria Trujillo*, Sentence of the Court, March 16, 1847.
  - *United States v. Antonio Maria Trujillo*, True Bill, March 1847.
  - *United States v. Antonio Ma Trujillo*, treason, March 9, 1847.
  - *United States v. Archuleta*, nolle prosequi, May 3, 1847.
  - *United States v. Archuleta*, plea, March 13, 1847.
  - *United States v. Barcelo*, nolle prosequi, March 24, 1847.
  - *United States v. Barcelo*, plea, March 13, 1847.
  - *United States v. Pantaleon Archuleta*, treason, March 11, 1847.
  - *United States v. Trinidad Barcelo*, treason, March 10, 1847.
  - *United States v. Trujillo*, plea, March 12, 1847.
  - *United States v. Trujillo*, appeal, March 1847.
  - *United States v. Trujillo*, verdict, March 15, 1847.
  - *United States v. Vigil*, indictment, March 17, 1847.
  - *United States v. Vigil*, plea, March 22, 1847.
  - *United States v. Vigil*, nolle prosequi, May 3, 1847.
- United States Supreme Court
  - *United States v. Wheeler*, 254 U.S. 281 (1920).

Arizona
- District Court, Third Judicial District, County of Yavapai
  - *Territory of Arizona versus Martin Duran*, trial transcript, November 14, 1887.
- Justice's Court, Maricopa County, Phoenix Precinct
  - *The People of the Territory of Arizona vs. Guadalupe Corrales*, Case no. 89, May 31, 1894.
  - *The People of the Territory of Arizona vs. Luz Miranda*, Case no. 108, August 14, 1893.
  - *The People of the Territory of Arizona vs. Manuela Cruz*, Case no. 1, January 23, 1893.
  - *The People of the Territory of Arizona vs. Manuela Pesquiera*, Case no. 109, August 14, 1893.
  - *Territory of Arizona v. Francisco Yanez*, Case no. 71, August 11, 1885.
  - *Territory of Arizona v. John Doe*, Case no. 61, July 20, 1885.
  - *Territory of Arizona v. John Doe, Tiburcio Ruiz*, Case no. 247, July 14, 1886.
  - *Territory of Arizona v. John Doe, a Mexican*, Case no. 175, March 16, 1886.
- Tombstone Courthouse, Justice Court of Register Actions
  - *Territory of Arizona v. John Doe (a Mexican)*, July 24, 1892.
  - *Territory of Arizona v. John Doe Mex.* (aka Ferdinand Rivera), April 30, 1893.
  - *Territory of Arizona v. John Doe Mex.* (aka Refugio Bernal), April 30, 1893.
  - *Territory of Arizona v. John Doe—Mexican, true name unknown*, May 8, 1895.
  - *Territory of Arizona v. John Doe unknown Mexican*, February 12, 1893.

California
- Court of Sessions, Los Angeles County
  - *People vs. Antonio Garcia*, Case no. 536½, February 28, 1861.
  - *People vs. Epifano Valdez*, Case no. 670, January 18, 1864.

      People vs. Gabriel Rodriguez, Case no. 632, August 17, 1863.
      People vs. Jose Machado, Case no. 565, November 13, 1861.
      The People vs. Juan N. Padilla, Case no. 343, motion
          to set aside indictment, March 4, 1861.
      People vs. Juan N. Padilla, Case no. 537, March 6, 1861.
      People vs. Mariano Villa, Case no. 563, nolle prosequi, November 7, 1861.
      People vs. Polonia Acosta and Josefa Ybarra, Case no. 568, November 16, 1861.
      People vs. Serrapio Navarro, Ramon Navarro, and Jesus Lopez,
          Case no. 561, nolle prosequi, November 7, 1861.
   District Court, Los Angeles County
      People vs. Vicente Ochoa, Case no. 557, nolle prosequi, August 24, 1861.
   Justice Court, Los Angeles County
      People vs. Isabella Esquerer, Case no. 604, October 15, 1862.
      People vs. Ramon Carrillo, Case no. 622, April 13, 1863.
New Mexico
   Court of the Police Magistrate, Santa Fe
      La Ciudad de Santa Fe vs. Nicolas Maes, Case no. 676, March 8, 1909.
   District Court, Bernalillo County
      Territory v. Elfego Baca, Case no. 526, grand jury indictment, March 23, 1885.
   District Court, Socorro County
      Territory v. Elfego Baca, Case no. 694, trial transcript, November 4, 1884.
      Territory v. Elfego Baca, Case no. 743, true bill, March 31, 1885.
   Justice of the Peace Precinct #3, Doña Ana County
      *Territory of New Mexico v. Albino Gomez and Juan
          Benavides*, Case no. 112, October 16, 1893.
      Territory of New Mexico v. Juan Villegas, Case no. 102, October 9, 1893.
      Territory of New Mexico v. Juan Villegas, Case no. 118, October 21, 1893.
   Justice of the Peace, Precinct #4, Santa Fe County
      *Territory of New Mexico vs. Juan Antonio Ortega, Emilio Gutierrez,
          and Cleofas Jimenez*, witness testimony, November 8, 1906.
   Supreme Court of the Territory of New Mexico
      Territory v. Chavez (8 N.M. 528), September 1, 1896.
Texas
   Criminal Court, Tarrant County
      State of Texas v. L. Reno, Case no. 10737, September 23, 1893.
      State of Texas v. L. Reno, Case no. 11334–11338, September 23, 1893.
      State of Texas v. "Mexican Antone," Case no. 3488, April 15, 1886.
      State of Texas v. Raul Orozco, Case no. 37696, September 7, 1909.
   San Antonio Corporation Court
      State of Texas vs. Andres Casteneda, Case no. 515, May 7, 1924.
      State of Texas vs. Isabela Rodriguez, Case no. 3000, December 31, 1915.
      State of Texas vs. Joe Sarromar and Jose Dan Ramon, Case no. 514, May 7, 1924.
      State of Texas vs. Jose Martinez, Case no. 3796, April 25, 1914.
      State of Texas vs. Jose Martinez, Case no. 3800, April 25, 1914.
      State of Texas vs. Maria D. Trevino, Case no. 502, July 19, 1920.
      State of Texas vs. Maria Ruiz, Case no. 2333, December 9, 1915.

  State of Texas vs. mex, Case no. 2245, December 6, 1915.
  State of Texas vs. unknown mex, Case no. 4013, October 14, 1924.
  State of Texas vs. Valentina Puente, Case no. 850, May 15, 1902.
  State of Texas vs. Victor Sanchez, Case no. 516, May 7, 1924.
San Antonio Recorder's Court
  State of Texas vs. Andreas Coy, Jr., Case no. 5115, August 29, 1899
  State of Texas vs. Josephine Gomez, Case no. 6203, November 28, 1899.
  State of Texas vs. Julia Martinez, Case no. 5277, September 11, 1899.
  State of Texas vs. Louisa Garcia, Case no. 5276, September 11, 1899.
  State of Texas vs. Rafael Garza, Case no. 5114, August 29, 1899
  State of Texas vs. Stella Ramirez, Case no. 6202, November 28, 1899.
Texas Court of Criminal Appeals
  Cortez v. State, 69 S.W. 536, 44 Tex. Crim. 169, June 24, 1902.
U.S. 37th District Court, Bexar County
  State of Texas vs. Antonio Bernal, Case no. 21944, August 6, 1913.
  State of Texas vs. Antonio Jesus Lopez, Case no. 19070, November 15, 1908.
  State of Texas vs. Antonio Torres, Case no. 21915, July 2, 1913.
  State of Texas vs. Andres Pena, Case no. 19479, November 1, 1909.
  State of Texas vs. Guillermo Rodriguez, Case no. 19018, September 19, 1908.
  State of Texas vs. Jesus Garcia, Case no. 21679, December 25, 1912.
  State of Texas vs. Juan Gutierrez, Case no. 19503, September 20, 1909.
  State of Texas vs. Louis Ramos, Case no. 18958, September 11, 1908.
  State of Texas vs. P. G. Garza, Case no. 24517, May 7, 1916.

NEWSPAPERS AND MAGAZINES

Abilene (Tex.) Morning News
Abilene (Tex.) Reporter-News
Albuquerque Citizen
Albuquerque Evening Citizen
Albuquerque Evening Democrat
Albuquerque Evening Herald
Albuquerque Journal
Albuquerque Morning Democrat
Albuquerque Morning Journal
Albuquerque Tribune
Albuquerque Weekly Citizen
Albuquerque Weekly Journal
Alpine (Tex.) Avalanche
Annals of Travis County (Austin, Tex.)
Arizona Champion (Flagstaff)
Arizona Citizen (Tucson)
Arizona Daily Star (Tucson)
Arizona Republic (Phoenix)
Arizona Republican (Phoenix)
Arizona Sentinel (Yuma)
Arizona Silver Belt (Globe)
Arizona Weekly Champion (Flagstaff)
Arizona Weekly Citizen (Tucson)
Arizona Weekly Journal-Miner (Prescott)
Arizona Weekly Republican (Phoenix)
Austin American
Austin American Statesman
Austin Daily Statesman
Austin Statesman
Austin Weekly Statesman
Bisbee Daily Review (Bisbee, Ariz.)
Borger (Tex.) Daily Herald
Breckenridge (Tex.) Daily News
Brownsville (Tex.) Herald
Brownwood (Tex.) Bulletin
Carlsbad (N.Mex.) Current-Argus
Clarksville (Tenn.) Weekly Chronicle
Clifton (Ariz.) Clarion
Corpus Christi (Tex.) Caller
Corpus Christi (Tex.) Caller Times
Corpus Christi (Tex.) Times
Corsicana (Tex.) Daily Sun

Cuero (Tex.) Daily Record
Daily Alta California (San Francisco)
Daily Herald (Chicago)
Daily Herald (Weatherford, Tex.)
Dallas Daily Herald
Dallas Weekly Herald
Democratic Review
Denton (Tex.) Record-Chronicle
Deseret Evening News
    (Salt Lake City, Utah)
El Fronterizo (Tucson, Ariz.)
El Horizonte (Monterrey, Mex.)
El Paso Herald
El Paso Morning Times
El Paso Times
El Regidor (San Antonio)
El Tucsonense (Tucson, Ariz.)
Fort Sumner Review (N.Mex.)
Fort Worth (Tex.) Register
Fort Worth (Tex.) Star-Telegram
Galveston (Tex.) Daily News
Golden West (Freeport, N.Y.)
Houston Daily Post
Houston Post
Jefferson (Tex.) Jimplecute
La Aurora (Santa Fe, N.Mex.)
La Crónica (Mexico City)
La Gaceta de Las Vegas
La Herencia del Norte (Sante Fe)
La Opinión Pública (Albuquerque)
La Prensa (San Antonio)
Laredo (Tex.) Weekly Times
La Revista Popular de Nuevo Mexico
    (Taos, N.Mex.)
Las Vegas Daily Optic
Las Vegas Gazette
La Victoria (Raton, N.Mex.)
La Voz del Pueblo (Las Vegas)
Liberty (Tex.) Vindicator
Lockhart (Tex.) Daily Post
Los Angeles Evening Express
Los Angeles Herald
Los Angeles Star
Los Angeles Times
Lubbock (Tex.) Morning Avalanche
Marshall (Tex.) Messenger
Marshall (Tex.) Morning News

Marshall (Tex.) News Messenger
McAllen (Tex.) Daily Press
Mercedes (Tex.) Tribune
Mohave County Miner
    (Mineral Park, Ariz.)
Mountainair (N.Mex.) Independent
Mountain View Telegraph
    (Moriarty, N.Mex.)
New Mexico Independent (Albuquerque)
New Mexican Review
    (Santa Fe, N.Mex.)
New Mexico State Tribune
    (Albuquerque)
New York Herald
Niles National Register (St. Louis, Mo.)
Palestine (Tex.) Daily Herald
Placer Herald (Auburn, Calif.)
Prescott Arizona Miner
Press (Fort Worth, Tex.)
Public Ledger (Philadelphia)
Pueblo (Colo.) Chieftain
Raton (N.Mex.) Daily Range
Refugio (Tex.) Review
Rockdale (Tex.) Reporter
Roswell (N.Mex.) Daily Record
Sacramento Daily Union
Salt Lake City Deseret Evening News
Salt Lake Telegram
Salt Lake Tribune
San Antonio Evening News
San Antonio Express
San Antonio Light
San Benito (Tex.) Light
San Francisco Call
San Francisco Chronicle
San Francisco Daily Examiner
San Francisco Examiner
Santa Fe (N.Mex.) Daily New Mexican
Santa Fe (N.Mex.) New Mexican
Santa Fe (N.Mex.) Weekly New Mexican
Shiner (Tex.) Gazette
Sierra County Advocate
    (Kingston, N.Mex.)
Southwesterner (Columbus, N.Mex.)
Spanish American (Roy, N.Mex.)
State Herald (Mexia, Tex.)
St. Johns (Ariz.) Herald

St. Louis (Mo.) Post-Dispatch
Taylor (Tex.) Daily Press
Temple (Tex.) Daily Telegram
Texas State Gazette (Austin)
Texas State Times (Austin)
Tombstone (Tex.) Daily Epitaph
Tombstone (Tex.) Weekly Epitaph
Tucson (Ariz.) Citizen
Tyler (Tex.) Morning Telegraph
Valencia County News-Bulletin
  (Belen, N.Mex.)
Valley Morning Star (Harlingen, Tex.)
Valley News (Lebanon, N.H.)
Victoria (Tex.) Advocate
Victoria (Tex.) Daily Advocate
Visions of the West Side
  (Rio Rancho, N.Mex.)
Waco News-Tribune
Waxahachie (Tex.) Daily Light
Weekly Arizona Miner (Prescott, Ariz.)
Weekly New Mexican Review (Santa Fe)
Wichita (Kans.) Daily Times
Willacy County News
  (Raymondville, Tex.)

GOVERNMENT DOCUMENTS

Mexico

Correspondencia Diplomática Cambiada entre el Gobierno de los Estados Unidos y los de Varias Potencias Extranjeras. Mexico: Tip. de Gonzalo A. Esteva, 1882.

United States

Executive Documents Printed by the Order of the House of Representatives during the First Session of the Thirty-Sixth Congress, 1859–60. Washington, D.C.: Thomas H. Ford, 1860.
Federal Writers' Project. Slave Narrative: A Folk History of Slavery in the United States from Interviews with Former Slaves, Volume XVI, Texas Narratives Part 1. Washington, D.C.: Library of Congress, 1941. https://memory.loc.gov/mss/mesn/161/161.pdf.
Investigation of Mexican Affairs: Hearing Before a Subcommittee of the Committee on Foreign Relations, United States Senate, Sixty-Sixth Congress. Part 8, Washington, D.C.: Government Printing Office, 1920.
The Pacific Reporter, Volume 45: Containing All the Decisions of the Supreme Courts of California, Kansas, Oregon, Washington, Colorado, Montana, Arizona, Nevada, Idaho, Wyoming, Utah, New Mexico, Oklahoma, and Courts of Appeals of Colorado and Kansas June18–October 1, 1896. St. Paul, Minn.: West Publishing, 1896.
Papers Relating to the Foreign Relations of the United States, Transmitted to Congress, with the Annual Message of the President, December 3, 1888, Part II. Washington, D.C.: Government Printing Office, 1889.
President's Mediation Committee. Report on the Bisbee Deportation. Washington, D.C.: Department of Labor, November 6, 1917.
Texas Frontier Troubles, Report No. 343, House of Representatives. Washington, D.C.: Government Printing Office, 1876.
Treaty of Guadalupe Hidalgo; February 2, 1848. Washington, D.C.: Government Printing Office, 1871. https://avalon.law.yale.edu/19th_century/guadhida.asp#art8.

Arizona

Acts, Resolutions and Memorials of the Fifteenth Legislative Assembly of the Territory of Arizona. Prescott, Ariz.: Office of the Courier, 1889.

Acts, Resolutions and Memorials of the Seventeenth Legislative Assembly of the Territory of Arizona. Phoenix: Herald Book and Job Office, 1893.

The Howell Code, Adopted by the First Legislative Assembly of the Territory, November 1863. Prescott: Office of the Arizona Miner, 1865.

Journals of the Thirteenth Legislative Assembly of the Territory of Arizona, January–March 1865. San Francisco: H. S. Crocker, 1885.

The Revised Statutes of Arizona Territory. Columbia, Mo.: Press of E. W. Stephens, 1901.

California

The Penal Code of California: Enacted in 1872; as Amended in 1881. San Francisco: Sumner Whitney, 1881.

The Penal Code of California: Enacted in 1872; as Amended up to and Including 1905. San Francisco: Bancroft-Whitney, 1906.

Sloat, John D., Commodore. *The Sloat Proclamation*. Monterey, Calif., July 7, 1846. www.militarymuseum.org/Sloat.html.

The Statutes of California Passed at the First Session of the Legislature Began the 15th Day of Dec. 1849, and Ended the 22nd Day of April 1850, at the city of Pueblo de San José. San José: J. Winchester, 1850.

Stockton, Robert F., Commodore. *The Stockton Proclamation*. Los Angeles, August 17, 1846. www.militarymuseum.org/Stockton.html.

Tays, George. "Pio Pico's Correspondence with the Mexican Government, 1846–1848." *California Historical Society Quarterly* 13, no. 2 (June 1, 1934): 99–149.

"Treaty of Cahuenga – January 12, 1847." *US Government Treaties and Reports* 7 (2016). https://digitalcommons.csumb.edu/hornbeck_usa_2_b/7.

New Mexico

Acts of the Legislative Assembly of the Territory of New Mexico, Twenty-First Session. Santa Fe, N.Mex.: Manderfield & Tucker, 1874.

Acts of the Legislative Assembly of the Territory of New Mexico, Thirty-Second Session. Santa Fe: New Mexico Printing Company, 1897.

"Laws for the Government of the Territory of New Mexico; September 22, 1846." *Kearny Code of Law*, Washington, D.C.: Government Printing Office. https://avalon.law.yale.edu/19th_century/kearney.asp.

Laws of the Territory of New Mexico, Passed by the Legislative Assembly, Session of 1858–9. Santa Fe, N.Mex.: A. de Marle, 1859.

New Mexico Territorial Laws, 5th Assembly, 1855–56. Santa Fe, N.Mex.: Santa Fé Weekly Gazette Office, 1856.

Report of the Governor of New Mexico to the Secretary of the Interior for the Years 1882 and 1883. Santa Fe: New Mexico Printing Company, 1884.

Texas

"Constitution of the Republic of Texas." *Constitutions of Texas 1824–1876.* http://tarlton.law.utexas.edu/constitutions/.

Constitution of the Republic of Texas to which Is Prefixed the Declaration of Independence, Made in Convention, March 2, 1836. Washington: Gales and Seaton, 1836.

Early Laws of Texas, General Laws from 1836 to 1879, Relating to Public Lands, Colonial Contracts, Headrights, Pre-emptions, Grants of Land to Railroads and other Corporations, Conveyances, Descent, Distribution, Marital Rights, Registration of Wills, Laws Relating to the Jurisdiction, Powers and Procedures of Courts, and all Other Laws of General Interest, Volume 1, 2, and 3. St. Louis, Mo.: Gilbert Book, 1891.

"Hispanic Beginnings of Dallas: Into the 20th Century, 1850–1976," *Hispanic Beginnings of Dallas Project*, booklet. January 22, 1990.

Journal of the House of Representatives of the Regular Session of the Forty-Fourth Legislature, Regular Session. Austin: Van Boeckmann-Jones, 1935. https://lrl.texas.gov/scanned/Housejournals/44/H_44_0.pdf.

Journal of the House of Representatives of the Regular Session of the Thirty-Eighth Legislature. Austin: Van Boeckmann-Jones, 1923. https://lrl.texas.gov/scanned/Housejournals/38/H_38_0.pdf.

Journal of the House of Representatives of the Regular Session of the Thirty-Ninth Legislature. Austin: Van Boeckmann-Jones, 1925. https://lrl.texas.gov/scanned/Housejournals/39/H_39_0.pdf.

Journal of the House of Representatives of the Regular Session of the Thirty-Seventh Legislature. Austin: Van Boeckmann-Jones, 1921. https://lrl.texas.gov/scanned/Housejournals/37/H_37_0.pdf.

Journal of the House of Representatives of the Regular Session of the Thirty-Sixth Legislature. Austin: Van Boeckmann-Jones, 1919. https://lrl.texas.gov/scanned/Housejournals/36/H_36_0.pdf.

Journal of the House of Representatives of the Third Called Session of the Thirty-Eighth Legislature. Austin: Van Boeckmann-Jones, 1923. https://lrl.texas.gov/scanned/Housejournals/38/H_38_3.pdf.

Journal of the Senate, State of Texas, Regular Session, Thirty-Sixth Legislature. Austin: A. C. Baldwin & Sons, 1919. https://lrl.texas.gov/scanned/Senatejournals/36/S_36_0.pdf.

The Laws of Texas, 1822–1897. Austin: Gammel Book, 1898.

The Penal Code of the State of Texas, Adopted by the Sixth Legislature. Galveston: Printed by the News Office, 1857.

Proceedings of the Joint Committee of the Senate and the House in the Investigation of the Texas State Ranger Force, Volume I. February 5, 1919, Adjutant General Records.

Proceedings of the Joint Committee of the Senate and the House in the Investigation of the Texas State Ranger Force, Volume II. February 5, 1919, Adjutant General Records.

The Texas Criminal Reports: Cases Argued and Adjudged in the Court of Criminal Appeals of the State of Texas during Austin Term 1909, Volume 56. Chicago: T. H. Flood, 1909.

Treaty of Velasco (private). May 14, 1836. www.tsl.texas.gov/treasures/republic/velasco-private-1.html.

Treaty of Velasco (public). May 14, 1836. www.tsl.state.tx.us/treasures/republic/velasco-public-3.html.

ORAL HISTORIES

Baca, Elfego. "Interview with Elfego Baca." By Janet Smith. New Mexico, Folklore Project, Life Histories, 1936–39, July 13, 1936. www.loc.gov/item/wpalh001292/.

Heacock, Mrs. William C. "Interview with Mrs. William C. Heacock." By Janet Smith. New Mexico, Folklore Project, Life Histories, 1936–39. www.loc.gov/item/wpalh001300/.

Serrano, Maria de Jesus Jimenez. "Immigration of the Domingo Serrano Family, Ameca, Jalisco, Mexico to Houston, Texas, 1920's–1930's." By Isabel S. Perales. Houston, Houston Metropolitan Research Center, April 1981.

PUBLISHED HISTORICAL DOCUMENTS AND BOOKS

Anderson, George B. *History of New Mexico: Its Resources and People, Volume 1.* Los Angeles: Pacific States, 1907.

Cook, James H. *Fifty Years on the Old Frontier: As Cowboy, Hunter, Guide, Scout, and Ranchman.* New Haven, Conn.: Yale University Press, 1923.

Crichton, Kyle S. *Law and Order, Ltd.: The Life of Elfego Baca.* Santa Fe, N.Mex.: Santa Fe New Mexican Publishing Corporation, 1928.

de Baca, Manuel C. *Historia de Vincente Silva sus Cuarenta Bandidos, sus Crimenes y Retribuciones.* Las Vegas, N.Mex.: Imprenta La Voz del Pueblo, 1896.

Gallagher, Bertrand E. *Utah's Greatest Manhunt: The True Story of the Hunt for Lopez.* Salt Lake City: F. W. Gardner, 1913.

Hertzog, Peter. *A Directory of New Mexico Desperados.* Santa Fe, N.Mex.: Press of the Territorian, 1965.

Paine, Albert Bigelow. *Captain Bill McDonald, Texas Ranger: A Story of Frontier Reform.* New York: J. J. Little & Ives, 1909.

Perales, Alonso S. *En Defensa de mi Raza.* San Antonio: Artes Gráficas, 1936.

Perales, Alonso. S. *"Juan N. Cortina, Bandit or Patriot?" an Address by J. T. Canales before the Lower Rio Grande Valley Historical Society, San Benito, TX, October 25, 1951.* San Antonio: Artes Gráficas, 1951.

Rickard, Thomas Arthur. *The Utah Copper Enterprise.* San Francisco: Abbott Press, 1919.

Ridge, John Rollin. *Life and Adventures of Joaquin Murieta: Celebrated California Bandit.* Norman: University of Oklahoma Press, 1955.

Ridge, John Rollin. *The Lives of Joaquin Murieta and Tiburcio Vasquez: The California Highwaymen.* San Francisco: F. MacCrellish, 1874.

Siringo, Charles A. *A Cowboy Detective: A True Story of Twenty-Two Years with a World Famous Detective Agency.* Chicago: W. B. Conkey, 1912.

Sumpter, Jesse. "Life of Jesse Sumpter: The Oldest Citizen of Eagle Pass, Texas." Unpublished manuscript, commenced to be written, May 30, 1902. Corrected copy.

Taylor, Paul S. *An American-Mexican Frontier: Nueces County, Texas.* Chapel Hill: University of North Carolina Press, 1934.

Twitchell, Ralph Emerson. *The History of the Military Occupation of the Territory of New Mexico from 1846 to 1851 by the Government of the United States Together with Biographical Sketches of Men Prominent in the Conduct of the Government during that Period.* Denver: Smith-Brooks, 1909.

INTERNET RESOURCES

"Babies behind Bars." CWLA. Accessed March 20, 2022. www.cwla.org/babies-behind-bars/.

Blake, Robert Bruce. "Córdova, Vicente (1798–1842)." *Handbook of Texas* (online). Updated September 9, 2020. www.tsha.utexas.edu/handbook/online/articles/CC/fco71.html.

Boardman, Mark. "The First Lincoln County War." *True West*. March 1, 2014. https://truewestmagazine.com/the-first-lincoln-county-war/.

Correia, David. "Las Gorras Blancas of San Miguel County." New Mexico History. 2020. http://newmexicohistory.org/people/las-gorras-blancas-of-san-miguel-county.

Groves, Melody. "Jerked to Jesus: Albuquerque's First Town Marshall Met His Maker on an Unusual Gallows." *True West*. November 17, 2017. https://truewestmagazine.com/jerked-old-west-outlaw/.

Gurza, Agustín. "The Mexican Corrido: Ballads of Adversity and Rebellion, Part 1: Defining the Genre." The Strachwitz Frontera Collection of Mexican and Mexican American Recordings. November 2, 2017. http://frontera.library.ucla.edu/blog/2017/11/mexican-corrido-ballads-adversity-and-rebellion-part-1-defining-genre.

Gurza, Agustín. "The Mexican Corrido: Ballads of Adversity and Rebellion, Part 2: Border Bandits or Folk Heroes." The Strachwitz Frontera Collection of Mexican and Mexican American Recordings. November 9, 2017. https://frontera.library.ucla.edu/blog/2017/11/mexican-corrido-ballads-adversity-and-rebellion-part-2-border-bandits-or-folk-heroes.

Gurza, Agustín. "The Mexican Corrido: Ballads of Adversity and Rebellion, Part 3: Two-Part Corridos." The Strachwitz Frontera Collection of Mexican and Mexican American Recordings. November 30, 2017. https://frontera.library.ucla.edu/blog/2017/11/mexican-corrido-ballads-adversity-and-rebellion-part-3-two-part-corridos.

Gurza, Agustín. "The Mexican Corrido: Ballads of Adversity and Rebellion, Part 4: Corridos of the Mexican Revolution." The Strachwitz Frontera Collection of Mexican and Mexican American Recordings. December 13, 2017. https://frontera.library.ucla.edu/blog/2017/12/mexican-corrido-ballads-adversity-and-rebellion-part-4-corridos-mexican-revolution.

Gutiérrez, Ramón A. "Mexican Immigration to the United States." *Oxford Research Encyclopedias, American History*. July 29, 2019. https://oxfordre.com/americanhistory/view/10.1093/acrefore/9780199329175.001.0001/acrefore-9780199329175-e-146.

"History of El Paso, Texas." El Paso County Sheriff's Office. Accessed March 20, 2022. www.epcounty.com/sheriff/history.htm.

Hurst, James W. "Jose Chavez y Chavez: Outlaw – Hombre Muy Malo," DesertUSA. Accessed March 20, 2022. www.desertusa.com/desert-people/chavez.html.

"Intimate Partner Homicide." *National Institute of Justice Journal* 250 (November 2003). www.ncjrs.gov/pdffiles1/jr000250.pdf.

Jones, Adam James. "New Mexico Massacre: The Taos Rebellion." *Adam James Jones* (blog). February 8, 2012. https://adamjamesjones.wordpress.com/2012/02/08/new-mexico-massacre-the-taos-revolt/.

"John O'Sullivan Declares America's Manifest Destiny, 1845." The American Yawp Reader. Accessed March 20, 2022. www.americanyawp.com/reader/manifest-destiny/john-osullivan-declares-americas-manifest-destiny-1845/.

Kirby, Robert. "Kirby: Remembering the Worst Day in Utah Law Enforcement." *Salt Lake Tribune* (Salt Lake City). November 20, 2013. http://archive.sltrib.com/article.php?id=57148093&itype=cmsid.

Krazmien, Mindy M. "Gold-Rush Era Prostitutes." FoundSF. Accessed March 20, 2022. www.foundsf.org/index.php?title=Gold-Rush_Era_Prostitutes.

"'A Little Standing Army in Himself': N. A. Jennings Tells of the Texas Rangers, 1875." History Matters. The U.S. Survey Course on the Web. Accessed March 20, 2022. http://historymatters.gmu.edu/d/6534/.

Moffitt, Mike. "Weighing August Vollmer's Tarnished Legacy: Should His Name Be Scrubbed from Peak." SFGATE.com, September 25, 2020. www.sfgate.com/bayarea/article/Berkeley-Vollmer-Peak-police-chief-eugenics-15597927.php.

Orozco, Cynthia E. "The Nuecestown Raid of 1875." *Handbook of Texas* (online). Updated August 3, 2020. www.tshaonline.org/handbook/online/articles/jcnnt.

Parra, Alvaro. "Tomás A. Sanchez: The Californio Sheriff of Los Angeles." KCET (online). August 22, 2013. www.kcet.org/shows/departures/tomas-a-sanchez-the-californio-sheriff-of-los-angeles.

"Plan de San Diego." San Diego, Tex. January 16, 1915. www.digitalhistory.uh.edu/disp_textbook.cfm?smtID=3&psid=3692.

Rescola, Bob, and Rusty Heckaman. *Austin Police Department Guide*. Austin: Austin History Center and Austin Public Library, Updated in 2018. https://library.austintexas.gov/library/austin_police_department_subject_guide.pdf.

Thompson, Jerry. "Cortina, Juan Nepomuceno (1824–1894)." *Handbook of Texas* (online). Updated November 2, 2020. www.tshaonline.org/handbook/entries/cortina-juan-nepomuceno.

Tórrez, Robert J. "Rebellion of 1847 Treason Trials." New Mexico History. 2020. http://newmexicohistory.org/people/revolt-of-1847-treason-trials.

———. "A Short History of New Mexico." Accessed August 27, 2019. http://lincolncountycousins.org/1home/5hist.htm (site discontinued).

Trimble, Marshall. "The Legend of Elfego Baca." *True West*. June 5, 2017. https://truewestmagazine.com/legend-elfego-baca/.

———. "Vigilante Committees: San Francisco's 601 Took the Law into Their Own Hands." *True West*. July 2, 2019. https://truewestmagazine.com/vigilante-commitees/.

Underwood, Marylyn. "Rodriguez, Josefa [Chipita] (unknown-1863)." *Handbook of Texas* (online). Updated December 8, 2020. www.tshaonline.org/handbook/online/articles/fro50.

Van Leer, Twila. "Where'd He Go? Killer Was Never Found." *Deseret News* (Salt Lake City). April 18, 1995. www.deseretnews.com/article/416035/WHERED-HE-GO-KILLER-WAS-NEVER-FOUND.html.

Wroth, William H. "1847 Taos Rebellion." New Mexico History. 2020. https://newmexicohistory.org/2013/11/21/1847-taos-rebellion/.

Zakharova, Lisa. "Throwback Thursday: Jack S. Howard." *Sul Ross University Library* (blog). Accessed March 20, 2022. https://athenaeum.sulross.edu/throwback-thursday-jack-s-howard/.

THESES AND DISSERTATIONS

Abney, David Lawrence. "Capital Punishment in Arizona (1863–1963)." Master's thesis, Arizona State University, August 1988.
Chapman, David L. "Lynching in Texas." Master's thesis, Texas Tech University, August 1973.
Guillow, Lawrence E. "The Origins of Race Relations in Los Angeles, 1820s–1880s: A Multi-Ethnic Study." PhD diss., Arizona State University, 1996.
Monticone, Joseph Raymond. "Revolutionary Mexico and the U.S. Southwest: The Columbus Raid." Master's thesis, California State University, Fullerton, 1986.
Paige, Thomas A. "'To Get Their Labor for Nothing': Criminal Courts and Jim Crow in Tarrant County, Texas: 1887–1908." Master's thesis, University of Texas at Arlington, May 2012.
Perez, Aminta Inelda. "Tejano Rangers: The Development and Evolution of Ranging Tradition, 1540–1880," PhD diss., University of Iowa, 2012.
Phelan, Kendall. "The Evolution of Rape Law Reform in the United States." PhD diss., Chicago School of Professional Psychology, 2019.
Powers, Allison. "Settlement Colonialism: Compensatory Justice in United States Expansion, 1903–1941." PhD diss., Columbia University, 2017.
Taylor, Travis. "Lynching on the Border: The Death of Antonio Rodríguez and the Rise of Anti-Americanism during the Mexican Revolution." Master's thesis, Angelo State University, 2012.

ARTICLES AND BOOK CHAPTERS

Bandes, Susan A. "Compassion and the Rule of Law." *International Journal of Law in Context* 13, no. 2 (May 2017): 184–96.
Behnken, Brian D. "Controlling Los Hombres: American State Power and the Emasculation of the Mexican Community, 1845–1900." In *Masculinities and the Nation in the Modern World: Between Hegemony and Marginalization*, edited by Pablo Dominguez Andersen and Simon Wendt, 129–48. New York: Palgrave Macmillan, 2015.
Blew, Robert W. "Vigilantism in Los Angeles, 1835–1874." *Southern California Quarterly* 54, no. 1 (Spring 1972): 11–30.
Brayer, Herbert O. "Could Gunfighters Really Shoot?" *Guns Magazine* 2, nos. 1–13 (January 1956): 1–74.
Carrigan, William, and Clive Webb. "The Lynching of Persons of Mexican Origin or Descent in the United States, 1848 to 1928." *Journal of Social History* 37, no. 2 (Winter 2003): 411–38.
———. "A Dangerous Experiment: The Lynching of Rafael Benavides." *New Mexico Historical Review* 80, no. 3 (June 2005): 265–92.
———. "Mexican Perspectives on Mob Violence in the United States." In *Globalizing Lynching History: Vigilantism and Extralegal Punishment from an International Perspective*, edited by Simon Wendt and Manfred Berg, 53–67. New York: Palgrave Macmillan, 2011.
———. "The Rise and Fall of Mob Violence against Mexicans in Arizona, 1859–1915." In *Lynching Beyond Dixie: American Mob Violence Outside the South*, edited by Michael J. Pfeifer, 110–31. Chicago: University of Illinois Press, 2013.

———. "'This Community Will Not in the Future Be Disgraced': Rafael Benavides and the Decline of Lynching in New Mexico." In *Swift to Wrath: Lynching in Global Historical Perspective*, edited by William D. Carrigan and Christopher Waldrep, 68–96. Charlottesville: University of Virginia Press, 2013.

Correia, David. "'Retribution Will Be Their Reward': New Mexico's Las Gorras Blancas and the Fight for the Las Vegas Land Grant Commons." *Radical History Review* 108 (Fall 2010): 49–72.

Glassburn, Ashley. "Settler Standpoints." *William and Mary Quarterly* 76, no. 3 (July 2019): 399–406.

Goff, John S. "William T. Howell and the Howell Code of Arizona." *American Journal of Legal History* 11, no. 3 (July 1967): 221–33.

Gómez, Laura E. "Race, Colonialism, and Criminal Law: Mexicans and the American Criminal Justice System in Territorial New Mexico." *Law & Society Review* 34, no. 4 (2000): 1129–202.

Graham, C. M. "Have You Ever Heard of the White Caps?" *New Mexico Genealogist* 6 (December 1967): 3–8.

Gratton, Brian, and Emily Klancher Merchant. "An Immigrant's Tale: The Mexican American Southwest 1850 to 1950." *Social Science History* 39, no. 4 (Winter 2015): 521–50.

Haverluk, Terrence. "The Changing Geography of U.S. Hispanics, 1850–1990." *Journal of Geography* 96, no. 3 (August 2007): 134–45.

Herrera, Carlos R. "New Mexico Resistance to U.S. Occupation." In *The Contested Homeland: A Chicano History of New Mexico*, edited by Erlinda Gonzales-Berry and David R. Maciel, 23–42. Albuquerque: University of New Mexico Press, 2000.

Hueston, Jamey, and Miriam Hutchins. "The Power of Compassion in the Court: Healing on Both Sides of the Bench." *Court Review* 54, no. 2 (2018): 96–100.

Hurt, Randolph D. "Determination of the Penalty – By Judge or Jury." *SMU Law Review* 1, no. 1 (1947): 124–36.

Johnson, Benjamin H. "The Plan de San Diego Uprising and the Making of the Modern Texas-Mexican Borderlands." In *Continental Crossroads: Remapping U.S.-Mexico Borderlands History*, edited by Samuel Truett and Elliott Young, 273–98. Durham, N.C.: Duke University Press 2004.

Johnson, Benjamin Heber, and Andrew R. Graybill. "Introduction: Borders and Their Historians in North America." In *Bridging National Borders in North America: Transnational and Comparative Histories*, edited by Benjamin H. Johnson and Andrew R. Graybill, 1–30. Durham, N.C.: Duke University Press, 2020.

Knight, Larry. "The Cart War: Defining American in San Antonio in the 1850s." *Southwestern Historical Quarterly* 109, no. 3 (January 1, 2006): 319–36.

Louzon, David. "Corpus Christi's Galvan Ballroom: Music and Multiculturalism in the 1950s." *Journal of South Texas* 20 (Spring 2007): 213–36.

Loyola, Mary. "The American Occupation of New Mexico, 1821–1852." *New Mexico Historical Review* 14, no. 3 (1939): 143–99.

McBride, James P. "The Liga Protectora Latina: A Mexican-American Benevolent Society in Arizona." *Journal of the West* 14 (October 1975): 82–90.

Mertz, Richard J. "No One Can Arrest Me: The Story of Gregorio Cortez." *Journal of South Texas* 1 (1974): 1–17.

Miles, Tiya. "Beyond a Boundary: Black Lives and the Settler-Native Divide." *William and Mary Quarterly* 76, no. 3 (July 2019): 417–26.

Peck, Gunther. "Divided Loyalties: Immigrant Padrones and the Evolution of Industrial Paternalism in North America." *International Labor and Working-Class History* 53 (Spring 1998): 49–68.

Rasch, Philip J. "A Mention of Jose Chavez y Chavez." *Corral Dust* 5, no. 4 (October 1960): 27–30.

———. "Taking a Closer Look at Cimarron Murders." *National Association and Center for Outlaw Justice and Lawman History* 3, no. 3 (Winter 1977–78): 8–9.

Roberts, Virginia Culin. "'The Women Was Too Tough.'" *Journal of Arizona History* 26, no. 4 (Winter 1985): 395–414.

Romero, Mary. "Class Struggle and Resistance against the Transformation of Land Ownership and Usage in Northern New Mexico: The Case of Las Gorras Blancas." *Chicano-Latino Law Review* 26, no. 1 (2006): 87–110.

Ross, Frank. "The Bad Man of Socorro." *Mankind* 4, no. 4 (December 1973): 53–57.

Rulska, Anna. "Taos Revolt." In *The Encyclopedia of the Mexican-American War: A Political, Social, and Military History, Volume 1*, edited by Spencer C. Tucker, 631. Santa Barbara: ABC-CLIO, 2013.

Sánchez, Rosaura, and Beatrice Pita. "Rethinking Settler Colonialism." *American Quarterly* 66, no. 4 (December 2014): 1039–55.

Shipman, Jack. "The Salt War of San Elizario." *Voice of the Mexican Border* 1, no. 4 (December 1933): 157–64.

———. "The Salt War of San Elizario." *Voice of the Mexican Border* 1, no. 5. (January 1934): 198–215.

Smallwood, Stephanie E. "Reflections on Settler Colonialism, the Hemispheric Americas, and Chattel Slavery." *William and Mary Quarterly* 76, no. 3 (July 2019): 407–16.

Spear, Jennifer M. "Beyond the Native/Settler Divide in Early California." *William and Mary Quarterly* 76, no. 3 (July 2019): 427–34.

Szasz, Ferenc Morton. "A New Mexican 'Davy Crockett': Walt Disney's version of the Life and Legend of Elfego Baca." *Journal of the Southwest* 48, no. 3 (Autumn 2006): 261–74.

Tórrez, Robert J. "Crime and Punishment in Spanish Colonial New Mexico." Research paper no. 34, Center for Land Grant Studies, Guadalupita, N.Mex., May 20, 1990.

———. "A Deceptive Silence." *Round the Roundhouse* February 18–March 18, 2013, 6.

———. "A Ruthless Suppression of the Insurrection." *Round the Roundhouse* March 18–April 15, 2013, 6.

———. "Tragedy at Los Valles." *Round the Roundhouse* April 19–September 16, 2013, 6.

———. "The 'Treason Trials' of 1847." *Round the Roundhouse* April 15–May 13, 2013, 6.

———. "The Trials at Taos." *Round the Roundhouse* May 13–June 24, 2013, 6.

Truett, Samuel. "Settler Colonialism and the Borderlands of Early America." *William and Mary Quarterly* 76, no. 3 (July 2019): 435–42.

Truett, Samuel, and Elliott Young. "Introduction. Making Transnational History: Nations, Regions, and Borderlands." In *Continental Crossroads: Remapping U.S.-Mexico Borderlands History*, edited by Samuel Truett and Elliott Young, 1–34. Durham, N.C.: Duke University Press 2004.

Weiss, Harold J., Jr. "The Texas Rangers Revisited: Old Themes and New Viewpoints." *Southwestern Historical Quarterly* 97, no. 4 (April 1994): 620–40.

Williams, Brie A., Rebecca L. Sudore, Robert Greifinger, and R. Sean Morrison. "Balancing Punishment and Compassion for Seriously Ill Prisoners." *Annals of Internal Medicine* 155, no. 2 (July 2011): 122–26.

Wolfe, Patrick. "Settler Colonialism and the Elimination of the Native." *Journal of Genocide Research* 8, no. 4 (2006): 387–409.
Woods, Clee. "Señor Americano." *True: The Man's Magazine* 18, no. 105 (February 1946): 60–75.
Zarbin, Earl. "Henry Garfias: Phoenix's First City Marshal." *Journal of Arizona History* 46, no. 1 (Spring 2005): 55–70.

BOOKS

Allen, O. Fisher. *The City of Houston from Wilderness to Wonder*. Temple, Tex.: self-published, 1936.
Alexander, Michelle. *The New Jim Crow: Mass Incarceration in the Age of Colorblindness*. New York: New Press, 2020.
Anderson, Gary Clayton. *Ethnic Cleansing and the Indian: The Crime That Should Haunt America*. Norman: University of Oklahoma Press, 2014.
Anderson, Parker. *Arizona Gold Gangster Charles P. Stanton: Truth & Legend in Yavapai's Dark Days*. Charleston: History Press, 2020.
Baker, Pascale. *Revolutionaries, Rebels and Robbers: The Golden Age of Banditry in Mexico, Latin America and the Chicano American Southwest, 1850–1950*. Cardiff: University of Wales Press, 2016.
Balderrama, Francisco E., and Raymond Rodriguez. *Decade of Betrayal: Mexican Repatriation in the 1930s*. Albuquerque: University of New Mexico Press, 2006.
Ball, Larry D. *The United States Marshals of New Mexico and Arizona Territories, 1846–1912*. Albuquerque: University of New Mexico Press, 1978.
———. *Elfego Baca in Life and Legend*. El Paso: Texas Western Press, 1992.
———. *Desert Lawmen: The High Sheriffs of the New Mexico and Arizona Territories, 1846–1912*. Albuquerque: University of New Mexico Press, 1992.
Bancroft, Hubert Howe. *History of Arizona and New Mexico, 1530–1888*. Albuquerque: Horn and Wallace, 1962.
Bauer, Karl Jack. *The Mexican War, 1846–1848*. Lincoln: University of Nebraska Press, 1974.
Baumgartner, Alice L. *South to Freedom: Runaway Slaves to Mexico and the Road to the Civil War*. New York: Basic Books, 2020.
Behnken, Brian D. *Fighting Their Own Battles: Mexican Americans, African Americans, and the Struggle for Civil Rights Movement in Texas*. Chapel Hill: University of North Carolina Press, 2011.
Behnken, Brian D., and Gregory D. Smithers. *Racism in American Popular Media: From Aunt Jemima to the Frito Bandito*. Santa Barbara, Calif.: Praeger, 2015.
Behnken, Brian D., and Simon Wendt, eds. *Crossing Boundaries: Ethnicity, Race, and National Belonging in a Transnational World*. Lanham, Md.: Lexington Books, 2013.
Benton-Cohen, Katherine. *Borderline Americans: Racial Divisions and Labor War in the Arizona Borderlands*. Cambridge, Mass.: Harvard University Press, 2009.
Berg, Manfred. *Popular Justice: A History of Lynching in America*. Lanham, Md.: Ivan R. Dee, 2011.
Beyreis, David C. *Blood in the Borderlands: Conflict, Kinship, and the Bent Family, 1821–1920*. Lincoln: University of Nebraska Press, 2020.
Blackhawk, Ned. *Violence over the Land: Indians and Empires in the Early American West*. Cambridge, Mass.: Harvard University Press, 2008.

Boessenecker, John. *Gold Dust and Gunsmoke: Tales of Gold Rush Outlaws, Gunfighters, Lawmen, and Vigilantes.* New York: Wiley, 2000.

———. *Bandido: The Life and Times of Tiburcio Vasquez.* Norman: University of Oklahoma Press, 2010.

———. *Texas Ranger: The Epic Life of Frank Hamer, the Man Who Killed Bonnie and Clyde.* New York: Thomas Dunne Books, 2016.

———. *When Law Was in the Holster: The Frontier Life of Bob Paul.* Norman: University of Oklahoma Press, 2018.

Brundage, W. Fitzhugh. *Lynching in the New South: Lynching in Georgia and Virginia, 1880–1930.* Chicago: University of Illinois Press, 1993.

Bryan, Howard. *Albuquerque Remembered.* Albuquerque: University of New Mexico Press, 2006.

Butler, Anne M. *Daughters of Joy, Sisters of Misery: Prostitutes in the American West, 1865–90.* Chicago: University of Illinois Press, 1985.

———. *Gendered Justice in the American West: Women Prisoners in Men's Penitentiaries.* Chicago: University of Illinois Press, 1997.

Byrkit, James W. *Forging the Copper Collar: Arizona's Labor-Management War of 1901–1921.* Tucson: University of Arizona Press, 1982.

Caffey, David L. *Chasing the Santa Fe Ring: Power and Privilege in Territorial New Mexico.* Albuquerque: University of New Mexico Press, 2014.

Caldwell, Clifford R. *Dead Right: The Lincoln County War.* Self-published, 2010.

Caldwell, Clifford R., and Ron DeLord. *Eternity at the End of a Rope: Executions, Lynchings and Vigilante Justice in Texas, 1819–1923.* Santa Fe, N.Mex.: Sunstone Press, 2015.

Campbell, Randolph B. *An Empire for Slavery: The Peculiar Institution in Texas, 1821–1865.* Baton Rouge: Louisiana State University Press, 1989.

Campney, Brent M. S. *This Is Not Dixie: Racist Violence in Kansas, 1861–1927.* Chicago: University of Illinois Press, 2015.

———. *Hostile Heartland: Racism, Repression, and Resistance in the Midwest.* Chicago: University of Illinois Press, 2019.

Cardoso, Lawrence. *Mexican Emigration to the United States, 1897–1931.* Tucson: University of Arizona Press, 1980.

Carrigan, William D., and Clive Webb. *Forgotten Dead: Mob Violence against Mexicans in the United States, 1848–1928.* New York: Oxford University Press, 2017.

Castro, Rafaela G. *Chicano Folklore: A Guide to the Folktales, Traditions, Rituals and Religious Practices of Mexican-Americans.* New York: Oxford University Press, 2000.

Chadwick, Bruce. *Law & Disorder: The Chaotic Birth of the NYPD.* New York: Thomas Dunne Books, 2017.

Chávez, Ernesto. *The U.S. War with Mexico: A Brief History with Documents.* New York: Bedford/St. Martins, 2008.

Chesney-Lind, Meda, and Lisa Pasko. *The Female Offender: Girls, Women, and Crime.* Los Angeles: Sage, 2013.

Cool, Paul. *Salt Warriors: Insurgency on the Rio Grande.* College Station: Texas A&M University Press, 2008.

Cooper, Jonathan A. *Twentieth-Century Influences on Twenty-First-Century Policing: Continued Lessons of Police Reform.* Lanham, Md.: Lexington Books, 2015.

Correia, David. *Properties of Violence: Law and Land Grant Struggle in Northern New Mexico.* Athens: University of Georgia Press, 2013.

Cox, Mike. *Time of the Rangers: From 1900 to the Present*. New York: Forge, 2009.
Crongeyer, Sven. *Six Gun Sound: The Early History of the Los Angeles County Sheriff's Department*. Fresno, Calif.: Craven Street Books, 2006.
de Aragón, Ray John. *New Mexico in the Mexican American War*. Charleston: History Press, 2019.
DeArment, Robert K. *Deadly Dozen: Twelve Forgotten Gunfighters of the Old West, Volume 1*. Norman: University of Oklahoma Press, 2003.
de la Teja, Jesús F., ed. *A Revolution Remembered: The Memoirs and Selected Correspondence of Juan N. Seguín*. Austin: State House Press, 1991.
DeLay, Brian. *War of a Thousand Deserts: Indian Raids and the U.S.-Mexican War*. New Haven, Conn.: Yale University Press, 2008.
De León, Arnoldo. *They Called Them Greasers: Anglo Attitudes Toward Mexicans in Texas, 1821–1900*. Austin: University of Texas Press, 1983.
———. *Ethnicity in the Sunbelt: A History of Mexican-Americans in Houston*. College Station: Texas A&M University Press, 2001.
DeSoucy, M. David. *Arizona Rangers*. Charleston: Arcadia Publishing, 2008.
Deverell, William. *Whitewashed Adobe: The Rise of Los Angeles and the Remaking of Its Mexican Past*. Los Angeles: University of California Press, 2005.
Dunbar-Ortiz, Roxanne. *Not "a Nation of Immigrants": Settler Colonialism, White Supremacy, and a History of Erasure and Exclusion*. New York: Beacon Press, 2021.
Escobar, Edward J. *Race, Police, and the Making of a Political Identity: Mexican Americans and the Los Angeles Police Department, 1900–1945*. Los Angeles: University of California Press, 1999.
Eustis, Robert, and Katharine M. Morsberger. *Lew Wallace: Militant Romantic*. New York: McGraw Hill, 1980.
Faragher, John Mack. *Eternity Street: Violence and Justice in Frontier Los Angeles*. New York: W. W. Norton, 2016.
Feagin, Joe R., and José A. Cobas. *Latinos Facing Racism: Discrimination, Resistance, and Endurance*. New York: Routledge, 2014.
Foley, Neil. *The White Scourge: Mexicans, Blacks, and Poor Whites in Texas Cotton Culture*. Berkeley: University of California Press, 1997.
Frantzen, Durant, and Marshall B. Lloyd. *Texas's Criminal Justice System*. Durham, N.C.: Carolina Academic Press, 2018.
Fulton, Maurice Garland. *History of the Lincoln County War*. Edited by Robert N. Mullin. Tucson: University of Arizona Press, 2008.
Gardiner, Christine L., and Pamela Fiber-Ostrow, eds. *California's Criminal Justice System*. Durham, N.C.: Carolina Academic Press, 2014.
García, Mario T. *Desert Immigrants: The Mexicans of El Paso, 1880–1920*. New Haven, Conn.: Yale University Press, 1981.
Glasrud, Bruce A., ed. *African American History in New Mexico: Portraits from Five Hundred Years*. Albuquerque: University of New Mexico Press, 2013.
Glasrud, Bruce A., and Harold J. Weiss Jr. *Tracking the Texas Rangers: The Nineteenth Century*. Denton: University of North Texas Press, 2012.
Goldfinch, Charles W., and José T. Canales. *Juan N. Cortina: Two Interpretations*. New York: Arno Press, 1974.
Goldstein, Alyosha, ed. *Formations of United States Colonialism*. Durham, N.C.: Duke University Press, 2014.

Gómez, Laura E. *Manifest Destinies: The Making of the Mexican American Race*. New York: New York University Press, 2018.
Gonzales, Manuel G. *Mexicanos: A History of Mexicans in the United States*. Bloomington: Indiana University Press, 2019.
Gonzales, Phillip B. *Política: Nuevomexicanos and American Political Incorporation, 1821–1910*. Lincoln: University of Nebraska Press, 2016.
Gonzales-Day, Ken. *Lynching in the West, 1850–1935*. Durham, N.C.: Duke University Press, 2006.
González, Gabriela. *Redeeming La Raza: Transborder Modernity, Race, Respectability, and Rights*. New York: Oxford University Press, 2018.
González-Quiroga, Miguel Ángel. *War and Peace on the Rio Grande Frontier, 1830–1880*. Norman: University of Oklahoma Press, 2020.
Grandin, Greg. *The End of the Myth: From the Frontier to the Border Wall in the Mind of America*. New York: Metropolitan Books, 2019.
Graybill, Andrew R. *Policing the Great Plains: Rangers, Mounties, and the North American Frontier, 1875–1910*. Lincoln: University of Nebraska Press, 2007.
Greenberg, Amy S. *A Wicked War: Polk, Clay, Lincoln, and the 1846 U.S. Invasion of Mexico*. New York: Vintage Books, 2012.
Griffin, Denny. *Policing Las Vegas: A History of Law Enforcement in Southern Nevada*. Las Vegas: Huntington Press, 2005.
Griswold del Castillo, Richard. *The Los Angeles Barrio, 1850–1890*. Los Angeles: University of California Press, 1982.
Groves, Melody. *When Outlaws Wore Badges*. Lanham, Md.: TwoDot, 2021.
Guardino, Peter. *The Dead March: A History of the Mexican-American War*. Cambridge, Mass.: Harvard University Press, 2017.
Guidotti-Hernández, Nicole M. *Unspeakable Violence: Remapping U.S. and Mexican National Imaginaries*. Durham, N.C.: Duke University Press, 2011.
Hanchett, Leland J. *Catch the Stage to Phoenix*. Phoenix: Pine Rim Publishing, 1998.
Harlow, Neal. *California Conquered: The Annexation of a Mexican Province, 1846–1850*. Los Angeles: University of California Press, 1982.
Harris, Charles H., III, and Louis R. Sadler. *The Texas Rangers and the Mexican Revolution: The Bloodiest Decade, 1910–1920*. Albuquerque: University of New Mexico Press, 2004.
———. *The Plan de San Diego: Tejano Rebellion, Mexican Intrigue*. Lincoln: University of Nebraska Press, 2013.
———. *The Texas Rangers in Transition: From Gunfighters to Criminal Investigators 1921–1935*. Norman: University of Oklahoma Press, 2019.
Hayes, Alden C. *A Portal to Paradise*. Phoenix: University of Arizona Press, 2000.
Haynes, Sam W., and Gerald D. Saxon, eds. *Contested Empire: Rethinking the Texas Revolution*. College Station: Texas A&M University Press, 2015.
Henderson, Timothy J. *Beyond Borders: A History of Mexican Migration to the United States*. Malden, Mass.: Blackwell, 2011.
Hernández, José Angel, *Mexican American Colonization During the Nineteenth Century: A History of the U.S.-Mexico Borderlands*. New York: Cambridge University Press, 2012.
Hernández, Kelly Lytle. *Migra!: A History of the U.S. Border Patrol*. Los Angeles: University of California, 2010.
———. *City of Inmates: Conquest, Rebellion, and the Rise of Human Caging in Los Angeles, 1771–1965*. Chapel Hill: University of North Carolina Press, 2017.

Hernández, Sonia, and John Morán González, eds. *Reverberations of Racial Violence: Critical Reflections on the History of the Border*. Austin: University of Texas Press, 2021.

Hill, Karlos K. *Beyond the Rope: The Impact of Lynching on Black Culture and Memory*. New York: Cambridge University Press, 2016.

Hietala, Thomas R. *Manifest Design: Anxious Aggrandizement in Late Jacksonian America*. Ithaca, N.Y.: Cornell University Press, 1985.

Hinton, Elizabeth. *From the War on Poverty to the War on Crime: The Making of Mass Incarceration in America*. Cambridge, Mass.: Harvard University Press, 2016.

Hixson, Walter. *American Settler Colonialism: A History*. New York: Palgrave Macmillan, 2013.

Hobbs, Tameka Bradley. *Democracy Abroad, Lynching at Home: Racial Violence in Florida*. Gainesville: University of Florida Press, 2016.

Hobsbawm, Eric. *Primitive Rebels: Studies in Archaic Forms of Social Movement in the 19th and 20th Centuries*. New York: W. W. Norton, 1959.

———. *Bandits*. New York: New Press, 2000.

Hopkins, Anthony G. *American Empire: A Global History*. Princeton, N.J.: Princeton University Press, 2019.

Hornung, Chuck. *Fullerton's Rangers: A History of the New Mexico Territorial Mounted Police*. Jefferson, N.C.: McFarland, 2005.

———. *New Mexico's Rangers: The Mounted Police*. Charleston: Arcadia Publishing, 2010.

———. *Cipriano Baca, Frontier Lawman of New Mexico*. Jefferson, N.C.: McFarland, 2013.

Horsman, Reginald. *Race and Manifest Destiny: The Origins of American Racial Anglo-Saxonism*. Cambridge, Mass.: Harvard University Press, 1981.

Hughes, John Taylor. *Doniphan's Expedition*. College Station: Texas A&M University Press, 1997.

Immerwahr, Daniel. *How to Hide an Empire: A History of the Greater United States*. New York: Farrar, Straus and Giroux, 2019.

Jacoby, Karl. *The Strange Career of William Ellis: The Texas Slave Who Became a Mexican Millionaire*. New York: W. W. Norton, 2016.

Jameson, W. C. *Border Bandits, Border Raids*. Guilford, Conn.: Lone Star Books, 2017.

Jett, Brandon T. *Race, Crime, and Policing in the Jim Crow South: African Americans and Law Enforcement in Birmingham, Memphis, and New Orleans, 1920–1945*. Baton Rouge: Louisiana State University Press, 2021.

Johnson, Benjamin Heber. *Revolution in Texas: How a Forgotten Rebellion and Its Bloody Suppression Turned Mexicans into Americans*. New Haven, Conn.: Yale University Press, 2003.

Johnson, David. *The Horrell Wars: Feuding in Texas and New Mexico*. College Station: Texas A&M University Press, 2014.

Jordan, Winthrop D. *Tumult and Silence at Second Creek: An Inquiry into a Civil War Slave Conspiracy*. Baton Rouge: Louisiana State University Press, 1995.

Kang, S. Deborah. *The INS on the Line: Making Immigration Law on the US-Mexico Border, 1917–1954*. New York: Oxford University Press, 2016.

Kloppe-Santamaría, Gema. *In the Vortex of Violence: Lynching, Extralegal Justice, and the State in Post-Revolutionary Mexico*. Oakland: University of California Press, 2020.

Lack, Paul D. *The Texas Revolutionary Experience: A Political and Social History, 1835–1836*. College Station: Texas A&M University Press, 1995.

Lamar, Howard R. *Charlie Siringo's West: An Interpretive Biography*. Albuquerque: University of New Mexico Press, 2005.

Lavender, David. *Bent's Fort*. Garden City, N.Y.: Doubleday, 1954.

Levario, Miguel Antonio. *Militarizing the Border: When Mexicans Became the Enemy*. College Station: Texas A&M University Press, 2015.

Levinson, Irving W. *Wars within War: Mexican Guerrillas, Domestic Elites, and the United States of America, 1846–1848*. Fort Worth: Texas Christian University Press, 2005.

Lim, Julian. *Porous Borders: Multiracial Migrations and the Law in the U.S.-Mexico Borderlands*. Chapel Hill: University of North Carolina Press, 2017.

Lowe, Sam. *Speaking Ill of the Dead: Jerks in New Mexico History*. Guilford, Conn.: Globe Pequot Press, 2012.

Luckingham, Bradford. *Minorities in Phoenix: A Profile of Mexican American, Chinese American, and African American Communities, 1860–1992*. Tucson: University of Arizona Press, 1994.

MacKell, Jan. *Red Light Women of the Rocky Mountains*. Albuquerque: University of New Mexico Press, 2009.

Magoffin, Susan Shelby. *Down the Santa Fe Trail and Into Mexico*. Lincoln: University of Nebraska Press, 1982.

Martinez, Monica Muñoz. *The Injustice Never Leaves You: Anti-Mexican Violence in Texas*. Cambridge, Mass.: Harvard University Press, 2020.

May, David C., Kevin I. Minor, Rick Ruddell, and Betsy A. Matthews. *Corrections and the Criminal Justice System*. Boston: Jones and Bartlett, 2008.

McDonald, Jason. *Racial Dynamics in Early Twentieth-Century Austin*. Lanham, Md.: Lexington Books, 2012.

McGrath, Tom. *Vicente Silva and His Forty Thieves: The Vice Criminals of the 80s and 90s*. Self-published, 1960.

McKanna, Clare V., Jr. *Race and Homicide in Nineteenth-Century California*. Reno: University of Nevada Press, 2002.

Meeks, Eric V. *Border Citizens: The Making of Indians, Mexicans, and Anglos in Arizona*. Austin: University of Texas Press, 2020.

Meléndez, A. Gabriel. *Spanish-language Newspapers in New Mexico, 1834–1958*. Tucson: University of Arizona Press, 2005.

Menchaca, Martha. *The Mexican Outsiders: A Community History of Marginalization and Discrimination in California*. Austin: University of Texas Press, 1995.

Miles, Elton. *More Tales of the Big Bend*. College Station: Texas A&M University Press, 1988.

Mitrani, Sam. *The Rise of the Chicago Police Department: Class and Conflict, 1850–1894*. Chicago: University of Illinois Press, 2013.

Montejano, David. *Anglos and Mexicans in the Making of Texas, 1836–1986*. Austin: University of Texas Press, 1987.

Mora, Anthony P. *Border Dilemmas: Racial and National Uncertainties in New Mexico, 1848–1912*. Durham, N.C.: Duke University Press, 2011.

Morales, Armando. *Ando Sangrando (I Am Bleeding): A Study of Mexican American-Police Conflict in Los Angeles*. La Puente, Calif.: Perspective Publishing, 1972.

Miller, Wilbur R. *The Social History of Crime and Punishment in America: An Encyclopedia*. Los Angeles: Sage, 2012.

Nielson, George R. *Vengeance in a Small Town: The Thorndale Lynching of 1911*. Bloomington, Ind.: iUniverse, 2011.

Nolan, Frederick. *The West of Billy the Kid*. Norman: University of Oklahoma Press, 1998.

Ore, Ersula J. *Lynching: Violence, Rhetoric, and American Identity*. Jackson: University Press of Mississippi, 2019.

Oropeza, Lorena. *The King of Adobe: Reies López Tijerina, Lost Prophet of the Chicano Movement*. Chapel Hill: University of North Carolina Press, 2019.

Orozco, Cynthia E. *No Mexicans, Women, or Dogs Allowed: The Rise of the Mexican American Civil Rights Movement*. Austin: University of Texas Press, 2009.

Palombo, Bernadette Jones. *Academic Professionalism in Law Enforcement*. New York: Garland, 1995.

Paredes, Américo. *"With His Pistol in His Hand": A Border Ballad and Its Hero*. Austin: University of Texas Press, 2004.

Paz, Ireneo. *The Life & Adventures of the Celebrated Bandit Joaquin Murrieta*. Houston: Arte Público Press, 2015.

Perales, Monica. *Smeltertown: Making and Remembering a Southwest Border Community*. Chapel Hill: University of North Carolina Press, 2010.

Perkinson, Robert. *Texas Tough: The Rise of America's Prison Empire*. New York: Metropolitan Books, 2010.

Pfeifer, Michael James. *Rough Justice: Lynching and American Society, 1874–1947*. Chicago: University of Illinois Press, 2004.

Polston, Cody. *Wicked Albuquerque*. Charleston: History Press, 2017.

Ramos, Raúl A. *Beyond the Alamo: Forging Mexican Ethnicity in San Antonio, 1821–1861*. Chapel Hill: University of North Carolina Press, 2009.

Raspa, Darren A. *Bloody Bay: Grassroots Policing in Nineteenth-Century San Francisco*. Lincoln: University of Nebraska Press, 2020.

Reséndez, Andrés. *Changing National Identities at the Frontier: Texas and New Mexico, 1800–1850*. Cambridge: Cambridge University Press, 2005.

Roberts, Calvin Alexander, and Susan A. Roberts. *New Mexico*. Albuquerque: University of New Mexico Press, 2006.

Rosales, F. Arturo, ed. *¡Pobre Raza!: Violence, Justice, and Mobilization among México Lindo Immigrants, 1900–1936*. Austin: University of Texas Press, 1999.

———, ed. *Testimonio: A Documentary History of the Mexican American Struggle for Civil Rights*. Houston: Arte Público Press, 2000.

Roth, Mitchel P., and Tom Kennedy. *Houston Blue: The Story of the Houston Police Department*. Denton: University of North Texas Press, 2012.

Rousey, Dennis Charles. *Policing the Southern City: New Orleans, 1805–1889*. Baton Rouge: Louisiana State University Press, 1997.

Roybal, Karen R. *Archives of Dispossession: Recovering the Testimonios of Mexican American Herederas, 1848–1860*. Chapel Hill: University of North Carolina Press, 2017.

Rubenser, Lorie, and Gloria Priddy. *Constables, Marshals, and More: Forgotten Offices in Texas Law Enforcement*. Denton: University of North Texas Press, 2011.

Sager, Stan. *¡Viva Elfego!: The Case for Elfego Baca, Hispanic Hero*. Santa Fe, N.Mex.: Sunstone Press, 2008.

Saito, Natsu Taylor. *Settler Colonialism, Race, and the Law: Why Structural Racism Persists*. New York: New York University Press, 2020.

Sánchez, Joseph P., Robert L. Spude, and Art Gómez. *New Mexico: A History*. Norman: University of Oklahoma Press, 2013.

Schrader, Stuart. *Badges without Borders: How Global Counterinsurgency Transformed American Policing*. Oakland: University of California Press, 2019.

Schweninger, Loren. *Families in Crisis in the Old South: Divorce, Slavery, and the Law*. Chapel Hill: University of North Carolina Press, 2012.

Secrest, William B. *Behind San Quentin's Walls: The History of California's Legendary Prison and Its Inmates, 1851–1900*. Fresno, Calif.: Craven Street Books, 2015.

Segrave, Kerry. *Lynchings of Women in the United States: The Recorded Cases, 1851–1946*. Jefferson, N.C.: McFarland, 2010.

Sides, Josh. *L.A. City Limits: African American Los Angeles from the Great Depression to the Present*. Berkeley: University of California Press, 2006.

Singletary, Otis A. *The Mexican War*. Chicago: University of Chicago Press, 1960.

Smith, Charles E. *The New Mexico State Constitution*. New York: Oxford University Press, 2011.

Sonnichsen, Charles L. *Tucson: The Life and Times of an American City*. Norman: University of Oklahoma Press, 1987.

Spellman, Paul N. *Captain John H. Rogers, Texas Ranger*. Denton: University of North Texas Press, 2012.

Taylor, Keeanga-Yamahtta. *From #BlackLivesMatter to Black Liberation*. Chicago: Haymarket Books, 2016.

Taylor, Orville. *Negro Slavery in Arkansas*. Fayetteville: University of Arkansas Press, 2000.

Telles, Edward E., and Vilma Ortiz. *Generations of Exclusion: Mexican-Americans, Assimilation, and Race*. New York: Russell Sage Foundation, 2008.

Thompson, Jerry. *Cortina: Defending the Mexican Name in Texas*. College Station: Texas A&M University Press, 2007.

Tolnay, Stewart E., and Elwood M. Beck. *A Festival of Violence: An Analysis of Southern Lynchings, 1882–1930*. Chicago: University of Illinois Press, 1995.

Torget, Andrew J. *Seeds of Empire: Cotton, Slavery, and the Transformation of the Texas Borderlands, 1800–1850*. Chapel Hill: University of North Carolina Press, 2018.

Tórrez, Robert J. *Myth of the Hanging Tree: Stories of Crime and Punishment in Territorial New Mexico*. Albuquerque: University of New Mexico Press, 2008.

Tsompanas, Paul L. *Juan Patron: A Fallen Star in the Days of Billy the Kid*. Richmond: Bell Isle Books, 2013.

Turk, David S. *Forging the Star: The Official Modern History of the United States Marshals Service*. Denton: University of North Texas Press, 2016.

Turner, Don. *The Massacre of Gov. Bent*. Amarillo, Tex.: Humbug Gulch Press, 1969.

Unterman, Katherine. *Uncle Sam's Policemen: The Pursuit of Fugitives across Borders*. Cambridge, Mass.: Harvard University Press, 2015.

Urbina, Martin Guevara, Joel E. Vela, and Juan O. Sánchez. *Ethnic Realities of Mexican Americans: From Colonialism to 21st Century Globalization*. Springfield, Ill.: Charles C. Thomas, 2014.

Van Ness, John R., and Christine M. Van Ness, eds. *Spanish & Mexican Land Grants in New Mexico and Colorado*. Manhattan, Kans.: Sunflower University Press, 1980.

Villanueva, Nicholas, Jr. *The Lynching of Mexicans in the Texas Borderlands*. Albuquerque: University of New Mexico Press, 2017.

Wadman, Robert C., and William Thomas Allison. *To Protect and to Serve: A History of Police in America*. New York: Pearson, 2003.

Wagoner, Jay J. *Arizona Territory, 1863–1912: A Political History*. Tucson: University of Arizona Press, 1970.

Waldrep, Christopher. *The Many Faces of Judge Lynch: Extralegal Violence and Punishment in America*. New York: Palgrave Macmillan, 2002.

Walker, Dale L. *Bear Flag Rising: The Conquest of California, 1846*. New York: Forge, 1999.

Walker, Samuel. *A Critical History of Police Reform: The Emergence of Professionalism*. Lanham, Md.: Lexington Books, 1977.

Webb, Walter Prescott. *The Texas Rangers: A Century of Frontier Defense*. Austin: University of Texas Press, 1965.

Weber, David J., ed. *Foreigners in Their Native Land: Historical Roots of the Mexican Americans*. Albuquerque: University of New Mexico Press, 1973.

———. *The Mexican Frontier, 1821–1846: The American Southwest Under Mexico*. Albuquerque: University of New Mexico Press, 1982.

Weiss, Harold J. *Yours to Command: The Life and Legend of Texas Ranger Captain Bill McDonald*. Denton: University of North Texas Press, 2009.

Welsome, Eileen. *The General and the Jaguar: Pershing's Hunt for Pancho Villa: A True Story*. Lincoln, Neb.: Bison Books, 2007.

Wilson, Lori Lee. *The Joaquín Band: The History Behind the Legend*. Lincoln: University of Nebraska Press, 2011.

Wilson, R. Michael. *Legal Executions in the Western Territories, 1847–1911: Arizona, Colorado, Idaho, Kansas, Montana, Nebraska, Nevada, New Mexico, North Dakota, Oklahoma, Oregon, South Dakota, Utah, Washington and Wyoming*. Jefferson, N.C.: McFarland, 2010.

Wilson, John Philip. *Merchants, Guns & Money: The Story of Lincoln County and Its Wars*. Santa Fe: Museum of New Mexico Press, 1987.

Wright, George C. *Racial Violence in Kentucky Lynchings, Mob Rule, and "Legal Lynchings."* Baton Rouge: Louisiana State University Press, 1996.

Yeatman, Ted P. *Frank and Jesse James: The Story Behind the Legend*. Nashville: Cumberland House, 2000.

Zack, Naomi. *White Privilege and Black Rights: The Injustice of U.S. Police Racial Profiling and Homicide*. Lanham, Md.: Rowman & Littlefield, 2015.

Index

Page numbers in italics refer to illustrations.

Acevedo, José, 200
Acosta, Jesus, 136
Adee, Alvey A., 77–78
Aguilar, Lauterio, 130–31
Aguirre, Anastacio, 113
Aguirre, Blas, 113
Aguirre, Celso, 113
Aguirre, Epitacio, 113
Aguirre, Martin, 110, *111*
Alarid, Eugenio, 103, *104*
Alarid, Laureano, 106
Albuquerque (New Mexico): Bernalillo County sheriff's Office, 84–85, 88–89, 197, 198; crime in, 85, 117–18; police department, 96, 184–85, 197–98, 198–99, 204–7. *See also* Armijo, Perfecto; Baca,

Elfego; Bernalillo County Sheriff's Office; Galusha, Jandon "J. R."
Albuquerque Police Department: formation of, 197–98; professionalization of, 198–99; rivalry with Bernalillo County sheriff, 206–7. *See also* Chavez, Dennis; Gallegos, Henrico "Henry"; Galusha, Jandon "J. R."; Yarberry, Milton
Allen, Tabe, 93
Allison, Clay, 63, 65, 66, 67, 82
Alta California. *See* California
Alvarado, Santiago, 111–12, 115
Álvarez, Manuel, 26
Alvarid, Juan, 52–53
Alvisa, Francisca, 122

Ancheta, Joseph, 105, 106, 109
Angney, William, 28
Archuleta, Diego, 27–28
Archuleta, Pantaleon, 30
Arizona: crime in, 117–18, 123–35; development of criminal justice system in, 44–45; extralegal justice in, 67–70, 73–74, 76–77; penal code of, 45; Territory of Arizona, 1, 6, 40, 44–45, 67–71, 117, 123–35. *See also* Armijo, Perfecto; Garfias, Enrique "Henry"; home guards; *Howell Code, The*; Welch, John; Yuma Territorial Prison
Arizona Territorial Legislative Assembly. *See* Arizona
Armendariz, Juan, 112
Armijo, Geronimo, 94
Armijo, Manuel, 22–23, 24, 26, 32
Armijo, Perfecto: background of, 84–85, 85; death of, 89; elections, 85, 88, 89; elimination of Leyba Gang, 85–87; involvement in Yarberry case, 88; reappointment as sheriff, 89; taxation problem, 88–89. *See also* Baca, Elfego; Chavez, Frank; Leyba, Marino; Yarberry, Milton
Arny, William, 41
Arroyo Seco (New Mexico), 157
Atchison, Topeka & Santa Fe Railway, 198
Atkinson, John G., 154
Austin (Texas): development of police department, 21; Mexican American police officers in, 200. *See also* Austin Police Department
Austin, Alfred, 174
Austin Police Department: arrests of Mexicans and Mexican Americans, 40, 137–38; development of, 21; Mexican American police officers, 200

Baca, Cipriano, 158
Baca, Conrado, 98
Baca, Elfego: background of, 90; death of, 101; defense of Mexican-origin community, 91–92, 96, 97–98, 215–16; election as sheriff, 98; and father jailbreak, 90; Frisco shoot-out, 81–82, 94–96, 215–16; Manzano Gang and, 98–99; other jobs in criminal justice, 96–98, 97; problems in Frisco (New Mexico), 91–92; relationship with Billy the Kid, 91; shoot-out at Saracino's home, 93; trials for murder, 95–96; views on law enforcement, 99, 100; vigilante justice and, 93, 95. *See also* Kelsey, Guy Franklin; McCarty, Charlie; San Francisco Plaza "Frisco" (New Mexico); Saracino, Pedro; Texas Cowboys
Baca, Francisco, 90, 91, 243n42
Baca, James, 108
Baca, Jose Sosteno, 157–58
Baca, Juanita, 90
Baca, Manuel, 125
Baca, Reyes, 125–26; disparaged in court, 126–27, 128
Baca, Santiago, 185
Bakersfield (California), 58
banditry, 8, 9, 11–12, 57, 114–15, 147–49, 155, 167, 170–74, 180, 186; as excuse for racial violence, 8, 58, 148, 149, 158, 161, 170–72, 175–78, 181, 203; as a law enforcement creation, 9, 12, 147–48, 149–52, 158–59, 167, 169, 170–72; leading to law enforcement careers, 82, 91, 101, 103, 217, 220. *See also* justice, extralegal: Mexican and Mexican American resistance to; *and names of specific bandits*
Bandit Wars, 115, 173, 218
Barcelo, Trinidad, 30
Barquello, Juan, 136
Barrera, Miguel, 86, 88
Barton, James, 35, 42, 56, 57
Bates, Sanford, 211
Bayard, Thomas F., 75, 77–78, 79
Bazán, Jesus 175–76
Bean, Joshua, 149, 259n12
Bear Flag Revolt, 32, 33
Beaubien, Charles, 26, 30
Beaubien, Narciso, 32
Becerra, Virginia, 191, 192, 193
Belen (New Mexico), 90
Benavides, Juan (arrested for resisting arrest), 136

Benavides, Juan (first lynching in Santa Fe), 49–50, 62
Benavides, Rafael, 207–8, 213
Benavides, Santos, 85, 86, 88
Bent, Charles, 21–22, 26–27, 28, 29
Bent, George, 30
Bernalillo County Sheriff's Office, 84–85, 89, 197, 198; fight with Albuquerque Police Department, 206–7, 213
Billy the Kid, 91, 101, 104, 242n23
Bingham Canyon (Utah), 167
Bisbee Deportation, 179–80
Biscailuz, Eugene, 110
Blancett, George, 208
Blankenship, J. W., 76, 77, 79, 240n109
Blaine, James G., 72, 73
Blair, Francis, 26–27, 30
Bledsoe, William, 187
Booth, Stephen E., 157
Border Patrol, 6, 46, 185, 212, 213, 235n158; Frontier Force as early example of, 153–54
Borrego, Juan, 63, 237n57
Borrego Gang, 105–6. *See also* Gonzalez y Borrego, Antonio; Gonzalez y Borrego, Francisco
Brandt, Frank, 195, 196
Brite Ranch raid, 176–77, 264n129
Brodie, Alexander O., 132
Brown, Herbert, 132
Browne, James, 151
Brownsville (Texas), 115, 150, 176; Cortina raid in, 150–51, 152. *See also* Cortina, Juan
Bryan, Thomas, 76, 78
Buchanan, James, 25
Bull, Mr., 209
Butarus, Feliciano, 63, 67

Cabrera, Tomás, 150–51
California: crime in, 120–22; development of criminal justice system in, 6, 16, 37, 42–44, 118; extralegal justice in, 53–58, 148–50; Mexican-American War and, 16, 21, 32–35; Mexican resistance to American encroachment in, 35–37; operation of criminal justice system, 120–22, 150, 211–12; penal code of, 44; policing in, 43–44, 57–58, 110. *See also* Aguirre, Martin; Los Angeles (California); Mexican-American War; Murrieta, Joaquin; Murrieta, Juan
California Joe, 86, 88
California Rangers, 6, 149
Cameron County (Texas), 60, 151, 190–91
Campbell, Charles, 88, 91. *See also* Yarberry, Milton
Canales, José Tomás "J. T.," 10, 150, 189, 219, 267n20.
Canales Investigation, 183–84, 185–87, 213, 218
Canales Reforms, 187–88, 189, 213, 218
Cano, Chico, 9, 147–48, 170–72, 171, 218, 229n21, 263n128, 264n129; and brothers, 170, 171; and Porvenir Massacre, 176–77
Cannon, Frederick, 54
Capitulation of Cahuenga, 37, 221
Cardenas, Manuel, 53, 65–66
Carr, Frank, 115, 173
Carriaga, Fernando, 57
Carrillo, Ramon, 121
Castellón, Aureliano, 60
Castro, José Antonio, 32–34, 35
Cardis, Louis, 153
Catron, Thomas B., 105, 106
Chabio, Susan, 133
Chacon, Adolfo, 113
Chapa, Francisco A., 165
Charlton, Russell C., 206, 207
Chaves, Labrada, 69
Chavez, Dennis, 199–200, 213, 219, 271n98
Chavez, Frank, 87, 88; and Joseph Ancheta case, 105–6
Chavez y Chavez, Jose, 90, 109, 115, 116, 155; early law enforcement work, 101–2; as Las Vegas deputy sheriff, 103–4, 246n109; role in Lincoln County War, 102–3
Chicano Movement, 223–24
Choate, Boone, 158–59, 160
Cimarron (New Mexico), 62, 67. *See also* Butarus, Feliciano; Griego, Francisco "Pancho"; St. James Hotel
citizens patrols. *See* justice, extralegal: citizens patrols

Index 303

City of Dallas Calaboose. *See* Dallas (Texas): calaboose
Civil War, 3, 22, 41, 152, 209
"Clipper," 71, 80
Cochise County (Arizona), 73, 74, 125, 128, 129, 180
Colquitt, Oscar, 160, 165, 166
Columbus Raid, 178–79
committees of public safety. *See* justice, extralegal: committees of public safety
compassionate release. *See* incarceration: compassionate jurisprudence
Contreras, Abram, 98–99
Cook, James, 93, 96
Coolidge, Calvin, 194
Cordero, Severo, 113
Cordova, Lazaro, 99
Cordova, Leocardo, 69–70
Cordova, Ramon, 69
corridos (ballads), 166–67
Cortéz, Gregorio, 9–10, 158, 162, 166, 170, 218, 222; death of, 161; defense committee of, 9–10, 159–60, 161; flight and manhunt, 159; shooting of Sheriff Morris, 158–59; trials, 160–61
Cortéz, Romaldo, 159
Cortina, Juan: background of, 150; role in Brownsville raid, 151; role in Cortina Wars, 151, 152; role in Nuecestown Raid, 151–52; shooting of Marshal Shears, 150–51. *See also* Cabrera, Tomás; Nuecestown Raid; Shears, Robert
Courtier, John P., 49, 50, 62
Cox, Frank, 77, 78, 124, 222
Cuarento, Antonio, 84
Curry, George, 104, 107

Dallas (Texas): calaboose, 139; city jail, 139, 140, 209; police department, 21, 140, 143, 144, 200; police professionalization in, 200, 201; racism in criminal justice institutions of, 139, 140, vigilance committee in, 21
Davis, Levi, 62–63
de Baca, Manuel C., 156
de la Torres, Eululotia, 202, 203
del Valle, José Maria, 46, 235n158

del Valle, Ygnacio, 121
de Soto, Dionicio, 113, 114
Doak, William, 212
Doña Ana County (New Mexico), 40, 105, 136
Dorame, Esteban, 125
Duarte, Manuel, 191
Duncan, David, 74–76
Duncan, Thomas, 74–75
Duran, Martin, 125–26; death of, 128; murder of Reyes Baca, 126; public support of, 127–28; trial of, 126–27. *See also* Baca, Reyes
Duran, Rosa, 133

Eagle Pass (Texas), 175; lynching of unknown Mexican man in, 59–60. *See also* Owens, Robert; Sumpter, Jesse; Wood family
Eggers, L. F., 127
El Burro, 92, 95, 215
Eldeo, Fermin, 58
"El Gran Centro," 209–10
Elias, Miguel, 58
Ellingwood, G. W., 71, 238n81
El Paso (Texas): constable's office, 112, 114; county sheriff's office, 112–13, 114, 153; police department, 111–12. *See also* Guadalupe Salt War
Embudo (New Mexico), 29
Encinas, Francisco, 58
Enriquez, Juan, 132
Escajeda, Juan Jose, 113
Esperanza, Frank, 69, 70
Estes, David, 71

Ferazon, Cayatano, 125
Ferguson, Dave, 115
Ferguson, Miriam, 194
Fimbrez, Manuela, 132, 255n103; incarceration at Yuma Territorial Prison, 132–33; murder of Ah Foy, 132; pardon and release of, 133. *See also* Enriquez, Juan; incarceration: compassionate release
Flores, Desiderio, 138
Flores, José María, 35–36

Flores, Juan (Flores Daniel Gang), 57
Flores, Juan (lost father in Porvenir Massacre), 177
Flores Daniel Gang, 42, 57
Fornoff, Fred, 107
Fort Worth (Texas), 138–39
Foster, Stephen C., 42
Fox, James M., 172, 175; involvement in Porvenir Massacre, 176–77, 178, 186. *See also* Cano, Chico; Porvenir Massacre; Texas Rangers
Foy, Ah "'Sullivan' the Chinaman," 132
Franco, Juan, 112, 114, 115, 116
Frémont, John C., 32, 33, 34, 35, 36, 73, 239n88
Frisco (New Mexico). *See* San Francisco Plaza "Frisco" (New Mexico)
Frisco shoot-out, 81, 82, 94–96, 215–16
Fritz, Mary, 73–74, 75
Fritz, Winfield, 73–74, 75
Frontier Force, 153–54
fuerzas nacionales, las, 36–37

Gabaldan, Eugenio, 49–50
Galeyville (Arizona), 71
Gallegos, Crespin, 49–50, 62
Gallegos, Gavino, 49
Gallegos, Henrico "Henry" "Lonesome Kid," 204–6, 207, 208, 213, 219
Gallegos, Jose Pablo, 22
Galusha, Jandon "J. R.," 198–99, 200
Galvan, Rafael, Sr., 201
García, Anastacio, 149–50
Garcia, Antonio, 120
Garcia, Cesario, 157
García, Florencio, 176, 184, 186, 187
Garcia, Jose, 98
Garcia, Tomas, 113, 115, 116
Garcia, Valerio, 117–18, 124, 125
Garfias, Enrique "Henry," 2, 9, 77, 78, 83–84, 83, 115, 116, 124, 222
Garza, Jose, 191
Gates, Thomas, 130, 131
General Claims Commission, 178
Genung, Charles, 76, 78
Giddings, Marsh, 101
Gillespie, Archibald, 35–36, 42

Gingguy, Mr. "Pata de Hule," 209
Glover, Robert, 159, 160, 161
Golden (New Mexico), 53, 87
Gomez, Albino, 136
Gómez, Antonio, 164–65, 165–66, 222
Gomez, Rafael, 109
Gonzales County (Texas), 38, 39, 58, 61, 158
González, Inocencio, 194, 195
Gonzales, Manuel, 125
Gonzales, Manuel C., 195
Gonzales, Martina, 125, 126
Gonzalez y Borrego, Antonio, 105–6
Gonzalez y Borrego, Francisco, 105–6
Gore, Z. T., 165
Gosper, John, 73, 239n88
Graham, Sam, 190
Grant, John, 169
Greaghe, St. George, 117
Great Depression, 210, 211, 212
Great Mexican Migration. *See* Mexico: law enforcement response to migration of Mexicans
Griego, Francisco "Pancho," 63–65, 66, 67, 82
Guadalupe Salt War, 152–54, 172, 221
Gutierrez, Emilio, 109
Gutiérrez, Faustino, 86, 88
Gutterson, Charles L., 117, 123, 124

Haas, Harlow, 206, 207
Hamer, Frank, 170, 185, 192
Hardcastle, Alfred, 95, 96
Hardmount, William, 150
Harvis, J. A., 170, 171
Hawkensmith, 75
Heacock, William, 96–97
Hearne, Bert, 94, 96
Henderson, Effie, 163, 164, 165
Henderson, Lemuel, 163, 164
Hernandez, Vicente, 69–70
Hinojosa, Daniel, 115, 116, 174
home guards, 179, 180, 198
Hoover, Herbert, 212
Horrell brothers, 101–2
Horrell War, 101–2
Houston (Texas), 5, 20, 37, 209, 223; citizen patrol, 20; police department, 5, 20

Howard, Charles, 153–54
Howard, Jack, 170, 171
Howell Code, The, 44–45
Hubbell, Frank, 117, 123, 124
Hubbell, Philip, 206–7
Hubbell, Thomas, 89
Hughes, Louis C., 125, 131
Hunter, Jim, 163

Idar, Jovita, 166, 180
incarceration, 18, 43, 128, 145, 212, 221; compassionate jurisprudence, 119, 120, 133, 135, 137, 142, 211, 222; development of jails, 5, 7, 18, 25, 37, 42, 43, 44, 118, 145, 211, 213, 221; development of prisons, 7, 18, 40–41, 118, 145, 210, 211, 213, 221; pardons, 31, 87, 119, 125, 129–30, 132, 133, 136, 137, 161, 200, 211; plantation jail, 7, 208–9; women and, 132–33, 134, 210. *See also* Dallas (Texas): calaboose; Leavenworth Penitentiary; Old Town Jail; Penitentiary of New Mexico; Santa Fe (New Mexico): jail; Socorro County Jail; Yuma Territorial Prison
Industrial Workers of the World, 179–80
Ingalls, Frank, 129–30
"Italian named John," 113

Jacomo, Carlos, 53, 87
Jenkins, William, 57–58
Jensen, Nephi, 169
Jimenez Serrano, Maria de Jesus, 208, 209, 210
Johnson, Frank, 163
Joint Committee of the Senate and the House in the Investigation of the Texas Ranger Force. *See* Canales Investigation
Jones, Jot, 191
justice, extralegal: anti-Mexican conventions, 37–40; citizens patrols, 7, 20, 51, 52, 157; committees of public safety, 5, 7, 42, 51, 62, 69–70, 150–51; definition of, 5, 7, 42–43, 50–52; kangaroo courts, 57, 95, 96, 103; lynch mobs, 2, 37–38, 41–42, 46, 51–53, 65, 68–72, 164–65, 169, 208, 216; Mexican and Mexican American involvement in, 47, 52, 69–71, 76–78, 85–86, 98, 103, 115, 217; Mexican and Mexican American resistance to, 5, 9, 53, 55–58, 60, 79–80, 123, 150–52, 155–58, 180–81, 217–19; problems with terminology, 7, 52–53, 217, 235–36n12; vigilance committees; 5, 20–21, 38–40, 42, 46, 50–52, 54–58, 62, 65, 67–70, 85–87, 149–53; White peoples' lies about, 7, 38–39, 46, 50–53, 58, 70, 219. *See also* violence
justice, legal: development of court system, 6–7, 18, 24, 43–44, 45; impartial operation of, 108–9, 120–21, 122, 124, 140–41, 142–43, 160–61, 221; Mexican Revolution impact on treatment of Mexican-origin people, 8, 112, 119, 131–32, 135, 136, 139–40, 141, 146, 218, 221; military kangaroo courts, 30–31; nolle prosequi cases, 30, 121, 123; railroading of Mexican and Mexican American defendants, 121, 130–31, 138, 140, 167; "unknown Mex." cases, 119, 135, 137, 139–40, 143, 145–50, 163; women and, 121–22, 124–25, 125–27, 138, 140, 141, 145. *See also* incarceration; law enforcement; violence

Karnes County (Texas), 158, 160
Kearny, Stephen Watts, 22–25, 23, 26, 32, 36–37
Kearny Code of Law, 24–25, 33, 34, 37, 40, 216, 221
Kerber, Charles, 153, 154
Kern County (California), 58
Knight, Robert E. Lee, 186–87
Krakauer, Adolph, 111–12, 249n147

La Agrupación Protectora Mexicana, 166, 180
Lackey, Joseph, 87
Laguna, Domingo, 125
La Liga Protectora Latina, 180
La Liga Protectora Mexicana, 166
Lambert, Fred, 22, 62–63
Lambert, Henry, 62, 63, 237n57. *See also* St. James Hotel
Lane, "old man Lane," 21
Lane, William Carr, 40

Las Gorras Blancas, 9, 102, 104, 105, 106, 148, 155–58, 180, 246n107, 260n37
La Sociedad de Bandidos, 103–4, 155
La Sociedad de Proteccion y Justicia, 157, 246n107
Las Vegas (New Mexico), 62, 86, 102–3, 155–56
law enforcement: development of, 5–6, 15, 17, 20–21, 41–45, 220; military as, 17, 20, 27, 35, 45, 59; participation in extra-legal justice, 59, 70, 103, 152, 175–77; perceptions of Mexican-origin people, 3, 4, 118–20, 148, 172–73, 178, 218; origins as vigilance committees, 20, 21, 41–42, 50; police in-fighting, 105–6, 206–7. *See also,* justice: legal; Mexican Americans: service in law enforcement; Texas Rangers; *names of specific officers; names of specific police departments; and names of specific sheriff's offices*
League of United Latin American Citizens, 189, 201
Leavenworth Penitentiary, 87, 196
Lee, Stephen L., 26, 28, 30, 31–31
Leon, Charles, 105
Lewis, Mrs. Charles, 207
Leyba, Marino, 52, 85, 86–87, 106
ley de fuga. *See* ley fuga
ley fuga (law of flight), 8, 148, 170–71, 175, 187, 216, 220
Lincoln County Mounted Rifles, 101, 102
Lincoln County Regulators, 101, 102
Lincoln County War, 101–2
Lomeli, Antonio V., 74
Long, E. J., 204
Longoria, Antonio, 175–76
Lopez (first name unknown), 92
Lopez, Clemente, 69, 70
Lopez, Lorenzo, 155–56
Lopez, Martin, 202–3
Lopez, Rafael "Red," 167–70, 185
Lopez, Severo, 162–63
Los Angeles (California), 5, 32, 37, 41, 42–43, 56–58, 120–21, 179, 204, 211, 223; City Guard, 42, 56, 57; county sheriff, 35, 110; police department, 41, 42, 57, 179, 204, 212, 213

Los Lunas (New Mexico), 90
Los Valles (New Mexico), 29–30
Lugo, Juan, 203, 204
Luna, Alfredo, 190
Luna, Fred, 199–200
lynching. *See* justice, extralegal
lynch mobs. *See* justice, extralegal: lynch mobs

Maes, Nicolas, 108, 109
Maes, Patricio, 103–4
Manifest Destiny, 3, 16
Manzano Gang, 98–99
Maricopa County (Arizona), 1, 124, 128, 129, 130, 135, 222; sheriff's office, 2, 69, 76, 77, 83, 84
Marino Leyba Gang, 85–86, 87–88
Mariscal, Ignacio, 78–79
Maron, Antonio, 58
Martin, Barney, 76, 77, 78, 79
Martinez, Epitacio, 92, 95, 215
Martinez (conflict with Lane), 22
Martinez Saloon, 88, 91
matanza. *See* Porvenir Massacre
May, Louis, 194, 195
McCarty, Charles, 92–93, 94
McCoy, Robert, 164–65, 222
McDonald, William, 162
McFarland, "Stormy" Jim, 74–75
McMains, Oscar P., 65, 66, 80
McMillen, Thomas, 198
Mejía, Manuel, 1–2, 76–79, 83, 124, 163, 222, 240n109
Mexican Americans: criminality, 4, 117–46; criminality as compared to other ethnic groups, 129, 131–32, 145–46, 210–11; resistance to abuse, 9–10, 79–80, 96, 152–54, 155–58, 159–60, 166, 185–89, 191–92, 203–4, 213–14, 215–16; service in criminal justice system, 9, 50, 105–7, 108–9; service in law enforcement, 2, 8–9, 47, 81–104, 108–16, 199–201, 217; treatment by criminal justice system, 118–20, 121, 124, 125–26, 128, 129, 138–39, 140–42, 210–11; use of extra-legal justice, 47, 52, 69–71, 76–78, 85–86, 98, 103, 115, 217; as victims of extralegal justice,

Index 307

Mexican Americans (*continued*)
  63–66, White racist views on, 4, 7, 118, 135, 148, 184, 217–18
Mexican-American War, 3, 7, 16, 17, 21–37, 46, 216–17. *See also* 1847 Treason Trials, Treaty of Guadalupe Hidalgo
Mexican Posse, 101–2
Mexican Revolution, 8, 9, 170, 172–73, 186, 208, Columbus Raid, 178–79; criminal justice response to, 118, 131–32, 136, 139, 140–41, 146, 217
Mexicans: opposition to slavery, 37, 38, 39–40, 58–59; opposition to U.S. military, 17, 21, 22–24, 27–30, 31–32, 32–34, 35–37; as refugees, 8, 119, 135, 136, 140, 146, 178–79, 208–9, 218; treatment of by criminal justice system, 118–20, 121, 125–26, 128–29, 131, 132, 135, 138–39, 140–42, 210–13; as victims of extralegal violence, 54–56, 57–62, 67–71, 74, 76–77, 91–92; White racist views about, 4, 7, 118, 135, 148, 217–18. *See also* Mexican-American War; Mexican Revolution
Mexico: aid to Mexican citizens in the U.S., 9, 71–73, 74, 76, 77–79, 165, 177–78, 192–93; alleged criminals escaping to, 58, 69, 118, 125, 135, 191; ambassadorial and consular work, 2, 46, 71–73, 75, 77–79, 113, 176, 178, 190, 192–94, 195, 202; law enforcement response to migration of Mexicans, 135, 136, 138–39, 211–12, 213, 218; loss of northern territory, 3, 16–17, 20, 25–26, 46, 221; Mexican-American War, 16–17, 21, 28–29, 46, 216, 221; resistance to American military, 22–24, 27–30, 31–34, 35–37; and Texas Revolution, 15–16; and treason trials, 28, 29, 30–31, 32, 216; violations of territorial limits by U.S. law enforcement, 69, 175, 176. *See also* Mexican-American War, Mexican Revolution, Taos Revolt, Treaty of Guadalupe Hidalgo
Miera, Pantaleon, 85–86, 88
Miller, Nathaniel, 199
Miranda, Luz, 124–25
Molina, Carmen, 132

Montoya, Joaquim, 53, 87
Montoya, Pablo, 28, 30
Morris, George, 151, 152
Morris, William, 158–59, 160, 161
Mulvenon, William J., 77, 222
Muñoz, Adolfo, 115, 174, 184
Muñoz, Carlos, 161–62
Murray, George, 106–7
Murphy, John, 62
Murphy, Nathan O., 75, 132
Murrieta, Joaquin, 148–49, 150, 158, 167, 170
Murrieta, Juan, 110, *111*, 248n144

Naranjo, Francisco, 94, 95
Neff, Pat, 188, 192
New Mexico, 10–11; development of criminal justice system in, 16, 24–25, 40–42; extralegal justice in, 49–50, 52–53, 62–67, 207–8; home guards, 179; Las Gorras Blancas, 155–58; Mexican-American War, 22–32; operation of criminal justice system, 135–37, 204–7, 210–11; policing in, 81–82, 84–110, 197–99. *See also* Kearny Code of Law; Las Gorras Blancas; 1847 Treason Trials
New Mexico Territory. *See* New Mexico
New Mexico Territorial Legislature. *See* New Mexico
New Mexico Territorial Mounted Police (rangers), 6, 41, 106–7, 157–58
news media: defense of extralegal justice, 39, 54–55, 58, 61, 68–69, 71, 86, 163–64, 174; opposition to extralegal justice, 55–56, 67, 74; as sympathetic to Mexican-origin people, 132, 159–60, 165, 166
1847 Treason Trials, 30–31, 32, 216
Noack, Garrett, 165
Norias Raid, 174–75, 184
Nuecestown Raid, 151–52
Nunez, Agapito, 137
Nuñez, Delancio, 194, 270n70
Nuñez, Jose, 194, 195, 270n70
Nuñez, Teresa, 194, 195, 270n70
Nuñez, Tomás, 194, 195, 202, 203, 270n70
Nunnas, Ventura, 71

O'Donel, C. M., 157–58
Old Town Jail, 95, 96, 97
Olivares, Enrique, 192
Ordoña, José, 72, 73
Ortega, Juan Antonio, 109
Ortega, Teodoro, 190
Ortiz, Santos, 108–9
Ortiz, Tomas, 27–28
Otero, Alfredo "Fred," 99, 245n87
Otero, Miguel, 89, 104
Owens, Robert, 59, 60
Oyervides, Miguel, 200

Pacheco, Manuel, 123
Padilla, Jose de Jesus, 98
Padilla, Juan N., 120–21
Padilla, Marta Abila de, 120–21
Padilla, Zacarias, 106–7
Padilla y Chavez, Manuel, 107
Pais, Jose, 49–50
Paul, Robert H. "Bob," 72, 73, 80
Payno, Manuel, 202
Penitentiary of New Mexico, 40–41, 87, 136, 145, 156, 210
Penny, G. W., 164–65
Peno, John, 143–44
Perales, Alonso, 193, 194, 195, 219
Perea, Escolástico, 86, 88
Perez, Jesse, 114–15, 250n173. *See also* Texas Rangers: Mexican American Rangers
Perham, Perry, 93, 95
Pesquiera, Manuela, 124–25
Phelps Dodge Corporation, 179–80
Phillips, John, 202, 203
Phoenix (Arizona); crime in, 123, 124, 128, 129, 130; extralegal justice in, 1–2, 68–69, 76–77, 179; police department, 2, 83, 83–84, 179; sheriff's office, 1–2, 69, 76, 77, 84. *See also* Garfias, Enrique "Henry"; Maricopa County (Arizona); Mejía, Manuel
Phoenix, William, 55
Pico, Pío de Jesus, 32–33, 34, 46
Pima County (Arizona), 44, 70, 73, 125, 128, 129, 132, 133

Pinkerton National Detective Agency, 105
Plan de San Diego, 148, 172–74
Planet (Arizona), 69
policing. *See* Arizona; California; justice, legal; law enforcement; New Mexico; Texas; Texas Rangers; *names of specific police departments; and names of specific sheriff's offices*
Polk, James K., 25, 31
Porvenir Massacre, 8, 176–78, 184, 185, 186, 187, 264n152
Potter, Charles, 52, 85, 86–87
Prescott (Arizona), 68
Price, Sterling, 26, 27–28, 29, 30, 31
Prince, L. Bradford, 105, 136, 156

Quiñones, Francisco, Jr., 73, 74, 75–76, 163
Quiñones, Francisco, Sr., 75

Rafferty, James, 73–74, 75
Ramos, Basilio, 173
Rancheria Massacre, 52, 54–56, 149
Ransom, Henry, 175–76
Raymond, Joseph, 73–74, 75
Republic of Texas. *See* Texas
Rincones, Guadalupe, 190
Rio Grande City (Texas), 160, 162
Robledo, Martin, 159, 161
Rodriguez, Almando, 193
Rodríguez, Antonio, 163–64, 165
Rodriguez, Francisca, 122
Rodriguez, Guadalupe, 211
Rodriguez, Josefa "Chipita," 52
Rogers, John, 159, 161, 222
Romero, Jesus (Bernalillo County sheriff), 89, 198
Romero, Jesus "saber slasher," 83–84
Romero, Matías, 75, 77, 78–79
Romero, Tomás, 28, 29
Romo, Jesus, 57
Ross, Frank, 95, 96
Ruiz, Antonio, 57–58
Ruiz, Bessena, 58
Ruíz, Enrique D., 192
Ruiz, Tiburcio, 124
Ryan, John, 144

Index

Saguaripa, Jesus, 69–71
Saiz, Antonio, 99
Saiz, Pancrasio, 99
Saiz, Pedro, 99
Salcido, Rafael, 72, 73
Salt War. *See* Guadalupe Salt War
San Antonio (Texas), 17, 39, 190, 193; Bexar County Sheriff's Office, 144; operation of criminal justice system in, 140–43, 159; marshal's office, 21; police department, 37, 114. *See also* La Agrupación Protectora Mexicana; Perez, Jesse
Sanchez, Tomás Avila, 110
Sanchez, Ventura R., 115
Sandoval, Gabriel, 104
Sandoval, Telesfora, 104
San Elizario (Texas), 112, 153–54. *See also* Guadalupe Salt War
San Francisco Plaza "Frisco" (New Mexico), 81, 91–94, 95, 96, 215–16, 243n46. *See also* Baca, Elfego; Frisco shoot-out
San Juan County (New Mexico), 42
San Juan Guards, 42
San Marcos (Texas), 60
San Miguel County (New Mexico), 42, 102, 103, 155–56
San Patricio (New Mexico), 102
San Patricio County (Texas), 52, 61
San Quentin State Prison, 100, 121, 122, 150
Santa Cruz de la Cañada (New Mexico), 29
Santa Fe (New Mexico), 24, 27, 62; county sheriff's office, 87, 88, 105–6, 108, 109; jail, 136; marshal's office, 197, 198; 1846 planned revolt in, 27–28, 30; operation of criminal justice system, 40–42, 108–9, 136–37, 145, 156, 210–11; police department, 5, 41, 46, 49–50; Santa Fe Ring, 65, 105
Saracino, Pedro, 91–92, 93, 96, 215
Saucedo, Pedro, 190
Saucedo, Salvador, 190
Schnabel, Henry, 159, 160, 161
Schroeder, Marie, 190
Segovia, Josefa, 54, 149
Seguin (Texas), 38

Sena, Amado, 109, 116
Serna, Nicolas, 108
Shaw, E. O., 125
Shaw, Leslie, 194, 195
Shears, Robert, 150–51, 152
Sheldon, Lionel, 42, 242n27
Sierra, Jose, 113
Silva, Vicente, 103–4
Simpson, Pete, 91, 92, 95
Siringo, Charles, 105
Sitter, Joe, 147–48, 170–72, 263n126
Slaughter, John, 91, 92, 93
Slidell, John, 25
Sloat, John D., 33, 149
Smith, Andrew, 169
Smith, Joe, 137
Socorro (New Mexico), 62, 90, 91, 95, 96, 97–98, 100, 104, 137, 243n46
Socorro Committee of Safety, 62, 64
Socorro County Jail, 95, 98
Sonora (Mexico), 34, 79, 148
Sorenson, Julius, 167, 169
Soto, Antonio, 78
Standfield, Emma, 60
Standfield, Hugh, 60
Standfield, Watson, 60
Stanton, Charles, 79, 240n109
Stephens, Ezra, 165
Stephens, William, 165
St. James Hotel, 62, 63, 65, 67
Stockton, Robert F., 32, 33–35, 36, 37, 42
Sugar Land (Texas), 209
Sumner, Edwin V., 40
Sumpter, Jesse, 59

Tafolla, Jesus, 24
Taos (New Mexico), 26, 28, 52; Las Gorras Blancas, 157; Taos Revolt, 28–30, 46
Tarrant County (Texas), operation of criminal justice system, 138–39; convict camp, 144
Tays, John B., 153–54
Teller, Raymond, 194, 195–96
Téllez, Manuel C., 192, 195, 202
Territory of Arizona. *See* Arizona
Territory of New Mexico. *See* New Mexico
Tessiere, Julian, 87

Texas: development of criminal justice system in, 3, 5, 17, 18–20, 37, 44, 118, 230n23; extralegal justice in, 37–40, 52, 58–61, 150–52, 161–62, 163–66, 190, 191, 208–10; massacres in, 152, 170, 174–75, 176–78; operation of criminal justice system in, 9–10, 137–44, 152–53, 158–61, 164, 170–71, 174–78, 193–96, 231, 251n9; penal code of, 19–20, 230n23; policing in, 10, 20–21, 37, 111–15, 170–71; Republic of Texas, 16, 18–20; Texas Revolution, 3, 15–16, 17. *See also* Porvenir Massacre, Texas Rangers

Texas Army, 3, 18

Texas Cowboys, 4–5, 72, 73, 81–82, 84, 90, 91–96, 101–2, 116, 215–16

Texas Department of Corrections' Central Unit Prison, 209–10

Texas Department of Public Safety, 188–89

Texas Rangers, 6, 14, 15–16, 18, 148, 153–54, 159, 162–63, 166, 193–94, 218; extralegal killings by, 60–61, 152, 173–74, 175–76; massacres by, 152, 170, 174–75, 176–78; Mexican American Rangers, 114–15; reforms of, 10, 183–84, 185–89, 219. *See also* Canales Investigation, Porvenir Massacre

Tijerina, Santiago, 185, 266n4

Tingley, Clyde, 206, 207

Tipton, Sam, 63, 67

Tolby, Franklin James "F. J.," 53, 65, 66, 67

Travis County (Texas), 39

treason trials. *See* 1847 Treason Trials

Treaty of Cahuenga, 37, 221

Treaty of Guadalupe Hidalgo, 8, 16, 37

Treaty of Velasco, 20, 37

Trujillo, Antonio Maria, 24, 31

Trujillo, Juan, 87

Trujillo, Julian, 103, 104

Trujillo, Placido, 136

United States: acquisition of Mexico's territory, 3–4, 17, 21, 22–26, 32–37; colonialism in the Southwest, 3, 4, 17, 24–25, development of criminal justice system in, 6, 16, 17, 40–41, 211–13, 221; interactions with Mexican government, 46, 71–72, 75, 77–79, 113, 177–78, 192

U.S. Army: as an agency of law enforcement, 3, 6, 16, 17, 32, 45–46, 59, 154, 176, 216; Mexican-American War, 22–37; murder of Mexican-origin people, 29–30, 46, 175, 176; treason trials, 28, 29, 30–31, 32, 216. *See also* 1847 Treason Trials; Kearny, Stephen Watts; Mexican-American War

U.S. Border Patrol, 6, 185, 212–13, 235n158; similar organizations predating, 46, 146, 153–54

U.S. Customs Service, 6, 114, 147, 170, 191

U.S. Marshals Service, 6, 97, 197

Utah's Greatest Manhunt, 167–70, 168

Valdez, Epifano, 122

Valdez, Jose, 103

Valdez, Juan, 167, 169

Valencia County (New Mexico), 87, 106–7

Valenzuela, Jesus, 123–24

Valles, Eliseo, 137

Varela, Cérbulo, 35–36

Vásquez, Tiburcio, 149–50, 167

Vega, Cruz, 65, 66, 67

Vega, Francisco, 79

Vigil, Donaciano, 26, 29, 32

Vigil, Pedro, 30

vigilance committees. *See* justice, extralegal: vigilance committees

vigilantism. *See* justice, extralegal

Villa, Francisco "Pancho," 178–79, 198

Villarreal, Andrés, 159

Villareal, Francisco, 60

Villegas, Juan, 136

Villareal Zárate, Elías, 191, 192, 193, 268n40

violence: beating, 1, 27, 60, 76, 77, 105, 109, 112, 120, 150, 165, 179, 185, 191–93, 195, 199, 202, 207; burning, 55, 60, 87, 163, 166; hanging, 1–2, 30, 31, 32, 50–51, 54–55, 56, 58, 60–61, 62, 63, 65, 69, 70, 72, 73, 76–77, 85–86, 88, 91–92, 103, 106, 115, 127–28, 152, 161, 164–65, 175, 199, 208; rape, 54, 122; shooting, 42, 53, 55–56, 57, 67, 77, 84, 88, 91–96, 105–6, 126, 150, 151, 159, 162, 171, 191, 194, 202–3; stabbing, 75,

Index

violence (*continued*)
84, 104, 114, 130, 164; torture, 59–60, 61, 65, 157, 188

Wallace, Lew, 101, 102
Wallace, William, 43, 53
Warren, Harry, 177
Welch, Barney, 202, 203
Welch, John, 185, 202–4, 213, 219
Welch, Stanley, 114, 160, 162
Wharton, Henry, 124–25
White, Ted, 94
White Americans: conquest of Mexico's territory, 16, 17, 21–37, 46, 216–17; as decent members of the criminal justice system, 11, 65–66, 71, 77, 124, 125, 130–31, 159, 164–65, 198–200, 222; justifications and lies about extralegal justice, 7, 38–39, 46, 50–53, 58, 70, 219; racism and, 3, 4, 8, 11, 12, 38–39, 46, 51, 56, 57, 90, 92–93, 115, 118, 134–35, 138, 145–46, 148, 154, 176; sympathy toward Mexican-origin people, 26–27, 42–43, 53–54, 57, 181; use of extra-legal justice, 2, 37–38, 41–42, 46, 51–53, 65, 68–72, 164–65, 169, 208, 216. *See also* justice: extralegal; justice: legal; violence

White Owls, 192, 193
Willacy County (Texas), 194, 195, 196
Williams, Robert, 68
Willis, John, 70, 71
Wilson, Wilford, 164–65
Winters, Ramon, 49, 50, 235n4
Witbeck, George, 169
Wood family, 59
Woods, W. T., 124
Wright, William Lee, 192–93
Wuensche, Harry 165

Yanez, Francisco, 124, 128
Yarberry, Milton, 88, 89, 91, 106, 197, 242n23
Yavapai County (Arizona), 1, 44, 68, 76, 77, 127, 128, 129, 130, 133; sheriff's office, 77, 78, 222
Young, William, 144
Yuma Territorial Prison, 40–41, 125, 128, 129–35, 134, 145

Zabaleta, Doroteo, 56
Zaller, Matt, 194, 195
Zamacona y Murphy, Manuel de, 72–73
Zeckendorf, William, 69–70, 238n79
Zieschang, Charles, 164, 165–66
Zulick, C. Meyer, 75, 78, 79, 127

www.ingramcontent.com/pod-product-compliance
Lightning Source LLC
Chambersburg PA
CBHW031756220426
43662CB00007B/426